REAL WORLD AFTER EFFECTS

Eric Reinfeld and Sherry London

LightSpeed Publishing
Glen Ellen, California

Peachpit Press
Berkeley, California

Real World After Effects
Eric Reinfeld and Sherry London

Peachpit Press

1249 Eighth Street
Berkeley, CA 94710
510/548-4393

Find us on the World Wide Web at:
http://www.peachpit.com

Peachpit Press is a division of Addison Wesley Longman

Packaged and edited by LightSpeed Publishing, Inc.
Cover design: Mimi Heft
Cover image created in After Effects by Auguste Design
Interior design and production: Evana Gerstman

ISBN 0-201-68839-5

9 8 7 6 5

Printed and bound in the United States of America

ACKNOWLEDGMENTS

From Eric Reinfeld:

This Book is dedicated to my grandfather Benjamin Bradly Kudin.

Thanks to Sherry London for asking me to work with her on this project, and the friend that I have made.

I would like to thank Victor Milt for providing much of the video footage used throughout this book. His video expertise and wisdom was truly helpful. I would also like to thank David Acosta and Claude Martin for coming through when the chips were down, Richard Lainhart for helping out with the sound and 3D chapters, and Josh Laurence for his help with the animation chapter.

Special thanks to the artists who contributed to our gallery: Dave Teich, Laurence Kaplan, Jaime Beauchamp and Marc Steinberg, and once again Richard Lainhart.

Special thanks to my sweetheart Linda Shishido. She put up with me, tested the book, and even held up her side of the conversation as I babbled in my sleep.

Thanks to the many friends and family that have been very patient and thoughtful during this adventure: Huggy Bear Ferris, who postponed lunch for 3 months, Deke McClellend, who tried to keep me calm through the tough days, Josephine Portnoy for watching out for me, and Robin Olson for being supportive to me and my cat Sweetie, when we both needed support. I'd also like to thank Ken Kinzer, who shined the light at the end of the tunnel, Joyce, Ed, Debbie, Danny, Tanya, Lielle and Eitan, O'ma Reinfeld, Barry and Amy Biedny, Etta and Herbie Berman, Dorothy Breading—all my ever growing family. Thanks to the pets in my life, Sweetie and Sampson, the world's most affectionate cats, and Kaya, the atomic tail. Finally, thanks to Joel Fugazzotto and Scott Calamar of LightSpeed Publishing, and to Truevision, ElectricImage, MetaCreations, and Adobe.

Extra special thanks goes to David Biedny and Bert Monroy for getting me started on this wonderful journey. Thanks guys, you're the best!!!

From Sherry London:

To Joel Fugazzotto—for causing this book to be.

To Eric Reinfeld—for friendship.

To my husband Norm, with love.

I would like to thank the folks at Adobe—Patricia Pane and Terese Bruno—for their help and encouragement throughout this project. I would also like to thank Scott Calamar for his wonderful developmental edits.

For the vendors who supplied us with demos and information—we could not have made this book as good without you.

INTRODUCTION

After Effects has quickly become the number one desktop package for adding effects to video and for compositing footage. In this book, we hope to give you a "beyond-the-manual" look at how you can use After Effects in the "real world."

We have tried to make the book easy to use. The chapters are broken down into specific functions. The CD contains the footage files for each of the chapters. Each chapter has a completed project as well as a completed movie. You can work in the completed project or work in your own project.

You may find it beneficial to remove the Adobe After Effects 3.0 preferences file before you start work on the exercises in this book. This will force the program to start with the default configuration—a "known state" which is the baseline system for all of our exercises.

After Effects and memory: The examples in this book are designed to use small amounts of memory. As you work through the book to the more advanced techniques, you may find it beneficial to increase After Effects' memory. Generally, the more memory the program has allocated to it (on the Mac—this is not an issue on Windows), the better it operates. The memory should be set somewhere between 25 and 50 megabytes for the larger chapters. Chapter 17, Working with Large Images, will require the most memory since the chapter discusses working with high resolution files. The filters chapters (Chapters 13-16) may also require larger memory configurations.

Each chapter contains a Footage folder that holds the footage (source material) used in that Project. The Done folder contains the finished Project so that you may refer to it. When you open the completed file, you will need to relink the objects with their sources. The sources are provided in the Foot folder for each individual project.

Enjoy!

CONTENTS AT A GLANCE

TABLE OF CONTENTS

Section 1
Basic Moves

After Effects Environment

Welcome to After Effects

Adobe After Effects is a video compositing program that is both fun to use and extremely powerful. With it, you can create QuickTime movies for output on the Web, CD-ROM, or monitor, or you can create full-motion broadcast quality video for output to high-end (or lower end) video components. Video effects that once cost hundreds of thousands of dollars now can be created at your own desktop workstation.

The amazing thing about After Effects is that it can be used by anyone—regardless of skill level with video. You don't even need a video capture card to produce visually exciting movies. All you really need are After Effects, Photoshop, and your imagination.

You can create cutting-edge work with After Effects using only still images—which you can animate with incredible ease. After Effects, therefore, becomes the perfect vehicle for print graphic artists who wish to move into a new direction—the area of motion graphics. If you love working with Photoshop, then you will find After Effects even more exciting. After Effects lets Photoshop dance.

What if you are already an accomplished user of Adobe Premiere? Does After Effects have anything for you? Yes, indeed. Premiere is a video editing program. It allows you to sequence your video clips and to create transitions from one clip to another. After Effects is the perfect companion to Premiere. You can use it before or after using Premiere to apply special effects to the video and to mix video clips together in ways that Premiere could not begin to match. Premiere only performs an AB roll (it can transition between Clip A and Clip B and then make the result the new Clip A so that you can add more footage). In After Effects, you can mix multiple layers of video together or with still images and use them all at the same time.

 # Preview

With just a little bit of introduction, let's jump right in and meet Adobe After Effects. In this first chapter, we wish to introduce you to the Adobe After Effects environment and show you the interface. Here is a list of things that you will learn in this chapter:

- Play a movie in the MoviePlayer Application.
- Open a project in After Effects.
- Display footage items in their Layer windows.
- Define and state the purpose of a Composition.
- Play a Composition.
- Show and collapse Layer information in the Composition Time Layout window.
- Identify In and Out points.
- Move to specific times along the time line.
- Define, create, and edit a keyframe.
- Render a movie.

In this chapter, we have already created a project for you. (Actually, we will let you "peek" at the projects for every chapter before you start them, so you can expect a Preview in every chapter.) The project for this chapter is called AECH01.mov (catchy title, isn't it!), and it's located on your CD-ROM in the Chap01 folder.

Double-click on the AECH01.mov icon. If you have a copy of MoviePlayer installed, it will launch. MoviePlayer is a part of the Apple QuickTime program. If you do not have a copy, then drag the one from the Utilities folder of the CD-ROM onto your hard drive.

Figure 1-1 shows the window that appears. You see just the MoviePlayer window and a small menu above it. Pull

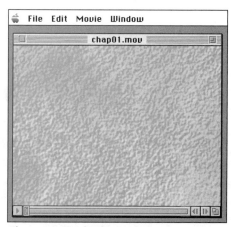

Figure 1-1: Movie Player window.

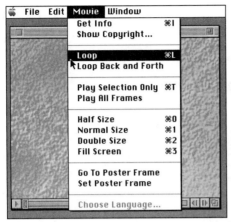

Figure 1-2: Movie menu.

Figure 1-3: Dragging the Movie slider.

down the Movie menu as shown in Figure 1-2. Select Loop. Open the Movie menu again and choose "Play all Frames." Drag the slider control at the bottom of the movie, about halfway toward the center—as shown in Figure 1-3. You can see that the movie displays the frame that is current at that point.

What is a frame?

A frame is the basic unit of measure in a movie. It is a single image. Animation is an illusion. It occurs because a large number of individual images are shown in a short period of time. Each image is slightly different from the one before it. As these images are displayed quickly, one after the other, our brain records "motion." In reality, no motion occurred. The movie in this chapter is recorded to play at 30 frames per second. That means that 30 individual images are supposed to appear in one physical second of time (though in practice, this rate will vary with your processor and hard drive speed).

Finally, play the movie. Do this by clicking on the arrow at the left of the slider, on the bottom of the Movie window. Notice that the text "Welcome to After Effects" appears one word at a time. It reaches full size and then begins to rotate and grow smaller. Finally, it grows back to full size as it fades out. The movie loops as you instructed it to, and will continue to play until you either quit the application, or click on the leftmost control near the slider (which looks like two upright lines as the movie plays) to stop it.

Feature Presentation

Double-click on the file "AECH01.aep" to open Adobe After Effects. The project will open and your screen should look similar to Figure 1-4. Let's look at this figure a bit more closely.

Figure 1-4: Adobe After Effects environment.

In the upper-left corner is the Project window. This is the main control for After Effects. A Project is the name given to a group of files that are meant to be used together. These files can be still images, QuickTime movies, video footage, or compositions. Saved together, they are a Project. Only one project can be open at any time, and the Project is the top of the After Effects hierarchy.

A Project is composed of Footage items and Compositions. A Footage item is a still image, a QuickTime movie, captured video, or audio to be used in a project. It is the building block of the project—the individual item itself.

You can use a number of footage items together in a Composition. The Composition is the place where the footage items are sequenced and effects are added. Compositions can in turn be used inside of other compositions.

The Project Window

Look at the contents of the Project window. There are three items:

- Comp 1
- Text.mov
- BITxtur.mov

The project contains two footage items—text.mov and BITxtur.mov, which are both QuickTime movies—and one composition, Comp 1, which uses the two movies.

The Project window also shows you other information. In addition to the file types, you can see the file size for the imported footage items. You can also see the duration (the length in time) of the items. Text.mov is six seconds and 15 frames long (6:15) while BITxtur.mov is 7 seconds long (7:00). If there are 30 frames per second, this means that Text.mov has 195 frames and BITxtur.mov movie has 210 frames. Both of the movies are actually longer than the composition in which they are used. Comp 1 is only five seconds long (150 frames). This means that you may use only part of a movie in a composition if you wish.

You can preview the footage items directly from the Project window. Double-click on the Text.mov Movie in the Project window. A new window appears that contains the movie. The first frame of the movie is totally black, so it looks empty. The controls are identical to the controls on the MoviePlayer application. Play the movie by clicking on the single arrowhead at the bottom left of the controls. This movie only contains the text from the AECH01.mov movie.

What do you think the BITxtur.mov Movie contains? Of course—it has the moving background. Double-click on it and see. Play the movie from the Project window.

Does it seem as if the movies play more slowly than in MoviePlayer, or are a bit choppy? The speed within After Effects is generally not as good as the speed you can get from playing the movies from within MoviePlayer. This is an expected slowdown and is perfectly okay. After Effects needs to think about what it is displaying much more than an application which only plays completed movies.

Double-click on Comp 1. This window is different. Let's take a closer look.

The Composition Window

Even though you see what looks like the original movie, the controls in this window are different. For one thing, there do not seem to be any video controls to play the movie. Actually there are—but not in the window. You can preview the material in the Comp 1 window by pressing the single right-pointing arrowhead in the Time Controls window. (If that is not visible in your system, select Window → Palettes → Show Time Controls or press Cmd-3 on the Mac or Ctrl-3 for Windows.)

Figure 1-5 shows the portions of the Composition window labeled. On the bottom of the window, starting at the left, is the Display control. Pull down the menu—you can view the composition at any magnification from 1:64 (very tiny) to 64:1 (64 times

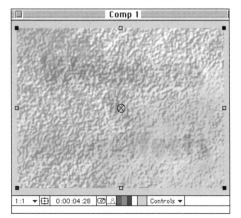

Figure 1-5: Composition window.

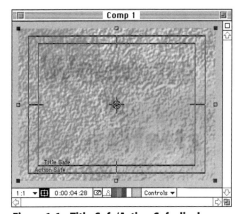

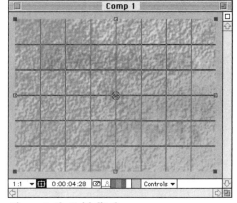

Figure 1-6a: Title-Safe/Action-Safe display.   **Figure 1-6b: Grid display.**

the actual size). Leave this set to 1:1 unless you need to change it for a special reason. When you change the magnification, all you are changing is the size at which you view the composition on the screen. You are not changing the actual image at all.

The next box is a three-way switch that lets you view the composition with nothing in front of it, or with either a Title-Safe/Action-Safe preview, or a Grid preview. Click on the switch and let it scroll though. Figure 1-6a shows the Title Safe preview and Figure 1-6b shows the Grid preview.

You will learn much more about the Title-Safe/Action-Safe areas, but for now, all that you need to know is that it shows the areas of the screen where you can be sure that your text or motion activity will be properly seen on a TV. The Grid display is useful for aligning things and spacing items properly.

Keeping Time

Time is a very important element in Adobe After Effects. Everything that happens in an After Effects composition is linked to the display of time. By default, After Effects uses SMPTE timecode. SMPTE refers to the Society of Motion Picture and Television Engineers. It is their default standard of encoding time. This standard encodes time based on Hours, Minutes, Seconds, and Frames. For this reason, you will see time written as 0:00:00:00.

The next control is the Time control. All time in After Effects uses the SMPTE time codes by default (see Sidebar). Figure 1-5 shows the time in the Composition window to be 0:00:04:28. This means that the frame displayed in the figure occurs four seconds and 28 frames into the composition—which in a five second Comp is almost at the very end.

Click on the time control—once. The dialog box shown in Figure 1-7 appears. This is the Go To Time window. You can go to any point along the timeline by typing it into the window. Type 28 in place of the 04, so that you move to frame 28 of the composition. Notice that it takes a few seconds for the display to catch up when you move the time. Also notice that the display in the Time Layout window moves to the new time as well.

For now, you really do not need any other of the controls along the bottom of the screen. You will meet them a bit later. Let's explore the Time Layout window next.

Figure 1-7: Go To Time dialog.

Time Layout Window

Figure 1-8 shows a close up view of the Time Layout window. This is the place where all of the action is defined. If you are familiar with MacroMedia Director, the Time Layout window is analogous to the Score. It is in the Time Layout window that you can specify effects and motion.

Let's simplify the view for a moment. Notice the small triangles in the leftmost column of Figure 1-8. Like the folder indicators in the Finder, these triangles swirl to reveal or hide the underlying hierarchy. Click on the triangles next to both film clips (1: Text.mov and 2: BITxtur.mov movie) and collapse both hierarchies. Your Time Layout window will then look like Figure 1-9.

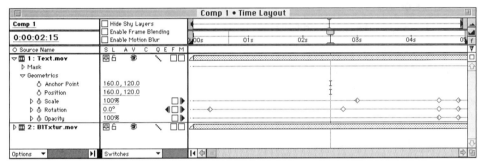

Figure 1-8: Time Layout window.

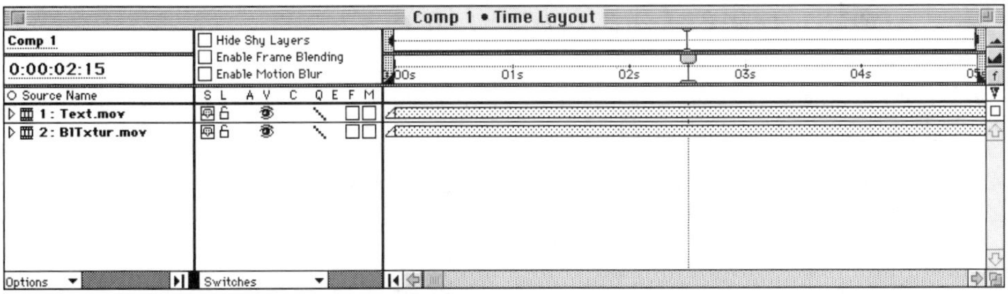

Figure 1-9: Time Layout window collapsed.

Notice the two long ribbon-like lines in the Time Layout window in Figure 1-9. The turned end at the left indicates the In Point of each layer—the starting point for the Footage in the Layer—which is at the very start of this Composition. You cannot see a matching "turned end" at the right of the time line because each layer is actually longer than the Composition, so the Out Point does not show.

The Time Layout display is divided into three sections at the moment. The first section (on the left) lists both Layers in the Composition. A Layer in After Effects is a distinct footage item to which effects can be applied over time independently of effects to any other footage item. In this sense, an After Effects layer serves the same purpose as a layer in Photoshop or Illustrator. As in both those programs, the order of layers can be changed, and you can hide or show layers as you wish.

The second area in the Time Layout window contains the Switches. You do not need to know about these yet, so we will simply name them for you right now. Starting with the icon of the left:

- **S:** Shy switch: This determines whether you can see all of the information about a layer.
- **L:** Layer Lock: If the layer is locked, you cannot move it or select it.
- **A:** Use Audio: Available only if there is audio in the footage item.
- **V:** View Video: Show it (Eye open), Hide it (Eye closed), or use a Transfer mode (Solid Eye).
- **C:** Continuously Rasterize image: Used when working with Illustrator images.
- **Q:** Quality setting: Solid is highest quality, dashed line is low quality, X is wire frame outline of layer.
- **E:** Show Effects applied to layer.
- **F:** Enable Frame Blending.
- **M:** Enable Motion Blur.

You will learn how, when, and why to use these switches as you progress through this book.

The third area of the Time Layout window is the time line itself. Currently, it is displaying the 5-seconds of the Composition. Try this:

 Studio Time: Changing Time Views

1. Press Cmd-G (Mac) or Ctrl-G (Windows) to open the Go To Time window. Type in 00 to go to the start of the Composition.

2. Click on the "large mountain" icon at the right of the Time Layout window (the second one down). Figure 1-10 shows the new Time Layout view, as the time line zooms in so that you can see increments in the Time Layout window that are smaller than seconds.

3. Click the large mountain icon a third time. Now, you see time in 10 frame increments.

4. Click on the f icon (the third one on the right edge of the window). This shows you time in individual frames—the smallest unit possible—as you can see in Figure 1-11.

5. Finally, click on the "small mountain" icon until you are back to the original view (this should be five clicks).

6. There is a faster way to set your zoom to wherever you want it. Look at the top "row" of Figure 1-11. It has a small white area bracketed by two small black half-circles. Now, look at your time line which shows the same two black half-circles with a much larger white area

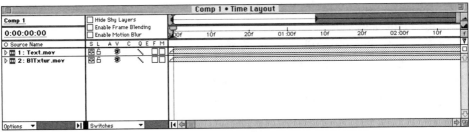

Figure 1-10: Time line zoomed in to 10-frame intervals.

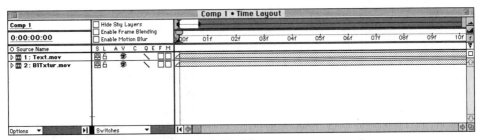

Figure 1-11: Time line zoomed in to see individual frames.

between them. Grab the right half-circle with the mouse cursor and pull it towards the left. Move it back towards the right. Notice that it almost works like a rubber-band as it expands and compresses the time line.

7. You can also expand the time line from the other end by moving the left half-circle towards the right. This is easier to do, however, when the Current Time is not set at the beginning of the Composition.

OK, so now that you know how to look at time, let's see how to set it and move through it. There are a number of ways to set the time.

 ## Studio Time: Setting Time

1. The easiest way to set the time (if you remember the command) is to press Cmd-G (Mac) or Ctrl-G (Windows) to bring up the Go To Time window. The mnemonic here is to associate "G" with "Go To." Use this method to set the time to 1 second by typing 100 into the dialog box (0:00:01:00).

2. Another way to set the current time marker is to drag it along the time line. Put your cursor on the blue Current Time indicator in the second "row" of Time Layout Window, and drag the marker (also referred to as the "Playback Head") to a new time. Drag it now to 2 seconds. This method is certainly easy, but it is not always as precise.

3. You can check the time, however, in the Current Time indicator box—the second "row" of the first column in the Time Layout window. It will always show you the Current Time setting. Notice that the box is underlined with a dotted line. This is a convention used in After Effects

to indicate that a field or item is clickable—you can make a dialog box pop up by clicking once in the underlined area. If you click on this indicator, the familiar Go To Time window appears. This now gives you a third easy way to set the current time. Set it to 3 seconds.

Why would one want to set the Current Time indicator? There are a number of different reasons, but the major one is so that you can add effects at specific points in time. These effects then occur at specific frames that are called keyframes.

Keyframes

The concept of keyframe is perhaps the most important one that you need to comprehend if you are going to work with After Effects. A keyframe is a specific frame in the Time Layout window that is linked to a specific action. Let's look at the actions and keyframes that are already in the Time Layout window.

To start, let's view the first footage item in the Layer window. Remember, double-clicking on the Text.mov movie in the Project window allowed you to play the movie using video controls in the Footage window. If you double-click on the Text.mov movie in the Time Layout window, you will see the Layer Window as in Figure 1-12. The Current Time is left at 3 seconds.

If you look at the entire application window shown in Figure 1-13, you notice something very interesting. The Time in all three windows (the Layer window, the Comp window, and the Time Layout window) is set

Figure 1-12: Layer window.

to 3 seconds. However, the text in the Comp window seems to be spinning where the same text at the identical time in the Layer window is still straight. How can that be?

The answer is that the rotation is not in the QuickTime movie Text.mov at all. It is added to the layer in Comp 1. Click on the arrowhead next to the Text.mov layer in the Time Layout window to expand the layer. Figure 1-14 shows you this view.

The Layer hierarchy shows that when you expand Text.mov, there are two headings beneath it: Mask and Geometrics. For now, nothing in the movie uses the Mask functions. However, the Geometrics section is also expanded. Under it are five more categories:

- Anchor Point
- Position
- Scale
- Rotation
- Opacity

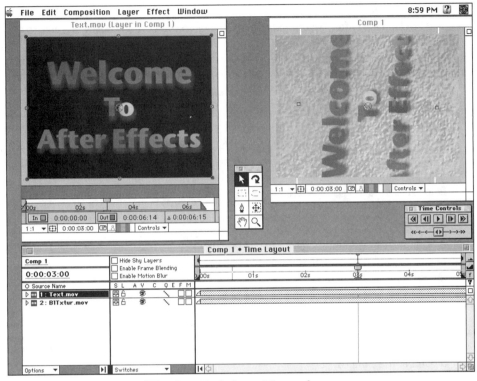

Figure 1-13: Layer, Comp, and Time Layout windows at 3 seconds.

These are the geometric attributes that you can set and change. Notice that the little stop watches next to Scale, Rotation, and Opacity have tiny hands in them. This shows that keyframes have been set for these attributes.

 Studio Time: Locating Keyframes

1. Notice that the Current Time indicator set to 3 seconds intersects a diamond icon along the line coming from the Scale attribute. An arrow next to the checked box beside Scale points towards the right. The underlined Scale field reads "100%."

Figure 1-14: Expanded Time Layout window.

2. Click on the right-pointing arrow. The Current Time moves to 4 seconds, 15 frames. The text "Welcome to After Effects" gets much smaller in the Comp window, as you can see in Figure 1-15. What has happened? Clicking on the keyframe arrow moves you from keyframe to keyframe for a specific attribute. At each keyframe, the value for that attribute changes. Clicking on the right arrow again shows you that the scale has returned to 100% (though you will notice that the opacity has decreased).

3. Let's add another keyframe for the Scale attribute. Use one of the methods that you have learned to set the Current Time indicator to 3 minutes and 15 frames (315 or 0:00:03:15). The Scale field value is an interpolated 73% at that point in time (an interpolated value is a value calculated from the values of the previous and next keyframes). Click on the underlined Scale field (remember, an underlined field reveals a dialog box when clicked). Figure 1-16 shows the dialog box.

4. Change the amount to 70% of Source and make sure that the Preserve Aspect Ratio is also checked. Figure 1-17 shows the Time Layout window with the new keyframe selected.

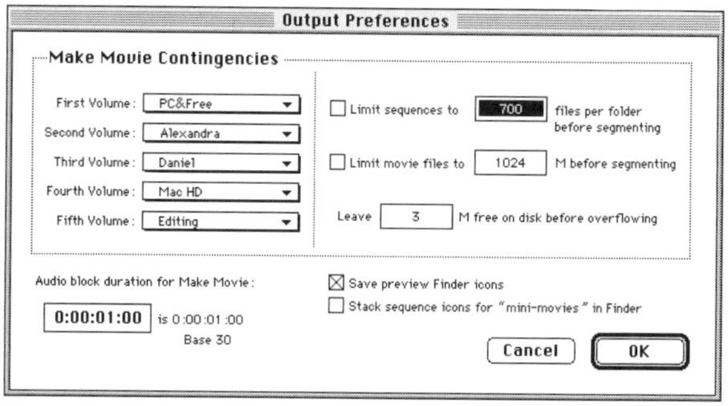

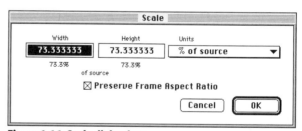

Figure 1-15: Comp Window at 4 seconds and 15 frames.

5. Drag the Playback Head to the left in the Time Layout window (so it is at 0 seconds). Play Comp 1 by clicking on the center control in the Time Controls window.

6. Watch the Time Layout window as the composition plays. Notice how the text starts to shrink at 3 seconds and then gets larger at 4 seconds, 15 frames.

Figure 1-16: Scale dialog box.

7. What other keyframes are set? Click in the checkbox next to the Rotation attribute. This sets the time back to 0 seconds. Follow the keyframes by clicking on the right arrow. The first two keyframes (after the 0 mark) are also set to 0 degrees of rotation. However, the keyframe at 4:15 shows that five rotations have occurred. Those five rotations start from the 0 point keyframe at 2:22. The final keyframe adds one additional rotation between 4:15 and 4:26.

8. Opacity stays at 100% until 4:15, when it declines to 15% at 4:26. Let's make the opacity move some more. Set the Current Time to 00 (Mac: Cmd-G, Windows: Ctrl-G, then type 0).

9. Click in the checkbox to the left of the right arrow in the Opacity time line. This leaves a keyframe set to 100% at Time=00.

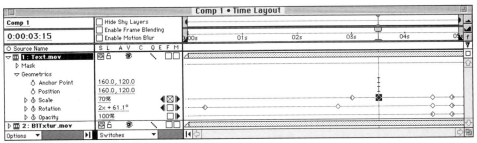

Figure 1-17: New Scale key frame.

10. Set the Current Time to 1 second (Mac: Cmd-G, Windows: Ctrl-G, and type 100 or just move the Playback Head until the Current Time reads 0:00:01:00). Add a keyframe with 50% opacity. (Remember, click on the underlined Opacity field.)

11. Bring the Opacity back to 100% at 2:00, and take it down to 75% at 3:00. (Add the keyframes by moving the Current Time indicator to the new time and clicking on the underlined Opacity field.)

12. Preview Comp 1 by playing it in the Time Controls window.

Rendering a Movie

Now that you have opened a project and added some keyframes to it, you need to re-create the finished movie—since it has changed. In this practice, let's choose some very simple options (they will get more complex later) and make a QuickTime movie.

You render a movie by selecting the Make Movie option in the Composition menu (Mac: Cmd-M, Windows: Ctrl-M). Depending upon the complexity of the effects that you have added, and the speed of your computer, this process can take anywhere from several minutes to several days! (Yes, this is not a typo, we did say days.) However, this movie will not take nearly that long. It will, however, eat up over 50 Mb of hard drive space, so be forewarned. Working with video is not for the short-on-disk-space! We will show you how to compress the finished video later in this book. We use an almost miraculous program called "Movie Cleaner" to perform this task. It is indispensable.

 Studio Time: Making a Movie

1. First, save this project as AECH01.aep.

2. Next, open the Output Preferences dialog in the File menu. Figure 1-18 shows this dialog. You may specify up to five hard drives that you wish to use to hold temporary material as the movie is rendered. The dialog shows our setup. Use your own.

3. Quit After Effects and then start it up again so that the Preferences take effect. Open AECH01.aep that you just saved.

4. Press Cmd-M (Mac) or Ctrl-M (Windows) to Make a Movie. Call the rendered movie "AECH01b.mov" in the Save dialog.

5. Next, the Render Queue dialog shown in Figure 1-19 appears. Click on the underlined area next to the Output Module. In Figure 1-19, it says "Based on Lossless." Your entry is likely to be different.

6. Figure 1-20 shows the Output Module Settings dialog. Select QuickTime movie as the format.

7. Click on the Format Options button in the Video section. Select None as the Compression (this is usually the wrong choice, but here, it is the best one since we don't want to explain compression to you just yet). Change the settings so that they look like the ones in Figure 1-21. Click OK.

8. Click OK to the Output Module Settings (make sure that they match Figure 1-20).

9. Finally, click on the Render button and let it rip!

Congratulations! You have just made your first movie. Double-click on it in the Finder so that it plays under MoviePlayer. You may also bring it back into After Effects as a footage item and view it there.

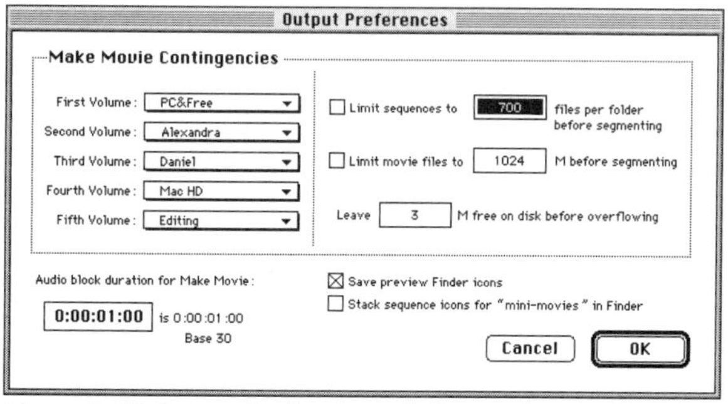

Figure 1-18: Output Preferences dialog.

 **Rewind**

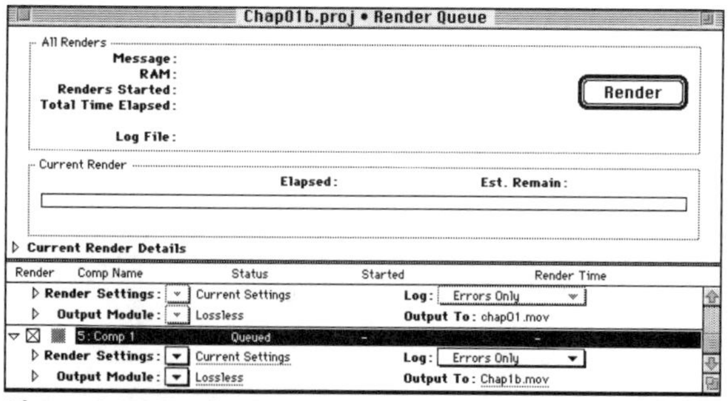

This chapter introduced you to the After Effects environment. You have learned how to open, save, and render a project, and how to create keyframes. You have also learned how to view Footage items, items in the Layer window, and how to preview a Composition.

Figure 1-19: Render Queue.

You have learned that a project is composed of one or more footage items which contain one or more Compositions, and Compositions contain one or more layers. You have also seen the Layer hierarchy in the Time Layout window and have practiced adding keyframes that change the geometric parameters or attributes of a layer. So, you've learned quite a lot in one session.

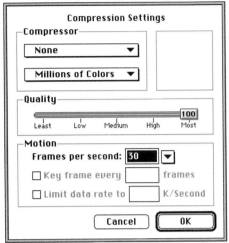

Figure 1-20: Output Module Settings.

Figure 1-21: Format Options window.

 # Coming Attractions

It was really easy to create this chapter's movie. What aren't we telling you? Actually, there is a lot that we didn't tell you about.

The two movies that are the basis for this project... How were they developed? What makes the "Welcome to After Effects" text vibrate and change color? Why does the Blue Texture background seem to move across the screen? Why does it look as if a light is moving across it? How did the Welcome to After Effects text acquire a shadow?

The secrets behind these effects we've created will be revealed to you in the chapters that follow. Stay tuned. The best is yet to come!

Using Still Images

 Preview

One of the many features that makes After Effects so exciting is its ability to make still images move. For the Photoshop artist, this opens up a whole new way of looking at, and working with, images. It becomes a pathway into motion graphics.

Another benefit for the traditional 2D artist, is that you don't need expensive video input equipment or a video camera in order to see results. You can make exciting, cutting-edge videos using only still images. Photoshop images can be used in layers—and you can animate the layers so that each one moves independently.

At the end of this chapter, you should be able to:

- Create a new After Effects project.
- Add Footage items to the project from the menu or by dragging them.
- Add a layered Photoshop file as a Composition.
- Tell After Effects how to treat the alpha channel information embedded in a file.
- Apply the last alpha setting to other footage items.
- Set key frames to change layer attributes.
- Set a Constant value for a layer attribute.

- Scale an image over time.

- Change the Opacity of an image over time.

- Change the Position of an image over time.

- Rotate an image over time.

- Add a Gaussian Blur effect.

The project for this chapter consists of three patterned After Effects layers that interact with one another as they move and rotate over a background. Double-click on AECH02.mov and launch the MoviePlayer application.

Change the settings in the MoviePlayer application so that you play every frame (Movie → Play all Frames), and Loop (Movie → Loop). Watch the movie a few times so that you understand what the final result of your efforts will be. Now, let's see how it was done.

Feature Presentation

In Chapter 1, you were introduced to the After Effects environment and learned about key frames and changing time lines and layer geometry.

Now you will learn how to import the layers by two different methods—from individual images or from a single Photoshop file (which contains all four layers) as a Composition.

Importing Individual Images

In Chapter 1, you did not get a chance to create a new project or to import footage items, since you worked with a project that was already in place for you. When you first open After Effects, a new, empty project is automatically created, unless you have launched After Effects by selecting a project as you did in Chapter 1. You need to add footage items to the empty project in order to have something to see.

You can add footage items in several ways:

- You can add one item at a time by selecting File → Import → Footage File. This gives you the normal Open dialog.

- You can add multiple items at one time by selecting File → Import → Footage Files (notice the "s" on "Files"). This gives you the normal Open dialog multiple times until you click "Done."

- You can drag multiple items onto the After Effects icon or alias (you might want to have one reside permanently on your desktop). After Effects needs to be loaded already for this to work as expected.

- You can drag multiple footage items into the Project window directly from the desktop. Figure 2-1 shows the setup for this. It is actually a bit tricky, but much faster than most other methods if all of your footage files are already in one folder. The Practice session below leads you through this method.

Let's first set up a new project and import each image on its own.

Studio Time: Creating a New Project and Getting Footage Items

1. Create a new Project (File → New Project). Save this into a new folder as Proj2.

2. You can bring all four starting images for this example into the Project window in one step. In the Finder, open the Project2 folder located on the CD-ROM. Select the four images as you normally would (click on one and then add the others by Shift-clicking).

3. Position yourself so that you are back in After Effects, but can still see the selected files on the desktop. From inside of After Effects, drag the files on the desktop into the Project window. For this to work, the files must be selected already. Figure 2-2 shows the Stony Texture file; Figure 2-3 shows the Cloud Puffs pattern, and Figures 2-4 and 2-5 show the Stars pattern and the Hearts pattern respectively.

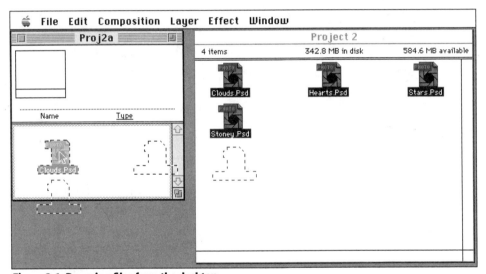

Figure 2-1: Dragging files from the desktop.

Shortcuts

Command	Mac	Windows
Open a new Project	Cmd-Opt-N	Ctrl-Alt-N
Add Single Footage Item	Cmd-I	Ctrl-I
Add Multiple Footage Items	Cmd-Opt-I	Ctrl-Alt-I

Figure 2-2: Stony Texture file for background.

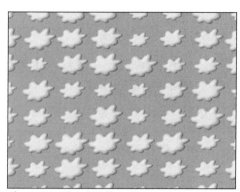

Figure 2-3: Cloud Puffs pattern.

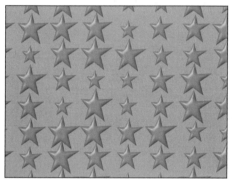

Figure 2-4: Stars pattern.

Figure 2-5: Hearts pattern.

There is one minor problem that occurs when you import footage by dragging. You are not asked how the footage item is masked. Masked??? What is that?

The subject of masking (mattes) and alpha channels is one that will be treated in much more detail as you progress through this book. A matte is a channel or image that helps to separate the part of the image that you want in the final movie from the parts that you don't want. For example, if you rendered a cat in a 3D program and wanted to animate it in After Effects, you would want to see only the cat—not the rest of the color background that came from the 3D program. All images are rectangular when they are imported. You need a matte to determine what you will see and what drops away.

If you are familiar with other graphics applications, this process is analogous to placing an image into QuarkXPress using a clipping Path or writing a transparent GIF so that you can see only the main motif on a Web page.

You may bring images into After Effects that have alpha channels already built into them (an alpha channel is a separate part of the image that carries transparency data—black areas will be transparent and white areas will be visible in After Effects). Some applications, however, produce images that are "premultiplied." This term means that the image already has a solid color in it where you wish the image to be transparent (this is the case with images that are created for viewing on the Web).

After Effects gives you the opportunity to specify what type of alpha channel or matting should be applied to each image that you import. In the dialog, you can specify one of three settings for the alpha channel.

- 📇 Ignore Alpha: This gives you a completely opaque image. No background is removed.

- 📇 Straight (unmatted): This option uses the alpha channel information to remove the image background.

- 📇 Premultiplied: This option allows you to drop out a single color in the image (presumably a solid background color) and shows the rest of the image as opaque.

If you import your footage items by dragging them from the desktop, however, you by-pass the dialog box that interprets the alpha channel information. When this happens, After Effects takes its best "guess" as to what you want it to do—and it may guess wrong!

Not to worry. The command "Interpret Footage" can fix it. Let's look at it now.

Studio Time: Interpreting Footage Items

1. Highlight the Clouds.psd image in the Project window (click once).

2. Open the Interpret Footage dialog (File → Interpret Footage → Main). Figure 2-6 shows the dialog box. Notice that the only choices not grayed out mostly concern the Alpha Channel interpretation. That is the only part of the dialog that concerns us as well!

3. Select the second radio button "Treat as Straight."

4. Click OK.

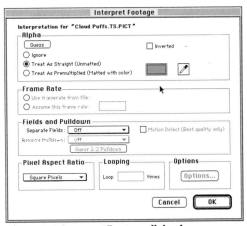

Figure 2-6: Interpret Footage dialog box.

Two other images need to be interpreted that same way. You could repeat Steps 1-4 for the Hearts.psd and the Stars.psd images, but there is an easier way. You can ask After Effects to "remember" your interpretation and then apply it to the remaining images.

5. Make sure that the Clouds.psd image is still selected. Select the File → Interpret Footage → Remember Interpretation command.

6. Highlight the Hearts.psd image in the Project window. Figure 2-7 shows that the alpha interpretation is incorrect on this image as well (it says "Millions of Colors + (Premultiplied)" next to the thumbnail of the footage item).

7. Now apply the File → Interpret Footage → Remember Interpretation command. This changes the alpha type to Straight. You can be sure of that by looking at the thumbnail area of the Project window with the footage item selected.

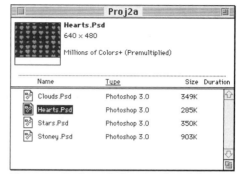

8. Select the Stars.psd image and apply the same setting to it as well (use the keyboard shortcut shown in the Sidebar).

9. Select the Stony.psd image. Look at the thumbnail area—it lists 16 million colors, but no alpha information. You do not need to interpret this footage item as there is no transparency present at all.

Figure 2-7: Project window showing alpha interpretation.

Shortcuts

Command	Mac	Windows
Interpret Footage → Main	Cmd-Shift-H	Ctrl-Shift-H
Remember Interpretation	Cmd-Opt-C	Ctrl-Alt-C
Apply Interpretation	Cmd-Opt-V	Ctrl-Alt-V

Since you have imported the four Photoshop files as individual images, you need to create a new Composition in which to store them. Let's create the new Composition and then go back and start over—using a single, layered Photoshop file as the starting point.

 Studio Time: Creating a New Composition

1. Create a new Composition (Composition → New Composition).

2. Figure 2-8 shows the Composition Settings window. You need to set the size of the Composition to 320 x 240 (which is one-half of the "traditional" screen size of 640 x 480). Set the Frame rate to 30 frames per second and the Duration of the Composition to 10 seconds (use the settings shown in Figure 2-8).

3. Click OK.

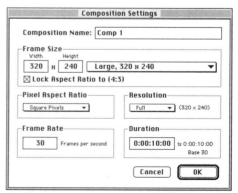

Figure 2-8: Composition Settings window.

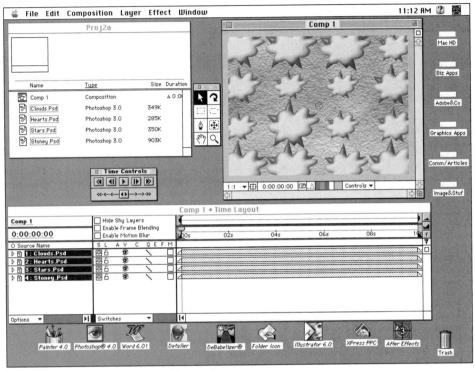

Figure 2-9: After Effects window with new Comp set up.

4. In the Project window, select all of the items except for Comp1 (the new Composition). You can do this by Shift-clicking on the items or by dragging a Marquee around them.

5. Once the items are selected, drag the entire group into the empty Composition window. You will feel them snap to the center of the window. When the images snap to center, release the mouse. Figure 2-9 shows how your screen should look. Notice that you can "see through" all of the layers except for the Stony texture. This is because of the alpha interpretation that you set.

Shortcuts

Command	Mac	Windows
Create a New Composition	Cmd-N	Ctrl-N

Using a Photoshop File as a Composition

Now that you have set up the After Effects environment by importing four separate files, it is time to see how this could have been done in one step—using a layered file created from the four individual Photoshop files.

Let's backtrack a bit first. What is the source of the images being used as footage files? We created the three pattern files in Specular TextureScape, a program that uses vector shapes (the type of shapes created in Adobe Illustrator or Macromedia Freehand) as the basis for making repeat patterns. TextureScape can add relief and lighting to the vector shapes, and render the final image at any resolution. It also produces an alpha channel that can be used to remove the pattern motifs (i.e. the vector shape object) from the background. It is very easy to open the rendered TextureScape file in Photoshop and use the alpha channel to remove its background (which is exactly how we prepared the layered Photoshop image, Shapetex.psd).

Because After Effects is manufactured by Adobe, its features are very integrated with other Adobe products such as Photoshop and Illustrator. One of the main problems presented by the layer structure in Photoshop is how to keep the transparency of the layers when the image is imported into another application. Most programs ignore the transparency and make the images opaque, or cannot read a Photoshop file at all (this is why you need a clipping Path in order to have a non-rectangular image in QuarkXPress).

After Effects, however, "knows" about Photoshop files and transparency—and even about the layer Transfer/Apply/Blending modes in Photoshop (they are called by so many different names). When you import a Photoshop file that has layers, After Effects is able to make it into one Composition so that the layers are maintained individually and the Apply mode information is respected. Try it now.

 ## Studio Time: Importing a Photoshop File as a Composition

1. First, select all of the items in the Project window and delete them (by pressing the Delete key or selecting Clear from the Edit menu). This leaves you with an empty project.

2. Import the file "Shapetex.psd" as a Photoshop Composition (File → Import → Photoshop 3.0 as Comp…). Figure 2-10 shows the Project window after the file has been imported. Notice that instead of four individual files as you had previously, you now have a folder (which contains the layers) and an already-created-for-you Composition with the same name as the file that you imported.

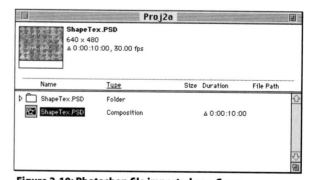

Figure 2-10: Photoshop file imported as a Comp.

3. The Photoshop file is actually 640 x 480, but a movie of that size takes far too many computer resources. You need to change the size of the Composition to a more manageable 320 x 240. Highlight the Shapetex.psd Composition name in the Project Window. Edit the Composition Settings (Composition → Composition Settings). Change the size of the Comp to 320 x 240 and set the duration to 10 seconds if it is not that way already (After Effects will remember your last setting).

4. Set the View for the comp to at least 1:2. Figure 2-11 shows the Comp window with the View size being set.

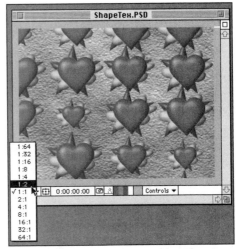

Figure 2-11: Setting the Composition View size.

Shortcuts		
Command	**Mac**	**Windows**
Edit Comp Settings	Cmd-K	Ctrl-K

Adding Key Frames and Effects

Finally! Bet you thought we'd never get to the point of actually doing something with the images…

Well, we will—in a few paragraphs! Let's think for a moment, though, of what we can do and why we (the authors) have created this project as a learning device. Still images present somewhat less of a challenge in compositing than moving images (i.e. video footage). That is why we are presenting this material early in the book, as an easy project. However, this type of project can become very complex and very interesting (we're going to keep it simple—but still interesting).

After Effects has many filters and effects that you can add to an image above and beyond the Mask and Geometrics categories that are shown in the Composition Time Layout window. However, for now, just think of these possibilities. You have four images, three of which have transparency and can interact with each other. For each image layer, you can change the following geometric attributes:

- Anchor Point: The position or point in the image around which the image rotates or scales (the default is the image center point).

- Position: The location of the image in the Composition window.

- Scale: The size of the image—it can be magnified or made smaller.

■ Rotation: The angle of the image and how many times it revolves between two key frames.

■ Opacity: The degree of transparency of the image in relation to the other images.

Changing these five attributes alone gives you several hundred different starting scenarios. You could easily spend years just exploring the creation of motion graphics using still images before you feel the need to move on!

But we need to move on… In the Studio Time that follows, you will get a chance to arrange these layers to move and interact. You will also get to apply your first filter. Along the way, you will meet a number of new commands and techniques. Rather than break up the flow of instructions, we will use the Rewind section as a way of helping you to remember the new items introduced here.

 Studio Time: Stony Texture Layer

1. Collapse the outline structure on the Composition Time Layout window by clicking on the triangles in front of each layer so that they point to the right.

2. Hide all layers except the Stony Texture layer. To do this, click on the Eye next to each layer's name in the center section of the Time Layout window. Figure 2-12 shows a portion of the Time Layout window with the top three layers hidden (the Eyes are closed).

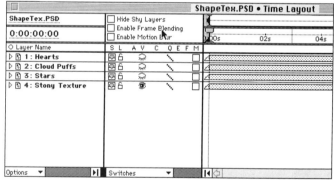

Figure 2-12: Hiding the top three layers.

3. The Stony Texture needs to be the bottom layer (it already is unless you have moved it). You make it the bottom layer by dragging the layer name to the bottom position (as you would in Photoshop) or by pressing Cmd-B (Mac) or Ctrl-B (Windows) to send it to the back.

4. Make sure that the Current Time is set to 0.

5. We are going to set the Position attribute for the Stony Texture layer. Press P to access the Position attribute.

6. Click inside the stop watch to set the first key frame at time 0:00:00:00.

7. Change the time to the Out point of the Composition. This happens to be 9.29 seconds.

You can change the time to the Out point by clicking near the 10 second mark on the dotted time line near the top of the Time Layout window (as shown in Figure 2-13). It is

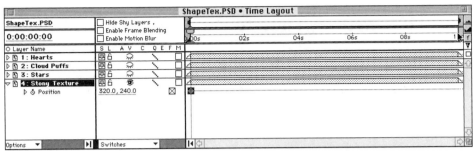

Figure 2-13: Setting the Current Time to the Out point (notice the cursor).

sometimes hard to get the time to be exact when you set it by clicking, however. A faster, more accurate way to set the time to Out point is to press the O key (the letter O, not the number zero).

8. Change the position of the layer to 160x by 120y (this centers the image in the Comp window).

You can do this visually, by dragging the center point marker (the x inside a circle) until it looks centered (as shown in Figure 2-14), or you can set it numerically by clicking on the underlined Position coordinates. Figure 2-15 shows the cursor in the correct position to click to set new coordinates.

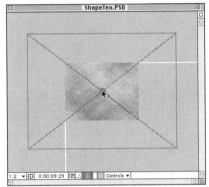

Figure 2-14: Dragging the Position Marker to set a new position.

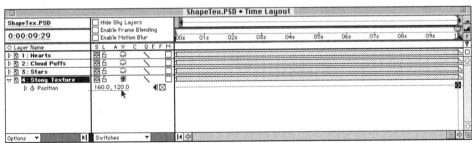

Figure 2-15: Clicking on the Position coordinates.

If you set the coordinates numerically, you see the dialog box shown in Figure 2-16. Figure 2-17 shows the Composition window once the ending position has been set.

9. Press the Tilde (~) key to collapse the Stony Texture hierarchy.

10. Press the Tab key to deselect all.

11. Save your work (Mac: Cmd-S, Windows: Ctrl-S).

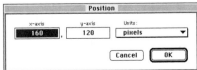

Figure 2-16: Setting a new position numerically.

Tip: Setting Time to the Out point

If you wish to set the Current Time marker to the Out point, so that you can set another key frame for a movement or effect, you can do it by typing the letter O (no need to press the Shift key—lowercase is fine). However, you do need to have the layer selected when you type, or else the time marker will not move.

Shortcuts

Command	Key
Set Current Time to Layer Outpoint	O
Collapse Layer Hierarchy	~ (Tilde)
Deselect All	Tab

Let's work on the Stars layer next. For this one, we will set opacity and rotation attributes.

 ## *Studio Time: The Stars layer*

1. Click on the Eye next to the Stars layer to turn it back on.

2. Make sure it is on top of the Texture layer (which it should be).

3. Set the Current Time to 0.

4. Click on the Stars layer to select it.

5. Type the letter T to bring up the Opacity settings (think "T" for "Transparency").

6. Press the Shift key and type the letter R to add a Rotation attribute for manipulation (the Shift key allows you to select and make visible more than one geometric attribute at a time).

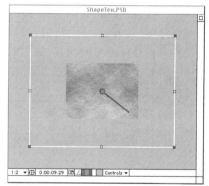

Figure 2-17: Composition window with new position set.

7. Click inside the stop watches for both attributes at the Current Time of 0.

8. The Rotation is fine at the original setting of 0.

9. Change the Opacity to 0% by clicking on the dotted line underneath the 100% setting. The cursor in Figure 2-18 shows the correct place to click. Figure 2-19 shows the Opacity dialog.

10. Set the time to 8 seconds (Mac: Cmd-G, Windows: Ctrl-G) and type 800 in the Time dialog box.

11. Set a new Opacity value the same way you did before. Make it 30%.

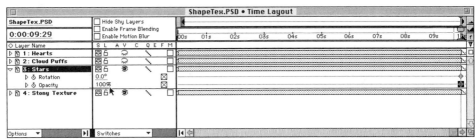

Figure 2-18: Clicking to bring up the Opacity dialog.

12. Change the time to 10 seconds.

13. Set a key frame for Opacity of 0%.

14. While at the 10 second time, also set a key frame for Rotation (click on the under lined Rotation amount to bring up the dialog box). Set the number of rotations to 1. Figure 2-20 shows this dialog.

15. Press the Tilde (~) to collapse the hierarchy.

16. Preview your movie to this point by clicking on the center button (the right-pointing triangle) on the top row of the Time Controls window. Make sure that you see a complete rotation of the Stars layer.

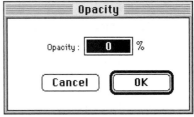

Figure 2-19: Opacity dialog.

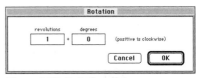

Figure 2-20: Rotation dialog.

There is a problem with the rotating Stars layer. Since it is in the upper left corner of the Composition window, there are times that the corners rotate off of the Composition so that no stars appear near the corners of the Comp. We need to fix this so that we always see stars in the movie. However, we do not want to change the position of the Stars layer through time. We need to change the position once and leave it that way—preferably without causing any key frames to be created for that attribute. It would also help if the layer were smaller. At 85% of its normal size, more stars would fit into the movie, but the image will still be large enough to keep stars visible the entire time that it rotates.

To change the initial value for any attribute without making any key frames, you need to set the Current Time to 0 and change the attribute value without clicking inside of the stop watch.

Studio Time: Setting Initial Values with No Key Frames

1. Click to select the Stars layer.

2. Click on the Triangle in front of the layer name to show all of the attributes.

3. Click on the Position attribute (on the dotted line) to bring up the dialog box. Set the values to 160x and 120y. Click OK.

4. Click on the Scale attribute. Set the Scale to 85%. Figure 2-21 shows the After Effects screen at this point. In the Time Layout window, notice that there are no key frames for the Position or Scale attributes and that there is also no mark inside of the stop watch in front of those attributes.

Next, let's turn our attention to the Cloud Puffs layer. In this layer, you will get to add your first effect—a Gaussian Blur.

 ## *Studio Time: The Cloud Puffs Layer*

1. Turn on the Clouds layer by clicking on the Eye icon next to the layer name. Make certain that the layer is positioned above the Stars layer and below the Hearts.

2. Click on the name of the layer to select the layer.

3. Set the Current Time to 0.

4. Reveal the Opacity (T) and Position (Shift-P) attributes. (Remember, you need to press the Shift key when you select a second attribute to add it to the first one shown rather than replace it.)

5. Set key frames for both Opacity and Position by clicking inside of the stop watches.

6. Set the starting Opacity to 30%.

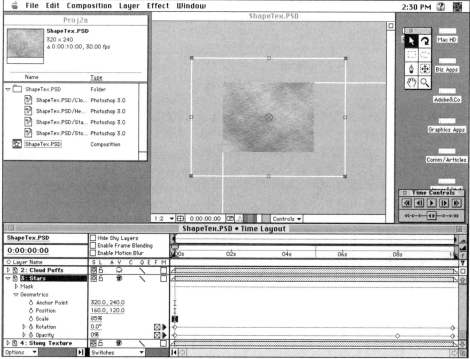

Figure 2-21: After Effects window with starting values set for the Stars layer.

7. Set the position to 0x and 240y. This moves the image to the upper right-hand corner.

8. Set the Current Time to the layer Out point (O). You could also get to the end of the Comp by pressing Cmd-Opt-Right Arrow (Mac) or Ctrl-Atl-Right Arrow (Windows).

9. Drag the layer diagonally towards the upper right. After you begin to drag, press the Shift and the (Mac) Opt or (Windows) Alt key. You will feel the image snap to a corner or center position as you drag. Drag it until it snaps to the lower left corner of the image. Figure 2-22 shows the Composition window with the Clouds layer in position. The Position coordinates should read 320, 0.

10. Change the Opacity to 40% as well while you are still located at the layer Out point.

11. Set the Current Time to 1 second (Mac: Cmd-G, Windows: Ctrl-G) by typing 100 into the dialog.

12. Create a key frame that sets the Opacity to 100% at 1 second. (Hint: click on the Opacity setting.) If you look at the key frames along the time line you will see that the clouds will gradually fade from 30% to 100% in 1 second of time. Then it will go from 100% opacity to 40% opacity in nine seconds time.

13. Set the Current Time to 0.

Let's add a Gaussian Blur effect to this layer that will change over time. It will be blurrier at the beginning and get cleaner as time goes on. This will help to create some spatial depth in the project.

14. From the Effects menu, select the Blur & Sharpen submenu. Drag down to the Gaussian Blur effect and release the mouse button. Figure 2-23 shows this menu.

15. The selection of the Gaussian Blur effect adds the window shown in Figure 2-24 to your screen. This is the Effect Control window. You can change the settings here rather than in the Time Layout window if you wish. However, you do need to

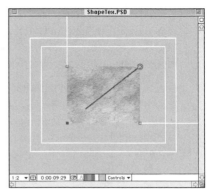

Figure 2-22: Clouds layer dragged to lower-left corner.

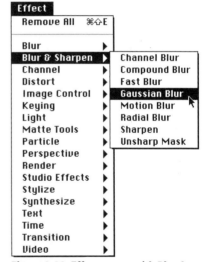

Figure 2-23: Effects menu with Blur & Sharpen submenu.

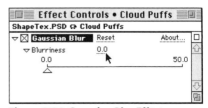

Figure 2-24: Gaussian Blur Effect window.

expand the effect in the Time Layout window so that you can see the stop watch and set the first key frame (click on the right-pointing arrow to make the hierarchy drop down).

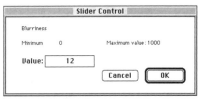

Click on the underlined Blurriness amount as shown by the cursor in Figure 2-24. Change the Blurriness to 12 in the resulting dialog box, which is shown in Figure 2-25. If you have not set a key

Figure 2-25: "Set Gaussian Blur Blurriness Amount" dialog.

frame by clicking in the stop watch, your settings are assumed to be Constants and will not change.

16. Set the Current Time to 6 seconds, 15 frames (Mac: Cmd-G. Windows: Ctrl-G) by typing 615 into the dialog. Set the Blurriness amount to 0. The effect remains at 0 for the rest of this Comp.

17. Use the Tilde (~) key to flatten the hierarchy.

18. Save your work.

"Reading" the Composition Window

It can be somewhat confusing to know what is happening when you change the position of a layer in the Composition window if the layer itself is larger than the Composition (as is the case in the current exercise). The layers are each 640 x 480 while the Composition is 320 x 240 (exactly half the size in each dimension).

When you first opened the Photoshop file as a Comp, After Effects placed it so that only the upper-left quarters of the layers were visible through the Composition window. That is why you saw a larger white square extending around the Composition. When you moved the Stony Texture layer's position, the white outline moved to the surround the visible composition. Changing the position of the Stars layer for the entire duration of the Comp placed the white outline equidistant from the image border (and reducing it to 85% made the outline smaller).

Therefore, when you look at Figure 2-22, you see the positions of the three layers that you have set so far as they appear at the Out point of the Comp. The Stony Textures and the Stars layers are centered, and the Puffy Clouds layer is moved so that the lower-left quarter of the image is visible in the Composition window.

One more layer remains. You will move the position of this layer to center it, and then add moving Scale and Opacity effects.

Studio Time: The Hearts Layer

1. Turn on the Hearts layer by clicking on the Eye icon next to the layer name. Make certain that the layer is on top.

2. Click on the name of the layer to select the layer.

3. Set the Current Time to 0.

4. Reveal the Opacity (T) and Scale (Shift-S) attributes. (Remember, you need to press the Shift key when you select a second attribute to add it to the first one shown rather than replace it.)

5. Set key frames for both Opacity and Scale by clicking inside of the stop watches.

6. Set the Scale to 50% and the Opacity to 0% (at the 0 time marker). Figure 2-26 shows the Scale dialog as it should be set.

7. Set the Current Time to 5 seconds (Mac: Cmd-G, Windows: Ctrl-G) by typing 500 into the dialog.

8. Set a key frame for Opacity of 50%.

9. Go to the Layer Outpoint (O) and set a key frame for Opacity of 100% and a Scale key frame of 85%.

Figure 2-26: Scale dialog.

10. It is painfully obvious after you have set the final key frame that you need to center the Hearts layer—since only part of the Composition is covered with hearts. Use the Tilde (~) to collapse the hierarchy and then expand it by clicking on the triangle. All of the Geometric attributes are shown.

11. Set the Current Time to 0.

12. Click on the Position attribute (but not the stop watch) to set a constant position of 160x by 120y, or drag the layer towards the upper-left and press the modifier key (Mac: Opt, Windows: Alt) after you start to drag. Let the layer snap to the center of the composition.

13. Press the Tilde (~) to collapse the layer hierarchy.

14. Save your work.

Shortcuts

Command	Mac	Windows
Constrain & Snap To	Shift-Opt-Drag	Shift-Alt-Drag
Go to End of Comp	Cmd-Opt-Right arrow	Ctrl-Alt-Right arrow
Go to Beginning of Comp	Cmd-Opt-Left arrow	Ctrl-Alt-Left arrow
Send Layer to Top	Cmd-F	Ctrl-F
Send Layer to Bottom	Cmd-B	Ctrl-B

You are now ready to render the file. You may wish to preview it first, but it will be very slow. The Gaussian Blur effect needs to be computed for each frame up until frame 6.15, and that slows down the preview considerably.

Render the file as you learned in Chapter 1.

 # Rewind

In this chapter you learned two types of skills for After Effects. You learned major concepts — such as setting keyframes and adding effects, and you learned productivity skills— such as keyboard shortcuts — to help you work faster and more efficiently.

Major Concepts

- Setting keyframes.
- Scaling an image over time.
- Changing the Opacity of an image over time.
- Changing the Position of an image over time.
- Rotating an image over time.
- Adding a Gaussian Blur effect.
- Setting a Constant value for a layer attribute.

Productivity Skills

- Moving to a layer Out point (O).
- Using the Go To Time command (Mac: Cmd-G, Windows: Ctrl-G).
- Sending a layer to the top (Mac: Cmd-F, Windows: Ctrl-F) or bottom (Mac: Cmd-B, Windows: Ctrl-B).

- Constraining the movement of a layer to the horizontal, vertical, or diagonal so that it snaps into position (Mac: Shift-Opt-Drag, Windows: Shift-Alt-Drag).

- Moving to the start (Mac: Cmd-Opt-Left arrow, Windows Ctrl-Alt-Left arrow) or end (Mac: Cmd-Opt-Right arrow, Windows Ctrl-Alt-Right arrow) of a Comp.

- Collapsing a layer hierarchy (Tilde).

- Deselecting all (Tab).

 # Coming Attractions

In Chapter 3, you will learn how to work with moving video and still images in one Composition.

Using Video and Still Images

 # Preview

In Chapter 2, you learned how to mix a number of still images together to create a moving texture. In this chapter, you will see how "live" video can be mixed with still images.

For this chapter, we edited the video footage and digitally spliced together a variety of clips—some footage taken in New York Harbor, and an angry, hurricane-lashed ocean taken in Margate, New Jersey.

In this chapter, you will use the footage as an already-prepared movie. In Chapter 4, we'll give you the original video footage (well…almost original—read on to see why) and show you how to put it together yourself.

Preview the movie AECH03.mov to see the finished project. We were feeling whimsical, but it is a really good use of still and video images.

In this chapter, you will learn these new tricks and techniques that allow you to:

- 🎬 Nudge a footage item into place using the arrow keys.
- 🎬 Use the Grid to help position an element.
- 🎬 Change the background color of a Comp.
- 🎬 Preview the Comp using the spacebar.
- 🎬 Create "sustaining" keyframes.

- Trim footage.
- Copy and Paste keyframes.
- Move the Layer Duration bar to set In points.
- "Reverse animate" to make sure your footage ends where it should.
- Split Layers.
- View a footage item's alpha channel.

Feature Presentation

The chapters in this section of the book follow a specific order. In using After Effects, you can composite still and/or video images. Therefore, one is left with three mathematical possibilities: use only still images, use still and video footage, composite video onto video. These possibilities occupy chapters 2, 3, and 4. We present the three topics in order of their increasing complexity. Since this is the first chapter in which you will use video captured from a video camera (as opposed to QuickTime movies built from other After Effects still-image composites), it is time to look at ways in which video footage differs from still images.

A Tale of Two Fields

Video differs from still images in a number of ways. The most obvious of them is, of course, that it moves—or at least appears to move. The apparent motion in video footage comes from the fact that every frame of the footage item is slightly different from the one that preceded it. When the frames are displayed at a fast rate (such as the 24 frames per second of standard film or 30 frames per second of video), it looks to the viewer as if something is actually moving. This, of course, is the principle behind animation, where motion is shown by flipping rapidly through a variety of still images. In video (or live movies), the motion is actually captured on videotape or film, and when the footage is digitized, it shows up as the series of slightly different images.

But you knew that already... So, why are we repeating it? When you capture live footage from a video camera, other complications arise:

- The footage now has a real, fixed length (still images take the length of the Composition into which they are placed).

- The footage has to be translated from an analog device to a digital device (unless you are using one of the new, expensive digital video cameras).

In the chapters to follow, you will learn how to change the time of a clip—to trim frames from the start or end of the footage, or to make the frames play faster or more slowly.

You will also learn about some of the technicalities of getting good video captures from your camera. However, you need to know a little bit of what is in store for you (threat or promise... you need to decide which!).

One of the problems with getting good video input is that each frame of NTSC video (the standard for video used in the United States—the acronym has a "formal" interpretation as well, but engineers claim it means "Never Twice the Same Color") is actually two frames. The video frame consists of two images (called fields—one containing the even rows and the other the odd rows) that are displayed one after another on the television screen. These images are said to be interlaced. In order to get good quality footage from them, you need to de-interlace them (even if you need to re-interlace them in order to write them back out to video tape).

The de-interlacing process is handled by After Effects when you select the Interpret Footage→ Main→ Fields and Pulldown command. In most of the footage in this book, we have already done that for you. We had to—because we needed to reduce the size of the video footage to fit it all on the CD-ROM. To reduce the size, we needed to select a different video compressor (codec), so we pre-built the footage for you at the highest quality-vs.-size setting that we could use. We will talk about preparing, capturing, and compressing video in later chapters. If you need more specific information now, read those chapters. For the moment, we just wanted to warn you that there is a major issue that we are glossing over because it is not the proper time to introduce you to the full complexities. (We will let you fall totally in love with After Effects before we show you some of the "gotchas.")

Setting the Scene

The project for this chapter is a movie that contains footage playing inside of an old television set. The set is showing the evening news—and all of it is bad. There is a "Special Report." A tidal surge is announced along with the news that a ferry is stranded. Finally, there is the announcement of a space invasion! And so it seems… You not only see the spaceship on the TV, it flies out of the TV right into your room!

Studio Time: Set Up and Import Footage

1. Create a new project (Mac: Cmd-Opt-N, Windows: Ctrl-Alt-N). Save it as AECH03.aep.

2. Import the entire footage folder at one time by using the Import Footage Files command (Mac: Cmd-Opt-I, Windows: Ctrl-Alt-I). Figure 3-1 shows the multiple footage open dialog. After you select each footage item, you are prompted for the alpha matte treatment that you want. Select Straight (not pre-multiplied) each time you are asked. Tip: Remember which

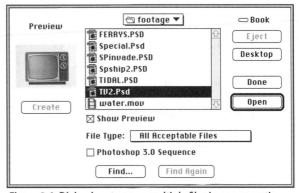

Figure 3-1: Dialog box to open multiple files in one operation.

files you have imported already because After Effects does not keep track and lets you import the same file multiple times.

3. Create a new Comp (Mac: Cmd-N, Windows: Ctrl-N). The Comp should be 320 x 240, 12 seconds long, and 30 fps.

4. Set the Current Time to 00 (Mac: Cmd-G, Windows: Ctrl-G, then type 0).

Now that the project is set up and all of the footage has been imported, you can arrange it in the Comp window. In the instructions that follow, you will see how to nudge your footage item if it is not exactly where you want it. You will also learn how to change the background color for a layer.

 ## Studio Time: Placing TV and Video layers

1. Drag the Tv2.psd image into the center of the Comp. Let it snap to the center. Notice that the duration of the image is the same as the duration of the Composition.

2. We want to position the TV, however, so that the TV screen, rather than the entire TV, is in the exact center of the Comp. You can use the arrow keys to nudge the footage left, right, up, or down by one pixel at a time. You can also you the Shift key with an arrow key to move ten pixels at one time. You need to position the TV with the Right arrow key.

3. How do you know if you have the TV screen centered? You can eyeball it, of course. You can also use the Grid feature on the Composition window. Click on the small rectangular control at the bottom of the Composition window (between the View control and the Current Time marker). The first click will cause the Title Safe area to appear, a second click will bring up a Grid. Centering the screen actually does not look good, so instead, position it so that the television control panel starts two grid squares to the right of center (as shown in Figure 3-2). Turn off the Grid when you have the image properly positioned.

4. Notice that the center of the TV is black. This is because it is masked. The background color of the Comp is black (by default) and that color shows through the screen area on the TV. You can change this background color if you wish. Pull down the Composition item on the menu and select Background Color. Figure 3-3 shows the dialog box.

5. Click on the Eyedropper and select a gray at the outer edge of the television image. The center of the screen turns gray. This actually has no effect on the Comp at all, as the background will not show anyway, but we wanted to make sure that you knew you could do this. If you click on

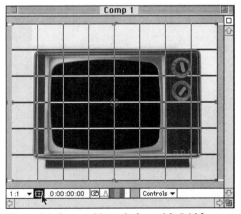

Figure 3-2: Composition window with Grid for positioning.

the color square instead of the Eyedropper, the standard system Color Picker appears. Click OK.

6. While still at 00, drag the video clip into the Comp window. Place it over the TV screen. Let it snap to the center of the Comp.

7. Send it to the back (Mac: Cmd-B, Windows: Ctrl-B). The video clip will appear as if it is in the TV screen. You can press the spacebar to play through the Comp frame by frame. The playback is much slower than it will be when the movie is rendered (or than it was when you previewed the finished movie in MoviePlayer).

8. Set the Current Time to 00 (Mac: Cmd-G, Windows: Ctrl-G, then type 0).

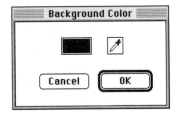

Figure 3-3: Change Background Color dialog box.

Shortcuts

Command	Mac	Windows
Change Bkg. Color	Shift-Cmd-B	Shift-Ctrl-B
Send Layer Backwards	Cmd-B	Ctrl-B

Making Headlines, Part 1

The next four Studio Time segments place the news headlines in their correct locations and set up the keyframes for those layers. Each type element will fade up, play for a bit, and then fade off.

Let's move the Special Report image in place first.

Studio Time: Special Report

1. Drag the Special.psd image into the Comp window. Position it over the TV screen so that it looks as if it is on the screen. Use the arrow keys as needed. The type is just a bit too large.

2. Type S to open the Scale property. Set the scale to 80%. Do not make the property key-frame-able (don't click in the stop watch). The scale will remain constant.

Figure 3-4: Special Report—correctly positioned.

3. Nudge the scaled image as needed to center it in the screen. Figure 3-4 shows the headline correctly positioned.

4. We do need to create a keyframe for the Opacity, however, as we want that to change over time. Press T to display the Opacity property. This closes the Scale property (since you didn't press the Shift key) but that's okay. The scale will remain at 80% and we don't need it cluttering up the time line since it does not change.

5. Click in the Opacity stop watch to make the property key-frame-able. Set the first keyframe at Time=00. The Opacity setting is 0% (click on the underlined opacity amount).

6. Set the Current Time to 15 frames (Mac: Cmd-G, Windows: Ctrl-G and type 15 or just move the Playback Head until the Current Time reads 0:00:00:15). This is the half-second mark.

7. Create another keyframe by setting the Opacity for the headline to 100%.

8. Set the Current Time to 115 frames (Mac: Cmd-G, Windows: Ctrl-G and type 115 or just move the Playback Head until the Current Time reads 0:00:01:15). This is the one and one-half-second mark.

9. Leave another keyframe at this point in time, but do not change the Opacity value. You can do this by simply clicking in the keyframe Navigation box to the right of the Opacity Amount setting. Figure 3-5 shows this location marked with an X in the correct spot and the cursor pointing to it.

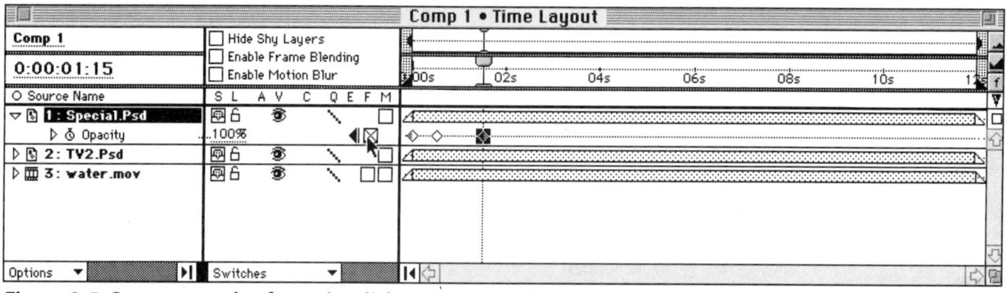

Figure 3-5: Create a new keyframe by clicking in the keyframe Navigation box indicated by the cursor.

10. Set the Current Time to 2 seconds (Mac: Cmd-G, Windows: Ctrl-G, and type 200 or just move the Playback Head until the Current Time reads 0:00:02:00).

11. Create a new keyframe. Make the Opacity 0%.

12. This is the end-of-the-line for this headline. Since there is no reason to keep it active at 0% Opacity, we need to tell After Effects that the headline's usefulness has ended and its length should be cut short. The process of removing frames from the beginning or end of a footage item is called trimming. Trim the headline to the Current Time by pressing the Option and Right bracket key (]) for Mac or Alt-] for Windows.

13. Preview the movie by pressing the spacebar. Press it again to stop the preview.

14. Set the Current Time to 00 (Mac: Cmd-G, Windows: Ctrl-G, then type 0).

Let's stop a minute and talk about the action in Step 9. We left a keyframe with the same Opacity setting as the one before. Why? What purpose did it serve?

The second keyframe with an Opacity of 100% ensured that the opacity of the headline would remain at that level for an entire second—the time between 0.15 and 1.1.5. Had that second keyframe not been set, the headline would have begun to fade as soon as it had reached full intensity. By using a matching keyframe, we made sure that no change would occur until a different point in time. The final keyframe, at 2.00, causes the opacity to move back to 0%, but the actual fading only occurs over the half second from 1.1.5 to 2.00.

Trimming Footage

In addition to learning to create a "sustaining" keyframe, the last Studio Time also showed you one way to trim footage. If you are a frequent Photoshop user (and we assume that most of you are), you have undoubtedly realized that Photoshop abounds with many different ways to accomplish the same task. After Effects does too. You have learned about a number of different ways to open footage items, that most menu commands have keyboard shortcuts, and that you can create keyframes using several different methods. It should not surprise you, then, to learn that you can trim footage in a variety of ways.

In the Studio Time just completed, you trimmed frames from the end of the Special Report headline by use of a key sequence (Mac: Opt-], Windows: Alt-]) in the Time Layout window. You can also trim footage in the Layer window. While that is not the most efficient place to trim footage for this project, the next Studio Time will show you how it is done.

You will also learn how to restore the footage that you have trimmed. Trimming does not actually remove anything at all. It only suppresses the viewing of the trimmed frames. You can restore them at any time you wish. Of course, once you render the movie, those frames are not included in the finished product at all; but they are never physically pulled from the original footage item.

Figure 3-6a: Layer window before trimming the duration of the footage item.

Studio Time: Trimming Footage in the Layer Window

1. Your Current Time should be set at 00 from the last Studio Time. Check to make sure that it is.

2. Drag the Tidal.psd image into the Comp window. The text is much too large, but let's ignore that for right now. Let the text snap to the center of the Comp window.

3. Double-click on the name Tidal.psd in the Time Layout window. This opens the

Layer window. Figure 3-6a shows the Layer window with the Layer Duration bar set to the full 12 second length of the Comp.

4.　Set the Current Time to 2 seconds (Mac: Cmd-G, Windows: Ctrl-G, and type 200 or just move the Playback Head until the Current Time reads 0:00:02:00).

5.　Click the red Out button. This snaps the Out point of the layer (the time that the layer ends) to 2.00 (Current Time marker). The layer has been trimmed to 2 seconds, as you can see in Figure 3-6b. Figure 3-7 shows the Time Layout window at this point. Notice that the gray Layer Duration bar is only 2 seconds long there as well. In both windows, you can see, by the dotted lines extending beyond the trimmed footage, that frames have been suppressed.

Figure 3-6b: Layer window after trimming.

6.　Drag the red Out point indicator on the Layer Duration bar in the Layer window so that it stretches back to 12 seconds again. This shows how you can restore the footage simply by dragging the Out point.

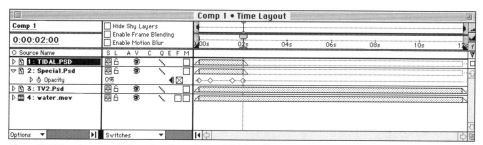

Figure 3-7: Time Layout window showing trimmed Tidal.psd layer.

7.　Undo (Mac: Cmd-Z, Windows: Ctrl-Z).

8.　We need to set the time to 12 seconds to show you another way to restore footage. Since 12 seconds is the Composition duration, here is another shortcut to getting there: press Cmd-Opt-Right arrow (Mac) or Ctrl-Alt-Right arrow(Windows). This key combination will always get you to the end time of a Comp.

9.　Click the red Out button again. This also restores the footage.

10. Set the Current Time to 2 seconds (Mac: Cmd-G, Windows: Ctrl-G, and type 200, or just move the Playback Head until the Current Time reads 0:00:02:00).

11. This time, trim the layer by pressing the same key combination that you used in the Time Layout window (Mac: Opt-], Windows: Alt-]). It works just as well in the Layer window.

Shortcuts

Command	Mac	Windows
Go to Comp start	Cmd-Opt-Left arrow	Ctrl-Alt-Left arrow
Go to Comp end	Cmd-Opt-Right arrow	Ctrl-Alt-Right arrow
Trim end to Current Time	Opt-]	Alt-]
Trim start to Current Time	Opt-[	Alt-[

Moving Time

In this section, we will show you how to move the Layer Duration bar to a new time (not an efficient way to work in this project—but this is a good spot to learn that it can be done).

You placed the Tidal.psd image in the Composition window while the Current Time was set to 00. Because of this, the Tidal.psd image was also given an In point of 00. It makes no sense to leave it there, since that two headlines ("Special Report" and "Tidal

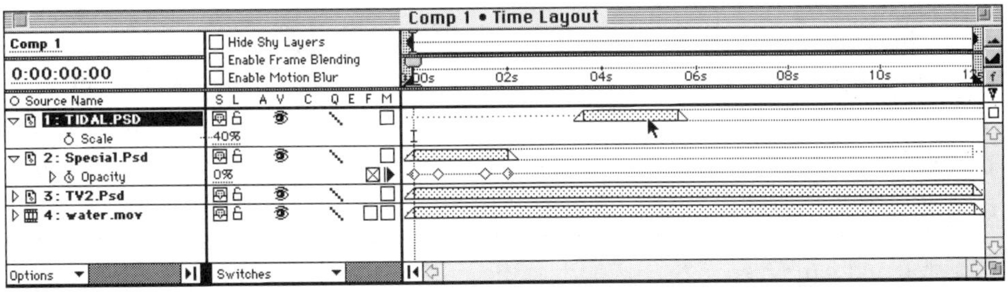

Figure 3-8: Moving the Layer Duration bar.

Surge") would conflict with one another. We need the Tidal.psd image to start at the Out point of the Special Report image.

In this Studio Time segment, you will learn to reposition the Layer Duration bar in several ways.

 Studio Time: Moving Time and Copying Key Frames

1. First, you need to set the scaling for the Tidal Surge text. Press S to show the Scale property. Set the amount to 40%. Do not click in the stop watch—you do not want to create a keyframe.

2. Center the text in the TV screen. You can do this by dragging, nudging, or using the Grid to help position the text. Tip: Press and hold the Opt key (Mac) or Alt key (Windows) as you drag to view the item as you drag it.

3. The Current Time should still be set at 2.00. If not, set it now.

4. Place your mouse on the Layer Duration bar for the Tidal.psd layer (the 2-second long ribbon-like bar that you shortened). With the mouse button pressed, you can drag it anywhere you wish along the layer time line. Figure 3-8 shows the Layer Duration bar as it is being moved.

5. Try to position it so that the dotted area on the ribbon starts at exactly 2 seconds.

Figure 3-9: Comparison of Time Layout window In and Out points with Layer window In and Out points.

Hmm… How can you tell? You can't—unless perhaps one of the other windows will show you the new time. Maybe the Layer window lets us see the new In point. Double-click the name in the Time Layout window to open the Layer window for Tidal.psd. Figure 3-9 shows a dilemma. It looks like the In point in the Layer window is still reading 00. Bad news—or is it?

Actually, it is not. You are looking at two different systems of telling time. The Layer window shows the In and Out points relative to the length of the footage item. The Time Layout window shows the In and Out points relative to the Comp.

Therefore, the Layer window correctly shows that the footage item is not trimmed at the start and is trimmed to two seconds at the end. Notice that the Playback Head in the Layer window is positioned at the beginning of the footage item—even though the Current Time is 2.00. This makes sense if you think about it; 2.00 is the time at which the footage item begins.

6. If you want to see where you are dragging the Layer Duration bar, you need to show the Info palette (Mac: Cmd-2, Windows: Ctrl-2). This little palette is as helpful here as the Info palette is in Photoshop. This time, drag the Layer Duration bar and read the numbers in the Info palette. Figure 3-10 shows the Layer Duration bar in motion and the Info palette above it. Using the Info palette and patience, you can properly align the Layer Duration bar by dragging.

There are easier ways.

7. Leave the Current Time set at 2.00. This time, drag the Layer Duration bar towards the right, and as you drag it back to the left again, press the Shift key. As the bar nears the Current Time marker, it will snap into place. If you wish to position by dragging, this method is somewhat easier to control.

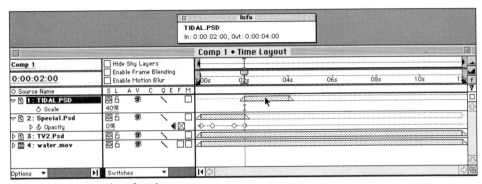

Figure 3-10: Reading the Info palette.

8. Drag the Layer Duration bar far to the right again. Leave the Current Time marker at 2.00. This time, simply press the Right bracket key (]). The Time Duration bar will fly to the Current Time marker. This is the most foolproof method of setting the correct In point (other than bringing in the Layer at the right time so that you don't need to fool around with it at all).

Copying keyframes

Now that we finally have the Tidal.psd layer positioned correctly in time, we will see how to copy the keyframes that you set up for the Special Report layer and paste them into Tidal layer. This makes repeat processing—which is what we are doing—much easier, because it allows you to re-use the timings that you previously set.

 Studio Time: Copying keyframes

1. Make sure that the Current Time is still set to 2.00.

2. Press T to bring up the Opacity property.

3. Drag a Marquee carefully around the four keyframe markers in the Special Report layer (use the same Pointer/Arrow tool that you have been using; press the mouse button down and drag just as you would to drag a number of icons on the desktop at one time). Figure 3-11 shows a detail shot of the Time Layout window with a Marquee around the keyframes. All four keyframes will darken to show that they have been selected.

4. Copy the keyframes to the clipboard (Mac: Cmd-C, Windows: Ctrl-C).

5. Click on the name "Tidal.psd" in the top layer. The layer name will turn black.

6. Paste in the selection from the clipboard (Mac: Cmd-V, Windows: Ctrl-V). There is no need click in the stop watch before you paste. The paste command creates the new keyframes. These keyframes bring the opacity of the image from 0 to 100 in .5 seconds, hold the opacity at 100 for 1 second, and the bring the opacity back to 0 in the remaining .5 second.

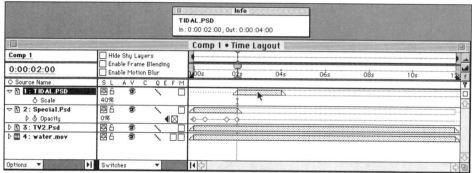

Figure 3-11: Marquee drawn around keyframes to be copied.

Making Headlines, Part 2

We need to add the remaining two headlines to the Comp. Each new one will begin where the previous headline ended, and last for 2 seconds. We will again copy the keyframes and re-use them.

Studio Time: Setting Two More Headlines

1. Set the Current Time to 4.00 (the Out point of the Tidal.psd layer).

2. Drag the Ferry.psd image into the Comp window. Notice, in Figure 3-12, that the In point of the layer is automatically set to 4.00 (the location of the Current Time marker).

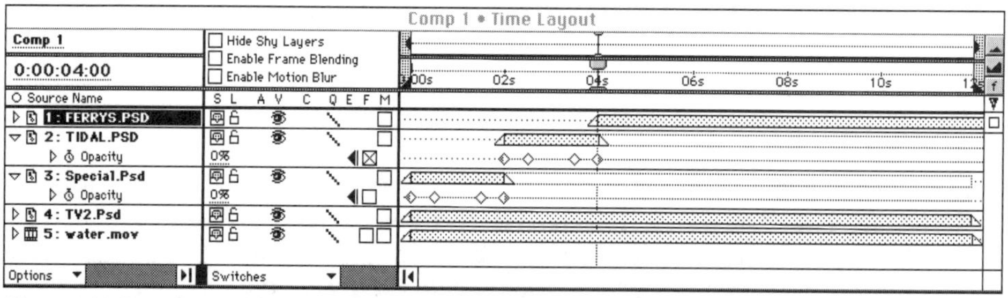

Figure 3-12: Ferry layer with In point at 4.00.

3. Press S to bring up the Scale property.

4. Scale the image to 60% and center it on the screen.

5. Press T to bring up the Opacity property.

6. The keyframes should still be on the clipboard. Make sure that the layer name is highlighted, and then paste in the selection from the clipboard (Mac: Cmd-V, Windows: Ctrl-V).

7. Click to deselect the keyframes, but click on the layer name to make sure that it is still selected.

8. Set the Current Time to 6.00.

9. Trim the footage to the Current Time marker (Mac: Opt-], Windows: Alt-]).

10. Drag the Spaceshp.psd image into the Comp.

11. Press S to bring up the Scale property.

12. Scale the image to 70% and center it on the screen.

13. Press T to bring up the Opacity property.

14. The keyframes should still be on the clipboard. Make sure that the layer name is high-lighted, and then paste in the selection from the clipboard (Mac: Cmd-V, Windows: Ctrl-V).

15. Click to deselect the keyframes, but click on the layer name to make sure that it is still selected.

16. Set the Current time to 8.00.

17. Trim the footage to the Current Time marker (Mac: Opt-], Windows: Alt-]). Figure 3-13 shows the Time Layout window at this point.

18. Set the Current Time to 00 (Mac: Cmd-G, Windows: Ctrl-G, then type 0). Press the spacebar to preview the movie.

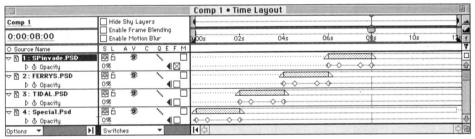

Figure 3-13: Time Layout window with four headlines positioned.

Visitor from a Weird Planet

In this final segment of the project, we will introduce our space visitor into the Composition. This image is part of the Classic Pio Nostalgia collection. He is the "Beer Guy," and is provided for your use by Classic Pio Partners.

You will also learn two new techniques. The first of them is what we call "reverse animation" and is possibly a philosophy or approach more than a technique. When you animate a still image, it is often much easier to place it where you want it to end up in the Comp rather than where it enters the Comp. In this case, you will place the final keyframe first. After the ending keyframe is positioned, you can set the Current Time back to the In point of the layer and drag the image to its starting position. We will have you do a lot of this type of animation throughout this book.

The second technique is called "layer splitting." We will create some of the keyframes for the space invader, and then break up the layer into two parts. When we created the project, we used two copies of the space invader file—one that looked as if it were inside of the television, and one that was on top of the TV so that it could zoom out. When we wrote the instructions, we looked and said "This is a perfect opportunity, not to be missed, to teach about splitting layers." So, the bottom line here is that the final facet of this project could be done either way—and both ways are totally "correct."

Studio Time: Placing the Visitor

1. The Current Time should still be set to 8.00.

2. Drag the Space2.psd image into the Comp. Let it snap to the center point. Figure 3-14 shows the space visitor. Gee that's big!

3. Press S to display the Scale property. Do not keyframe. Set the scale to 15%.

4. Press P to display the Position property. Click in the stop watch to make the property key-frame-able.

Figure 3-14: Space visitor.

5. Set the Current Time to 9 seconds (Mac: Cmd-G, Windows: Ctrl-G, and type 900, or just move the Playback Head until the Current Time reads 0:00:09:00).

6. Click inside the Position keyframe Navigation box to leave a keyframe at this position. Figure 3-15 shows where to click (the X).

7. Return the Current Time setting back to 8 seconds. The easiest way to do this is to click on the left arrow next to the Position box. The arrows next to the property boxes let you easily navigate from one keyframe to another. This is certainly the most accurate way to make sure that you return to the exact place where a keyframe has been set.

8. Change the View for the Comp to 1:2 so that you can see the pasteboard around it.

Figure 3-15: The Position box.

9. Drag the space ship directly to the right. Place it out on the pasteboard so that it is near the right side of the Comp. Figure 3-16 shows you this view.

10. Press the spacebar to preview the movie.

11. Set the Current Time to 9.15 seconds (Mac: Cmd-G, Windows: Ctrl-G, and type 915, or just move the Playback Head until the Current Time reads 0:00:09:15).

12. Split the layer at this point (Edit→ Split Layer). Figure 3-17 shows the Time Layout window with two copies of the Space2.psd image on top of the layer stack.

13. The small time line (the 1.15 second piece) is now the top layer on the stack. This is the small bit of footage that needs to be placed behind the television. Drag this layer to the near bottom of the stack. It needs to be positioned above the Water.mov and below the Tv2.psd image.

14. Drag the Current Time back to about 7 seconds and press the spacebar to preview the movie.

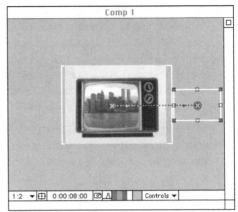

Figure 3-16: Positioning the space ship on the pasteboard.

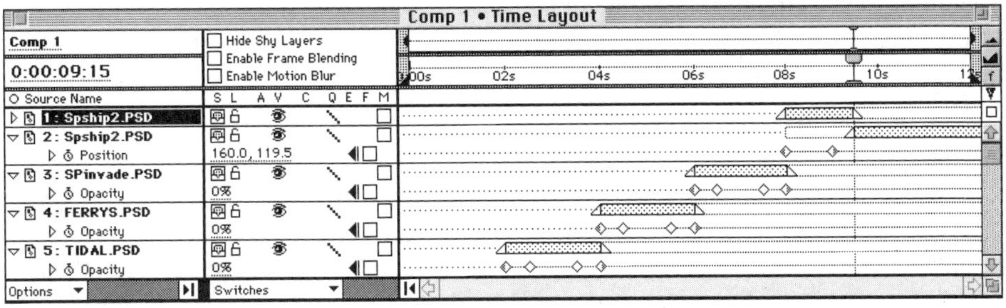

Figure 3-17: Space ship layer split.

15. Let's return to the new top layer (it is also called Space2.psd). Click on it to select it. Notice that the Layer Duration bar shows that it has been trimmed on the front to this point. It also shows the two keyframes already set up for Position.

16. Set the Current Time back to the In point of the current layer by pressing the letter "I." This sets the Current time to 9.15.

17. The Position property is displayed. Press Shift-S to display the Scale property as well.

18. Click inside of the Scale stop watch to make the property key-frame-able and leave a keyframe at the Current Time.

19. Click in the Position keyframe Navigation box to leave a Position keyframe at the Current Time as well. (If you wish, you may delete the two keyframes left over from the layer split. Highlight them by clicking, Shift-clicking, or by encircling them with a Marquee. Then press the Delete key.)

20. Set the Current Time to 11 seconds (Mac: Cmd-G, Windows: Ctrl-G, and type 1100 or just move the Playback Head until the Current Time reads 0:00:11:00).

21. Change the Scale to 100%. This leaves a keyframe.

22. Press the Opt key (Mac) or Alt key (Windows) and drag the little man to a location in the window where you can see the most of him. This is his moment (and the last Position keyframe in the movie)! Figure 3-18 shows you this frame. The act of moving the image creates a new keyframe.

23. Set the Current Time to 00 (Mac: Cmd-G, Windows: Ctrl-G, then type 0). Press the spacebar to preview the movie.

Figure 3-18: Space visitor correctly positioned.

Did you notice that you could "see though" the bubble on the space ship as the ship zoomed out of the television set? How is that possible? The Space2.psd image contains an alpha channel that is part of the image as it is sold by Image Club. It is the alpha channel that allows the background to appear through the image. After Effects, like Photoshop, uses an 8-bit grayscale alpha. Anything that is solid white in the channel shows up as opaque in the Comp. The black areas in the channel are totally transparent. Areas that are gray are partially transparent.

You can view the alpha channel for the space ship by double-clicking on the layer name to open the Layer window (or you could view it by double-clicking on the footage name in the Project window). In either case, at the bottom of the window, there is a series of four colored rectangles: red, green, blue, and white. When you press and hold the mouse button on the white rectangle, it becomes black and you can see the alpha channel contents (the red, green, or blue rectangles show the red, green, or blue channels of the image). Figure 3-19 shows the Layer window with the alpha channel displayed. Notice the bubble area is in shades of gray, so part of the background can show through.

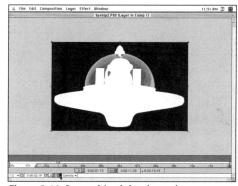

Figure 3-19: Space ship alpha channel.

Why is the Space Visitor File so Large?

At the end of this animation, the space ship zooms out of the TV so that the little man inside of it fills up the entire 320 x 240 area. While resolution is not quite as much of an issue in After Effects animations as it is in images destined for print media, you are nonetheless working with raster (pixel-based) graphics. You need to size your original footage at least as large as the largest size at which you will display it.

Raster images should not be scaled to more than 100% or they begin to break up and look awful. The solution is to use a large file and scale it down—which is what we have been doing in most of the examples so far (even if we have not made an issue out of it).

Adding a Motion Blur Effect

As a final step, we need to add a motion blur to bottom space ship layer as it moves from the pasteboard onto the screen. We will add two types of motion blur—one of them is a filter, and the other is a "real" blur that will be added when the movie is rendered.

 Studio Time: Adding Motion Blurs

1. Click on the lowest space ship layer (the one near the bottom of the layer stack) to select it.

2. Press "I" to go to the layer In point.

3. Add a Motion Blur effect (Effects➔ Blur&Sharpen➔ Motion Blur).

4. The Motion Blur dialog shown in Figure 3-20 appears. You also need to expand the layer to see the Motion Blur effect, and expand the Motion Blur effect in the layer to see the stop watches. (Reminder: click on the small triangles to expand the hierarchy.)

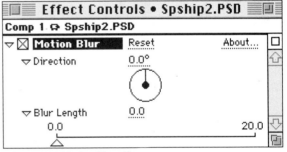

Figure 3-20: Motion Blur effect.

5. Set the direction to 0 rotations and 90 degrees. Do not set up a keyframe for the direction as it will remain constant. This setting leaves the motion blur "trail" on the right side of the space ship—exactly where it logically should be if the space ship is moving to the left.

6. Click in the Blur Length stop watch. Set a value of 7.8 for the keyframe.

7. Go to the layer Out point (O). Set a keyframe for Blur Length of 0. Warning: We probably need to introduce you to a new sight—if it looks as if the screen did not move when you pressed O, take a careful look at the cursor arrow. If the arrow head is cycling between white and black, then the program is "thinking." This is the equivalent of the wonderful spinning clock that you get to see so much of in Photoshop. The motion blur is a slow effect. When it is used, the entire calculation process is slowed. Just be patient and wait for it.

8. Click in the "Enable Motion Blur" switch at the top of the Time Layout window as shown in Figure 3-21. Also click in the box under the M column in the Time Layout window as shown in Figure 3-22. This enables the "real" motion blur at render time.

9. Select all of the layers (Mac: Cmd-A, Windows: Ctrl-A). Press the Tilde (~) to collapse them all. Press Tab to deselect.

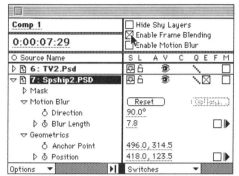

Figure 3-21: Enable Frame Blending switch.

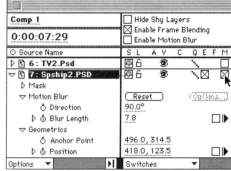

Figure 3-22: Add "real" Motion Blur to layer.

10. Set the Current Time to 00 (Mac: Cmd-G, Windows: Ctrl-G, then type 0). Press the spacebar to preview the movie. (You may get very tired of waiting for the Motion Blur to calculate. If you do, just move the Playback Head to skip over those frames.)

11. Render the movie (Mac: Cmd-M, Windows: Ctrl-M).

 # Rewind

We really covered a lot of new material in this chapter—even though the project was simple and easy to do. You learned how to:

- Nudge a footage item into place.
- Change the background color of a Comp.
- Preview the movie.
- Trim footage in both the Layer and Time Layout windows.
- Copy and Paste keyframes.
- Set layer In points.
- Split Layers.
- View a footage item's alpha channel.

In most cases, you learned multiple techniques for performing the same actions. A movie can be previewed using the Time Controls palette or by pressing the spacebar. You can make multiple layers from one footage item by splitting layers, duplicating the layer, or dragging the footage item to the Comp multiple times. You can trim footage in two different windows or by using several different key commands.

Coming Attractions

In the next chapter, you will build the Water.mov footage from the original component clips. You will also learn how to display moving video inside of other moving video and work with a number of movies at one time.

Video on Video

 Preview

Layering video footage is one of the many strengths of the remarkable After Effects program. If you want one video to play inside of another, you need to use After Effects to build it— this is something that Premiere cannot do! In this chapter, you will have your first taste of working with multiple clips inside of one another. It's no more difficult than the techniques that you have mastered so far, but it is certainly a creative leap forward.

Preview the movie AECH04A.mov in the MoviePlayer application. This movie shows the skyline of New York City, and features four other views of the river that emerges from the skyline. Finally, a sixth video pops out in the center. The four river views grow to touch one another, and the last video casts a drop shadow over the backdrop.

This chapter actually has two projects. In addition to the AECH04A.mov file, there is a AECH04B.mov movie. This contains the footage that you placed inside of the television in Chapter 3 (remember… we promised we'd show you how to do it).

In this chapter, you will learn how to:

- Trim video footage.

- Position multiple layers at one time.

- Create and hide Shy layers.

- Lock layers.

- Set keyframes for multiple layers at one time.

- Apply a drop shadow.

- Change layer In and Out points.

- Stretch Time.

- Use the In/Out controls in the Time Layout window.

- Create seamless fade-ins to transition video clips.

You will also learn a bit more about the rendering pipeline and how (and why) to add rendering considerations into the design process.

Feature Presentation — Part 1

AECH04A.aep uses a lot of video footage—six different video clips. It has a background piece of video, four small zooming footage items, and a final piece of video. Let's start by placing the background piece of footage. It needs to be trimmed and placed in the correct starting location.

Studio Time: Getting Started

1. Open After Effects and create a new Comp (Mac: Cmd-N, Windows: Ctrl-N). Make the Comp 320 x 240 and 20 seconds long. This is longer than the finished movie will be, but we need to leave room for trimming the footage.

2. On the desktop, open the Chapter 4 source folder (AE04Foot) and highlight all of the source footage items in the CH04foot folder.

3. Return to After Effects and drag the items from the desktop into the Project window.

4. Drag Skyline.mov into the Time Layout window. Let After Effects automatically center it in the Comp window. The clip is approximately 19 seconds long.

5. Save the changes to your project.

Looking at Time

We need to trim the Skyline.mov because the first several frames are bad. You learned a number of ways to trim footage in Chapter 3. Trimming frames from the beginning of a footage item sets the In point of the item to the new starting frame. If it started at Time=0:00:00:00 before trimming, it will now start later because you removed frames from the front. Actually, those frames are still there; they are just not shown. Therefore, if you want to both trim the footage and have the first visible frame appear at a specific In point, you need to perform two actions: trim the footage and deliberately change the In Point. In the next Studio Time, we will do both.

The other thing that we will do in the Studio Time is to change our view of time as we trim so that we can see each frame of the video on the time line. This makes it much easier to see what is happening. In Chapter 1, you were briefly introduced to this ability (i.e. to change your view of the time line), but this is the first time that we have actually used it in a project.

Studio Time: Trimming Footage and Zooming in on Time

1. Figure 4-1a shows the Time Layout window. Notice the location of the cursor. The black semi-circles (proper name: Viewing Area brackets) on either end of the top bar can zoom in as close as you want to reveal the detail on selected areas of the image. The cursor is located

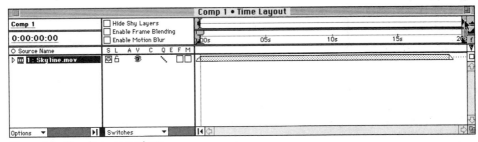

Figure 4-1a: Time line zoomed out.

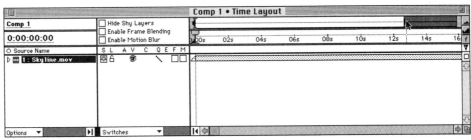

Figure 4-1b: Time line zoomed to 2-second increments.

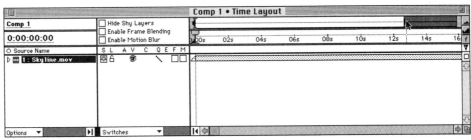

Figure 4-1c: Time line zoomed to 1-second increments.

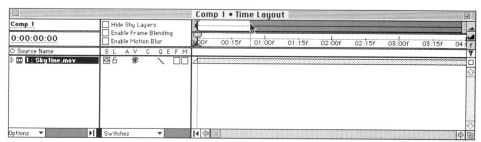

Figure 4-1d: Time line zoomed to 15-frame increments.

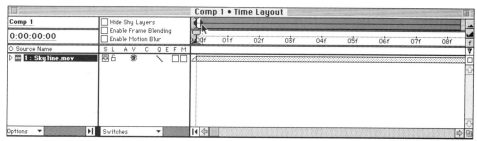

Figure 4-1e: Time line zoomed to 1-frame increments.

at the right Viewing Area bracket. By moving it towards the left, you can change your view of Time. Figures 4-1b through 4-1e show successive views of the Time Layout window as you compress the viewing area. Observe that you change from looking at seconds to looking at frames. When the two brackets meet, you can see every frame on the time line.

Figure 4-1e shows the way your time line should look as we begin. Drag the right Viewing Area bracket as far left as it will go.

2. Set the Current Time to 00 (Mac: Cmd-G, Windows: Ctrl-G, then type 0).

3. You need to position the Current Time marker to 3 frames. That should be really easy for you now, but let's pretend for a moment that you do not know where the first "good" frame is located, and you need to search for it. Here are two ways:

Figure 4-2: Time Controls palette showing "forward-one-frame" arrow.

Press the "forward one frame" arrow (that's the second arrow from the right) on the Time Controls palette (Window →Palettes →Time Controls). Each quick-but-firm press should take you one frame forward. Check the Current Time to make sure that it has. Figure 4-2 shows this control with the cursor positioned at the correct button.

Move the large Playback Head on the time line forward one frame at a time by dragging it. At your current zoom level, it will easily snap forward to each successive frame. Figure 4-3 shows the large Playback Head being moved.

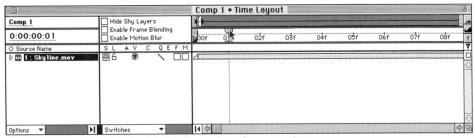

Figure 4-3: Large Playback Head being dragged one frame at a time.

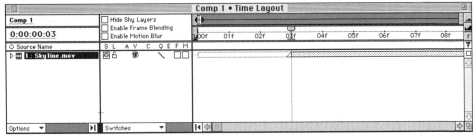

Figure 4-4: Time Layout window showing trimmed layer.

4. At 3 frames (0:00:00:03), trim the footage (Mac: Opt-[, Windows: Alt-[). Figure 4-4 shows the time line with the trimmed footage. Observe that the In point now starts 3 frames later.

You can confirm this by double-clicking on the layer name to bring up the Layer window. As you can see in Figure 4-5, the In point is now set to 3 frames.

5. Set the Current Time to 00 (Mac: Cmd-G, Windows: Ctrl-G then type 0).

6. Press the Left bracket key ([) to move the In point of the layer to the Current Time. Figure 4-6 shows the new location. If you

Figure 4-5: Layer window with new footage In point.

Figure 4-6: Trimmed footage at new In point.

double-click on the layer to open the Layer window, you will see that it still lists the In point at 3 frames. Remember, the Layer window does not show the starting time of the footage item in the layer. It only shows the In point in relation to the entire length of the original footage item.

7. Move the right Viewing Area bracket towards the right until you can see the time line displayed in 1-second increments.

Shortcuts

Command	Mac	Windows
Tools palette	Cmd-1	Ctrl-1
Info palette	Cmd-2	Ctrl-2
Time Controls palette	Cmd-3	Ctrl-3
Audio palette	Cmd-4	Ctrl-4

Positioning the Rest of the Footage Items

Your next task is to move the remaining five pieces of video into their correct positions in the Comp. This is a practice of skills that you have already learned. You need to bring one item to the top of the layer stack and hide it temporarily. The other four items need to be distributed into the four corners of the Comp. You can do this by dragging the item and then nudging it in place with the arrow keys, or by constraining the motion of the item as you drag it.

Studio Time: Placing the Footage items

1. Set the Current Time to 1 second (Mac: Cmd-G, Windows: Ctrl-G, and type 100, or just move the Playback Head until the Current Time reads 0:00:01:00).

2. Drag a Marquee around the un-placed five video items in the Project window or Shift-click to add each one to the selection.

3. Drag all five items to the center of the Composition window. Notice that all of the In points start at 1 second.

4. Press the Tab key to deselect everything.

5. Click on the Bridge.mov layer to select it. Bring it to the top of the layer stack by dragging or by using the keyboard shortcut: Cmd-F for the Mac, Ctrl-F for Windows. This layer is now in its correct position.

6. Click on the Eye in the Video column to hide the layer from view for the moment.

7. You can also remove the layer from the Time Layout window temporarily. The only reason to do this is to conserve viewing space. Since the window is a bit crowded, let's try it.

The S switch in the Switches column (it is the first column in the Switches section, as you can see in Figure 4-7a) is the "Shy" switch. Clicking on the "little man peeking over the wall" in the S column makes a layer shy. You can see this in Figure 4-7a as the little man hides behind the wall. If you then click on the "Hide Shy Layers" box as shown in Figure 4-7b, the little man becomes too timid to appear at all—the layer is removed from the Time Layout window completely (until you uncheck the Shy layers box or give the layer more courage).

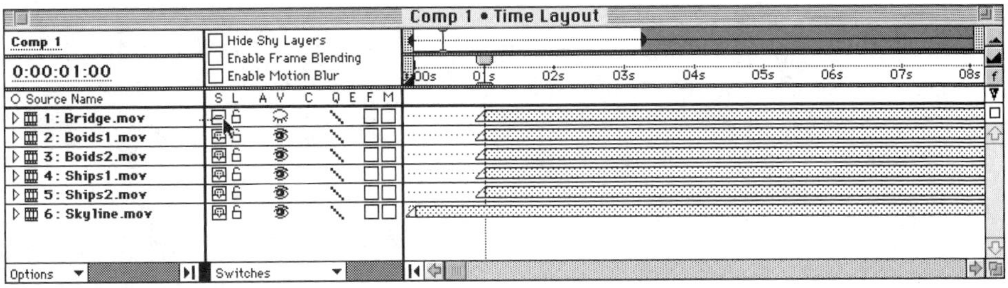

Figure 4-7a: Making a layer "Shy."

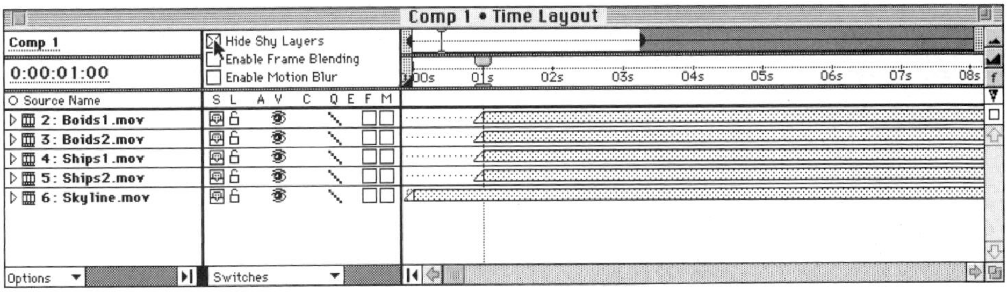

Figure 4-7b: Hiding the Shy layers.

Warning: Making a layer shy does not lock it. If you select all of the layers to make a change, you will change every layer—including the shy ones that you cannot see. If you need to make a layer temporarily shy, you probably ought to lock it at the same time.

8. If you have hidden the shy layer, uncheck the Hide Shy Layers box so that Bridge.mov is again visible. Now, click on the lock icon in the L column to lock the layer. Figure 4-8 shows

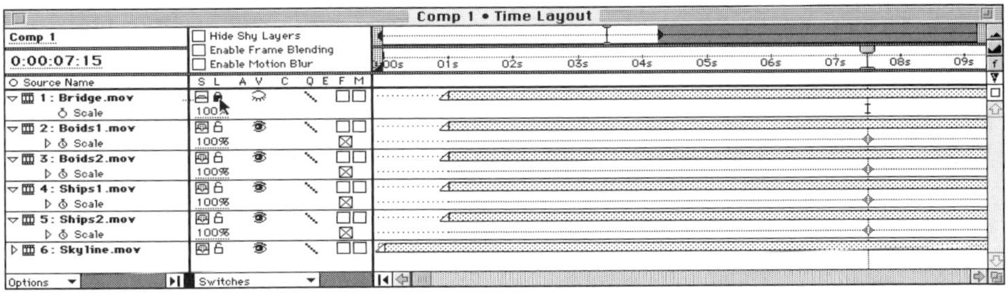

Figure 4-8: Locking a layer.

the cursor over the lock icon just after the layer has been locked. Notice that the lock has turned black and the handle fits into the body of the lock.

9. Click on the Hide Shy Layers box again to remove the top layer from the Time Layout window temporarily.

10. Drag the new top layer (Boids1.mov) to the top left corner of the image so that the upper-left corner of the movie aligns with the upper-left corner of the Comp. Use the arrow keys to nudge the item in place.

11. Drag Boids2.mov to the bottom-right corner of the Comp. Remember, you can snap the item into the corner by pressing the Shift key after you start to drag it. If you press the Option key (Mac) or Alt key (Windows) as well, you can view the item as you position it (otherwise, all you see is the wireframe view).

12. Drag Ships1.mov to the upper-right corner, and Ships2.mov to the lower-left corner of the Comp. Figure 4-9 shows the Composition window with the layers correctly arranged.

Figure 4-9: Composition window with four movies arranged correctly.

Tip: Nudging Footage

The arrow keys can nudge a footage item one pixel in any direction when you are at a 1:1 zoom level. If you press the Shift key as you use the arrow keys, the footage item moves in 10-pixel increments.

Scaling and Zooming Movies

Do you find it tedious to scale each layer separately? You can do many of the editing moves at one time with multiple layers selected. The one "fiddley" thing that you cannot do, unfortunately, is set the stop watch to enable keyframes for a property, but once that has been done, you can set keyframes at the same location in multiple layers. The next Studio Time shows you this shortcut as you set the four small videos to scale up from nothing so that they look as if they are zooming out onto the main screen.

 Studio Time: Setting Properties for Multiple Layers

1. Select all of the layers (Mac: Cmd-A, Windows: Ctrl-A).

2. Deselect the Skyline.mov layer by clicking on its name in the Time Layout window while pressing the Shift key.

3. Type S to bring up the Scale property for all four selected layers.

4. Set the Current Time to 7.15 seconds (Mac: Cmd-G, Windows: Ctrl-G, and type 715, or just move the Playback Head until the Current Time reads 0:00:07:15).

5. Set the stop watch in each layer to make Scale a keyframeable property.

6. Select all again (Mac: Cmd-A, Windows: Ctrl-A). You need to remove the Skyline.mov layer from the selection again, as well. If this becomes annoying, lock the layer. Then it cannot be selected.

7. Set the Scale property to 80%. With the four layers selected, when you click on one scale setting, you will set them all.

8. Leave the layers selected and press I to take you to the layer In point. Click on a scale setting and set it to 0. This will set the scale of all four items to 0 at their In point. It will take them 6.15 seconds to scale up to 80%.

9. With the layers still selected, set the Current Time to 9.00 seconds (Mac: Cmd-G, Windows: Ctrl-G, and type 900, or just move the Playback Head until the Current Time reads 0:00:09:00). Click on one of the scale settings, but do not change it from 80%. This will set all four selected layers (this is a sustaining keyframe—one to keep a setting at a constant level long enough for it to be noticed).

10. Set the Current Time to 11 seconds (Mac: Cmd-G, Windows: Ctrl-G, and type 1100, or just move the Playback Head until the Current Time reads 0:00:11:00).

11. Change the scale setting to 100%. The four movies now meet in the center and cover the entire image.

Rendering Pipeline and Trimming Layers

"The time has come, the walrus said, to talk of many things…" One of those things, right now, is a very brief discussion about the way that After Effects renders your movie. When you render a movie, After Effects adds it to the Render Queue. As each movie is rendered, it is processed in a very specific order. After Effects starts with the bottom layer in the stack and first calculates the mask, then all of the applied effects, and finally, all of the geometry information such as Scale, Opacity, Position, etc. It then moves up the layer stack to preform the same actions on the next layer, and blends the results with the layer below. This is called the render pipeline, and the more you understand about how it works, the better you will be at optimizing your projects for rendering efficiency.

Rendering efficiency is needed. We once tried to render a two minute movie that processed for a full twenty-four hours! (We decided not to include that one in this book.)

What this points out, however, is that rendering a movie can take a lot of time (and hard drive space—but that is a different story). Efficiency pays here. If you can manage to save even one-half of a second of time in rendering each frame, over a movie of two minutes, you would have saved half an hour of rendering time. It helps to know what After Effects does when it renders a movie. (By the way, we have only begun to cover the subject of efficient rendering. This will be a continuing theme throughout the book.)

After Effects creates each movie frame by calculating the value of each active layer and then outputting the result. If you have five layers and the top layer covers all of the other layers, After Effects calculates the result of each underlying layer anyway. This can be very time consuming—especially if a slow filter like a Gaussian Blur is applied to an unseen layer.

It is the equivalent of the two imagesetter horror stories told by Service Bureau support people in the print world. One is when the client places into QuarkXPress a file inside of a clipping path where the file is much larger than the clipping path area that will be seen. This forces the imagesetter to image enormous amounts of data and then toss away most of it. The ultimate horror story is the told of the file that contained a very simple element but simply refused to image—causing a PostScript limitcheck or out-of-memory error every time it ran. The support group finally discovered that the client kept covering over previous work with an opaque white box before dragging the "simple" element into the picture. The stuff that could not be seen was horrendous and was the culprit choking the RIP.

You won't get a PostScript error in After Effects (since it is not a PostScript program), but you will pay, none-the-less, for inefficiency. Your movie will take much longer to render if you force After Effects to do extra and unnecessary work. So—you've been warned.

How does this apply to the current exercise? In the last Studio Time, you scaled the four movies so that they eventually covered the background movie. Therefore, you don't need the background movie (Skyline.mov) once you can no longer see it. A layer is "active" if the time in question is between the In point and the Out point of the layer. Makes sense…if the layer is "playing," it is active and will be rendered. The solution here is to trim the Skyline.mov layer so that its Out point is reached when the four other movies cover it up. Let's do it. This is a really short exercise!

 Studio Time: Trimming Unnecessary Footage

1. Deselect all of the layers (Tab).

2. Select the Skyline.mov layer. If you locked it, unlock it. If you made it shy, show it and then unlock.

3. Trim the Out point of the layer to the Current Time of 11 seconds (Mac: Opt-], Windows: Alt-]).

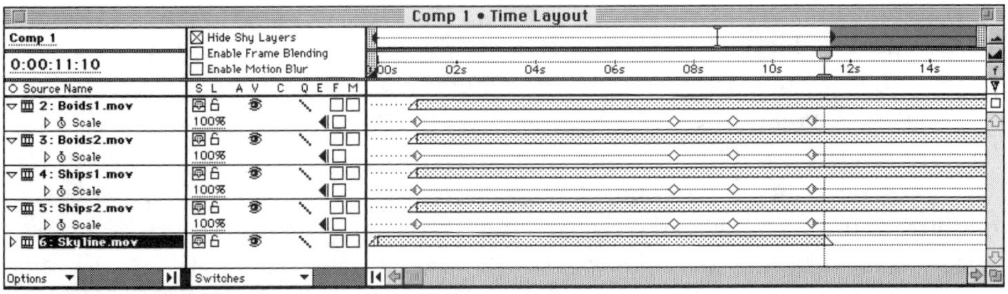

Figure 4-10: Trimmed Skyline.mov layer.

Warning: make sure that you have trimmed the footage—not just moved the entire time line. The Layer Duration bar "ribbon" will show a double dotted line that continues from the end of the bar, as shown in Figure 4-10, if the layer has been properly trimmed.

Adding a Drop Shadow Effect

If you are accustomed to Photoshop, and the numerous steps that it can take to create a drop shadow, you will enjoy After Effect's automatic handling of this task. In the next Studio Time, you will create four drop shadows, and sequence the layers so that the drop shadows make sense when the layers are completely zoomed out.

 Studio Time: Adding Drop Shadows

1. Use the Shift key to select each of the four zooming layers and add them to the selection (click on the Boids1.mov layer name in the Time Layout window, and then press and hold the Shift key as you click on the name in the Boids2.mov, Ships1.mov, and Ships2.mov layers).

2. Select the Drop Shadow effect from the Perspective effects submenu on the Effects menu. This action places four Drop Shadow dialog boxes into your interface. Figure 4-11 shows the dialog box.

3. Unfortunately, you cannot set all four of these at one time. They need to be set one by one. In each dialog box, set the Color to black (which is the default), the Opacity to 50%, Direction to 135 degrees, Distance to 13, and Softness to 12. If the Drop Shadow effect is using its default values, you will only need to change the Distance and the Softness. These values are constant; *do not set a keyframe.*

4. Figure 4-12 shows the Composition window after all four drop shadows are added. Hmmm… there's a bit of a problem. It looks a trifle peculiar to have one drop shadow covering the others like that. When all four layers are at their maximum speed, no drop shadow should be visible.

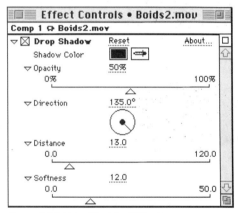

Figure 4-11: Drop Shadow dialog box.

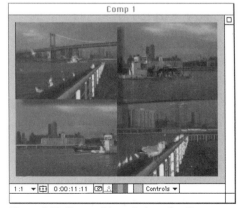

Figure 4-12: Composition window after Drop Shadow effect is added.

You need to move the offending layer (the top, left one which is the Boids1.mov) so that it is the lowest of the four movies in the layer stack.

Click on the top left movie in the Comp window to select it (if you didn't already know which one it is, this action would tell you that). Drag the layer name in the layer stack until it is below the Ships2.mov and above the Skyline.Mov.

5. Set the time back to 00 and press the spacebar to preview the movie to this point.

Earlier in this chapter, we spoke about the rendering pipeline and the need to work efficiently. The Drop Shadow effects have created a rendering inefficiency. When the four movie elements are fully zoomed, you cannot see the drop shadow at all. Therefore, you do not really need the Drop Shadow effect once the images are at 100% size. If we set values of 0 for all of the effect parameters, we can "shut-off" most of the filter calculations. This would make the movie render more efficiently.

We had a trade-off to make here, though. It was ease-of-working versus rendering efficiency. We chose the ease-of-working, as the "cost" of inefficiency was not terribly high. We had no need to set a keyframe for the Drop Shadow effect—the drop shadows are constant. In order to shut off the drop shadow, however, we would have needed to create keyframes. If you wish to test the difference in rendering speed, you can go back and create a starting keyframe at the In points of the four layers. Set it to the values the you used for the constants. Set a "sustaining" keyframe (by clicking in the boxes) at Time=00:00:11:00. Move the Playback Head forward one frame (to Time=00:00:11:01) and create a keyframe that sets as many of the parameters as possible back to 0. Render the movie a second time and see if you have saved much (you can tell by reading the rendering times in the Render Queue log). There is only one second to the movie after the four smaller movies zoom out. It should not make a significant difference here.

Setting the Bridge

It is time to let our shy layer take center stage. The final Studio Time for this example shows you how to let the top layer zoom into the image and how to finish up the movie.

 Studio Time: Finishing Up

1. Click to turn off the Hide Shy Layers box.

2. Remove the Shy flag from the Bridge.mov layer, unlock it, and turn the Eye icon back on so that the layer becomes visible in the Comp window.

3. Set the Current Time to 5 seconds (Mac: Cmd-G, Windows: Ctrl-G, and type 500, or just move the Playback Head until the Current Time reads 0:00:05:00).

4. Click on the Bridge.mov layer name to select it.

5. Press the Left bracket key ([) to set the In point of the Bridge.mov layer to the Current Time.

6. Type S to open the Scale property and click in the stop watch to make it keyframe-able. Set the scale to 0. (You are still at 5 seconds.)

7. Set the Current Time to 8 seconds and make a keyframe with a value of 100.

8. Set the Current Time to 10.15 seconds (Mac: Cmd-G, Windows: Ctrl-G, and type 1015, or just move the Playback Head until the Current Time reads 0:00:10:15). Click in

Figure 4-13: Proj4a—last frame.

the box to make a sustaining keyframe that will keep the same 100% value as the previous keyframe.

9. Set the Current Time to 13 seconds and make a keyframe with a value of 80.

10. Add a Drop Shadow effect for the Bridge.mov layer exactly as you did for the other layers. It is a constant (no keyframes). Use the same settings as well. Figure 4-13 shows the last frame of the video.

11. Preview the movie and then render it (if you wish). Close the Project.

Feature Presentation — Part 2

In Chapter 3, you placed a short video clip inside of a television set. The clip was a actually three video clips "glued" together in After Effects. The "glue" is called a transition—it is the area of overlap between two pieces of video. If you use Adobe Premiere (or other video editing software), there are a large number of canned (pre-recorded) transition effects that are possible. You can also use After Effects to create your own. This movie uses opacity changes as the transition method.

In addition, you will also learn how to time-stretch video. The term "time-stretching" actually means exactly what it says. It is a way to take a piece of video that is too short and re-map it on the time line so that it becomes longer. In this example, you will time-stretch the surf video so that the area of the video that is the most useful lasts for a bit longer.

Studio Time: Setting up the Comp

1. Create a new Project (Mac: Cmd-Opt-N, Windows: Ctrl-Alt-N).

2. On the desktop, open the Chapter 4 source folder (AE04Foot) and highlight all of the source footage items in the 4proj4b folder.

3. Return to After Effects and drag the items from the desktop into the Project window.

4. Save the Project as Proj4b.

5. Create a new Comp (Mac: Cmd-N, Windows: Ctrl-N). Make the Comp 320 x 240, 30 frames per second, and 12 seconds long.

6. Drag all of the footage items into the Composition window so that they are centered.

7. Move the Skyline.mov layer to the top of the layer stack (Mac: Cmd-F, Windows: Ctrl-F).

Stretching Time

"Stretching Time" is a problem that we never seem to have in the real world. Time usually needs to be compressed so that more will fit into the hours available (yes…After Effects can do that too!). However, in this section we need to take a segment of a video clip and stretch it out so that it plays longer. In doing so, it will also seem to play more slowly. Why? The answer should be evident—you are taking a specific set of actions (the frames in the video clip) and making them play for more time. The information or actions have not grown, so the action that once took 30 frames to show, for example, now takes 45 frames. You are still looking at the same sequence of events, only now they seem to appear slower.

Why do we need to stretch time here? The movie is supposed to look as if it was taken in deep water. If you play the original footage item (Surf.mov) by double-clicking on the name in the Project window, you will see that it was clearly shot at ocean's edge. Furthermore, there is a good look at the boardwalk in Atlantic City (well, Ventnor, but that is just a few miles downbeach). The boardwalk is not a sight that works well near the New York skyline! The time stretching will allow us to use the "good" footage and lengthen it to the needed number of frames.

 ## Studio Time: Stretching Time

1. Turn off the Eye icon on the top two layers so that only the surf is visible.

2. Set the Current Time to 2.11 seconds (Mac: Cmd-G, Windows: Ctrl-G, and type 211, or just move the Playback Head until the Current Time reads 0:00:02:11).

3. Trim the footage to the layer In point (Mac: Opt.-[, Windows: Ctrl-[).

4. Set the Current Time to 00 (Mac: Cmd-G, Windows: Ctrl-G, then type 0).

5. Move the layer In point to the Current Time by pressing the Left bracket key ([).

6. Set the Current Time to 4.15 seconds (Mac: Cmd-G, Windows: Ctrl-G, and type 415, or just move the Playback Head until the Current Time reads 0:00:04:15). Notice that you can just begin to see the corner of the railing for the boardwalk in the bottom right corner of the clip.

7. Trim the Out point of the layer to this time (Mac: Opt-], Windows, Alt-]). Figure 4-14 shows the Time Layout window after the Surf.mov layer has been trimmed.

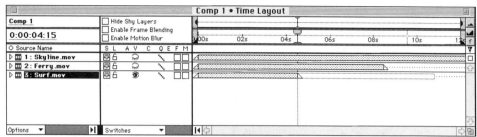

Figure 4-14: Time Layout window with trimmed Surf.mov layer.

8. Add a Time Stretch to the layer by selecting the option from the Layer menu as shown in Figure 4-15.

9. The Time Stretch dialog appears. Set the Stretch Factor to 125%. This gives the clip a new duration of 5:20. Set the Hold In Place location to Layer In point. This will keep the current In point for the layer and move the Out point. Figure 4-16 shows the dialog, and Figure 4-17 shows the Time Layout window with a new Layer Duration bar for the Surf.mov layer.

Figure 4-15: Layer menu showing Time Stretch.

Now that you have applied the time stretch to the layer, is there a way to see, numerically, what has been done? Of course. There is another group of settings embedded in the Time Layout window that we have not yet mentioned at all. This is the In/Out Control area and it is hidden between the Switches and the time line. You can reveal it by clicking on the left-pointing arrow at the bottom of the time line section of the Time Layout window (the location is shown highlighted by the cursor in Figure 4-18).

This control area shows that Surf.mov is time stretched by 125%. You can edit this amount at any time that you wish by clicking on the under-lined control, as shown by the cursor position in Figure 4-19.

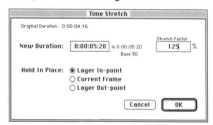

Figure 4-16: Time Stretch dialog.

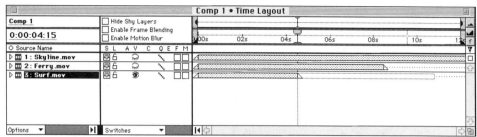

Figure 4-17: Time Layout window after time stretch.

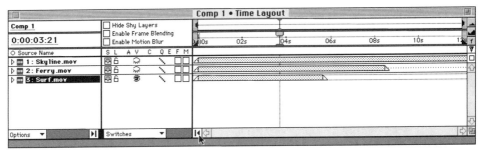

Figure 4-18: Click location to show In/Out settings.

Figure 4-19: In/Out settings showing time stretch amounts.

Finishing Up

We need to create the transitions and keyframes for the remaining two layers of video. This requires using the skills learned in Chapter 3 to drag and snap Layer Duration bars to specific points in time. By way of review, several methods are used.

 Studio Time: Transitions and Finishing Touches

1. Turn on the Eye next to the Ferry.mov layer. Click to select the layer.

2. If you have opened your Time Layout palette to show the In/Out controls, click on the arrow to hide them again. This gives you more working space.

3. Set the Current Time to 2.15 seconds (Mac: Cmd-G, Windows: Ctrl-G, and type 215, or just move the Playback Head until the Current Time reads 0:00:02:15).

4. Drag the Layer Duration bar so that the new In point becomes 2:15. Press Mac: Cmd-2 or Windows: Ctrl-2 to show the Info palette, and drag the bar until the Info palette reads 2:15.

5. Press T to bring up the Opacity property (remember: think Transparency!!!). Click in the stop watch to make it keyframeable. Set the property to 0%.

6. Set the Current Time to 5.20 seconds (Mac: Cmd-G, Windows: Ctrl-G, and type 520, or just move the Playback Head until the Current Time reads 0:00:05:20).

7. Create a new keyframe with a value of 100%. This allows the layer to softly merge with the Surf movie from 2.15 to 5.20 on the time line. Time=5:20 is where the Surf movie ends—just as the Ferry layer reaches full opacity. The Ferry layer needs no additional keyframes.

8. Set the Current Time to 7:00 seconds (Mac: Cmd-G, Windows: Ctrl-G, and type 700, or just move the Playback Head until the Current Time reads 0:00:07:00).

9. Turn on the Skyline.mov layer by clicking on the Eye icon. We want this layer to start at 7:00. Drag the Layer Duration bar towards the right. After you start to drag, press the Shift key. You will feel the Layer Duration bar snap to the Current Time marker as it gets close to it.

10. Oh no! We have those few bad frames in this footage again. Not to worry. Since we are setting the initial layer opacity to 0, there is no need to trim the footage. All will be well.

11. Press T to bring up the Opacity property. Click in the stop watch to make it keyframeable. Set the opacity to 0.

12. We want a two second overlap, so set the Current Time marker to 9:00.

13. Click on the Opacity property and set it to 100.

14. Finish up by trimming the Ferry layer to enhance rendering efficiency. We can trim the layer (Mac: Opt-], Windows: Alt-]) to the Current Time of 9:00 since it is no longer visible. Remember to click to select the Ferry layer before you press the Command key. Otherwise, you will trim the wrong layer!

Shortcuts

Command	Mac	Windows
Trim start of video	Opt-[	Alt-[
Trim end of video	Opt-]	Alt-]
Set In Point to Current Time	[	[
Set Out Point to Current Time	]	]

"We want a two second overlap." How do we know we want a two-second overlap? Or, the better question to ask is "How does one determine the correct timing on layer transitions and effects?" It is a good and valid question, and one which we will discuss in more detail as the chapters become more complex. This is where experience and trial and error count.

In some of the earlier examples, we used sustaining keyframes to keep certain properties, such as scale, constant for a brief period of time. The period of static is necessary for the viewers to perceive the activity in the video. If a scene appears, it needs to stand still for a while so that you can see what it is. The amount of time to "stand still" will vary based on the specific circumstance. In Chapter 3, we "held" the headlines for 1 second. The headlines were still images, and only needed to stay at full opacity long enough to be read.

Moving video, however, needs to have some time to run if it is to be meaningful. You can see by "reading" the time line in Figure 4-20, how we have scheduled the In and Out points and keyframes of the video in Proj4b.

In the chapters that follow, we will discuss again some of the factors that necessitate shorter or longer amounts of sustaining actions. It still takes trial and error—and render and re-render—until we are happy with the results, but it takes much less of it than it did when we first began to use After Effects. Principles of traditional animation are very useful in this context (i.e. figuring out how long an action or activity needs to be held), and we will pass along those tips as well.

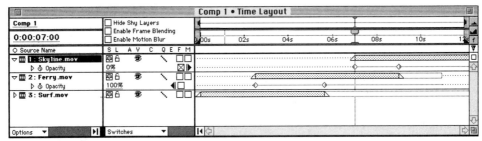

Figure 4-20: Time Layout window for completed Proj4b.

Making a Smaller Version

One final thought: the movie in Chapter 3 that played through the television was smaller than this Composition. How was that done?

Compositions can be placed inside of other Compositions. In order to create a Comp that is 240 x 180 and 12 seconds long, you simply need to create a new Composition with those settings. Drag the first Comp into the center of the new Composition window and set the Scale property to 80%. Now render the new Comp. Your movie will be at the smaller size.

 Rewind

We've accomplished a lot in this chapter. You have learned how to work with multiple video clips and composite or transition them together. You have learned how to apply keyframes to several layers at one time, and how to stretch a piece of video footage so that it plays for a longer amount of time. You have had a chance to practice several methods of changing the In and Out points of layers and of trimming the video footage. In addition, we have also begun to discuss two themes which will be expanded upon throughout the book: how to render a movie efficiently, and how to animate a movie so that the audience has enough time to absorb what it is trying to say.

Coming Attractions

This chapter concludes the first section of this book: Mastering the Basics. In the four chapters so far, you have learned to use the After Effects interface and to set up Projects and Compositions. You have learned the different basic techniques of using still video, compositing still video with moving footage, and working with multiple "live" video clips.

In the next section, Working with a Variety of Inputs, you will learn about using Illustrator images, working with layered Photoshop images, how to create and use mattes, how to work with Transfer modes, and how to use audio in your projects.

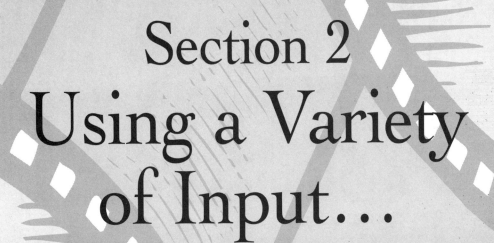

Section 2
Using a Variety of Input...

Using Illustrator Files

 Preview

How do you create a very complex project? The answer: one step at a time. The first four chapters of this book have shown you the basics of using After Effects. This chapter builds on that background. You may feel as if you have moved suddenly from kindergarten to post-graduate work when you see the project for this chapter, but there are only a few things in here that you have not already done.

Before we frighten you any further, preview AECH05.mov in the MoviePlayer application. It consists of a variety of words and type elements moving across the screen in a number of directions at varying opacities and speeds.

How many elements are there? There are twelve Illustrator files used in this project, and some of them are used multiple times. This makes the project very complex—even if nothing fancy were done with these elements. In order to use this many images as input, you need to organize your project. Therefore, one of the major new skills to be learned here is the trick of nesting Compositions. You will build several small, easy-to-manage, Comps and place them inside of one "master" Comp. This both helps to organize the project and to change the order of processing in the rendering pipeline.

In addition to nesting Compositions, you will learn how to:

- Continuously rasterize vector images.

- Pre-compose layers ("Compify" is another name for this process).
- Change the quality of the preview and rendering.
- Collapse Geometrics before previewing or rendering.

These five new skills represent a major leap in your understanding of what you can do with After Effects.

 # Feature Presentation

This is the first time that we have used Illustrator elements in this book. As you probably know, Adobe Illustrator is a popular drawing program for the Mac and Windows. We'll assume you are experienced with it, as most After Effects users began their graphics work in other applications such as Illustrator or Photoshop. If you need help with Illustrator, there are many fine books out, including *Real World Illustrator 7*, by Deke McClelland, also published by Peachpit Press. Adobe After Effects is as capable of working with vector files (generated by Illustrator, and occasionally by other vector programs as well) as it is with Photoshop files. It is a little trickier working with vector (path-based) images than it is with raster (pixel-based) images. This chapter will help you master the finer points.

Using Vector Files

After Effects is a pixel-based program. It does not work with PostScript Paths even though it is capable of importing them. For those of you who are not as familiar with one of the major headaches of the print world, the advantage of a PostScript path when printing is that the path (or vector art) prints nicely at any printer resolution. It is capable of smooth printing on a 300 dpi laser printer or a 2400 dpi linotronic. Pixel-based (raster) images—such as images created in Photoshop, are not so fortunate. If you enlarge them at print time, you are likely to make them very jagged-looking, leaving a stair-step effect around edges that should be smooth.

This is not as much of an issue in After Effects, since the actual image size does not get very large, but this problem surfaces in the way in which Adobe Illustrator files are handled. Figure 5-1a shows the Switches section of the Time Layout window with a raster image layer. The C switch stands for Continuously Rasterize, and in this case it is blank. The switch is only operative when the layer consists either of a vector image or of a Comp. For now, let's just consider the instance when a layer is a vector image.

Figure 5-1b shows a vector image added as a new layer. The C switch shows a dot surrounded by a circle of dots. This is the Off stage of the Continuously Rasterize switch. It is the default condition. To rasterize means to convert an image from its vector form into pixels (which happens when you open an Illustrator image within Photoshop). With the switch set off, After Effects imports the vector art and rasterizes it at 100% of its original size. It does not use the image paths again. If you scale the image larger than 100%, you will create a jaggy image. However, if you turn the Continuously Rasterize switch on, as

Figure 5-1a: You cannot Continuously Rasterize a raster image.

Figure 5-1b: Continuously Rasterize switch turned off for vector image.

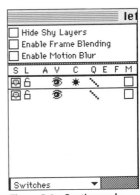

Figure 5-1c: Continuously Rasterize switch turned on for vector image.

shown by the asterisk in the C column in Figure 5-1c, After Effects will go back to the original Illustrator outlines and re-rasterize the image as the size changes. This gives you the best quality possible although it makes for slow rendering and previewing.

The other issue of concern with vector images is anti-aliasing. If you are familiar with Photoshop, then this is not a new topic for you. Anti-aliasing is a technique that makes the edge of an element look smooth. This process creates pixels at the edge of the shape to produce a transition from the color of the shape to the color of the background in approximately three pixels. This edge makes the shape seem smooth when it really is not. Figure 5-2a show a portion of aliased (jaggy) text and Figure 5-2b shows a piece of text that has been anti-aliased. Both are at 600% enlargement.

There is no flag in After Effects to determine if you want aliased or anti-aliased text. However, if you set the Quality switch (Q column in the Switches area of the Time Layout

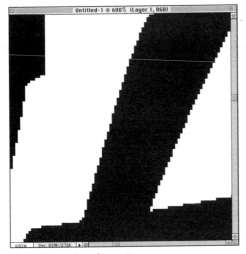

Figure 5-2a: Aliased text.

Figure 5-2b: Anti-aliased text.

Figure 5-3a: Wireframe Quality setting.

Figure 5-3b: Draft Quality setting.

Figure 5-3c: Best Quality setting.

window) to Best, the vector images will be anti-aliased as they are rasterized. The Quality switch has three settings: Wireframe (shown in Figure 5-3a as an X), Draft (shown in Figure 5-3b as a forward slash), and Best (shown in Figure 5-3c as a backward slash). Notice both the icons used and the effect produced in the Comp window. As you can see, only in Best mode is the image anti-aliased.

Setting Up

You are now ready to start this chapter's project. There are a number of small Compositions to create, and one final Comp where everything comes together. The first Comp that we will make is very simple. It contains three words, and the action is to move the words across the Comp and back again.

 Studio Time: Left to Right Comp

1. Create a new Comp (Mac: Cmd-N, Windows: Ctrl-N). Make it 320 x 240, 12 seconds long, 30 frames per second. Name the Comp " Left Right Type" and set the background color to white (Mac: Shift-Cmd-B, Windows: Shift-Ctrl-B).

2. Set the Current Time to 00 (Mac: Cmd-G, Windows: Ctrl-G, then type 0).

3. In the AE05Foot folder, on the Mac, highlight the Ink.ai, Paint.ai, and Pencils.ai images. Return to After Effects and drag the footage items into the Project window. If you are using Windows (or prefer this method), import the files with the File → Import → Footage Items command.

4. Save the project.

5. Select the three Illustrator images and drag them to the center of the Composition window. (Hint: if you don't see the text, you have forgotten to change your background to white!) Press the Tab key to deselect.

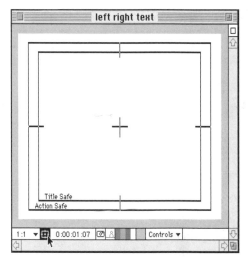

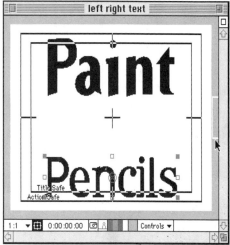

Figure 5-4: Title Safe/Action Safe guides turned on.   **Figure 5-5: Ink, Pens, Paint temporarily positioned.**

6. Turn on the Title Safe/Action Safe guidelines in the Comp window. (Figure 5-4 shows where to click in case you have forgotten.)

7. The Ink layer is on top. Click on the text in the Comp window to select it. Drag it to the right. After you start to drag, press the Shift key to keep the text horizontally constrained. Slide the text to the right just outside of the frame.

We need to move the words "Paint" and "Pencils" to the top and bottom of the screen and them off to the left. This is a two-step process—position vertically and then move to the side.

8. "Paint" is the next layer. Select the text and drag it up until the wireframe box is halfway between the upper Title Safe and Action Safe lines. Press the Shift key after you start to drag to keep the text centered.

9. Drag the "Pencils" layer to the bottom of the frame, halfway between the lower Title Safe and Action Safe guide lines. Press the Shift key after you begin to drag to keep the text centered. Figure 5-5 shows the Comp window at this point. Note that you can see the Paint and Pencils text, but the Ink text is in a box off to the right (and all you can see of it is the start of a white outline).

10. Now that Paint and Pencils are centered top to bottom, select both text objects (click on Paint, press the Shift key and click on Pencils). Drag the Pencils layer to the left until it is just off of the frame (as shown in Figure 5-6). Press the Shift key after you

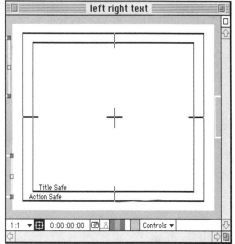

Figure 5-6: Pencils, Paint, and Ink correctly positioned at Time=0.

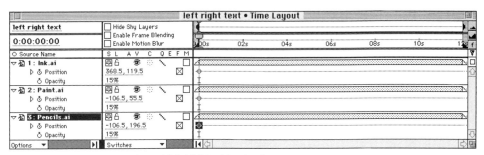

Figure 5-7: Time Layout window with initial Position keyframes set.

start to drag the items to keep the items horizontally constrained. Although it looks as if you are dragging only one item, both of them move when you are done.

11. Select all of the layers (Mac: Cmd-A, Windows: Ctrl-A).

12. Press T to open the Opacity property and Shift-P to add the Position property.

13. Click on one of the Opacity settings and change it to 15%. This will be a constant.

14. Press the Tab key to deselect, and click inside each of the Position stop watches to create an initial keyframe. Figure 5-7 shows the Time Layout window.

15. Go to the layer Out point (O). Click inside of the Keyframe Navigation box for each layer's Position property to leave an ending keyframe at the same location as the initial keyframe (see Figure 5-8).

16. Set the Current Time to 6 seconds (Mac: Cmd-G, Windows: Ctrl-G, and type 600, or just move the Playback Head until the Current Time reads 0:00:06:00).

17. Change the Comp window to 1:2 view so that you can see the text elements on the pasteboard.

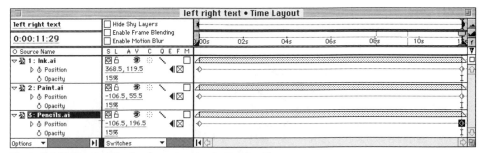

Figure 5-8: Ending Position keyframes set to starting locations.

18. Select the Paint and Pencils layers, and move them to the right until they are just off of the right edge of the frame. Press the Shift key after you begin to drag to keep the items horizontally constrained.

19. Select the Ink layer, and move it to the left until it is just off of the left edge of the frame. Press the Shift key after you begin to drag to keep the layer horizontally constrained. As you can see in Figure 5-9, you have exchanged the positions of the text layers.

20. Change your view back to 1:1. Set the Current Time to 00 (Mac: Cmd-G, Windows: Ctrl-G, then type 0).

21. Set the Quality to High and preview the Comp. You may turn on the Continuously Rasterize switch, but since we have not changed the scale of the layers, it should not make any difference to the quality of the output.

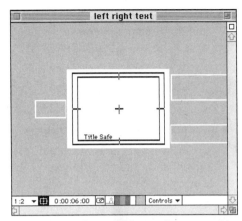

Figure 5-9: Text layer positions exchanges at mid-point.

22. Close the Composition (Mac: Opt-click, Windows: Alt-click on the Time Layout window or Comp window close box). Both the Comp window and the Time Layout window close. The Comp is ready to be nested.

Creating the Sun Background

If you have previewed the finished project, you know that it uses a graphic of the sun as a background. This background is built up of three different Compositions. The first Comp creates the sun face and rotates the rays around it. The second Comp uses five copies of the rotating sun to make an overall background image. The third Comp uses two copies of the second Comp and adds a fast blur effect to one of them.

As you will see when you re-create the sun background, by preparing the pieces and incorporating them into a Comp which is then treated as a single unit, you can organize your work and preserve your sanity. Let's begin with the sun face itself—our starting point for the other Comps in this section.

The Sun Face

You will use two Illustrator files: Face.eps and Sunrays.ai. Figure 5-10 shows the single Illustrator image which was used to create the two files. The image is 01F11 5.0 from the Design Elements Sampler set by Ultimate

Figure 5-10: Sun image from the Design Elements collection by Ultimate Symbol.

Symbol; included on the CD-ROM for this book. We've separated the face from the sun's rays, and duplicated, colored, and rotated the rays. The files included here are the ones that have already been manipulated to work with this exercise.

 Studio Time: Building the Sun Comp

1. Drag the files Face.eps and Sunrays.ai into the Project window.

2. Create a new Comp (Mac: Cmd-N, Windows: Ctrl-N). Make it 320 x 240, 12 seconds long, 30 frames per second. Name the Comp "Sunface1" and set the background color to white (Mac: Shift-Cmd-B, Windows: Shift-Ctrl-B).

3. Set the Current Time to 00 (Mac: Cmd-G, Windows: Ctrl-G, then type 0).

4. Drag Face.eps and Sunrays.ai into the Composition window. Let them snap to the center of the window.

5. Deselect (Tab).

6. Press R to show the Rotation property. Click in the stop watch to make it keyframeable. Leave the rotation amount alone (it defaults to 0 rotations and 0 degrees).

7. Go to the layer Out point (O). Set a new keyframe for Rotation to 0 rotations and 180 degrees. This will make the sun's rays rotate very slowly throughout the movie.

Figure 5-11: Sun Face 1 Composition complete.

8. Crop the Comp close to the sun elements by changing the size of the Comp (Mac: Cmd-K, Windows: Ctrl-K) to 210 x 200.

9. Select all of the layers (Mac: Cmd-A, Windows: Ctrl-A). Press the Opt key (Mac) or Alt key (Windows) and drag the layers towards the center point. Press the Shift key after you begin to drag to snap the elements to the center point.

10. Preview the Comp (press the spacebar).

11. Set the Quality to Best and set both items to Continuously Rasterize. Preview again. It's much slower now.

12. Close the Composition (press the modifier key - Mac: Opt, Windows: Alt–and click on the Time Layout window or Comp window close box). Both the Comp window and the Time Layout window close.

Building the Sun Background Composition

Now that the basic sun has been cropped, we can create a new Comp that uses five copies of this image. The sun is already rotating in the Sun Face 1 Comp, so there is no need to make each of the copies rotate. That is one major advantage in using a nested Composition.

 Studio Time: Building the Sun Background Composite

1. Create a new Comp (Mac: Cmd-N, Windows: Ctrl-N). Make it 320 x 240, 12 seconds long, 30 frames per second. Name the Comp "Sun Background" and set the background color to white (Mac: Shift-Cmd-B, Windows: Shift-Ctrl-B).

2. Set the Current Time to 00 (Mac: Cmd-G, Windows: Ctrl-G, then type 0).

3. Drag the Sun Face 1 Comp into the center of the new Comp so that it snaps to the center point.

4. Press S to show the Scale property. Set the Scale amount to 85%. This is a constant, so do not click in the stop watch.

5. Duplicate the layer (Mac: Cmd-D, Windows: Ctrl-D).

6. Press the Opt key (Mac) or Alt key (Windows) and start to move the image. Press the Shift key after you have started to drag the layer to make it snap to the upper-left corner of the Comp window.

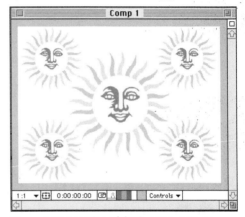

Figure 5-12: Location of the Sun Face 1 Comp images in the Sun Background Comp.

7. Change the Scale property to 50%. It is also constant.

8. Duplicate this layer three more times. Snap a copy to the other three corners of the Comp window as shown in Figure 5-12.

9. You may wish to give a slightly different name to each layer to help distinguish them. Select each layer name in the Time Layout window and press the Return key. This makes the layer name editable. If you simply start typing at this point, you replace the entire name. Place your cursor to the right of the text and click. Now you can add on to the current name. Either give each layer an additional number or identify it by place UL for Upper Left or LR for Lower Right, etc. after each name. You can switch back to the original Source names

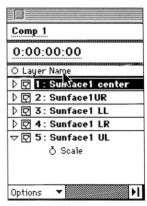

Figure 5-13a: Displaying the custom layer names.

at any time by clicking on the words "Layer Name" under the Go To Time setting on the Time Layout window (shown by the cursor location in Figure 5-13a). This re-displays the original Source name as you can see in Figure 5-13b.

10. Set the Quality switch to Best.

11. Close the Composition (press the modifier key—Mac: Opt, Windows: Alt–and click on the Time Layout window or Comp window close box. Both the Comp window and the Time Layout window close. The Comp is ready to nest.

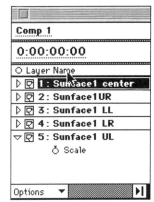

Figure 5-13b: Displaying the original Source names.

Shortcuts

Command	Mac	Windows
Duplicate a layer	Cmd-D	Ctrl-D
Change the layer name	Return	Enter

Building the Sun Bkg2

You are almost there! Only one more Comp remains until the Sun layer is complete. This time, we will place two copies of the Sun Background into a new Comp.

 Studio Time: Finishing the Sun

1. Create a new Comp (Mac: Cmd-N, Windows: Ctrl-N). Make it 320 x 240, 12 seconds long, 30 frames per second. Name the Comp "Sun Bkg2" and set the background color to white (Mac: Shift-Cmd-B, Windows: Shift-Ctrl-B).

2. Set the Current Time to 00 (Mac: Cmd-G, Windows: Ctrl-G, then type 0).

3. Drag the Sun Background Comp into the Comp window so that it snaps to the center of the window.

4. Press T to show the Opacity property. Set the value to 40% but do not set a keyframe—the Opacity is constant.

5. Duplicate the layer (Mac: Cmd-D, Windows: Ctrl-D).

6. Add a Gaussian Blur effect (Effects → Blur & Sharpen → Gaussian Blur). Set the value of the blur to 3. Do not create a keyframe. The blur is to remain constant. All it does is soften the Composition a bit.

7. Set the Quality switch to Best for both layers.

8. You may preview this if you wish, but it will be slow.

9. Close the Composition (Mac: Opt-click, Windows: Alt-click on the Time Layout window or Comp window close box). Both the Comp window and the Time Layout window close. The Sun is finished! Now let's move on to some other elements that will join the sun in the final project.

The Graphic Background Comp

The Graphic Background Composition is formed from a number of duplicates of a single typographic element from the Design Elements Sampler set by Ultimate Symbol. Six copies of this element are used to form a design that rotates and moves across the image like the June Taylor dancers or the Rockettes, performing a precise ballet of transition.

This Composition is difficult to design–but we've already done the hardest part for you, which is the design process itself. Once you know where each element will go, the rest is mechanical. The "reverse animation" technique is used here. Place the elements first in the ending position and then move backwards in time to place their starting positions.

 Studio Time: Building the Background Graphic

1. Create a new Comp (Mac: Cmd-N, Windows: Ctrl-N) that is 5 seconds long, 30 frames per second. Change the background color to white (Mac: Shift-Cmd-B, Windows: Shift-Ctrl-B).

2. Import the file 02N09.ai (File → Import → Footage File).

3. Set the Current Time to 00 (Mac: Cmd-G, Windows: Ctrl-G, then type 0).

4. Drag the 02N09.ai image into the Comp. Let it snap to the center point.

5. Duplicate the layer (Mac: Cmd-D, Windows: Ctrl-D) five times. Add an identifying number to each layer. (Click on the layer name and press the Return key on the Mac or the Enter key

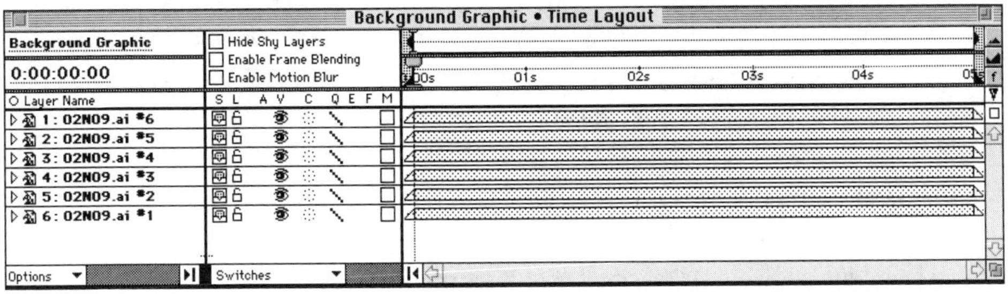

Figure 5-14: Layers named with identifying numbers.

on Windows.) The lowest layer (Layer 6) should be names 02N09.ai #1. Number consecutively from there to the top. Figure 5-14 shows the correctly named layers in the Time Layout window.

6. Set the Current Time to 1 second (Mac: Cmd-G, Windows: Ctrl-G, and type 100, or just move the Playback Head until the Current Time reads 0:00:01:00). This is the point at which all of the elements should form their major pattern, so that it is here that we begin to build the graphic.

7. Bring up the properties for Opacity, Rotation, and Scale (T, Shift-R, Shift-P). Use table 5-1 to set the 1-second values for each layer. KF stands for keyframe. An asterisk (*) means that you should click in the stop watch to set a keyframe for that property. If there is no asterisk, the property is constant. Figure 5-15 shows the Comp window with the elements in position at 1 second.

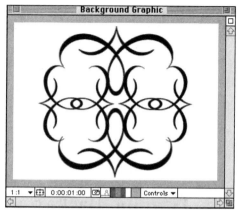

Figure 5-15: Composition window at 1 second.

Layer Name	Opacity	KF	Rotation	KF	Scale	KF	Position	KF
02N09.ai #1	100%	*	0		100%		160,183.5	*
02N09.ai #2	100%	*	180		100%		160,57.5	*
02N09.ai #3	100%	*	90	*	65%	*	198.5, 123.5	*
02N09.ai #4	100%	*	-90	*	65%	*	123.5, 123.5	*
02N09.ai #5	100%	*	90	*	65%	*	73.5, 123.5	*
02N09.ai #6	100%	*	-90	*	65%	*	245.5,123.5	*

Table 5-1: Opacity, Rotation, Scale, and Position at 1 second.

7. Set the Quality on each layer to Best. You also need to set the Continuously Rasterize flag, but you can do this at the end if you find that it slows your machine too much.

8. Set the Current Time to 1.15 seconds (Mac: Cmd-G, Windows: Ctrl-G, and type 115, or just move the Playback Head until the Current Time reads 0:00:01:15). Create sustaining keyframes for all of the keyframeable properties in each layer.

9. Set the Current Time to 00 (Mac: Cmd-G, Windows: Ctrl-G, then type 0).

10. Use table 5-2 to set all of the initial values. These value will place most of the layers off-screen. With all layers at Opacity=0% to start, the entire design will gain in opacity as it moves into its first major position. It is easiest to copy a keyframe that is the same in several

layers and paste it into the next layer that needs it. For example, at Time=0, all of the opacities are 0. Set the first one and copy it to the clipboard (Mac: Cmd-C, Windows: Ctrl-C). Click on the next layer down (or up) and click in the Opacity Keyframe Navigation box to set the keyframe. Then paste in the keyframe from the clipboard (Mac: Cmd-V, Windows: Ctrl-V). Figure 5-16 shows the Composition window at Time=0. The Comp window is at 1:2 so that you can see the position of the layers that are out of the frame.

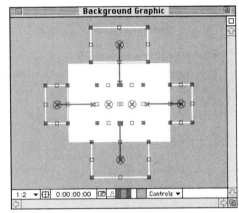

Figure 5-16: Composition window at Time=0.

Layer Name	Opacity	KF	Rotation	KF	Scale	KF	Position	KF
02N09.ai #1	0%	*					160,293.5	*
02N09.ai #2	0%	*					160,-57.5	*
02N09.ai #3	0%	*	90	*	65%	*	198.5, 123.5	*
02N09.ai #4	0%	*	-90	*	65%	*	123.5, 123.5	*
02N09.ai #5	0%	*	90	*	65%	*	-36.5, 123.5	*
02N09.ai #6	0%	*	-90	*	65%	*	354.5, 123.5	*

Table 5-2: Opacity, Rotation, Scale, and Position at Time=0.

11. There are two other times at which keyframes are set—2.05 and 3.05. In both remaining time changes, the two large type elements move completely out of the Composition. The four smaller elements look as if they are doing a square dance as they pull apart, rotate around one another, and move into the corners of the movie frame. (Watch the preview movie again to see this action.) They then shrink in size while they sit in the corners. Tables 5-3 and 5-4 give you the information to set up the remaining two times. It is completely your choice whether to place all of the keyframes by time or by layer. Either way is correct. Remember to only set a keyframe where there are

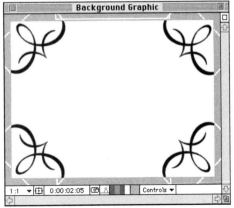

Figure 5-17: Composition window at 2.05 seconds.

asterisks in the KF column. Opacity does not change in either of the two tables. Figure 5-17 shows the final positions of the typographic elements in the Comp window.

Layer Name	Opacity	KF	Rotation	KF	Scale	KF	Position	KF
02N09.ai #1	100%						160, 293.54	*
02N09.ai #2	100%						160, -56.5	*
02N09.ai #3	100%		46	*	65%	*	290, 33.5	*
02N09.ai #4	100%		-135	*	65%	*	32.5, 208	*
02N09.ai #5	100%		-41	*	65%	*	34, 31	*
02N09.ai #6	100%		-225	*	65%	*	287, 207	*

Table 5-3: Opacity, Rotation, Scale, and Position at Time =2.05.

Layer Name	Scale	KF
02N09.ai #3	50%	*
02N09.ai #4	50%	*
02N09.ai #5	50%	*
02N09.ai #6	50%	*

Table 5-4: Scale changes at Time=3.05.

12. Turn on Continuously Rasterize (and Best Quality if you have not already done so). Preview the motion in the Comp window. The Comp is now ready to be nested into the final Comp–when we get to it. Close the Composition (press the modifier key–Mac: Opt, Windows: Alt—and click on the Time Layout window or Comp window close box. Both the Comp window and the Time Layout window close.

As we said at the start of this section, it is long and involved but not difficult to place all

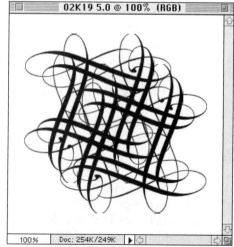

Figure 5-19: Design composed of eight copies of the original swash character.

Figure 5-18: Swash character from Design Elements by Ultimate Symbol collection.

of the elements and set their keyframes. It is much more difficult to design the layout yourself. For practice–and to give yourself the thrill of total accomplishment–you might want to attempt a project similar in concept to this Composition when you have finished the chapter. In the Ultimate Symbol folder on the CD-ROM, there is another swash character in file 02K19.ai. This element, as shown in Figure 5-18, is used to form the design in Figure 5-19. That is one suggestion as to how to use the element.

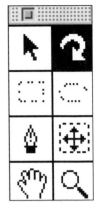

You can work in Illustrator, Photoshop, or directly in the After Effects Composition window to design your effect. You can easily rotate any element in the After Effects Comp window numerically or by using the Rotate tool (shown selected in Figure 5-20).

Figure 5-20: After Effects Tools palette showing Rotate tool selected.

Building the Photos and Graphics Elements

If you preview the chapter project, you can see the word "Photos" zoom out until only the center "o" is showing. This element is created in two stages–a Composition that controls the Scale and Position properties and a second Composition that adds Opacity changes and a Gaussian Blur effect.

Photos Composition

The text, "Photos," set in Illustrator, is the next element to be designed. The word appears slowly in the frame and then zooms out very large. It goes from 0% Scale to 700% Scale. The only reason that we can do this is because the text is in vector format and we are telling After Effects to continuously rasterize the image. If After Effects rasterized the text only once, at 100% size, then the text would be so pixelized at 700% Scale that it would be ugly and unreadable.

 Studio Time: Creating the Photos Composition

1. Create a new Comp (Mac: Cmd-N, Windows: Ctrl-N) that is 5 seconds long, 30 frames per second. Change the background color to white (Mac: Shift-Cmd-B, Windows: Shift-Ctrl-B).

2. Import the file Photos.ai (File → Import → Footage File). Figure 5-21 shows this image in the Footage window.

3. Set the Current Time to 00 (Mac: Cmd-G, Windows: Ctrl-G, then type 0).

4. Drag the Photos.ai image into the Comp. Let it snap to the center point.

5. Display the Scale and Position properties (S, Shift-P). Click in the stop watch to make both properties keyframeable.

6. Set the Scale to 0%. The Position is fine in the center (160, 120).

7. Set the Current Time to 2 seconds (Mac: Cmd-G, Windows: Ctrl-G, and type 200, or just move the Playback Head until the Current Time reads 0:00:02:00). When the image is zoomed to 700%, it needs to be in a specific spot, so let's set that keyframe now.

8. Set the Scale to 700%.

9. Center the "o" in "Photos." Set a keyframe for Position at approximately 195, 60. Figure 5-21 shows the Comp window.

10. Turn on Continuously Rasterize and Best Quality. Preview the Comp.

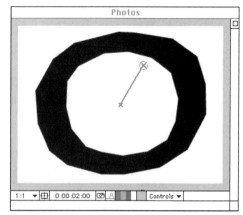

Figure 5-21: "Photos" Scaled 700%.

11. Close the Composition (press the modifier key–Mac: Opt, Windows: Alt–and click on the Time Layout window or Comp window close box). Both the Comp window and the Time Layout window close.

Starting the Photo/Graphics/Zoom Comp

We need to nest the Photos Composition into another Comp. Why? Because we want to add an effect to the image. Even though Photos was a very simple Comp consisting of only one layer, it has to be continuously rasterized for best effect. If you re-open the Photos Comp for a moment, you will see that the Continuously Rasterize flag shows an asterisk (*)–to indicate that it is on. Pull down the Effects menu as if you wished to apply a special effect. It's gray–every choice is dimmed. After Effects allows you to either apply an effect or to continuously rasterize. You cannot do both. But you can nest the Comp that has been continuously rasterized inside of another Comp–and that Comp may have effects applied to it.

 ## Studio Time: Creating the Photo/Graphics/Zoom Comp

1. Create a new Comp (Mac: Cmd-N, Windows: Ctrl-N). Make it 320 x 240, 12 seconds long, 30 frames per second. Name the Comp "Photo/Graphics/Zoom" and set the background color to white (Mac: Shift-Cmd-B, Windows: Shift-Ctrl-B).

2. Set the Current Time to 00 (Mac: Cmd-G, Windows: Ctrl-G, then type 0).

3. Drag the Photos Comp into the Composition window. Let it snap to the center of the window.

4. Set the Current Time to 1:00 seconds (Mac: Cmd-G, Windows: Ctrl-G, and type 100, or just move the Playback Head until the Current Time reads 0:00:01:00). Press T to bring up the

Opacity property. Click in the stop watch to make Opacity keyframeable. Set the value at 100%.

5. Go to 3:00. Set the Opacity keyframe value to 0%.

6. Set the Current Time to 00 (Mac: Cmd-G, Windows: Ctrl-G, then type 0).

7. Let's add a Gaussian Blur to the type (Effects → Blur & Sharpen → Gaussian Blur). Click in the effect stop watch in the Layer area of the Time Layout window to make the Gaussian Blur keyframeable. Set an initial keyframe of 0%.

8. Go to 00:00:00:15 and make a sustaining keyframe of 0% for the Gaussian Blur by clicking in the Keyframe Navigation box.

9. Go to 3:00. Set a keyframe of 20 for bluriness.

10. Save your work.

Compifying

The ability to nest Compositions is very important. It helps you to organize your footage files so that you have fewer items to juggle in the final Comp. It allows for convenience–if you need to apply the same keyframe times and settings to a group of layers, you can place all of the layers into a single Composition and then place that Comp into a new one to which one set of keyframes is applied. It also allows for re-usability. If you need five copies of a layer to which a variety of keyframes have been applied, you can create one Comp and place it five times in the final Comp. No keyframes are needed as they are contained in the one original. Should you need to change those settings, the change only needs to be made to the original–not the five nested Comps. Finally, creating a nested Comp allows you to change the rendering order of the layer. All items in the placed Composition are rendered before any keyframes that have been applied to the nested Comp.

There is another way to nest Compositions. You can build a layer (or layers) in the final Comp and then replace that layer with a new Composition that contains the original layer(s). This process is called pre-composing and is usually referred to by experienced After Effects users as compifying.

Here's a fairly simplistic analogy of what happens when you compify. Picture this: You go into a supermarket and purchase six small bottles of beer and thirty-six tiny Nestle's Crunch miniatures. The check-out person rings up each individual item and places them into a bag for you to take home. Back up a bit. You are in the same supermarket with the same things in your grocery cart. But this time all of the items are placed in a bag. Before they are rung up on the cash register, a "packer" looks to see what you have and organizes them. She "creates" a six-pack of beer and a bag of Nestle's Crunch miniatures. Now the check-out person rings up only two items and when you get home, you have only two items to unpack. However, these two items contain everything that you originally purchased, and are inside of the same bag; the only change is the purchase is arranged differently. In addition, if it were possible to have set each beer bottle spinning continuously, now that you have a six-pack, you could spin that as well (while the individual bottles continued to spin around their own axes).

In last Studio Time, you created a Comp called "Photo/Graphics/Zoom." It currently has only one layer–the Comp containing "Photos" text. You used a nested Comp here because it was not possible to maintain the high quality and continuous rasterization of the text and apply a Gaussian Blur at the same time. We need to do much the same type of thing to a new piece of text, the word "Graphics." "Photos" zooms out with a very large letter left in the center of the image. As it zooms out, "Graphics" zooms in. The "o" in "Photos" and the "P" in "Graphics" need to zoom past one another (the "o" zooms through the center of the bowl of the letter "P." Because of this, the "Graphics" image needs to be arranged in the same Comp as the "Photos" image to get the size and timing correct. We will position the text and create the keyframes in a new layer of the Photo/Graphics/Zoom layer, and then pre-compose the layer to remove the keyframes and substitute a new Composition to which another set of keyframes may be added. The Pre-Compose command places the original layer (Graphics.ai) into a new Comp (Graphics.ai Comp 1), and that Comp is the one used in the Photo/Graphics/Zoom Comp.

Ugh…Is your head whirling? It is really easier to do than to explain, and once you see it in action, it makes sense. Promise.

 ## *Studio Time: Creating the Graphics.ai Layer*

1. Import the Graphics.ai file from the AE05Foot folder (Mac: Cmd-I, Windows: Ctrl-I).

2. Set the Current Time to 1 second (Mac: Cmd-G, Windows: Ctrl-G, and type 100, or just move the Playback Head until the Current Time reads 0:00:01:00).

3. Drag the Graphics.ai image into the Comp. Let it snap to the center point.

4. Press P and Shift-S to show the Position and Scale properties. Click in the stop watch to make both properties keyframe-able. Set the Position property to 232x, 210.5y. Set Scale to 1000%. This places the top portion of the "P" in "Graphics" directly in the center of the frame at the same time that the "o" in "Photos" is starting to zoom out. The "o" shows through the center of the "P" as you can see in Figure 5-22.

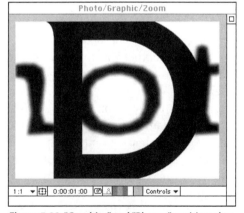

Figure 5-22: "Graphics" and "Photos" positioned to zoom through each other.

5. Set the Current Time to 2.00 seconds (Mac: Cmd-G, Windows: Ctrl-G, and type 200, or just move the Playback Head until the Current Time reads 0:00:02:00). Set a keyframe for Position at 162x ,119.5y. Create a Scale keyframe with a value of 75%. This sets the word "Graphics" the

same width as the zoomed out "O" (see Figure 5-23).

6. Set the Current Time to 2.15 seconds (Mac: Cmd-G, Windows: Ctrl-G, and type 215, or just move the Playback Head until the Current Time reads 0:00:02:15). Set an additional sustaining Scale keyframe of 75%.

7. Set the Current Time to 3.15 seconds (Mac: Cmd-G, Windows: Ctrl-G, and type 315, or just move the Playback Head until the Current Time reads 0:00:03:15). Set a Scale keyframe of 0%. Set the layer to Continuously Rasterize and set the Quality to Best.

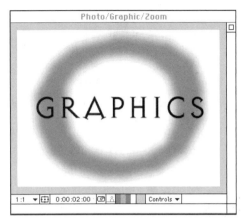

Figure 5-23: "Graphics" set to same width as the "o" in "Photos."

Creating the Graphics.ai Comp 1 Comp

You have created a layer named Graphics.ai. This layer contains keyframes for two geometric properties. The layer starts at Time=1:00. Let's compify this layer.

Studio Time: Compifying the Graphics Layer

1. Figure 5-24 shows the Time Layout window before we pre-compose the Graphics.ai layer. Note: The terms "pre-compose" and "compify" are deliberately being used interchangeably as they are synonyms and you will hear both. The Compify command in After Effects 2.0 was replaced by the Pre-Compose command in After Effects 3.0, which is how the concept got its multiple names.

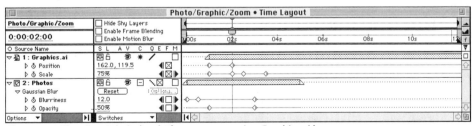

Figure 5-24: Time Layout window before pre-composing Graphics.ai layer.

2. Select the Layer → Pre-compose command (Mac: Shift-Cmd-C, Windows: Shift-Ctrl-C). Figure 5-25 shows the dialog box. You have two options: Leave all attributes in Photo/Graphic/Zoom, or Move all attributes into the new Composition. Select the latter. (We'll explain why in a little while.) Click OK.

The Comp, Graphics.ai, no longer is part of the Photo/Graphics/Zoom Comp. It still appears in the Project window, but the new Comp, Graphics.ai Comp 1, is the top layer in the currently-open Composition.

3. Set the Current Time to 1 second (Mac: Cmd-G, Windows: Ctrl-G, and type 100, or just move the Playback Head until the Current Time reads 0:00:01:00).

4. Press T to bring up the Opacity property. Set the Opacity property to 0%.

5. Go to 3 seconds. Set the Opacity to 100%.

6. Set the time to 2 seconds and preview the Comp. (It will play slowly.)

7. Close the Composition (Mac: Opt-click, Windows: Alt-click on the Time Layout window or Comp window close box). Both the Comp window and the Time Layout window close.

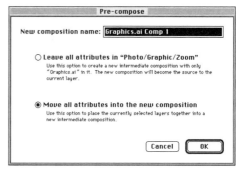

Figure 5-25: Pre-compose dialog.

Shortcuts

Command	Mac	Windows
Pre-compose (i.e. compify)	Shift-Cmd-C	Shift-Ctrl-C

What did we do? What happens when the Pre-compose command is used? Figure 5-24 shows the Time Layout window before the layer is compified. Figure 5-26 shows the Time Layout window just after the Pre-compose command is executed. The "before" figure shows the layer In point as 1:00; the "after" In point is Time=00. However, the Comp window at 2:00 is identical to Figure 5-23 both before and after compifying.

The Pre-compose command removes the original layer and replaces it with the newly-created Comp. By selecting the option to Move all attributes into the new Composition, you are telling After Effects to place all of the keyframes, masks, and effects into the inter-mediate Composition that it creates and to place a reference to the new Comp—with a

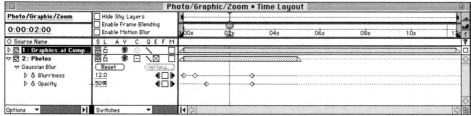

Figure 5-26: Time Layout window after the Pre-compose command is used.

"clean" time line–as a layer in the current Time Layout window. If you double-click on the Graphics.ai Comp 1 Comp, you see the original keyframes that you created.

However, Pre-compose uses the length of the current (master) Comp as the length of the new Comp that it creates, and it places it at Time=0. The keyframes created originally can no longer be seen, but they exit at the correct times in the underlying Comp and allow the new time line to produce the same results.

The other option, "Leave all attributes in Photo/Graphic/Zoom," would have left the keyframes and only removed the source image (Graphics.ai) to an intermediate Comp. This option is only available when compifying single layers, and is not nearly as useful as the "Move all attributes into the new Composition" option.

The Elements of Design Comp

When you preview the AECH05.mov movie, you see a rotating element saying "Elements of Design" that looks as if it was rendered in a program such as LogoMotion. It wasn't. You will learn to create this by applying a 3D effect to flat, vector text. Here is another opportunity to practice the skills you have learned.

 Studio Time: Centering an Element

1. Create a new Comp (Mac: Cmd-N, Windows: Ctrl-N). Make it 320 x 240, 12 seconds long, 30 frames per second. Name the Comp "Elements of Design" and set the background color to white (Mac: Shift-Cmd-B, Windows: Shift-Ctrl-B).

2. Set the Current Time to 00:00:00:15 (Mac: Cmd-G, Windows: Ctrl-G, then type 15).

3. Import the three files that comprise this Comp: Elements.ai , Of.ai, and Design.ai (Mac: Cmd-Opt-I, Windows: Alt-Ctrl-I).

4. Drag Of.ai into the Composition window. Let it snap to the center of the window. Since this is the central element, we position it first.

5. Show the Scale and Opacity properties. Click in the stop watches to make them keyframeable. Set the Scale value of to 0%, and the Opacity value to 10%.

6. Go to 2:15. Set a Scale keyframe value of 70% and an Opacity keyframe of 50%.

7. Set to Continuously Rasterize and set Quality at Best.

8. Compify the layer (Mac: Shift-Cmd-C, Windows: Shift-Ctrl-C). Accept the default name (Of.ai Comp 1). Select "Move all attributes into the new Composition." Click OK.

9. Set the Current Time to 00 (Mac: Cmd-G, Windows: Ctrl-G, then type 0). We are going to add effects to this layer from this point in time even though the underlying source to the Comp really doesn't start until 15 frames in.

10. Set an initial Opacity keyframe value of 75. Also add a Gaussian Blur with a keyframe value of 20 (Effects → Blur & Sharpen → Gaussian Blur).

11. Go to 2 seconds and set a blurriness keyframe with a value of 7.

12. Go to 4:00 and set a sustaining blurriness keyframe by clicking the Keyframe Navigation box for the Fast Blur effect. This centers the "Of" as you see in Figure 5-27.

13. Go to 6:15. Set a Blurriness keyframe with the value of 25%.

14. Now let's set some Opacity keyframes. Go to 6:00 seconds. Set a sustaining Opacity keyframe.

15. Go to 7:00 and set an Opacity keyframe value of 0%. The element fades off to nothing as the blur continues.

16. Set the Quality to Best.

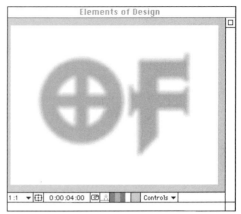

Figure 5-27: "Of" centered in the Comp window.

Shortcuts

Command	Mac	Windows
Add Single Footage Item	Cmd-I	Ctrl-I
Add Multiple Footage Items	Cmd-Opt-I	Ctrl-Alt-I

 Studio Time: Elements and Design

1. Set the Current Time to 00 (Mac: Cmd-G, Windows: Ctrl-G, then type 0).

2. Drag the Design.ai and Elements.ai images into the Comp. Let them snap to the center point. Leave both layers selected.

3. Press S and Shift-P to show the Scale and Position properties. Set the Scale to 63%. Do not create a Scale keyframe as the Scale remains constant. Deselect (Tab).

4. Set a Position value of 161x, 103y for the Elements.ai layer. Give the Design.ai layer a position of 160x, 137y. No keyframes are needed as the Position property also remains constant. Set both

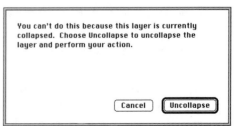

Figure 5-28: Error message reporting that effects cannot be applied to layers that are continuously rasterized.

layers to Continuously Rasterize, and set the Quality to Best.

5. Set the Current Time to 00 (Mac: Cmd-G, Windows: Ctrl-G, then type 0).

6. We are going to apply the Basic 3D effect to the two layers. Choose Effects → Perspective → Basic 3D. Uh-oh! Figure 5-28 shows the error message that appears. Click the Uncollapse button. Notice that the Continuously Rasterize switch turns into a box with a minus sign in it. (An explanation of this follows at the end of the Studio Time.)

7. Figure 5-29 shows the Basic 3D effect settings. Click in the stop watches in both layers to make them keyframeable for Swivel and Distance to Image. (Remember, you need to click on the arrowhead next to the effect in both layers to reveal the effect properties so that you can add keyframes.) Either follow the directions in Steps 8-11 or use Table 5-5 below to set the needed keyframes.

8. Set a Distance to Image value of 50 and a Swivel -90° for Design.ai. Give Elements.ai a Distance to Image value of 60 and a Swivel setting of 90. It looks as if both elements disappear from the screen. This is correct, because the settings of 90° and -90° turn the text around so that you are looking at the thickness of the text on edge–and it has no thickness.

9. Go to 2:00. Change the Distance to Image and Swivel settings to 0 for both layers. This makes the text face forward as shown in Figure 5-30.

10. Go to 4 seconds. Make sustaining keyframes for Swivel and Distance to Image in both layers.

11. Go to 6:15. Give Design.ai a Distance to image setting of 50 and a Swivel keyframe value of 90°. Give Elements.ai a Distance to Image value of 60 and Swivel value of -90°.

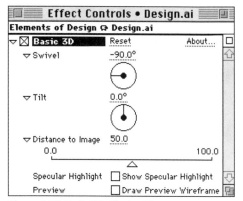

Figure 5-29: Basic 3D effect settings.

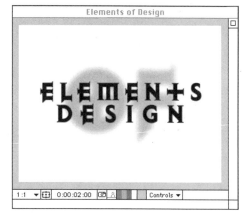

Figure 5-30: Comp window at Time=2 seconds.

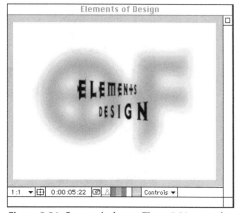

Figure 5-31: Comp window at Time=5:22 seconds.

These Swivel settings are the reverse of the first values and bring the text around to the opposite direction. (But you can't see it again!) Figure 5-31 shows the Comp window at 5:22. You can clearly see how the text revolves in virtual 3D space.

Layer Name	Distance to Image	Swivel
Time=00		
Design.ai	50	-90
Elements.ai	60	90
Time=2 seconds		
Design.ai	0	0
Elements.ai	0	0
Time=4 seconds		
Design.ai	0	0
Elements.ai	0	0
Time=6:15 seconds		
Design.ai	50	90
Elements.ai	60	-90

Table 5-5: Settings for Basic 3D effect.

Step 6 produced an error message saying that the layers were collapsed and you could not apply an effect to a collapsed layer. This probably made no sense to you at all. All shall be explained...

If you recall our earlier discussion about the Continuously Rasterize switch, we said that you could continuously rasterize an image or you could apply an effect–but not both. In this instance, we tried to do both, hence the error message. However, After Effects has two names for the same switch. It is also referred to as the Collapse Geometrics switch. While it might be more correct to say that Continuously Rasterize applies to an Illustrator image that is its own layer, and Collapse Geometrics applies to a Comp being used as a layer, the error message is general–it makes no distinction and refers to both instances as Collapse Geometrics.

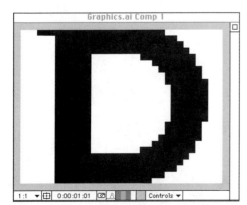

Figure 5-32a: 1000% Scale with Continuously Rasterize off; Draft Quality.

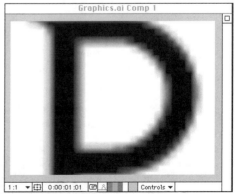

Figure 5-32b: 1000% Scale with Continuously Rasterize off; Best Quality.

This leaves us with several questions:

- What does Collapse Geometrics mean?

- Why did we add an effect if we had to sacrifice the continuous rasterization?

- How could we get continuous rasterization and still apply the effect?

Collapse Geometrics is a method used to speed the rendering of a Composition. Instead of calculating each geometric transformation as it is applied, the switch allows After Effects to calculate a "net" state for the frame. For example, if you had a frame that is supposed to be rotated 90° and displayed at 600% Scale and 0% Opacity, After Effects would have a lot of work to do for nothing. It would need to rotate the image, scale it way up, and then output nothing since the Opacity is set to 0. However, if the Collapse Geometrics switch is on, After Effects looks at all of the settings and determines that the result is a blank frame, so it does not need to perform any massive calculations.

The explanation of how Collapse Geometrics is a bit simplistic–you cannot apply this switch to a single raster layer; it is unavailable. It only shows up on the Time Layout window if a layer either contains a vector image or another Composition. The

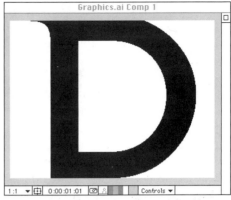

Figure 5-32c: 1000% Scale with Continuously Rasterize on; Draft Quality.

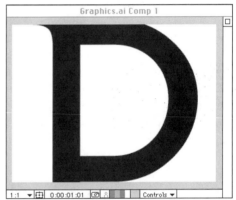

Figure 5-32d: 1000% Scale with Continuously Rasterize on; Best Quality.

same logic applies, though, if the Composition contains multiple layers. If one layer in the Comp rotates an element but another layer higher in the stack places an element on top of it that completely covers the lower element, the Collapse Geometrics switch forces evaluation of the result before the first rotation is done–so there is no need to waste processing on an element that is not visible. Using the switch can help significantly shorten processing times.

The manual also states that it can result in higher quality output, but this really refers to the switch when it is acting in Continuously Rasterize mode. As we have seen earlier in this chapter, if you need to scale your vector images beyond the 100% Scale, you will get a massive quality improvement. Examine Figures 5-32a through 5-32d. The "P" in Graphics is at almost 1000% Scale. In Figure 5-32a, Continuously Rasterize is off and Quality is set to Draft. The image is extremely jagged. When the Quality is set to Best, as it is in Figure 5-32b, it almost looks worse. The enlarging that occurs on the anti-aliased text is even uglier than the jaggies. The jagged image at least looked clean! Figure 5-32c shows the importance of the Continuously Rasterize switch even when the image is aliased. It looks remarkably better that the two previous figures. Finally, Figure 5-32d shows the improvement when the Quality is set to Best.

This brings us to the next point—why did we set an effect if it meant losing the continuous rasterization for the layer? The answer is easy: the Scale of the image did not exceed 100% in this example. There was no quality loss when the image was reduced to 63%.

If we needed to both scale the image over 100% and add an effect to it, what could we do? Hopefully, you already know the answer, because this situation has occurred several times in this chapter. You either create an new Comp to hold the effect or compify the one that you are creating and place the Continuously Rasterize switch in that one. Either technique allows After Effects to first perform the continuous rasterization of the element, and then process it again to add the effect. You have actually changed the rendering order to work in your favor so you meet both needs.

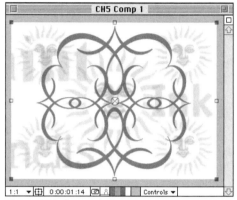

Figure 5-33: Comp window at 1:14.

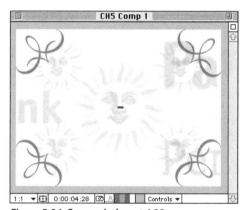

Figure 5-34: Comp window at 4:28.

The Master Comp

Believe it or not—we are actually ready to finish this up! This final Comp is anti-climactic. After all of this work, most of this Comp involves simply placing the other Comps into it.

Studio Time: Placing the Finished Comps

1. Create a new Comp (Mac: Cmd-N, Windows: Ctrl-N). Make it 320 x 240, 12 seconds long, 30 frames per second. Name the Comp "Ch5 Comp 1" and set the background color to white (Mac: Shift-Cmd-B, Windows: Shift-Ctrl-B).

2. Set the Current Time to 00 (Mac: Cmd-G, Windows: Ctrl-G, then type 0).

3. Drag the Sun Back #2 Comp into the Time Layout window so that it snaps to the center point.

4. Select the layer. Set an Opacity keyframe with a value of 100%. (Type T to show the Opacity property.)

5. Go to 2:00. Set an Opacity keyframe value at 45%. Also set a keyframe for Scale with a value of 100%. (Type Shift-S to add Scale to the items shown.)

6. Go to 2:15. Set a sustaining Scale keyframe value of 100%.

7. Go to 6:00 and set a Scale keyframe value of 85%.

8. Press the Tilde (~) key to collapse the hierarchy for this layer.

9. Go back to 00. You can press the Home key on an extended keyboard as a shortcut, or type "I" to take you to the layer In point if a layer is selected.

10. Drag in the Left Right Text Comp. Set its Opacity to 75%. Do not create a keyframe for Opacity. Add a Fast Blur of 2.5 that remains constant (Effects → Blur & Sharpen → Fast Blur). This is similar to a Gaussian Blur but takes less time to apply and is not as clean.

11. Press the Tilde to collapse the layer hierarchy.

12. Drag in the Background Graphics Comp. Set its Opacity to 50%. This is constant. Press the Tilde to collapse the layer hierarchy.

13. Go to 1:14 and drag in the Photo/Graphics/Zoom. Set the Opacity value to 85%. Press the Tilde to collapse the layer hierarchy. Figure 5-33 shows the Comp window at this point.

14. Go to 4:28 and drag in the Elements of Design comp. It needs nothing added to it. Figure 5-34 shows the Comp window at this time.

Surely you didn't think that we'd let you off the hook this easily! There is still one more type element that needs to be created. If you preview the AECH05.mov movie, you will see the word "Curves" appear in a swinging arc coming from a pivot point near the center-top of the movie. It is this element that still needs to be created. The text swings from its anchor point–and this is the first time that you are asked to change a layer's anchor point.

The anchor point is the position from which an element rotates or scales. You can picture this quite literally by its name–imagine a sheet of paper with a pin stuck into the center of it. If you want to rotate the sheet of paper, you can only revolve it around the point where the pin is located; the paper is fastened (or anchored) by the pin–its anchor point. In After Effects (as in Illustrator), the anchor point defaults to the center point.

In order to get something to rotate differently, you need to move the anchor point (a feature we've longed for but not yet gotten in Photoshop). We need the word "Curves" to look as if it has been suspended in a hammock and id being rocked to sleep. We need to change the anchor point so that it becomes the place where the "strings" on each end of the Curve "hammock" attach to the "tree."

You can do this numerically by changing the Anchor Point property in the Time Layout window, or you can drag the anchor point directly in the Composition window by using the Pan-Behind tool (the tool highlighted in Figure 5-35). This ought to be easy, and it is–but it is tricky as well. The problem is that changing the anchor point numerically moves the element, but not the physical location of the anchor point in the Comp window. Also, the anchor point coordinates are always in reference to the image as it appears in the Layer window–not the Comp window–so moving the anchor point with the Pan-behind tool is not possible if you are trying to move it to follow numeric instructions. The instructions in the Studio Time will work with no trouble (you are told to position the element where you want the anchor point to remain, and then set the anchor point numerically–which forces the text lower in the image). However, try moving the anchor point with the Pan-Behind tool and see what happens. After Effects is forgiving of several instructions as it has more than one level of Undo.

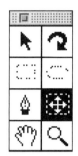

Figure 5-35: The Pan-Behind tool in the Toolbox.

1. Import the file Curves.ai (Mac: Cmd-I, Windows: Ctrl-I).

2. Set the Current Time to 3:06 seconds (Mac: Cmd-G, Windows: Ctrl-G, and type 306, or just move the Playback Head until the Current Time reads 0:00:03:06).

3. Drag the Curves.ai file into the center of the image.

4. Press P to show the Position property. Change the Position to 156x, -2y. This moves the text to the center top of the image as you can see in Figure 5-36.

5. Next we will change its anchor point. We will do this numerically. Press Shift-A to show the Anchor Point property. Set new the value to 118x, -105.5y.

6. Position and Anchor Point are constants, you do not need to set keyframes. However, you do need set keyframes for Scale (Shift-S) and Rotation (Shift-R). Set the Scale value to 30% and the Rotation value to 138°. The Opacity (Shift-T) is set at a constant of 40. Figure 5-37 shows that these new settings move the image off the frame.

7. Go to 5:14. Set the Scale to 50% and the rotation to -136.0.

8. Set the layer switches to Continuously Rasterize and set the Quality to Best.

Figure 5-36: Curves.ai positioned with default anchor point location.

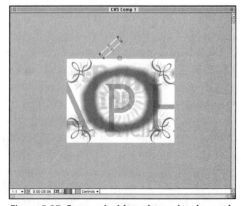

Figure 5-37: Curves.ai with anchor point changed.

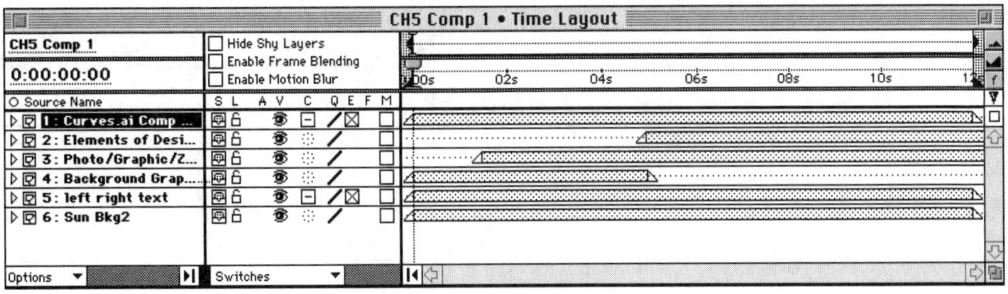

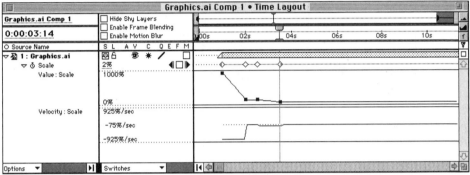

Figure 5-38: Curves.ai in starting position.

Figure 5-39a: Time Layout window with velocities unedited.

9. Compify the layer (Mac: Shift-Cmd-C, Windows: Shift-Ctrl-C). Accept the default name (Curves.ai Comp 1). Select "Move all attributes into the new Composition." Click OK.

10. Set the Opacity at 40%. Add a Fast Blur of 3 (Effects → Blur & Sharpen → Fast Blur). This is constant.

11. Press the Tilde (~) to collapse the layer hierarchy.

12. Finally, set all of the Quality switches to Best. Figure 5-39a and b shows the finished Time Layout window.

13. Render the movie while you're out for lunch and a relaxing cocktail. You deserve it!

 **Rewind**

That was a very long project–though it is a short one compared to the complexity of many projects that are created by After Effects artists. As projects become longer and more complex, it is critical that you learn to organize them properly, and to take advantage of any way to optimize their rendering time while still producing quality work.

One of the major new understandings that you should have from this chapter is the way in which you can change the rendering order for a layer within a Comp by pre-composing it. In addition to helping to organize a long project, pre-composing makes it

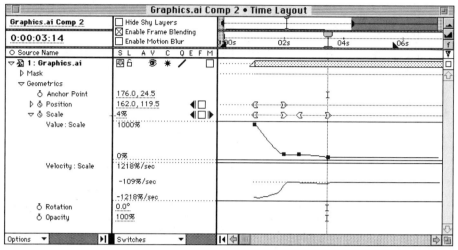

Figure 5-39b: Time Layout window with velocities edited.

possible to perform actions on actions–things that you could not do otherwise (such as rotating a Comp that contains images that are already rotating).

You also have learned how to work with vector images, how to keep them at their highest quality, and some of the trade-offs and issues that occur when you use vector images. You have learned what the Continuously Rasterize switch does, and how its meaning changes when it becomes the Collapse Geometrics switch. You have learned about anchor points and how and why to change them.

 # Coming Attractions

If you render your work as a movie and compare it to the AECH05.mov movie that we provided, you may notice a difference in the quality of the movement of different elements. Our movie is very smooth; your movie may be much more abrupt. Compare Figures 5-39a and 5-39b. You may have wondered about the reason for the little arrowhead next to the geometric properties. It controls the velocity of the motion into and out of the keyframes. These velocities can be edited in a manner similar to editing Bezier curves. Figure 5-39a contains a section from the project that you created which has had no velocities changed. Figure 5-39b shows the same segment of the Time Layout window from the project that created the AECH05.mov movie. Note the subtle differences in the lines in the Motion Graph.

You will learn how to tweak the Motion Graphs in Chapter 12. In addition, you will learn more about the principles of animation to make motion look more realistic, natural, and smooth.

In the next chapter, we will talk again about input from Photoshop, with some new twists.

Using Photoshop Comps

 Preview

What is it about a Photoshop Comp that makes it different than working with any other type of Photoshop file in After Effects? The most noticeable difference is that you need to import it into After Effects using a special menu item. Although you can select File→Import and open a "normal" (i.e. flattened) Photoshop file, in order to use all of the layers that are embedded in a Photoshop file, you need to specifically tell After Effects that you want to see all of the layers. You signal this by using the command File→Import→Photoshop 3.0 as Comp.

This brings us to the second immediate difference. After you have imported the Photoshop file as a Comp, you see two items in the Project window, where you would normally only see the footage item itself. You see a folder that contains all of the layers in the file—each as a separate image—and a second item, which is the Composition with each of the layers already placed in the same relationship to each other as they were in the original Photoshop file.

You would not see the third difference unless your Photoshop file employs *clipping groups*. A clipping group is a very useful feature in Photoshop that allows you to cut out a group of layers into the shape of the bottom layer. The easiest way to understand this, if you have not used the feature, is to pull an analogy from your childhood. Picture a sheet of construction paper, a tube of glue, and a box of variously colored glitter. If you draw the letter S on the construction paper with your tube of glue, and then pour glitter on top it, the glitter only sticks to the paper where it contains glue.

A clipping group works in much the same way. The bottom layer in the group is the "construction paper" and its opacity is the "glue." If you draw anywhere in the layer with 100% opacity (the color does not matter), it will leave glue for the clipped layers. The layers that you place above this bottom one can be clipped to the glue layer by designating it as part of the group (as a keyboard shortcut or a single checkbox in the Layers Option dialog for the to-be-clipped layer). The only part of the clipped layer that remains visible is the portion of the layer directly above the glue (i.e. the opaque pixels on the bottom layer). Unlike working with glitter (which is both difficult and messy to move once you have sprinkled it), you can move the clipped layers until you find just the "right" spot for them over the glue.

That was a long explanation of a feature in Photoshop—but what relevance does it have to After Effects? When you import a Photoshop file as a Comp and it contains clipping groups, each group becomes its own Comp in the folder that holds the Photoshop layers. This is a logical and extremely useful/friendly/intelligent way of handling what could be a sticky problem. Each group is presented in After Effects as a unit which can be placed and manipulated as one item.

It is this function of opening a Photoshop file as a Comp that we shall discuss in this chapter. Chapter 2 introduced you to working with Photoshop files (and to importing layered files as Comps). Chapter 12 picks up the Photoshop saga again when we look at using transfer modes within After Effects. Therefore, the "new" content in this chapter is the care and handling of Photoshop files that contain clipping groups.

Open and play the movie, AECH06.mov using the MoviePlayer application. The project concerns words—both literally and figuratively. The letters in the word "words" rotate and move onto the screen, and then the textures inside of each letter start to move once the letters themselves come to a stop.

In this chapter, you will learn how to:

- Open and import a Photoshop file that contains a clipping group.
- Recognize the correspondence between the file in Photoshop and in After Effects.
- Locate and use the Preserve Transparency flag.
- Open the source footage for a Comp nested within a Composition.
- Move textures through a clipping group.
- Define a Work Area and render only that portion of the image.

 # Feature Presentation

Photoshop files form the mainstay of a "typical" After Effects artist's daily work. The most common uses for After Effects are for titling and bumpers (the header or trailers before and after a TV program) or for animations in commercials. If the source footage isn't live video or an Illustrator file, then it is likely to be a Photoshop file (of course, there aren't many other choices!).

The first Studio Time helps you to see the differences and similarities between a file that contains clipping groups as it is displayed in Photoshop, and as it is displayed in After Effects. The first challenge is to determine exactly what the groups in the Photoshop file are doing, so that you relate this to the behavior in After Effects. Subsequent Studio Time segments discuss the creation of the actual After Effects project.

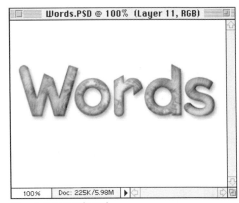

Figure 6-1: Words.psd.

Studio Time: Viewing the Clipped Photoshop File

1. Open the file Words.psd in Photoshop. Figure 6-1 shows the Photoshop file. Figure 6-2 shows the Layers palette.

2. Make Layer W the active layer by clicking on its name in the Layers palette. You will see a brush icon in the second column of the Layers palette (next to the Eye icon).

3. Click in the second column of the Layers palette for each of the three layers directly above Layer W (Texture 1 W, Texture 2 W, Type Shape W). You will leave a link icon in each layer's second column.

4. Create a new document (Mac: Cmd-N, Windows: Ctrl-N). From the Window menu, select Words.psd. A new image that is the same size and color mode of the Words.psd image will appear.

5. Click on the Words.psd image to make it active. Press the modifier key (Mac: Cmd, Windows: Ctrl) and Shift key and drag the image from the Words.psd document into the newly created Untitled image. The W layer and its three linked layers will come along (as long as you drag from the

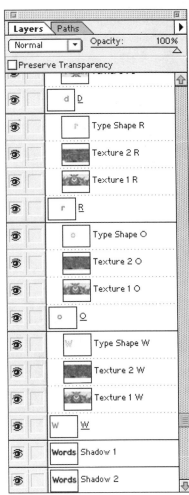

Figure 6-2: Layers palette for Words.psd.

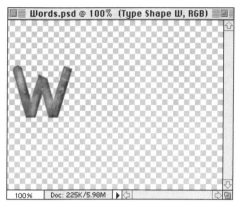

Figure 6-3: W group before ungrouping.

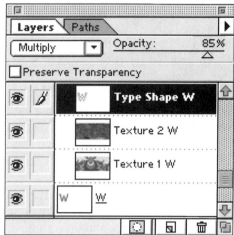

Figure 6-4: Layers palette with ungrouped layers.

image rather than from the Layers palette). Figure 6-3 shows the new image.

6. Hold down the (Mac) Option or (Windows) Alt key and move the image over a dashed dividing line between the layers in the Layers palette (the Untitled image is active). When the cursor icon changes to two overlapping circles, click on the dividing line. This removes the clipping group. (You can tell that it is gone because the dividing line becomes solid and the image preview in the Layers palette is no longer indented.) Figure 6-4 shows the Layers palette of the Untitled image with the groups removed.

7. Let's look at how the image was constructed. When these layers were grouped, they formed the letter W. Press the modifier key (Mac: Option, Windows: Alt) and click on the Eye icon next to the W layer. It becomes the only visible layer, as shown in Figure 6-5.

8. Press the modifier key (Mac: Cmd, Windows: Ctrl) and click on the *name* of the W layer in the Layers palette. This loads a selection based on the opaque pixels of the image. In this case, the selection outline looks like the letter W. The entire letter has 100% opacity even though the color values

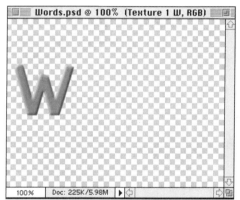

Figure 6-5: Layer W.

Figure 6-6: Texture 1 W layer.

in the layer differ. This letter, then, provides the glue.

9. Press the modifier key (Mac: Option, Windows: Alt) and click on the Eye icon next to the Texture 1 W layer. Figure 6-6 shows this layer, which is mostly opaque and contains a texture. If you highlight the Texture 1 W layer, you see that it is in Screen mode—that is, it gets lighter as it is placed over the layer below. (You will not "see" the Screen mode result unless the Eye icon for the W layer is turned on.) This layer has 100% opacity.

10. Press the modifier key (Mac: Option, Windows: Alt) and click on the Eye icon next to the Layer Texture 2 W layer. Figure 6-7 shows this layer. This layer also contains a texture. If you highlight the Texture 2 W layer, you see that it is in Overlay mode— that is, it colors the layer below, making the colors more intense.

11. Finally, press the modifier key (Mac: Option, Windows: Alt) and click on the Eye icon next to the Type Shape W copy layer. Figure 6-8 shows this layer. This layer contains another W—lighter than the original one and shadowed on the edges. If you highlight the Type Shape W layer, you see that it is in Multiply mode at 85% opacity. Its purpose is to give definition and shading to the letter W. You can verify this by turning on the Eye icon next to the W layer, and then switching the Eye icon next to the Type Shape W off and on again.

12. You can close the Untitled image now without saving it. The purpose was to show you exactly how each clipping group is constructed. All five groups in the Words.psd image follow the same format—bottom layer letter followed by two textures, and topped with a lighter shaded version of the letterform for emphasis.

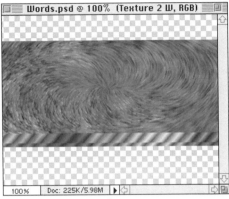

Figure 6-7: Texture 2 W layer.

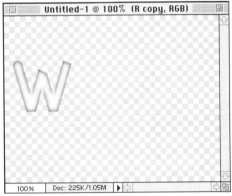

Figure 6-8: Type Shape W layer.

13. This leaves the bottom three layers in the Words.psd image unexplored. These layers are not members of a clipping group. Shadow 1 contains a solid black version of the word "Words" that acts to further define the shapes. Shadow 2 copy is a shadow for "Words" that is a blurred version of Shadow 1 at 50% opacity. WhiteBG is a white solid that functions as the image background.

Now that you know what the Photoshop file is doing, it becomes easier to understand the behavior of the file in After Effects. Let's turn our attention to that now. In this Studio Time, you will open the Photoshop file and see how it is displayed in After Effects.

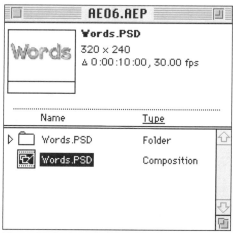

Figure 6-9: Project window with Photoshop Comp.

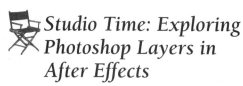 *Studio Time: Exploring Photoshop Layers in After Effects*

1. Create a new project (Mac: Cmd-Option-N, Windows: Alt-Ctrl-N). Name it AECH06.aep.

2. Import the Words.psd file from the AE06Foot folder (File → Import → Photoshop 3.0 as Comp). Figure 6-9 shows the Project window as it appears immediately upon import.

3. Turn down the arrow on the Words.psd folder in the Project window. Figure 6-10 shows this action. The first five items in the folder are Comps, followed by an entry for every layer in the original Photoshop file. Unfortunately, After Effects truncates the names so that the layers are not easily identifiable.

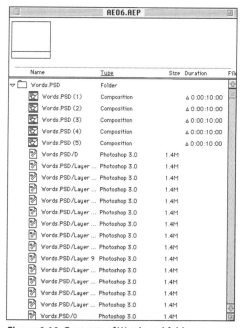

Figure 6-10: Contents of Words.psd folder.

4. Double-click on the Words.psd (1) Comp inside of the folder. Figure 6-11 shows the Comp window and Figure 6-12 shows the Time Layout window. Look familiar? This is the same clipping group that we used in the last Studio Time. Oddly enough, however, *then* it was near the bottom of the layer stack and *now* it is at the top. It has also acquired a name, which it lacked as part of the Photoshop file. It is not a descriptive name, true, but it is a name (which you will change in the next Studio Time). The only thing that looks is different is that it had

no black background in Photoshop. Here, it shows the color of the background Comp (which you can change by pressing Shift-Cmd-B on the Mac or Shift-Ctrl-B under Windows.

5. As you would expect, Words.psd (2) is the grouping for the letter O, and Words.psd (5) contains the group for the letter S. You can check this if you want by opening the Comps from within the folder.

6. Where is the entire word—the whole Photoshop file? It is in the Comp that is *outside* the folder. The Comp is labeled Words.psd. Close the Comp and Time Layout windows and close up the folder again by clicking on its arrow.

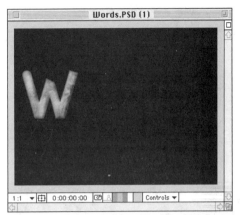

Figure 6-11: Comp window—Words.psd (1) Comp.

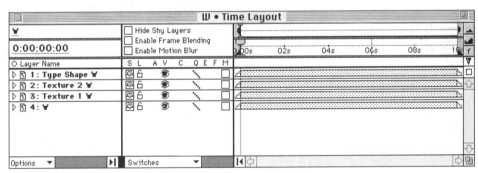

Figure 6-12: Time Layout window—Words.psd (1) Comp.

7. Double-click on the Words.psd Composition in the Project window to open it. Figure 6-13 shows the Comp window. It looks just like the original Photoshop file—complete with white background.

8. You can easily determine which layer is which by selectively turning off the Video switch (the Eye icon under the letter V in the Switches area) for each layer. Make sure that you turn them all back on when you are finished playing.

9. One final thing to notice in the Time Layout window is the length of the Comp.

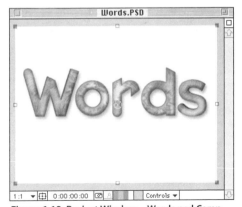

Figure 6-13: Project Window—Words.psd Comp.

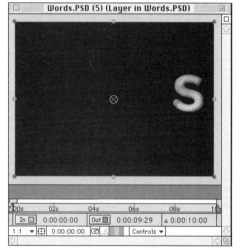

Figure 6-14: Time Layout window—Words.psd Comp.

Figure 6-15a: Layer window showing Words.psd (5).   Figure 6-15b: Alpha channel for Words.psd (5).

If you look at Figure 6-14, you'll notice that it is 10 seconds long. Your mileage, however, may vary. Because the Comp is a still image, and you never explicitly created the Comp, After Effects uses the last duration that it has in the Prefs file (i.e. the last duration that was created). If your Comp is also 10 seconds long, it is a fortuitous accident.

10. The only major unanswered question that remains is how After Effects handles the transparency issue for the clipping groups. You may have guessed that answer by now. It creates an alpha channel for each group that is partially responsible for the same output as a clipping group. To verify this, double-click on the Words.psd (5) Comp in the Time Layout window. Figure 6-15a shows the Layer window, and Figure 6-15b shows the alpha channel in effect (which you can see by clicking and holding the mouse down on the white-turned-black square at the location shown by the cursor).

11. There is one more piece to the transparency puzzle. Highlight the Words.psd (5) layer in the Time Layout window. Open the Source footage (Mac: Ctrl-double-click on the layer name, Windows: Alt-double-click on the layer name). This opens the underlying source Comp and its companion Time Layout window. Change the Switches to Transfer Controls as shown in Figure 6-16.

12. The Transfer Controls area is shown in Figure 6-17. Notice that the Mode column contains the same transfer modes (Blending/Apply modes in Photoshop) as the original Photoshop file. The final piece of the mystery of how After Effects simulates a clipping group, however, is revealed by the X in the boxes under the T (the column next to Mode). That is the Preserve Transparency box. When it is on, the layer respects the transparency of the layer beneath it. Layer 4 (the S) has an alpha channel in the shape of the letter S. It protects the transparency of that layer.

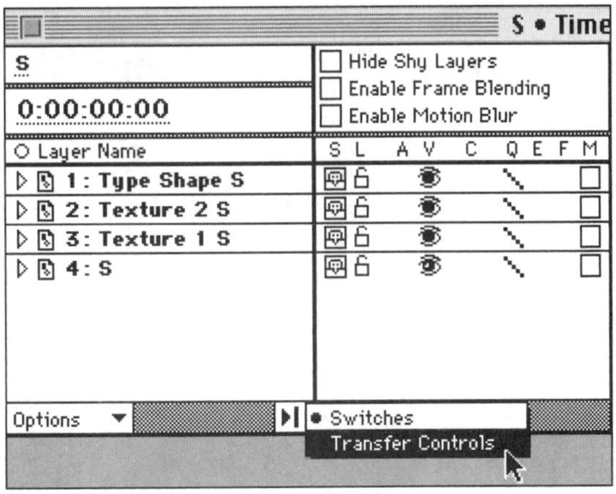

Figure 6-16: Switches to Transfer Controls.

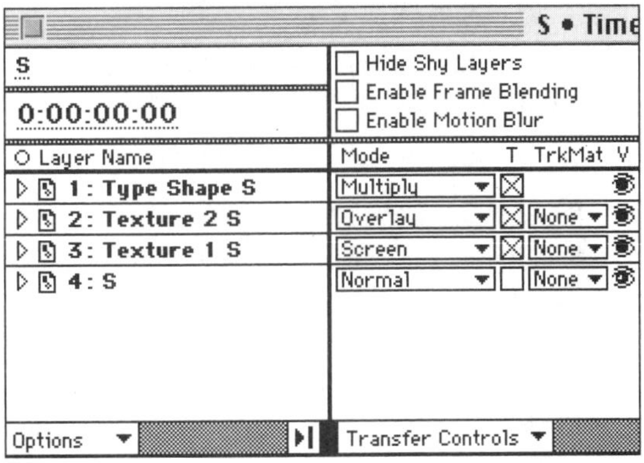

13. Click on the T box next to the Texture 1 S layer (Layer 3) to turn it off. Figure 6-18 shows the result. The layer spreads out over the Comp and no longer honors the transparency on the layer below. Click on the box again to preserve the transparency.

14. Press the Option (Mac) or Alt (Windows) key to close the Words.psd (5) Comp.

Figure 6-17: Transfer Controls.

You are finally ready to start the actual project. After all of this build-up and exploration, the project itself is fairly simple. In this Studio Time, you will set the Comp duration, rename the layers, and set keyframes to move the letters onto the screen and into position.

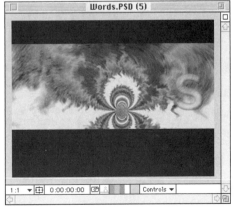

Figure 6-18: Turning off the Preserve Transparency flag.

Studio Time: Building Words

1. Change the Composition duration to 10 seconds (Mac: Cmd-K, Windows: Ctrl-K). While the Composition Settings dialog is open, also check to make sure that the Comp is 320 x 240 pixels and running at 30 frames per second.

2. Highlight each of the Words.psd layers in the Words.psd Comp, and change their names to reflect the letter that they contain. Start by selecting layer 5: Words.psd (1). Press the Return/Enter key and replace the number in parenthesis with a W. Press Return/Enter to exit typing mode.

Figure 6-19: Renamed layers in the Time Layout window.

3. Change the name of Layer 6 (Shadow 1) to Black Text.

4. Change the name of Layer 7 (Shadow 2) to Drop Shadow.

5. Change the name of Layer 8 (WhiteBG) to Background. Figure 6-19 shows the renamed layers in the Time Layout window.

6. Set the Current Time to 4:00 seconds (Mac: Cmd-G, Windows: Ctrl-G, and type 400, or just move the Playback Head until the Current Time reads 0:00:04:00). This is the time where all of the letters appear in the correct positions. Therefore, this is the place to begin to set their keyframes.

7. Select all of the layers (Mac: Cmd-A, Windows: Ctrl-A). Shift-click on the Background layer to deselect it. Press P, Shift-A, and Shift-R to show the Position, Anchor Point, and Rotation properties for the still-selected layers.

8. Click the Position and Rotation properties stop watch of the letter layers to make them keyframeable.

9. Click the Position stop watch for the Black Text and Drop Shadow layers to make that property keyframeable.

10. Leave all of the Rotation keyframe values at 0.

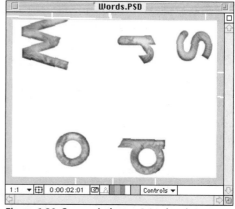

Figure 6-20: Comp window at 2:01 showing rotating text.

11. Set the values for the Position property as follows:

- Words.psd (S):Position= 282x, 122y

- Words.psd (D):Position= 223x, 122y

- Words.psd (R):Position= 163x, 104y

- Words.psd (O):Position= 122x, 119y

- Words.psd (W):Position= 55x, 127y

- Black Text:Position= 157.5x, 101y

- Drop Shadow: Position= 157x, 101y

12. Set the value for all of the Anchor Points in the letter layers to the same value as the Position property for that layer. (For instance, Words.psd (S) has a position value of 282x, 122y. Give it an Anchor value of 282x, 122y.) The Anchor Point value is a constant.

13. Set the Current Time to 00 (Mac: Cmd-G, Windows: Ctrl-G, then type 0).

14. You need to set the starting positions and rotation for the letters, and the starting position for the Black Text and Drop Shadow. Follow the chart below.

- Words.psd (S): Position= 263x, -41y Rotation=180°

- Words.psd (D):Position= 223x, 302y Rotation=-180°

- Words.psd (R): Position= 237x, -37y Rotation=180°

- Words.psd (O): Position= 85x, 276y Rotation=-180°

- Words.psd (W): Position= -5x, -63y Rotation=180°

- Black Text: Position=157.5x, 101y

- Drop Shadow: Position=160x, 105y

15. The starting positions place all the text off-screen. However, you need to set keyframes for opacity for the Black Text and Drop Shadow layers. It is obvious that the these layers cannot be seen at the start of the movie. Highlight the Black Text layer and press Shift-T to show the Opacity property. Click in the stop watch to make it keyframeable and give the layer an initial Opacity value of 0.

16. Set an initial Opacity keyframe for the Drop Shadow layer to 0; the same way that you did for the Black Text layer.

17. Go to Time=4 seconds.

18. Set sustaining keyframes (0% Opacity) for the Opacity property of the Black Text and the Drop Shadow.

19. Set the Current Time to 5:00 seconds (Mac: Cmd-G, Windows: Ctrl-G, and type 500, or just move the Playback Head until the Current Time reads 0:00:05:00).

20. Now that the letters are in place, the Black Text and the Drop Shadow can become visible. Set an Opacity keyframe of 100% for the Black Text layer, and an Opacity keyframe of 65% for the Drop Shadow layer. The Black Text layer gives added definition to the text.

21. Set a Position keyframe for the Drop Shadow text of 160, 105. This brings it back to its original position in the Photoshop file. After the text moves into place, the Drop Shadow layer fades in and slowly moves into the offset position typical of a shadow. Figure 6-20 shows the Comp window at Time=2:01. At this point, you can see the text rotating into position.

22. Set all of the Quality switches to High and preview the movie.

Shortcuts		
Command	**Mac**	**Windows**
Open the Comp Setting dialog	Cmd-K	Ctrl-K

The final Studio Time for this chapter shows you how to scroll or move the textures through the letterforms. When you view the finished movie, it is obvious that the textures continue to move after the letterforms stop. In reality, the textures are moving through the letterforms during the entire animation.

If you think for a moment about how the moving textures are done, you should realize that the only way to move the textures *inside* of each letter is to animate the layers that hold the two textures for each layer—i.e. the center two layers of the four-layer "sandwich" that constitutes each completed letter. Furthermore, it should be clear that you cannot place animation keyframes in the Words.psd Comp (the Comp that you used to set keyframes to bring the text into position). Keyframes in the Words.psd Comp affect the *entire* letterform rather than just a part of the make-up of the letter. Therefore, you need to drop back one level and animate the textures that are in separate layers inside of each letter's own Comp (the Words.psd (W) Comp, etc.).

This Studio Time shows you how to get "inside" of a nested Comp directly from within your main Comp, and how to set a Work Area and render only that portion of the movie.

 Studio Time: Finishing Up

1. Press the modifier key (Mac: Control, Windows: Alt) and double-click on the Words.psd (W) layer in the Words.psd Comp's Time Layout window. This opens both the Comp window and the Time Layout window for the letter W.

2. Set the Current Time to 00 (Mac: Cmd-G, Windows: Ctrl-G, then type 0). Remember, you are working in the nested Comp, so it is the *Current Time for the letter W* that needs to be set to 0.

3. Click on the second layer to highlight it (Texture 2 W). Press the Shift key and highlight the layer beneath that, as well, to select it (Texture 1 W). Press P to display the Position property.

4. Click in each Position stop watch to make the property keyframeable and set the initial keyframe. The Time=0 keyframe does not change from the original settings.

5. Go to the layer Out point (press O).

6. Set a Position keyframe for Layer 2 (Texture 2 W) of 48x, 100y.

7. Set a Position keyframe for Layer 3 (Texture 1 W) of 48x, 90.5y.

8. Press the modifier key (Mac: Option, Windows: Alt) and click the close box on the Time Layout window to close both the Time Layout and Comp windows for the letter W.

9. Repeat Steps 1 though 8 to set the texture keyframes for the remaining letters. Use the chart below to obtain the values for Time=10 seconds (Time=0 values are always the values that were present in the Comp when you opened it). You may, of course, select your own values for the moving textures and experiment as much as you want.

- Letter O (Words.psd (O))

- Layer 2 Position at Time=10 seconds: 73x, 116y

- Layer 3 Position at Time=10 seconds: 73x, 101.5y

- Letter R (Words.psd (R))

- Layer 2 Position at Time=10 seconds: 274x, 133y

- Layer 3 Position at Time=10 seconds: 273x, 101.5y

- Letter D (Words.psd (D))

- Layer 2 Position at Time=10 seconds: 250x, 75y

- Layer 3 Position at Time=10 seconds: 250x, 65.5y

- Letter S (Words.psd (S))

- Layer 2 Position at Time=10 seconds: 241x, 136y

- Layer 3 Position at Time=10 seconds: 284x, 126.5y

The letterforms arrive in their final position at 4 seconds, and the drop shadow and black text are in place at 5 seconds. The Comp is 10 seconds long. That leaves 5 seconds in which to watch the textures scroll across the letters. Five seconds is too long for most people to watch moving textures. The Comp can easily be cut to 7 or 8 seconds without losing any major part of the action.

10. Set the Current Time to 8:00 seconds (Mac: Cmd-G, Windows: Ctrl-G, and type 800, or just move the Playback Head until the Current Time reads 0:00:08:00).

Look carefully at Figure 6-21. It shows the top portion of the Time Layout window. The top line controls the view of the time line. By moving one of the half-circle icons at either end of the scale, you can change the increments that mark the time (which you have already learned how to do). The next line down contains the numeric time increments. The triangle icons at each end of that time line are the Work Area indicators. By setting these, you can easily control which portion of the movie is to be rendered. This is a very convenient shortcut when you do not want to either change the Comp settings or shorten the footage.

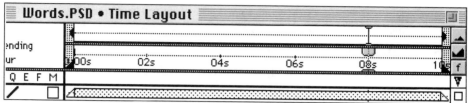

Figure 6-21: Work Area indicators—the black triangles at each end of line 2.

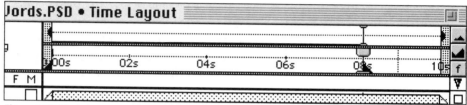

Figure 6-22: Work Area set to 8 seconds.

It results in fewer changes if you render and decide that you don't like it (it is also good for targeting a spot within a Comp for a fast test render).

11. Press the Shift key and drag the right Work Area triangle icon until it snaps to the Current Time marker, as shown in Figure 6-22.

12. Render the movie (Mac: Cmd-M, Windows: Ctrl-M). Click on the underlined Current Settings next to Render Settings in the dialog. This opens the Render Settings Options. Set the Time Span to Work Area as shown in Figure 6-23.

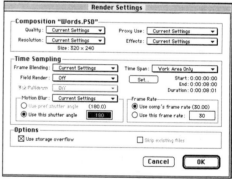

Figure 6-23: Time Span set to render Work Area only.

Shortcuts

Command	Mac	Windows
Open a nested Comp	Ctrl-Double-Click	Alt-Double-Click

This is a final "design note" to tell you a bit more about the logic behind the movement of the textures. If you had selected both Layer 2 and Layer 3 at one time in one of the nested Comps, after the keyframes were set for the moving textures, you would have seen that the two layers did not move though the letterform together. Each layer was moved a slightly different amount. This gives the textures a bit more liveliness and variety. In addition, the textures in all of the Comps did not move in the same direction. If you were setting up a similar project by yourself, you should set the positions for the textures by physically dragging them into the Comp window rather then by setting them by number as we did in this example. A good way to do this would be to select both Layer 2 and 3 and move them together. Then, deselect the bottom layer and move the top one a little more in one direction or another. If you look carefully at the movement of the textures, you will also see that some of them travel in a straight line and some move slightly on the diagonal.

 # Rewind

The key element taught in this chapter is the way in which After Effects handles a layered Photoshop file that contains clipping groups. In addition, you learned how to open nested Comps, set and render a Work Area, and create textures that move across an object protected by the Preserve Transparency flag.

 # Coming Attractions

Chapter 7 continues the saga of working with a variety of input sources. It takes an in-depth look at working with sound and audio input. It will help you add music tracks to your animations and to synchronize the action of the movie to rhythm of the music.

Audio Tools and Resources for After Effects Artists

 Preview

Audio (including music) is an important but often-overlooked component of desktop video production. Yet an effective sound track can mean the difference between the success or failure of a video or multimedia production. Fortunately, desktop audio production tools have come a long way since their inception, and it's possible to produce fully-professional audio for video without an enormous investment in hardware.

In this chapter, we'll:

- Present some basic concepts of sound.

- Give you an overview of audio hardware and how it works.

- Discuss some important desktop digital audio production tools and techniques you can use with After Effects for both broadcast and multimedia production.

- Let you try working with audio directly in After Effects.

 Feature Presentation

Let's start by looking at the big picture. What exactly is audio?

Basic Audio Concepts

Sound is a physical vibration that moves your eardrums; nerves attached to your eardrums send information to your brain. This information is then interpreted as a particular audio event. Sound is mechanical; that is, it requires the movement of a physical medium. Without that physical medium (air, water, or some other substance), there is no sound, which is why there is no sound in space, "Star Wars" notwithstanding. We hear periodic vibrations as pitches; aperiodic or random vibrations as noise. Natural sounds almost always contain some mixture of each type, which gives each sound its unique character.

The faster the rate of a periodic vibration, the higher the pitch sounds to us. Human beings can't hear the entire range of possible vibrations; our range of hearing is from 20 vibrations per second, or 20 Hz (Hertz, the standard unit for sound frequencies), to 20,000 vibrations per second, or 20 kHz (kilohertz). Actually, many people can't hear much above 15 kHz or so. Many computer systems can't reproduce sounds higher than 11 kHz without special hardware, and many consumer speaker systems struggle to reproduce frequencies below 100 Hz or even higher. We'll go into more detail about this later, but you should be aware of these limitations when you design your own audio tracks.

As mentioned, natural sounds consist of some combination of pitch and noise. Even relatively pure pitched sounds, like flutes, contain breath noise and a complex mix of pitched tones. These tones, called harmonics or overtones, are usually not individually audible but combine together to form a sound's distinctive tone color, or timbre.

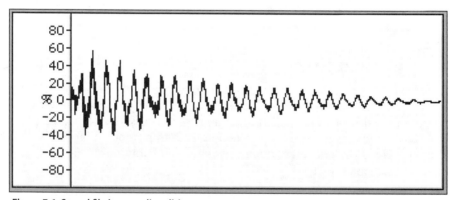

Figure 7-1: Sound file in an audio editing program.

Any sound, no matter how complex, can be represented as a waveform, which is a graph of changes in loudness, or amplitude, over time. Take a look at Figure 7-1, which is a graphic representation of a digital sound file as shown in an audio editing program.

After Effect's audio waveform display looks very much like this. What you see here is a waveform representing the sound of a plucked string. Amplitude is the vertical axis, time is the horizontal. You'll notice that the sound starts out with a fairly sharp onset, or attack, representing the initial plucking of the string, and then fades away, or decays, slowly. Figure 7-2 shows a few beats of a drum kit phrase in stereo.

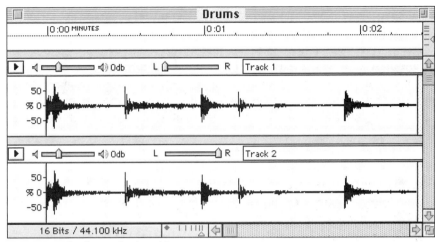

Figure 7-2: A few beats of a drum kit.

You see an individual track for each channel of the stereo signal. Note that you can clearly see the main beats of the music. Here, the attacks are sharper and the decays much faster than the plucked string, as you would expect with drum sounds. It takes a little practice to get used to knowing how these waveforms graphs represent sound, but you'll find that skill invaluable once you start editing digital audio. The ability to identify beats in music is especially useful for music video editors.

Acoustic sound is inherently an analog signal; that is, it changes continuously over time. In order to record and manipulate acoustic sound, it needs to be converted into an electronic signal so that audio equipment can work with it. Turning an acoustic signal into an analog electronic signal is called *transduction*, which means the conversion of one form of energy into another. A device that transduces is called a transducer; microphones and speakers are among the many types of transducers.

A microphone converts acoustic energy into electrical energy, while a speaker (or headphone set) converts electrical energy back into acoustic energy. Both are essential pieces of gear for an audio producer, especially the speakers. A microphone (or mic) works a lot like your ears; a thin diaphragm contained in the mic housing is attached to a wire which is surrounded by a magnetic field. Sound makes the diaphragm move back and forth, and the movement of the wire in the field generates an electronic signal that mimics the movement of the air that produced the sound. If graphed, that signal looks like our sound file from Figure 7-2. This type of microphone is called a dynamic mic, and it's the cheapest and most common type. Dynamic mics are often used in live sound applications because they're relatively sturdy, foolproof, and can withstand very high sound levels.

Another common type is the condenser mic. These are usually much more expensive and more sensitive than dynamic mics, and are a good choice for recording voices or acoustic instruments in a studio setting. In a condenser mic, two thin charged plates, one fixed and one movable, are placed close to each other. The movable plate serves as the diaphragm. As it moves back and forth in relation to the fixed plate, the changing distance between the two generates an electrical signal. Because the plates need to be continuously charged, a condenser mic needs an internal or external power supply to work. Most recording studios will have both dynamic and condenser mics on hand for different uses.

The signal coming from a mic is usually very low amplitude and needs to be preamplified to bring it up to a high enough level to be processed in an analog or digital environment. By contrast, signals coming from most electronic audio equipment are "hot" enough to not require preamplification.

A typical speaker or headphone set works exactly the opposite of a dynamic mic. A varying electrical signal causes the speaker diaphragm to move back and forth, displacing the air in sound waves. Because the electrical signal from a piece of audio gear like a mixer or computer isn't strong enough to push the speaker diaphragm by itself, a power amp is necessary to amplify the signal to the point where it can push the speaker. The more power the amp supplies, the louder the sound (until the speaker blows up, that is).

An analog tape deck like the familiar cassette recorder is another common type of transducer. Here, the electrical signal from a mic preamp, for example, gets converted into magnetic energy that displaces metal particles on a piece of recording tape. This displacement is more or less permanent, so the tape can store the transduced audio signal for playback at a later time by reversing the recording procedure and turning the magnetic patterns back into an electrical signal.

Multitrack tape recorders take this concept a step further and allow you to record tracks separately while listening to previous takes. This way, a single producer can assemble a piece of music by recording each part individually and mixing them in a final *mixdown* to produce the finished master recording. In fact, this is a very common technique in all phases of modern music and audio production.

Mixing down the individual tape tracks to a stereo master requires running the tracks through a *mixer*, as you might guess. A mixer basically consists of multiple individual inputs, each with its own volume, stereo placement, and effects controls, all running into a final (usually) stereo output. The mixer is usually the centerpiece of a recording studio, since it's used to route and control every audio source in the studio. The mixer's stereo output is typically split into two pairs, one feeding a power amp and pair of speakers or headphones, the other connected to a two-track mastering deck, DAT tape recorder, video deck, or CD-A (audio CD) burner.

Most professional mixers have some sort of *equalization* controls for each input. Equalization, or EQ, is the emphasis or suppression of selected frequencies in a sound. The familiar bass and treble controls on your stereo are the most basic form of EQ. Turning down the treble engages an electronic filter that reduces high frequencies while leaving lower frequencies alone. The bass control reduces or increases lower frequencies while letting higher ones pass. More sophisticated EQs, like those found on quality audio mixers, let you control middle frequencies or several different bands, or let you adjust the high and low-pass filters' cutoff frequencies. The purpose of EQ is to let you change the tonal colors of the sound's quality so that the tracks blend better in a mix. EQ also is used to compensate for shrill or muffled recordings, and for special effects.

As you can imagine, these various conversions and transductions of the original sound are not perfect. Every time the sound energy gets translated into another form, or gets patched through another piece of audio gear, some change happens to the original sound–elements of the sound are lost, and new elements are introduced. A multi-million dollar audio industry has dedicated itself to trying to minimize that change, and now analog audio gear is so good that at the highest levels of the industry, the changes are inaudible to all but trained ears.

The audio industry has largely moved to digital audio formats in the last ten years, and that move has opened up audio production to the use of the computer and software-based production tools, which in turn has lead to the desktop audio revolution. It's now possible for musicians (and video producers) to produce fully professional audio in home studios for a fraction of what it used to cost in recording studios, and without the need for specialized, and expensive, technicians. That's not to say that analog audio is dead–we still need to deal with acoustic sound, so mics and speakers will be with us for a while yet. However, digital tools and techniques are definitely taking over the audio world, and desktop producers are members of the digital vanguard.

Digital Audio Concepts

Like all digital information created and processed with a computer, digital audio consists of bits of data–ones and zeros. An analog or acoustic sound first needs to be *digitized*, or converted to digital data, before it can be worked on in the computer. The hardware that does this is called an *analog to digital converter*, or *A-to-D*. Many multimedia computers now have a built-in A-to-D, which lets you record via a microphone directly onto the computer's hard drive, or allows the computer to recognize your spoken commands.

Unlike analog sound, which varies continuously, digital sound always consists of discrete steps. The fineness of these steps, and consequently the accuracy of the reproduction of your sound, is determined by the *sample rate* and *bit-depth* used during the digitizing process. The higher the sample rate, the higher the frequencies you can record, and the higher the degree of the sound's natural brightness and "air" you'll be able to retain. The higher the bit-depth, the more detail and dynamic properties in the sound that will be preserved. CD-quality stereo audio is sampled at 16 bits, 44.1 kHz, in two interleaved tracks, which, incidentally, represents a data rate of about 150 KB per second. Multimedia audio is often 8 bit, 22.05 kHz, mono or stereo. Sometimes you'll come across lower sample rates, like 11 or even 8 kHz on the Web, but rarely lower than 8-bit resolution.

Tip:
For broadcast video production, you'll almost always use a 44.1 kHz sample rate, and 16 bits bit-depth.

What does this all mean? Something called the Nyquist Theorem states that a digital signal can't reproduce any frequencies higher than one half its sample rate. Stated another way, audio sampled at 44.1 kHz can't contain overtones higher than 22 kHz (half of 44.1). Audio sampled at 22 kHz can't contain overtones higher than 11 kHz (half of 22). You'll recall that the upper limit of human hearing is about 20 kHz, so that it seems that you would always want to sample at 44.1 or higher for the most realistic sound. In fact, projects where audio is critical should be produced at 16 bits, 44.1 kHz.

However, there is relatively little meaningful sound info in speech information above 10 kHz, so, with careful management, you can still have perfectly usable sound for most multimedia projects recorded at 22 kHz, with half the data rates and disk space required for 44.1 music audio. With the right software tools, you can even get acceptable 11 kHz audio–perfect for tight-bandwidth Web delivery.

Equally important in determining the quality of your final sound is its bit-depth. A sound sampled at 16 bits of resolution has 32,768 different amplitude levels with which to accurately reproduce a sound. An 8-bit sound, by contrast, has only 256 different amplitude levels. As you can see, 8-bit is going to be much coarser and less able to capture the details of a sound. Of course, 16-bit sound takes up twice as much space as 8-bit, and many multimedia machines can only reproduce 8-bit sound anyway, so for multimedia production sometimes you have no choice. Luckily, there are some good software tools for making decent 8-bit audio, and this seems like a good time to introduce the best.

Software Tools for Multimedia Audio

Software-based digital audio tools have come a long way in the last ten years. Fully professional applications with a wide range of plug-ins allow the desktop producer to record in a full multitrack environment with completely non-linear access, synthesize unique sounds, design sound effects, and edit music, voice, and video tracks all on the desktop. These tools divide into four broad categories: digital audio editors, multitrack recorders, MIDI sequencers with digital audio capabilities, and audio-for-video tools.

Digital Audio Editing Tools

Every multimedia producer at some point has to edit a digital audio track–to cut a breath out of a narration or substitute one word for another, to make a music bed twice as long, or to create a seamless loop for a multimedia wait state. Fortunately there are some good tools available on different platforms to do all these things. Computer-based graphic editing makes it easy to locate the offending breath, for example, by playing the track, stopping playback when you hear it, selecting it with the cursor, and deleting it with a key stroke or replacing it with a sound you've copied and pasted from another file. These tools are also useful for translating audio between the many formats you're likely to encounter for use in broadcast, CD-ROM, and the Web, since they can all read and write a wide variety of formats.

Waves' WaveConvert for Mac and PC (Figure 7-3) is an essential tool for multimedia audio producers. It lets you batch process audio conversions, has superior sample-rate and bit-depth conversion algorithms, makes cross-platform compatible files, and is pretty cheap besides. One function that is especially beneficial for After Effects users is that it lets you optimize QuickTime movie soundtracks in place. This means that WaveConvert will let you dither down just the audio portion of a QuickTime movie

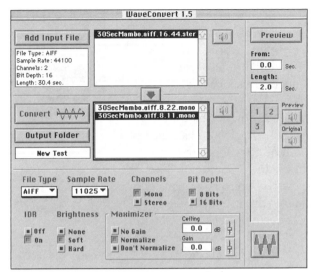

Figure 7-3: Waves' WaveConvert for Mac and PC.

and save it back into the movie without recompressing the video track. In fact, this is the best method for producing low-res multimedia files directly from After Effects–use After Effects to scale and compress the movie but leave the audio at CD quality (44.1 kHz/16 bit/stereo), then dither the audio in WaveConvert. WaveConvert can even make decent-sounding files at very low sample rates for Web delivery, better than any other software tool at this time. It's highly recommended.

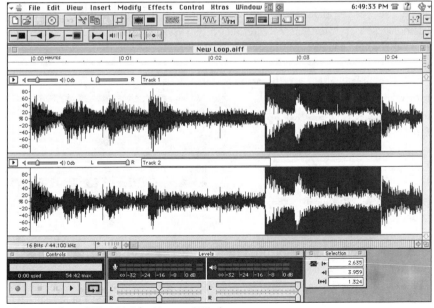

Figure 7-4: SoundEdit 16 2.0 for Macs and Windows.

Macromedia's SoundEdit was one of the first software-only audio editors available on any desktop platform. It was initially developed for the Mac and used the Mac's barely-adequate audio hardware for output. It always had decent audio editing tools, though, and has since matured into a powerful application equally at home editing QuickTime audio, CD-quality tracks, and low-res multimedia audio. The current version, SoundEdit 16 2.0 (Figure 7-4), is available for

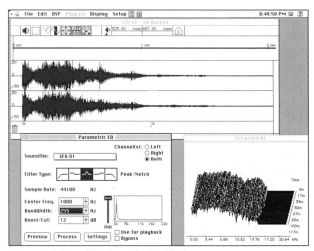

Figure 7-5: Sound Designer, by Digidesign.

Macs and Windows. With it, you can record and edit multiple tracks, edit QuickTime audio tracks, apply a variety of special effects to the audio, and output a wide range of files types and formats. You can also easily create loops for multimedia background tracks, and SoundEdit lets you save 44/16 audio in the new high-quality IMA compression format, whose 4:1 compression gives you CD-quality audio in the space of 8/22 audio. You can also use SoundEdit to produce highly-compressed ShockWave audio files for the Web in either streaming or downloadable formats.

Sound Designer, by Digidesign (Figure 7-5), was primarily responsible for the Mac's ascendance as the platform of choice for professional digital audio production. The original Sound Designer, intended for interfacing with sampling keyboards, also proved valuable for editing digital master recordings for CD.

More powerful auxiliary hardware allowed more record and playback tracks, and third-party developers began to produce plug-ins for the Sound Designer environment, such as Waves' S1/L1/Q10/C1 series of professional signal-processing tools (Figure 7-6).

Sound Designer features extremely precise and flexible editing tools, with markers, memory locations, and multiple loop support. Digidesign later

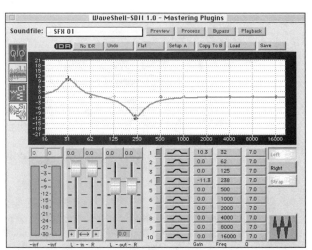

Figure 7-6: Waves' S1/L1/Q10/C1 professional signal-processing tools

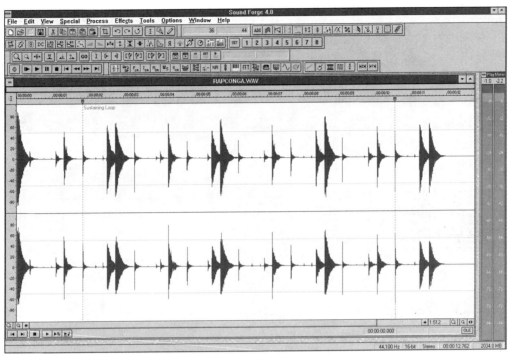

Figure 7-7: Sonic Foundry's SoundForge, the best choice for desktop audio.

introduced the highly successful ProTools hard-disk based multitrack recording and editing environment, which is in use in many recording and audio-for-video studios. Another new but powerful Mac editing application is BIAS Peak, which runs in native mode on a PowerMac and so is particularly fast for editing sound.

On the Windows NT side, Sonic Foundry's SoundForge is the best choice for desktop audio production (Figure 7-7). It has many of the same editing features as SoundEdit, such as graphic selection, cut, copy, and paste, normalizing, equalization, and a wide range of special effects like excellent quality reverb, delays, flanging, and so on. It also accepts third-party plug-ins from Waves and others. SoundForge works with a wide variety of sound cards, including the standard Sound Blaster-compatibles as well as higher-end products like Turtle Beach's Tahiti and Digital Audio Lab's CardD systems. It also produces RealAudio output for streaming Web delivery and supports Microsoft's ActiveX format plug-ins.

Multitrack Recording Software

One real breakthrough in desktop audio production has been the introduction of computer-based multitrack recording systems. These allow for full random access to all audio tracks and much more flexible editing than tape-based systems can provide. The first versions of these systems were from Digidesign and eventually developed into their industry-standard ProTools product line. ProTools and other related systems formerly required specialized and

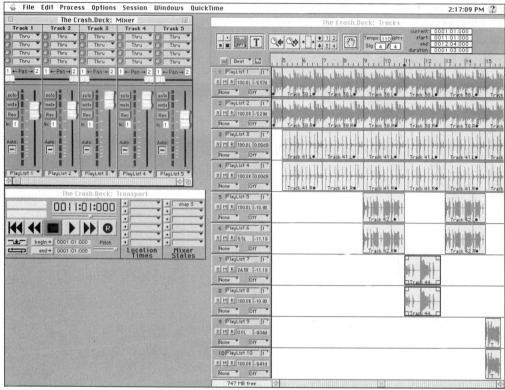

Figure 7-8: Macromedia Deck II, version 2.5 for the Macintosh.

relatively-expensive computer audio hardware installed in your system; without this hardware (essentially audio accelerator cards) the software was useless. With the hardware (and fast hard drives–a minute of 44/16 stereo audio requires 10 MB of disk space), you're guaranteed glitch-free playback with real-time signal processing and special effects, as well as top-quality analog and digital audio conversion and I/O.

Recently, though, desktop computers and hard drive systems have gotten fast enough to allow multitrack recording and playback without the need for additional hardware. Such systems currently exist for the Mac, which has its own built-in 44/16 audio system. PCs still require at least a basic audio card, so some additional expenditure is necessary for these systems. The amazing thing is that most of this new crop of multitrack software is quite cheap–between $200 and $500, as compared to $1500 to $8000 or more for hardware-based systems.

One of the first software multitrackers was Macromedia Deck II, currently at version 2.5 for the Macintosh (Figure 7-8) and soon to be available for Windows. On the fastest Power Mac with an accelerated hard drive, Deck can play back 32 tracks of 44/16 digital audio with real-time mixing. Deck has sophisticated built-in real-time EQ and special effects, and can accept third-party Adobe Premiere-compatible audio plug-ins. These,

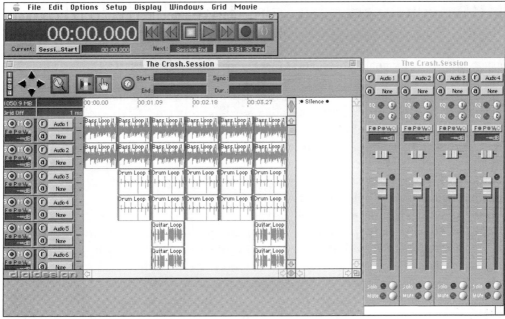

Figure 7-9: Digidesign's Session Software.

however, need to be applied to a track and rendered–they can't be used for real-time playback.

Deck's only real drawback is that the Mac's audio outputs, except on the most recent machines, are fairly low fidelity stereo mini plugs, rather than the more professional style RCA or XLR balanced audio connectors. The most recent PCI Power Macs at least have RCA I/O, but lack any kind of digital audio output, so even if your audio sources are entirely digital, you have to output in an analog format for your final recording, thereby losing a little quality. Fortunately, some inexpensive add-on cards are on the way from Apple and other manufacturers that allow for digital audio I/O using the Mac's native audio processing.

Note that in the pro audio industry this I/O is considered the critical component, like a drum scanner is considered critical in the digital imaging arena.

Another powerful software multitrack recorder is Digidesign's Session Software, which provides 16 tracks of playback with real-time mixing and EQ on Power Macs with no extra hardware (Figure 7-9). It's available for Windows too, but requires a sound card; when used in conjunction with Digidesign's Audiomedia III PCI audio card, eight tracks of real-time audio with digital audio I/O is possible.

Innovative Quality Software's SAW Plus is a popular Windows-only multitrack application that works with most standard Windows audio cards and provides more playback tracks than any other Windows multitrack program. SEK'D's Samplitude Studio, also exclusively for Windows, can give you up to 16 monophonic audio tracks on a Pentium-level PC with a fast hard drive and standard audio card.

MIDI Sequencers with Digital Audio

The development of MIDI (Musical Instrument Digital Interface) changed the music business forever and was the main reason computers infiltrated recording studios in the first place. MIDI was originally intended as a standard control language to allow synthesizers from different manufacturers to interface with and control each other. Because MIDI is a digital protocol, it soon became evident that personal computers could be used to control synthesizers, and the first MIDI sequencing programs appeared.

The great advantage of MIDI over live recording is that MIDI is a control language–it contains only instructions on how to play sounds, not the sounds themselves. The sounds themselves were created externally on synthesizers in real time as early as 1986. This makes MIDI a much more compact way to record music than recording audio tracks. Because it's purely digital data, MIDI can be manipulated in the computer just like text or graphics–cutting, pasting, duplicating, inverting, and so on. A MIDI sequencer is a kind of word processor for music, allowing a single performer to record unlimited virtual tracks and create perfect takes with simple editing techniques, or even construct complete performances note-by-note.

Of course, since MIDI doesn't make any sound on its own, you need synthesizers to perform the MIDI recorded music. There are literally hundreds of different synths available, in all price ranges. The number of sounds and voices available in a synth, and its overall sound quality, will determine the final quality of the MIDI score being played by the sequencer. It is not uncommon to see a small project studio with a dozen or more synths and special effects boxes, all MIDI controllable. With MIDI, it is possible for an individual to create a convincing music score with synthesizers only; in fact, many multimedia soundtracks are composed just this way, with the final output being a digital audio file.

On the PC platform, MIDI is also used in soundtracks, especially for games with sound designed to be played by the onboard synth in a standard PC audio card. As mentioned, MIDI's compact file size frees up disk space for graphics, and MIDI can also be programmed to higher levels of interactivity than digital audio can at this point. Some disadvantages of the on-board MIDI approach are that the composer is at the mercy of the MIDI sounds in whatever sound board the user has (and they vary widely in quality), and that MIDI cannot reproduce human voices or actual acoustic instruments well without a lot of expensive sample playback gear. MIDI will always be used to compose, but as multimedia computers get more powerful, you should expect to see MIDI soundtracks begin to disappear in favor of digital audio soundtracks.

There are many MIDI sequencing programs available, but of particular interest to those producing multimedia audio are sequencers that combine digital audio recording and playback capabilities with the standard MIDI features. Opcode's StudioVision for Mac and Windows is one of the more capable (Figure 7-10). StudioVision lets you view MIDI data tracks as text for easy editing, in a piano-roll format, and as music notation. It features unlimited tracks, rules-based editing (being able to make selections and perform operations based on criteria you set), and integration with Galaxy, Opcode's universal synth sound management program.

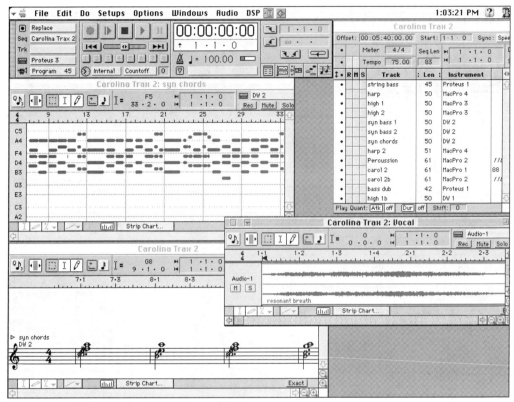

Figure 7-10: Opcode's StudioVision for Mac and Windows.

Beyond that, with a Power Mac by itself or with the addition of an approved sound card on other CPUs, StudioVision can record, playback, and edit up to 16 tracks of digital audio, depending on the capabilities of your hardware. This makes it easy to sync audio tracks, like voice-overs or live instrumental tracks, with your MIDI tracks. StudioVision also features some remarkable DSP (digital signal processing) functions, such as the ability to turn digital audio into the equivalent of MIDI data (which lets you edit it with all the standard MIDI editing tools like quantization) and back again.

Some other capable MIDI sequencers with digital audio capabilities for Mac and PC: Mark of the Unicorn's Digital Performer, Steinberg's Cubase Audio, Voyetra's Digital Orchestrator Plus, Cakewalk's Cakewalk Pro Audio, and Emagic's Logic Audio.

Audio for Video Applications

Many standard desktop video editing applications have excellent audio editing capabilities, and should not be overlooked by desktop video producers. An outstanding example is Adobe Premiere (Figure 7-11), shown here in audio editing mode.

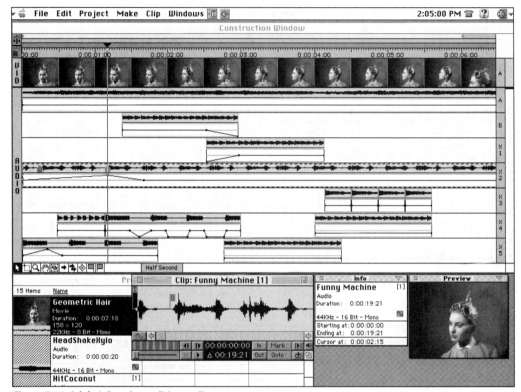

Figure 7-11: Adobe's Premiere, editing audio.

Premiere is available for both Macintosh and Windows NT. You can use Premiere to record audio directly into your computer from an external mic, tape, or CD, and save it as an audio-only QuickTime movie or in the standard AIFF audio file format. Once you've captured or imported your audio files, you can layer up to 99 tracks of mono or stereo audio, mix their levels with flexible graphic "rubber-band" controls, apply a variety of effects to any file and set keyframes to have the effect automatically change over time, and output the whole thing in a variety of sample rates and file formats.

Premiere features some decent sample rate conversion algorithms, so you can use it to optimize audio for low-res QuickTime playback. Adobe has developed an open plug-in standard for Premiere, and some interesting third-party plug-ins have appeared, including CyberSound FX from Invision and versions of Waves' Sound Designer plug-ins. One highly recommended Waves plug-in is AudioTrack 1.0 (Figure 7-12). This plug-in features the professional-level graphics EQ, compression, and noise gate algorithms found in Waves' much more expensive ProTools plug-ins, all in one reasonably-priced program. AudioTrack is invaluable for removing hiss and rumble from raw video tracks, as well as emphasizing voice-overs and punching up music beds.

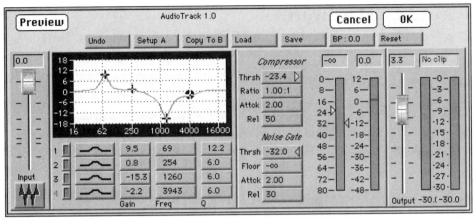

Figure 7-12: Waves' AudioTrack 1.0 plug-in for Digidesign's Sound Designer.

It would be nice if After Effects supported Premiere's plug-in architecture, wouldn't it? That way, we could have access to high-quality audio processing tools running in After Effects. Maybe in the next major revision.

All the same, the file formats that are supported make for flexible production. This is especially true as most audio professionals have very sophisticated tools to handle this for you. Additionally a tremendous quantity of Mac and PC tools exist, so you can do this yourself. When selecting software to import into After Effects, make sure you can read and export the following formats:

- Audio Interchange File Format (AIFF). After Effects uses QuickTime to convert this file type to QuickTime format before importing, or it can import AIFF directly if QuickTime 2.0 is installed.

- System 7 sound file (SFIL) format. This can also be converted to a QuickTime format.

- QuickTime (including both MACE and AU files).

Recording Audio for Video and Multimedia

Most producers coming to digital audio via the computer don't have the traditional analog recording studio background you find in many audio engineers. In fact, in many projects (particularly those where time hasn't been well budgeted) a graphics producer suddenly gets an order from on high to "throw some sound effects and music in there, and don't forget the voice-over." Needless to say, this is a recipe for instant stress. In an effort to relieve this stress, here's a highly condensed primer on recording audio in the computer environment– especially when using a computer's built-in audio. We'll use the Mac as our example platform, but most of what we relate here will translate to the PC.

Recording Hardware

First, there are some basic hardware issues to address. One–you need a good-quality audio monitoring system, so you can hear what you're editing. At the least, this should include a compact mixer and a pair of powered speakers. A number of companies including Apple, Yamaha, and Acoustic Research make stereo powered speakers designed for computer use. These speakers are magnetically shielded, so you can place them near your computer monitor without distorting its image. They also have the right connectors to plug directly into your CPU. The amplifiers in these speakers tend to be a little weak, however, so that increased distortion at higher listening levels becomes a problem.

A better solution is separate studio-quality near-field monitors (designed for close listening at relatively low volume levels) and a power amp to drive them. Yamaha NS-10s are a common studio standard; Tannoy and JBL near-fields are also popular. Any studio-grade power amp of at least 100 watts RMS per channel is a good match for these. Professional-quality speakers like these are important for detailed sound editing and music production, but you should have a pair of multimedia speakers on hand as well to test your mixes, since this is what many multimedia users will be using. For the same reason, you should listen to your mixes through the computer's built-in speaker as well. (Music industry professionals typically mix on expensive professional studio monitors, but most test and adjust their mixes on boom boxes and car stereos before final release, based on where they feel the music is most likely to be heard, and on the equipment that is likely to be used.)

At least as important as good monitor speakers is a clean, high-quality compact mixer to pre-amplify, mix, and route your audio signals. Many audio producers overlook this crucial piece of gear, even though a good one can be had for $300 or so. One of the best for multimedia is Mackie's 1202 VLZ. It features 12 input channels, an extremely clean sound, can amplify microphone signals and supply power for those mics that need it, and, perhaps most importantly, has multiple busses for routing audio to different locations. At the higher end, but still under $2000, is Yamaha's Pro-Mix 01 digital mixer. This is a 16-channel MIDI-controllable mixer with moving faders and an all-digital internal signal path. It has two built-in digital effects processors, eight mic preamps, internal memory to record mixer states, and is an excellent choice for those wanting to create a totally-automated studio.

A mixer bus is simply a discrete signal path. A multiple bus mixer lets you switch an input or group of inputs to any output or combination of outputs while controlling the levels of those outputs independently. This is important because any audio you process usually has to go to at least two different places–the monitor speakers and the record input. The record input itself might be the computer's audio input, a cassette or DAT deck, a video deck, or any combination of these. Without a multiple bus mixer, you'll constantly have to repatch input and output cables or use clumsy splitters to route your audio, and you still won't have independent level control.

Another advantage to running all your audio through a mixer is that the mixer will give you much finer input level control than is usually available in the computer itself. The Mac, for instance, has only seven different audio input levels in its built-in hardware. Seven levels is just too coarse a resolution to properly set input levels. Why is this important? Because when you record, you usually want to get the hottest possible signal on disk below distortion, and sometimes you need to set the input in between the Mac's allowable levels to get the best recording. (More on this follows.) An analog mixer, with its continuously variable controls, lets you tweak the inputs to your heart's content for the best results.

Another essential piece of gear is at least one good microphone for recording acoustic sources. Unfortunately, there is no single mic available that is ideal for every purpose, and there are hundreds of different models to choose from, but we can narrow down the choices a little. Probably the most common type of acoustic recording for multimedia is voice-over or narration reading, most often of a single voice. For this, you'll want a professional large-diaphragm condenser mic, such as the classic Neumann condensers. These mics aren't cheap (in fact, they range up to several thousand dollars, although a decent one can be had for well under $1000), but if you're doing a lot of voice recording, it's an investment that will really pay off in the much higher audio quality these mics provide. They're also excellent for recording sound effects and acoustic instruments, although their large size and extreme shock sensitivity make them less suitable for field recording and amplified instruments.

Be aware that any microphone you use will need to be preamplified before you can record from it into the computer. The signal from a microphone is actually very low–too low to be directly registered by most recording devices, in fact. Most recording devices, be they CPU, video deck, or tape machine, expect a line-level source that is of a certain minimum voltage level. (There are actually two standards for line-level signals, professional and consumer, but we won't get into that now.) The direct mic output is much less than line-level, so it needs to be preamplified before the recorder can sense it. The Mackie mixer mentioned above has nice clean sound and built-in mic preamps, which is another reason why it's a good choice for multimedia production.

If you do find yourself recording a lot of voiceovers in house, another important consideration is acoustic isolation. Obviously, you don't want a lot of traffic noise in the background of your narration track, but even a quiet space has a certain amount of ambient noise, and that goes double for computer rooms. Hard drives and their cooling fans tend to make a lot of noise, some monitors emit high-pitched frequencies, and even keyboard clicking and disk insertions can ruin a good take. So, whenever possible, you'll want to isolate the voice artist in a quiet room with as little ambient sound as possible, and ideally with some added acoustic isolation. This can be as simple as closet with a door (although your voice talent may not be too thrilled about that), or as elaborate as an installed isolation booth with its own lighting and ventilation.

Contrary to popular belief, acoustic isolation is not simply a matter of slapping some egg cartons up on a storage room's walls. Egg cartons and their more sophisticated counterparts, acoustic foam panels like Sonex, do very little to block external noise. Their only function is to reduce high-frequency reflections from interior walls, which cuts down on the reverberation in a room and gives it a "deader" sound. This gives the recording engineer more flexibility to control the reverberation ambience of the final mix. To truly cut down on external sound leakage, your space needs to be as airtight as possible and have walls as massive as possible. The more mass in the walls, the greater the sound blockage. So if you're thinking of turning a spare storage room into an isolation booth, an airtight door and an extra layer of inside wallboard will be a much better investment than covering the walls with foam (although you'll probably want to do that too, if you can). Professionals use a room within a room concept, but the cost can be prohibitive.

An alternative to a built-in isolation booth is a portable isolation booth, essentially a closet on wheels. The more elaborate portable booths have their own lighting and ventilation, with easy access for cabling in and out. They can be a good solution to modify an existing space or when building a new one isn't possible.

In any case, if your isolation area ends up being down the hall or even on another floor, you'll need to have a way for the voice artist to hear herself and any instructions from you. Again, a Mackie-type compact mixer is a good solution. Plug the mic into the mixer, run a line from it to your location and another one back into a second input, and plug headphones into the mixer's headphone monitor output. The talent will be able to control her own headphone level and hear what's going on at the recording station as well; and you won't have to run long mic-level signals from the isolation area to the recording area, thus reducing the risk of signal loss and extra line noise.

A final important hardware consideration is good cabling. Avoid cheap, thin cabling—heavier cabling means heavier shielding, which cuts down on possible noise interference. By the same token, look for heavy-duty metal connectors, with one important exception. The input connection on most Macs is a stereo mini jack which is recessed on the back panel behind a plastic housing. Only thin-profile mini plugs will snap fully into the mini plug jack; if you seem to only get one input channel, check this connection. Happily, the newest higher-end Macs have more professional RCA jacks for audio I/O.

Recording

With the right equipment in place, you're ready to rock and roll. If at all possible, it's usually better to first record acoustic audio on a high-quality tape system, such as DAT or a multitrack digital audio machine like Tascam's DA-88, instead of recording directly to hard disk. There are several reasons for this. One is that tape is much cheaper than drive space, and you can record essentially unlimited versions or takes by switching tapes. If you take notes as you record, and you should, you can easily find the good take and just record that one to the drive. Beyond that, a desktop computer-based hard disk recording system is inherently less stable than the average tape environment, and there is unfortunately a much greater chance of losing the perfect take to a hard disk crash or weird system error.

The most important reason for recording to tape first is that it provides much more control over your input levels than does recording directly to hard disk.

If you try to push the digital recording environment past its highest levels, the signal gets clipped out, resulting in horrendous digital distortion. Refer to Figures 7-13 and 7-14.

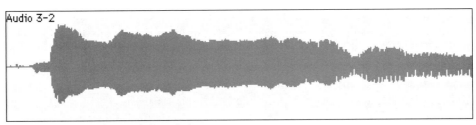

Figure 7-13: A correctly recorded vocal phrase.

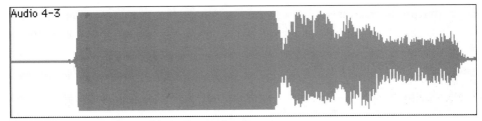

Figure 7-14: The same phrase with the first section clipped.

Note that 7-13's highest peak is near, but not over, 100%.

Figure 7-14 shows the same phrase with the first section clipped. The audio effect of this clipping is a disgusting crackling or crunching sound that completely obliterates the original signal. If any of your tracks look like this, throw them out and start over – they can't be repaired.

It's all too easy in the heat of a live recording to speak, sing, or play louder than you did in rehearsals or even the previous recording, possibly overloading the input and ruining the track. By recording to tape first, once you've isolated the desired take, you can simply play it all the way through before recording and set your levels interactively for the best possible signal, then rewind and record. If you set it too hot, just reset and re-record; it's much less stressful than trying to record live into the computer. Of course, if you record too hot to tape, you may still have to redo it.

However you decide to record, live or from tape, you'll need to set the Mac's hardware input level to 0 or 1 before setting the input level of your recording software. This is because the Mac's audio input is actually a microphone input that has its own rather inadequate preamp. On the Power Mac, the input level in the Sound control panel should be set to 0 (zero); this doesn't actually disable the input, but does bypass the mic preamp and brings the signal straight in at line-level. On AV Macs, setting the Sound input to 1 essentially does the same thing. Since your mixer output is line level, you want the audio input to be as close to line level as possible. Otherwise, it will be much too easy to overload the input and cause that nasty digital distortion. (By the same token, an output level of 1 is also line-level, which is what you want if you're going back out to the mixer.)

Once you've correctly set the hardware input, you can adjust the recording level with the software's input controls, if it has them, or the external hardware mixer. Again, because of the hardware mixer's greater sensitivity, adjusting externally is usually better. In many programs, the software input meters are inaccurate, to say the least; it's a good idea to record some test tracks at different input levels until you find where distortion occurs.

After you've recorded your tracks, inspect them visually to find any clipped areas. A slight amount of clipping may not be audible, so give a test listen to any clipped tracks. If you're satisfied with the results, you might want to normalize any tracks that don't hit 100%. Normalizing searches the audio file and looks for the highest peak, then amplifies the entire file proportionally so that the peak hits 100%. The relative levels between different parts of the track remain the same, so this isn't an audio compression function. Because no peak is over 100%, no distortion occurs, and you've got the hottest possible signal to work with. (You can think of this as applying Photoshop's Equalize filter to sound. The concept is basically the same.) Normalizing is most effective with tracks whose peaks are relatively close to 100%; if you normalize a very low-level track, you run the risk of dramatically increasing the noise level in the track. It's better in that case to re-record the track.

Normalizing is very important for 8-bit output, by the way. 8-bit audio has such a limited dynamic range compared to 16 bit that any low-level 8-bit signal usually gets lost in general background noise; you'll want to crank it up as much as you can get away with.

Finally, be aware that mixing tracks adds the levels of the various tracks together. This may seem painfully obvious, but what isn't so obvious is that many relatively low-level tracks mixed together can add up to a clipped final mix, especially if you have many virtual tracks in your mix that you can't play back live to hear the results. And, most programs can't figure out what's going to happen before you mix down and thus warn you about clipped output. In this case, it's probably best to look through your aggregate tracks and try to identify areas where clipping might occur, then select just those areas and do test mixes of them.

Mixing tracks also adds their combined noise, so getting quiet tracks to begin with is crucial.

Audio in After Effects

Now that we've gotten the recording tools and theory behind us, let's look at After Effects' own audio tools and what you can do with them. First of all, After Effects, strictly speaking, only supports one audio file type: QuickTime movies. Fortunately, QuickTime 2.5, the current version, has some versatile audio conversion tools built in, and After Effects can take advantage of them to import several different types of audio files. In this manner, After Effects is able to seamlessly open AIFF files, the current cross-platform standard, and WAV files, commonly used on Windows platforms. You'll notice that when you import one of these foreign file types, the Open button in the Open dialog changes to a Convert button, indicating that After Effects is converting the file into a QuickTime movie. QuickTime can do this without writing a new copy of the file, so you don't lose any disk space in the conversion process.

Once you've imported an audio file, you can drag it into a composition just like any other layer element and work with it in the time line. Rolling down the twirly arrow for the

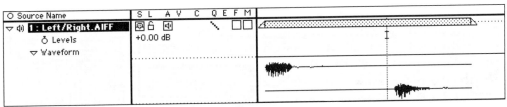

Figure 7-15: Waveform for two channels of a stereo file.

audio layer will let you see the file's waveform; if it's a stereo file, you'll see both channels of the waveform (Figure 7-15).

However, there isn't much else you can do with audio in (as opposed to before bringing it into) After Effects, especially when compared to the program's graphic power. The only keyframeable audio function is audio level, which you adjust in After Effects' audio palette (Figure 7-16).

If you're working with a stereo audio file, you can control each channel level independently by dragging the channel sliders; you can change the stereo levels together by dragging the center slider. Audio levels can vary from between 0 (no audio) to 398% of the original level, although amplifying the audio this much almost always results in the kind of digital distortion we discussed earlier.

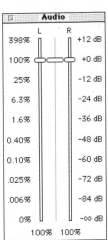

Setting audio keyframes lets you fade audio layers up and down or crossfade between two layers, allowing for a basic form of mixing. Once you've set level keyframes, you can adjust their velocities with the velocity graphs just like any other layer (Figure 7-17). This lets you create logarithmic fades that more naturally mirror the human ear's loudness response. You can also edit layers by setting in and out points for them with the standard layer tools, but After Effects is at best a rudimentary audio editing environment. For serious editing, use one of the professional tools mentioned previously, or premix with your mixer.

Figure 7-16: Audio level controls in the audio palette.

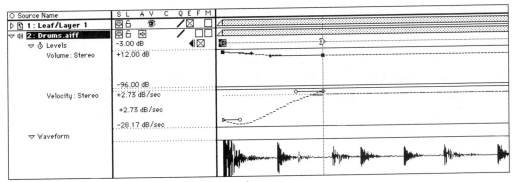

Figure 7-17: Audio level keyframes and Velocity Graphs.

After Effects lets you preview motion with or without audio; choose Composition → Preview → Motion and Audio (Work Area) to hear audio in your motion preview. You can also preview audio by itself by choosing Composition →Preview → Audio (Here Forward). You set the length and quality of this preview in File → Preferences → General; it defaults to 4 seconds, so you will want to increase this value to hear longer clips.

While you're previewing, you can drop audio layer markers on the beat of the music, or anywhere you want, by tapping the asterisk key on the keypad as the music plays. When you stop the preview, you'll see the unnumbered layer markers in the audio layer at the times you tapped. You can tighten up the synchronization by dragging these markers in the layer to line up with peaks in the waveform to, and then snap layers or keyframes to these markers for easy sync.

Audio Motion Math

As we mentioned, After Effects does not do a good job editing or modifying audio, but there is one extremely wonderful thing you can do in After Effects that uses sound in a way that no other commercial application can. We'll close this chapter with an explanation of the technique and offer some tips on how to apply it. In addition, you'll find a sample project and files on the companion CD to help get you started. To use this technique, called Audio Motion Math, you'll need the After Effects Production Bundle.

We won't go into the details of using Motion Math here–that's discussed in the Motion Math section in Chapter 16. However, even without an extensive knowledge of Motion Math, you should be able to create the Audio Motion Math effect if you follow these steps exactly. First, let's explain what we're going to do and how it works.

Example 1—Synching to a Beat

As you may know, Motion Math lets you take the values from one parameter, or property, in a layer and apply it to a property in another layer. For example, you can take the changes in rotation you've applied to one layer and translate those rotation changes to the vertical motion of another layer, so that as the first layer spins to the left, and the second one moves up, without you having to keyframe the second layer. Motion Math also lets you apply mathematical formulas to the translation process, so that you can have the second layer move down instead of up as the first layer spins, or scale the movement of the second layer in relation to the first.

In After Effects, the level of an audio layer is a property; in fact it's about the only property audio layers have. So, we can use Motion Math to figure out the level of the audio layer for each frame and apply it to a property in a second layer, thus having the second property change in time with the music. Instant audio sync without keyframing! Once you learn how to do this, you should be able to think of many uses for effects synched to audio. All right, let's get down to specifics.

Studio Time: Setting up for Audio Motion Math

1. Launch After Effects and open the project titled AECH07a.aep. It contains a composition and two files—Drum/Leaf Twirl, Drums.aif, and Leaf.psd.

2. Open the Drum/Leaf Twirl comp; you'll see that Leaf.psd layer and the Drums.aif layer.

3. Select the Leaf.psd layer and choose Layer → Open Effects Controls. Note that the leaf has a twirl effect applied to it.

4. With the Leaf.psd layer still selected, choose Layer → Keyframe Assistant → Motion Math to open the Motion Math dialog (Figure 7-18).

You are now set up to apply the Motion Math script. Notice that the dialog is laid out in a logical progression to help you apply the audio to the property of your choice.

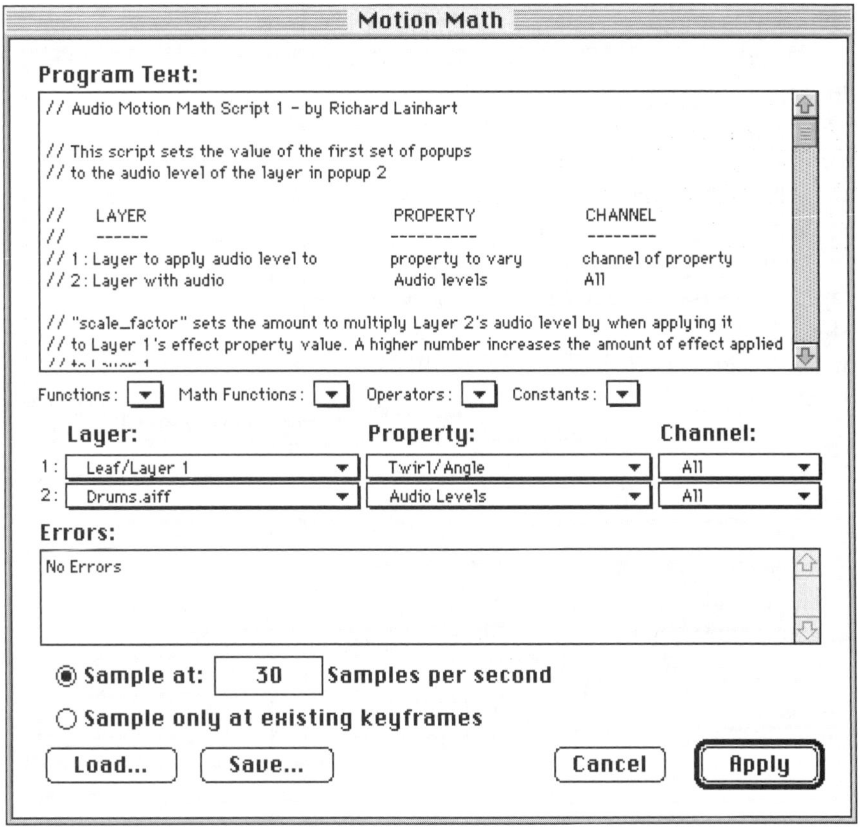

Figure 7-18: The Motion Math dialog.

Studio Time: Setting the Parameters

1. First, click the Load button and load the script titled "Audio Motion Math Script 1."

2. Click on the Layer pop-ups and make sure that Leaf.psd is Layer 1 and Drums.aif is Layer 2.

3. Set Layer 1's Property to Twirl/Angle and Layer 2's property to Audio Levels.

4. Set both Channel pop-ups to All. This script will, when executed, automatically copy the values from the audio layer's level at each frame and paste them into the Twirl Angle value for each frame. So, as the drum beat gets louder, the twirl increases.

5. Click on Apply to calculate the Motion Math. If you render the resulting movie, you should see something like the Beat1.mov you'll find on the CD.

Looking at Audio Motion Math Script 1 again, note that the variable "scale-factor" is set to 400. Audio levels in After Effects are calculated on a scale from 0 to 1; that is, the loudest audio gives a value of 1. Obviously, if you apply values between 0 and 1 to the twirl value, you won't see much action. You need to increase the value so that the twirl value is set to a more useful range. The "scale_factor" multiplies the value derived from the audio layer's level by the number after the equal sign. Try increasing or decreasing that number and reapplying the script to the Leaf layer, then rendering the results. Also try setting the audio level to effect other Leaf Layer 1 properties like Position or Rotation by selecting them from Layer 1's Property pop-up.

The next step is to modify the Motion Math script a bit to exaggerate the twirl motion as the beat gets louder. Our hearing is not linear; that is, as a sound's energy increases, our perceived loudness of that sound doesn't increase in a straight line, as it does in the graph in Figure 7-19.

Our hearing response is more like Figure 7-20.

A linear audio response applied to imagery looks somewhat unnatural. To create

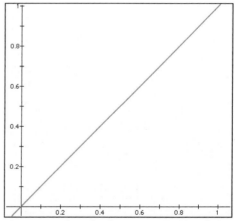

Figure 7-19: Linear loudness, as applied by a fader or volume slider.

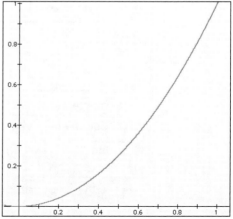

Figure 7-20: Human hearing, perceived loudness is non-linear.

a non-linear response, in this case an exponential relationship between the audio layer's loudness and the twirl, all we need to do is multiply the audio layer's level by itself, that is, squaring it, before we multiply it and apply it to the twirl value. Audio Motion Math Script 2 is set up to do this already. Rendering this movie will give you results something like the Beat2.mov on the CD. Here the twirl's response to the audio layer's level is more exaggerated, emphasizing the strong beats more strongly.

The Drums.aif file has been designed to loop smoothly, so you can extend it easily by highlighting the Drums.aif file in the project window and choosing File → Interpret Footage → Main…Set the file to loop the desired number of times. Another method is to duplicate the audio layer and snap it to the end of the layer you duplicated it from, repeating this process as many times as necessary. Try this loop with other footage of your own, using the level to change various distortion filters. If you have the Final Effects or Studio Effects plug-ins, use the loop to change the velocity of a particle system, to create instant synched explosions.

Example 2

The second example comes from a multitrack song and is a more musical construction. On the CD you will find an instrumental tune that was a concept test for a website promo piece. (In the footage folder, double-click the file named Popcorn.mov to launch MoviePlayer and play the file to hear the completed mix of the song. This is a single-file stereo track.)

The music is an ambient theme with sparse notes for the mere suggestion of a melody and rhythm. Notes and beats were left out to leave breathing space for the many tracks to be heard clearly.

As we have stated, the digital manipulation of audio precedes the widespread use of digital image effects processing; Jimi Hendrix used early devices of this kind to get his distinctive guitar sound. He used the effects boxes as musical additions to his guitar's sound, often filtering and distorting his sound beyond all recognition. Digital audio effects are used throughout contemporary audio production. Special "black boxes" give a performer or composer his unique sound and our composer is no exception.

The composer of our piece had After Effects image effects in mind as he wrote, conceiving his instrumentation and performances visually, manipulating audio channel operations and mattes with his selection of notes and rhythm. This song, though sparse, was composed with Motion Math in mind.

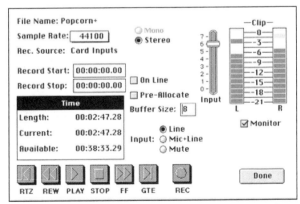

Figure 7-21: Digidesign's Sound Tools' flexible input and recording dialog.

The song was recorded one track at a time using Digidesign's Sound Tools (Figure 7-21) to capture individual files of each instrument's performance. The recordings were saved directly to the hard disk as AIFF audio files. (No audio cables were disconnected or harmed in the making of these recordings.)

Sound Tools is extremely flexible for this kind of repetitive recording process from a digital source. The tool offers various ways to synchronize to the composer's Music Sequencing system (another Macintosh running Studio Vision). A blended mix of the all tracks was then recorded to get a "mixed" and complete copy of the song. (This is usually best done in pro-audio gear, for reasons such as degree of control, as explained earlier.)

A total of 23 tracks were saved as AIFF files. Twenty-one of these were saved in mono, and one of them was a stereo track so it counts as two tracks. The stereo track named Popcorn.mov (Figure 7-22) is a mix of the 21 mono track files as a finished stereo program.

Twenty of the tracks were Motion Mathed and pre-rendered for you. Now we'll show you how to animate the 21st and final track representing wood block percussion performance.

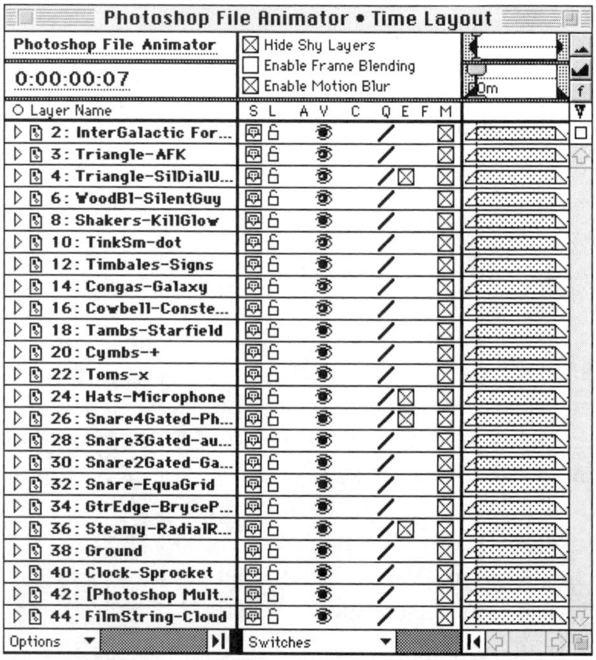

Composing the Picture

We placed each audio file associated with an instrument into a different layer in the After Effects project that was used to make the

Figure 7-22: The 21 recorded tracks, including the Popcorn.mov movie

Figure 7-23: The Photoshop layers.

Figure 7-24: The 21 audio files and the Photoshop Comp, with layers for each, in After Effects Time Layout.

background movie for this example. The Photoshop file that we animated contained many layers. Figure 7-23 shows the Layers palette and the composite image ("Guy.pic"), which has not yet been applied to the background movie we have supplied Photoshop Comp support was covered in detail in Chapter 6.

A layer was designated for each instrument track. Figure 7-24 shows the Photoshop file with all the above-listed layers turned on. You see part of the After Effects time line of the Photoshop file. The sound files are part of this Composition, one for each of the layers pictured here. (Actually the sounds have already been hidden. If you notice the Hide Shy

Layers button is enabled. This allows you to work on the layers you need, without filling your time line with layers you might not need to see.)

Since you can have unlimited layers, you can, in theory, mix an infinite number of audio tracks.

Part One

Part One of this lesson assumes that you have the production bundle installed. If you do not, you should read through this part anyway. You can still do Part Two after that.

The Bottom.mov file shown in Figure 7-25 was created with the technique you will now use. Your task is to animate the last layer, the Guy.pic, in synch with his instrument, the Woodbloc.aif sound file. Part Two is the final touch to the project, fading the video and audio to match each other.

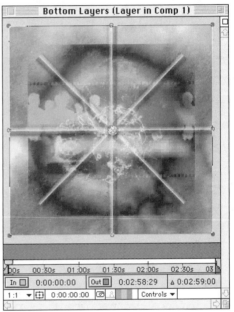

Figure 7-25: Bottom.mov.

 Studio Time: Animating the Guy.pic

1. Create a new project (Mac: Cmd-Opt-N, Windows: Ctrl-Alt-N), and in it a new Comp (Mac: Cmd-N, Windows: Ctrl-N) of 240 x 180 for a duration of 2:59 at 30 frames per second.

2. Import Bottom.mov, Popcorn.mov, Woodbloc.aif, and Guy.pic into your project. The Woodbloc.aif file will convert, but will not have to be written out as a new file.

3. Click Done.

4. Drag all four elements to the Time Layout window of the new Comp. Hit the Tab key to deselect all layers.

5. Highlight the Guy.pic layer and select Keyframe Assistant → Motion Math from the Layer menu. The Motion Math dialog can seem daunting at first. Continue the steps as indicated and observe what happens.

6. Click the Load button at the bottom left corner of the Motion Math Dialog to select the Layer audio.mm file layer from the Sample Motion Math Scripts folder that accompanies the Production Bundle.

7. Select Opacity under the property menu for the Guy.pic layer.

8. Select the sound file Woodbloc.aif for Layer 2.

9. The property of Layer 2 defaults to Audio Levels. This means the loudness of the wood block will drive the opacity of the Guy.pic layer.

10. Click Apply to compute the keyframes.

Part Two

Open the project named AE07MM.AEP if you were not able to do Part One of this exercise. If you just completed Part One, then we'll continue with the project you're using.

 Studio Time: Finishing Up

1. Set the Current Time to 2 minutes 11:00 seconds (Mac: Cmd-G, Windows: Ctrl-G, and type 21100, or just move the Playback Head until the Current Time reads 2:11:00).

2. Click the layer, Popcorn.mov to select it. Press the L key to expose After Effects' Levels controls.

3. Click the stopwatch icon to set a keyframe at 2:11:00.

4. Type the letter O on the keyboard to move to the end of the sound file.

5. Click the Levels value to open the Audio dialog box.

6. Set an ending keyframe by dragging the middle fader to 12%. This moves both the left and right levels together.

7. Type the letter J to go to the previous keyframe.

8. Select Preferences → General from the File menu (Mac: Cmd-;, Windows: Ctrl-;) and notice the default Duration setting of four seconds. For the Audio preview you will need to set these to your needs.

9. Double-click the 04 in 0:00:04:00 and change it to 60. Click OK.

10. Type the decimal point on the numeric keypad to preview the audio fade. Press Cmd-. (Mac), or Ctrl-. (Windows) to cancel the playback, or wait for the preview to finish.

11. If you previewed, type the J key to go to the previous keyframe (at 2:11:00).

12. Select the Bottom.mov layer and press T to bring up the Opacity property.

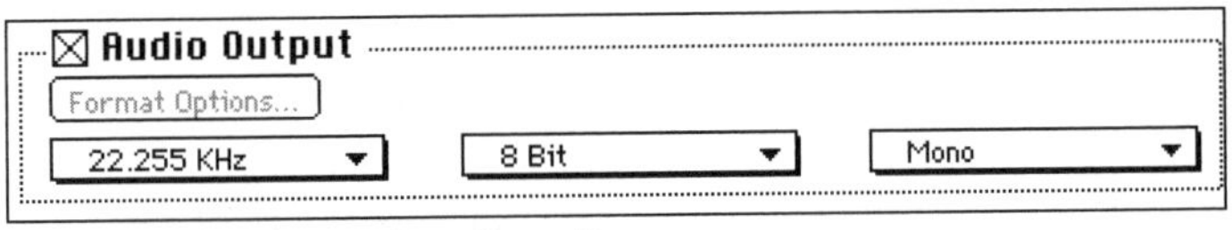

13. Click the stopwatch icon to set a keyframe at 2:11:00.

Figure 7-26: Output settings for audio.

14. Type the letter K to go to the end of your work area.

15. Click the Opacity value and type 0 in the Opacity dialog.

16. You should now render the movie (Mac: Cmd-M, Windows: Ctrl-M).

Other settings are described in the Output Setting section of Chapter 17. Use the settings in Figure 7-26 for this audio and execute the render.

As the project renders you should see successive frames modulating the brightness of the Guy.pic layer.

When you have finished, you will have a movie resembling the first one you opened at the beginning of the example, with the addition of your animated layer.

When you output your movie, it will be accompanied by an audio file that plays back with it.

Final Thoughts

Here are some key concepts that provide a final reinforcement to the information in this chapter.

Fading between Tracks

All your keyframing techniques can be used to fade and crossfade audio to your delight. Review what you have learned about manipulating them with this audio information in mind.

Previewing Audio

When you preview audio, you have control over the quality and length of the preview. The audio preferences you set do not affect rendering audio quality as render is set by the Output Module you select. We will cover those in a moment.

You can also preview audio synchronized with layer motion. This looks just like previewing without audio, as you have seen elsewhere in this book and in the manual.

To set preferences for audio preview:

1. Choose File → Preferences → General.

2. In the Audio Preview section, choose an audio sample rate from the first pop-up menu. Compact-disc quality sound is 44.1 KHz

3. Choose an audio sample size from the second pop-up menu. Compact-disc quality is 16-bit. Note: You may want to choose Allow Sample Rate to reduce the amount of time and memory required to preview.

4. Choose Stereo or Mono playback from the third pop-up menu.

5. Enter a duration for the audio preview. An audio preview begins at the CurrentTime marker and continues for the duration you specify here. This option is useful when you are checking short passages of a composition, although you can interrupt an audio preview at any time.

6. Click OK.

To Preview audio:

1. In the Composition window or Time Layout window, select the layers you want to preview.

2. Move the CurrentTime marker to the time where you want the preview to begin.

3. Choose Composition → Preview → Audio (Here Forward).

Scrubbing Audio

After Effects 3.1 lets you *scrub audio*, making easier to identify and mark a location in an audio layer to synchronize audio and visual effects. This means working back and forth across a sound until you find the exact place that you need. Instead of using the wave form, you can identify a location in the layer by moving the CurrentTime marker in the Time Layout window and listening to audio playback.

To scrub composition audio:

In the Time Layout window, move the Current Time marker while holding down the Control key. After Effects plays segments of the audio as you move across time. You can play the audio forward or backward.

Changing Audio Output Module Settings

The Audio Output options let you specify the sample rate (from 5.564 to 48.048 KHz), sample depth (8 bit or 16 bit), and the playback format (Mono or Stereo).

1. Choose a sample rate that corresponds to the capability of the output format. A sampling rate of 22.050 kilohertz is a standard for movies on Macintosh computers, IBM PCs, and compatibles. The standard for compact disc is 44.100 kilohertz, and the standard for digital audio tape (DAT) is 48 kilohertz.

2. Choose 8- or 16-bit sample depth, depending on the expected output format of the movie.

3. Choose an 8-bit sample depth for Macintosh or PC playback, and a 16-bit sample depth for compact disc and digital audio playback, or for hardware that supports 16-bit playback.

 Rewind

This chapter takes an in-depth look at audio-digital and analog audio editing in general, and using audio in After Effects. If you are not familiar with audio concepts, this chapter may have been rough going. However, when you need to use the information it will be here

Coming Attractions

We hope that this chapter has given you some insight into how to work with audio on the desktop and integrate sound with After Effects.

Next, we'll explore the world of 3D in After Effects. We will discuss the 3D programs available for Mac and Windows, what you should expect from them, and we'll show you how to combine 2D and 3D elements in your project. We'll provide you with some background on 3D, and a project that lets you place a finished 3D element into a composition.

3D Tools and After Effects

 Preview

This chapter talks about 3D and After Effects. Its format is a little bit different from that of most of the chapters in this book. In other chapters we show you features as you learn how to master them. However, After Effects has very few native 3D features. Therefore, most of this chapter is expository. It has been written based on the contributions of two experts in the field of 3D, David Acosta and Richard Lainhart. After you've digested the concepts, you can try the Studio Time—which gives you a chance to practice adding a 3D element to an After Effects project.

 Feature Presentation

After Effects is one of the most powerful desktop animation production tools available on any platform, but it can't do everything. In particular, since After Effects is really a 2D program, it can't process imagery in a true 3D space. What do we mean by this? The "true 3D space" in the computer world isn't *real* 3D space; after all, a seemingly solid, multi-sided 3D object on the screen doesn't exist in reality and has no dimensions, any more than the particle snowstorms created in After Effects. It's just a flat, 2D image.

In the computer animation world, imagery is categorized more by how and where it's created than by its final format. This is because anything displayed on a computer screen or in print is, by definition, a flat grid of pixels—a 2D, bitmapped image, no matter where it came from. So 2D digital animation differs from 3D digital animation not so much in its final form, since in each case you're producing a QuickTime or AVI movie—or a series a numbered, sequenced image files, but in how it's produced.

Programs are classified as 2D if their original sources are flat images, rather than 3D *geometry*. 3D programs, on the other hand, use mathematical, or geometric, descriptions of object shapes, rather than bitmapped images. These shapes are described in three dimensions (height, width, and depth) and don't exist as imagery until the final output is rendered. Since these shape descriptions (called *models*) aren't limited to any fixed size, they may be rendered at any chosen resolution—unlike bitmapped images, which have fixed resolutions.

Beyond that, a 2D program can only move images along the horizontal (X) and vertical (Y) axes. A 3D program understands and can move objects or its camera along the Z axis, or depth axis, as well, and correctly control perspective and the relationships of objects and lighting in the 3D space. Some 2D programs like After Effects can simulate Z-axis motion, as with the Basic 3D effect which is built-in to After Effects; programs like this are sometimes called "2 1/2D" applications. Adding more powerful and sophisticated 3D capabilities is a growing trend with 2D animation developers; a good example is the recently released Denim Illuminaire Paint and Composition suite.

3D Background

In the dim and distant past, all of 15 years ago, 3D animation was so expensive and complicated to produce that its use was reserved exclusively for feature films and network television. Computer animation systems cost hundreds of thousands or even millions of dollars, with the software not much cheaper, and usually required on-site programmers to get them to work at all. A little later, desktop workstations with more or less off-the-shelf software began to replace the old closed systems; these workstations and their programs could be had for as little as $100,000—chump change. Somewhere along the way, personal computers began to get more powerful, and 3D animation capabilities began to filter down to ordinary mortals. Recently we've begun to see reasonably-priced desktop systems that can do nearly all that the workstations could do, at a fraction of the price.

At the same time that computers and 3D software have been getting cheaper and easier to use, there's been a corresponding explosion of 3D production for film and video—it seems like every ad and "big" movie these days features elaborate 3D environments or special effects. Each phenomenon feeds the other, so there's an increasing need for reasonably-priced, full-featured 3D applications and the people to use them.

3D graphics is a broad topic, and there are least three different disciplines you would need to master to produce professional results on your own: modeling, animation, and rendering. We'll discuss each of these disciplines in turn, and as we do, we'll also define some other terms you may have come across—exotica like *polygonal geometry, spline geometry, Phong shading, ray tracing, Boolean modeling, deformations, particle systems,* and *inverse kinematics.*

Shapes and Modeling

Modeling, the process of creating 3D objects in the computer, is akin to sculpting, except with software tools. You may start with basic shapes (cubes, spheres, and so on), vary their scale and dimensions, and combine them in various ways to build up the model from smaller components. Another common modeling technique is *extrusion*, where you begin with a 2D outline and "push" it into 3D space. Yet another standard technique is *skinning* or *lofting*, in which you create a series of 2D profiles that define the skeleton of a shape (like the ribs of a ship, for example) and stitch a geometric skin over the profiles in order to create the solid shape.

Until recently, almost all 3D modeling programs worked with *polygonal* geometry exclusively. This means that all object surfaces are described as finite groups of two-dimensional flat planes, or *polygons*—usually triangles or quadrangles, but sometimes more complex shapes. The math required to describe a shape from polygons is pretty simple, which is why polygonal geometry is so popular, but flat shapes don't lend themselves well to describing curved shapes, as you can imagine. A cube is easily defined as six planes, but approximating a sphere requires many small polygons arranged to simulate the spherical shape. The more polygons you use to describe the sphere, the closer you can approximate its shape, but you can never truly create a smooth curve with polygons. The closer you get to such a shape, the more obvious its straight edges become. And, of course, the more you increase the resolution of your shape by increasing its polygon count, the more memory and CPU power are required to manipulate and push those polygons around.

Splines (variable curves) are a relatively new way to describe complex, organic geometry which defines curves as mathematical formulas rather than a collection of small shapes. *NURBS* (Non-Uniform Rational B-Splines) are a refinement of basic splines that are used in a number of newer modeling programs. Because a NURBS shape is a formula, it has infinite resolution and is always smooth at any zoom factor. Spline math is considerably more complex than polygon math, so splines are used less often at this time, although their acceptance is increasing in the 3D world. Of course, if you send a spline-based model from one program to another, the second program needs to understand the spline math correctly to handle the model.

This is somewhat like the difference between a paint program, such as Adobe Photoshop, and a draw program, like Adobe Illustrator. Photoshop uses finite bitmapped pixels (the equivalent to polygons) to define an image; you can only zoom into such an image so far before seeing the individual pixels and losing the overall picture. Illustrator uses 2D PostScript splines (very much like NURBS) to create an image at any desired resolution, but your output device needs to understand PostScript to render the Illustrator file. (If you have worked with Illustrator to any significant degree, you will recognize the controls provided by a NURBS modeler immediately. Most seasoned Illustrator users feel right at home in a NURBS modeler.)

The more advanced 3D applications also have more advanced modeling tools. *Boolean modeling* is a powerful technique based on logical operations performed on the intersections of models. Boolean modeling lets you take two spheres, for example, position them so that they overlap, then cut away the first sphere in the shape of the second sphere where they intersect, leaving a dimple in the side of the first sphere. It's ideal for cutting holes and tunnels in simple or complex objects, and in the hands of a skilled artist becomes a powerful sculptural tool. True Boolean modeling is difficult to implement in software, and so relatively few programs support it.

Metaballs (not meatballs) are usually spherical objects that have built-in characteristics and attraction to each other, so that when they get near each other their surfaces join together, somewhat like the molten wax in a LavaLite. The more sophisticated metaball modelers let you adjust the attraction of the balls to make smooth-surfaced models. When you combine metaballs of different attraction your smoothness varies according to these differences. The results can be quite amazing.

Modeling is often the most labor-intensive step of the 3D process. As a result, there are many third-party companies which sell ready-made models to those too busy (or too unskilled) to make their own. Such models are typically available in several different resolutions, ranging from simple, low-detail objects designed for video games and virtual reality applications, to exact and highly detailed planes, cars, and buildings for film production.

Animation, making things move around, is another skill set entirely. Here, the animator isn't so much concerned with the realism and detail of his models as in making them and the camera move convincingly, whether it's realistic motion or exaggerated cartoon antics. The standard 3D animation program is based on keyframes, just like After Effects, although some of the newer physics-based animation types don't implement keyframes. Again, as with models, it's possible to buy pre-fab motion data sets—such as all the keyframes necessary to animate a golf swing—which can not only recreate the motion convincingly but serve as good material for analysis by the animator. These data sets aren't as widely available as pre-fabricated models, though, and you need to buy the models and motion data separately.

One popular 3D animation operation is *deformations*—the ability to bend, twist, bulge, or otherwise warp an object's geometry into new shapes. Most programs featuring deformations will let you keyframe these changes over time, which enables you to create the kind of "squash and stretch" animation made popular by Warner Brothers cartoons and also seen today in commercials with dancing cars and cereal boxes.

Inverse Kinematics, or *IK*, sets up hierarchies of motion between parent and children models (models attached to parents), thus making it easier to simulate natural movement. Basically, IK lets models that are low in a hierarchy affect models higher in the hierarchy. For example, a correctly configured IK link will let you pull on a figure's foot and have the lower and upper legs follow along naturally, so that you don't need to individually animate the leg components.

Additionally, most IK systems employ sophisticated physics tools for the detection of collisions between objects. Such systems are capable of determining, without keyframing, when a ball meets the surface of the floor in a scene. IK is an important addition to the animator's arsenal, but isn't necessary or even desirable for creating convincing movement. Pixar's phenomenally successful 3-D movie *Toy Story*, for instance, was created without IK animation.

Particle systems are a special animation effect in which hundreds or thousands of points—or other shapes or objects—spray from a surface, each one following specified behaviors, collision-capable physics, and with built-in randomness. You set up the basic parameters, like gravity, initial direction, and velocity, and the program calculates the rest, without the need to individually animate all those points. With the right tweaks, particle systems can simulate water, smoke, fire, and other natural phenomena. There are some excellent third-party particle systems available for After Effects in the form of MetaCreations' Final Effects and Studio Effects (see Chapter 14), both of which include superb particle generators.

Rendering and Shading

Rendering, under which we will classify skills like texture mapping and lighting, is the last step in the 3D graphics process. During the rendering stage, the user assigns surface materials, or *texture maps*, to models. It is at this stage that the scene is lighted to create the desired mood or effect, and camera angles and moves are set up. Finally, the user sets up the rendering parameters and leaves the computer to crank out the frames. Rendering can take between seconds and hours (or sometimes days) per frame. This is based on the complexity, number of lights, textures, and size of the frame. It is often the most technical step of the process. And of course, we're talking about 24, 30, or even 60 frames per second of animation.

There are different types of rendering and shading for the scene. *Phong shading* renders the shading of a surface by calculating the color of each individual polygon based on its surface textures and lighting parameters. It then smooths the surfaces of adjacent polygons together to create the final image. Phong rendering can create very realistic images when set up correctly, and generally renders much faster than ray tracing (defined below). Phong's main limitations are that it cannot calculate reflections or refraction, which is the bending and distortion of light as it passes through transparent objects. To create these effects in with a Phong renderer, you have to fake them with texture maps. Some of the renderers based on the Phong shading technique are quite convincing, as you'll see later on in this chapter in when we work with "ElectricImage" in the Studio Time exercise.

Ray tracing simulates the physics of light, which is a completely different procedure than Phong shading. In ray tracing, surfaces are calculated by tracking virtual rays of light throughout a scene as they bounce off objects (reflection) or pass through objects (refraction). The advantage of ray tracing is that shadows, reflections, and refractions are calculated as part of the ray-tracing process, so it's generally easier to create more convincing photo-realistic images with ray tracing than with Phong shading. The disadvantage of ray tracing is that the computer has to calculate potentially millions of virtual light rays bouncing around the scene, so ray tracing is usually significantly slower than Phong shading.

In addition to its relative slowness, ray tracing has another significant limitation. In a real environment, even non-specular (not shiny) objects like walls and furniture reflect some light and color from their surfaces, and this diffuse light affects the surfaces of nearby objects. Hold a red ball near a white wall and you'll see a red glow on the wall near the ball, even in a room without direct light. Or, for more subtle example, look in the upper corner of the room you're in now. Unless the lighting in your space is extraordinarily even, each wall segment is a slightly different shade from the others, which is why we see the corner in the first place. If the walls are different colors, the colors will interact to some extent. Interior spaces rendered without these diffuse inter-reflective and ambient differences tend to look flat and "computerish." This ambient light is called inter-object illumination, or a "glow," that ray tracing does not calculate.

The *radiosity* rendering technique was created specifically to address ray tracing's inter-object illumination problem and increase the realism of rendered scenes. Basically, it works by dividing the surfaces in the scene into many small elements, and calculating how much each element affects the surface of every other element, based on the overall lighting in the scene. Since these interactions are calculated for the scene as a whole, the radiosity solution is not dependent on a particular view—in other words, as long as lights and objects in the scene don't change position and orientation, you can look at the scene from any angle in more or less real-time, since every element interaction has been pre-calculated. With enough hardware support this lets you generate real-time walkthroughs of surprisingly realistic spaces, or create real-time virtual sets for broadcast applications.

As you can see, there's a lot to do to produce 3D animation, and the tasks are often divided up among specialists for maximum efficiency, especially in big, expensive productions. Also, it's rare to find 3D artists who are equally accomplished in modeling, animation, and rendering. So, in the credits for most 3D effects extravaganzas, for example, you'll often see many separate modelers, animators, texture mappers, and even lighting and camera operators, all working in the same 3D project.

3D Programs

3D programs cover a wide range of platforms and price points, ranging from $100 to $100,000. Of course, for more money you get more features, although in general the prices of 3D applications are going down as their performance and capabilities go up. Let's take a closer look at some popular 3D applications and see how they interact with After Effects. There are a huge number of 3D applications at all levels of sophistication currently available; we're going to focus on the most important ones for the Windows/NT and Macintosh platforms in this overview.

NT Programs

The big advantage NT 3D programs have over their Mac counterparts is not NT's ease of use or superior rendering speed—in fact, the current PowerPC chips are generally faster at most rendering tasks than the equivalent Intel Pentium Pros. NT's superiority for 3D work lies in its implementation of *OpenGL*. OpenGL, originally developed by Silicon Graphics for its high-end graphics machines, is a set of libraries (system-level code that can easily be used by different programs) that lets 3D programs directly access hardware designed to accelerate 3D texturing and geometry manipulation. In combination with the right hardware display card, OpenGL lets a 3D artist see objects on the screen in fully-shaded lit views, instead of wireframe images without textures or lighting. This speeds up the modeling and animation process because you can see your models much more accurately and play back animations in something approaching real-time, without having to stop and render a finished scene for previewing. Apple's response to OpenGL, QuickDraw 3D, is a promising new technology that is still too immature for widespread professional hardware and software support. All the NT programs we'll discuss below implement OpenGL.

The best-known and most-used 3D application on the PC is Autodesk's 3D Studio, which has recently been completely revised and released as 3D Studio Max for NT (Figure 8-1). 3D Studio has been around for years and enjoys wide third-party developer support because of its open plug-in architecture. 3D Studio Max features a completely integrated interface—the old one was a series of modules—with many high-end features like network

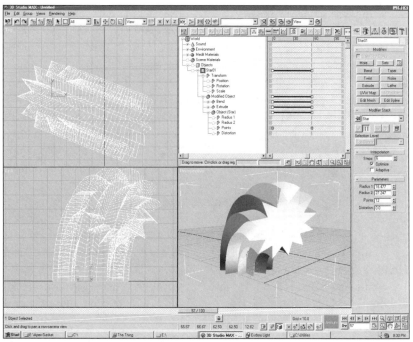

Figure 8-1: 3D Studio Max NT interface.

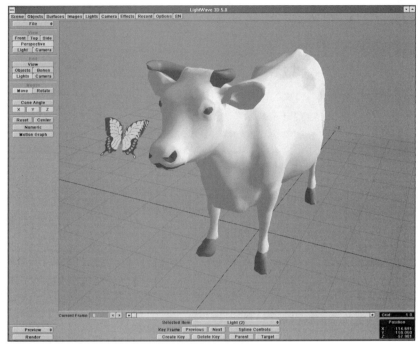

Figure 8-2: LightWave 3D.

rendering, visible lights, fog and smoke, inverse kinematics, object-oriented modeling, and particle systems. At around $3500, it's a professional tool in price and performance.

NewTek's Lightwave 3D 5.0, shown in Figure 8-2, runs on more platforms than any other 3D app—you can get it in identical versions for Windows NT on Intel, DEC Alpha, MIPS, and PowerPC chips, Power Mac, SGI, and Amiga. Originally developed for the Amiga as part of the original Video Toaster, LightWave 3D at $1495 is one of the least expensive full-featured professional 3D programs around. It comprises two modules: Modeler, for creating 3D geometry, and Layout, for lighting, animating, rendering, and applying texture to your scenes. LightWave includes sophisticated character animation controls, special effects like particle systems, fog, glows, and depth-of-field rendering, and a high-quality ray-tracing renderer. The ScreamerNet distributed rendering architecture built into the program lets you render scenes on any number of machines on a network, and due to LightWave's cross-platform compatibility, these computers can be a mix of any of the CPUs mentioned above. LightWave has enjoyed particular popularity in Hollywood for film and television special effects, and several popular current TV shows feature LightWave effects exclusively.

Softimage 3D is the 800-pound gorilla of the current crop of desktop 3D programs. Originally available only for SGI, Softimage was purchased by Microsoft in 1996 and ported to Windows NT, and was recently responsible for NT's swift acceptance as a viable solution for high-end 3D production work. Softimage is a tremendously powerful integrated package with a steep learning curve and the most flexible animation controls of any of the programs mentioned here. The basic version of the application features modeling, keyframe and physics-based animation, a huge variety of modeling tools, inverse kinematics and skinning, motion capture, decent ray tracing, and unique special effects. While Softimage's price has come down considerably from its SGI heights, Softimage 3D is still almost $8000, and you need to shell out an additional $7000 for the Extreme version, which includes Mental Ray (a high quality programmable renderer), particles, and MetaClay, a metaball modeling tool. Still, you can do nearly anything imaginable with Softimage, and it remains the program of choice for many top professional production facilities.

Alias/Wavefront is worth mentioning. This tool sports features comparable to Softimage. In fact, Alias has been with us since the beginning of the 3D revolution, bringing us liquid metal men and digital dinosaurs. This software has yet to be ported out of the Hallowed Halls of SGI, (SGI now owns the company) and onto to other platforms. Even so, the natural physics capabilities of Alias now sport technology enough for tornadoes, explosions, and earthquakes. It is the other 800-pound gorilla.

The latest generation of powerful desktop CPUs have made radiosity more practical for use by architects and animators. Lightscape Technologies' Lightscape Visualization System (shown in Figure 8-3) is the best radiosity rendering engine for those desktops. Its combination of radiosity processing and ray tracing allows experienced users to render scenes of unparalleled realism. No other desktop application renders light as beautifully as

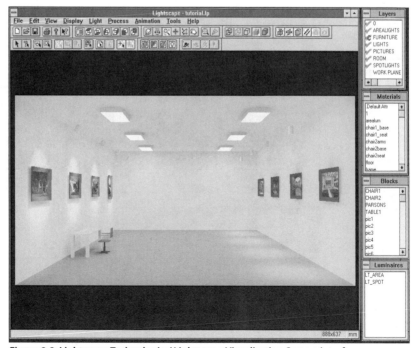

Figure 8-3: Lightscape Technologies' Lightscape Visualization System interface.

Lightscape does, and for that reason alone the program is worth having, especially for architects, display visualizers, and other "real-world" designers. Its limited camera-only animation capabilities make it less of a must-have for broadcast animators and game designers, although it was recently used effectively for interiors in Martin Scorcese's *Casino*. The program is rather technically oriented, so those without architectural or engineering training may find it a little dense at first, but overall, its spectacular results make any inconveniences worthwhile.

Mac Programs

ElectricImage Animation System, shown in Figure 8-4, is the premiere animation application for the Mac. For a long while, it also was the most expensive at $7500, but a lower-priced version has recently been released to counter market share pressure from Softimage for NT and 3D Studio Max. It features one of the fastest renderers on any platform, superior anti-aliasing, and many special effects. These features, previously only found in workstation-class applications, have been in ElectricImage for some time. It will include a modeler in a future version, so until then, models must be created in another application and imported into ElectricImage. AutoDesSys formZ, one of the best modeling programs around for Mac and Windows NT, is often preferred as a modeling front end for ElectricImage.

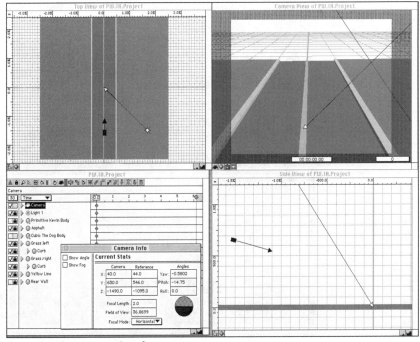

Figure 8-4: ElectricImage interface.

Figure 8-5: Strata Studio Pro interface.

Strata StudioPro, shown in Figure 8-5, is an integrated modeling/animation/rendering program. An earlier version of this program was used to created the phenomenally successful CD-ROM game Myst. It has a high-quality ray-tracing rendering engine and extensive modeling tools including Booleans, deformations, and particle systems. Recent versions are also among the first to support Apple's new QuickDraw 3D (QD3D) system software, which provides real-time shading, lighting, and texture mapping of models on PowerPCs.

Fractal Design's Poser 2, pictured in Figure 8-6, is an interesting one-trick pony that generates natural or fantastic human body models in correct anatomical positions for rendering in other 3D programs. The new 2.0 version also allows for simple animation and rendering within the program itself. You can define the body type you want to create (male, female, child, superhero) and then implement inverse kinematics to put the body model into any pose you like.

Fractal has also recently introduced Detailer for Mac and Windows NT (shown in Figure 8-7). Based on Painter, Fractal's natural-media paint program, Detailer lets you create accurate texture maps for 3D models. Texture mapping is one of the most important skills for a 3D artist to master, because good textures can add a lot of detail to simple models and greatly enhance the realism of a scene. It's easy enough to make good maps for models that consist of simple shapes joined together—you just isolate the shapes and apply flat, spherical, cylindrical or cubic maps to them. However, it's always been a struggle to

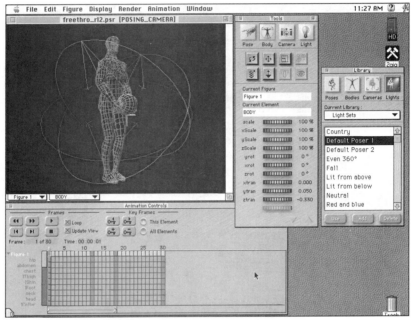

Figure 8-6: Fractal Design's Poser.

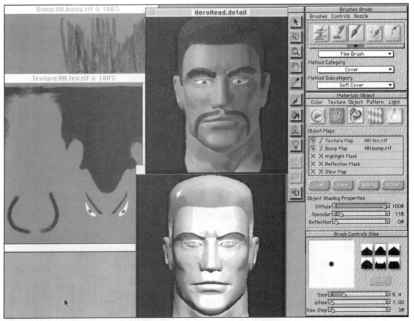

Figure 8-7: Fractal Design Detailer.

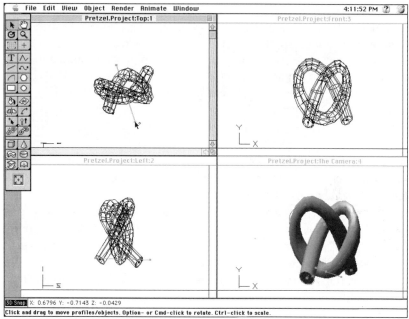

Figure 8-8: Macromedia Extreme 3D.

create accurate maps for complex objects, especially animals and human faces. A human face needs to be smooth, without obvious edges or seams where sections join together, and ideally, it should consist of a single object. An irregular model is the hardest to map, though, because its shape doesn't conform to any of the standard mapping methods. Detailer solves this problem by letting you paint directly onto the model surface and extracting the resulting texture map for use in a 3D rendering program. This makes it much easier to align the important areas of the face map to the face itself. 3D paint programs have been available for a while for expensive high-end workstations, but Detailer is the first useful desktop 3D paint application.

Macromedia's Extreme 3D, for Windows and Mac, is another new integrated release that incorporates modeling, rendering, and animation. Figure 8-8 shows the interface. Almost every parameter can be animated, and the program features a fast Phong renderer that is suitable for most multimedia work. Extreme 3D has an excellent integrated help system, and, for a 3D program, it is fast and easy to learn. At around $400, it's a good entry-level application, especially for those new to 3D, but it's powerful enough to be used for professional-quality work, particularly in multimedia production.

3D and After Effects

Well, now that we've given you a background in 3D and 3D programs, let's get back to After Effects. As we mentioned a 2D program like After Effects can't create true 3D environments on its own. However, most Mac-based animators consider After Effects an essential part of their software arsenal (and we expect the NT version of After Effects will prove just as essential to Windows-based animators). First, After Effects is great for making animated texture maps to be applied to 3D models. Moving Video mapped to a 3D TV screen, animated water, fire, and smoke maps, and even grayscale animations for surface displacement are common applications for After Effects animations in a 3D production.

Second, After Effects can generally render its footage faster than most 3D applications, so many 3D animators cut their production time by rendering 3D imagery in layers and compositing the layers in After Effects, often with a 2D background layer created directly in After Effects. In order to composite layers successfully, the 3D animator must rely on producing accurate alpha channels, which After Effects handles superbly. All of the 3D programs mentioned can produce and save alpha channels; but the trick is knowing what *kind* of alpha channel each produces.

For example, if you wanted to create a 3D outdoor scene and render the sky as an alpha channel in order to composite the scene against a video layer of moving clouds, you leave the sky empty and tell the 3D app to render the background as alpha. The program will render an anti-aliased edge to blend the two together. If the program shades the edge pixels into transparency, so that the edge pixels in the foreground aren't affected by the background color, it's creating a *straight* alpha channel. If the program shades the edge pixels into the background color, it's creating a *premultiplied* alpha channel.

Internally, After Effects only works with straight alpha channels. Normally, After Effects can identify the type of alpha channel the imported image uses, but some programs create *unlabeled* alpha channels—channels which are unidentified. ElectricImage is one of these, and it happens to create premultiplied alphas, usually matted against black. When you import an ElectricImage file for compositing, you'll need to identify it as matted with black. Fortunately, the other programs listed here can render PICTs and TIFFs (on the Mac side) and TIFF and Targa files on the NT side, all of which use straight labeled alpha channels. Avoid rendering to the common Windows BMP format; it doesn't support alpha channels at all.

Third-Party 3D Filters

All this talk about integrating 3D renders with After Effects makes it sound like After Effects can't generate any 3D imagery at all. While this is true of the program itself, there are some third-party filters which allow you to create true 3D graphics in After Effects without any other software, and we'll take a look at them next. Even with third-party plug-ins, After Effects' 3D capabilities are rather limited right now, but that situation won't last forever, and we'll close this chapter with a glimpse of the future.

MetaCreations' FE Sphere filter operates in true 3D space, and allows for some interesting 3D manipulation of text, among other things. MetaCreations' particle systems in their Final Effects and Studio Effects, especially the Studio Effects Particle World filter, also work in 3D space, and let you project imagery and 3D primitive shapes into Z space for some fascinating effects.

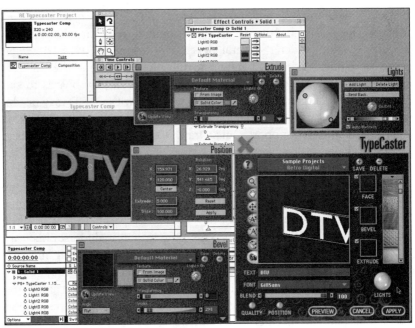

Figure 8-9: Xaos Tools TypeCaster interface.

You have, however, relatively little control over individual particles in these systems, and you certainly can't import 3D objects or text into After Effects and manipulate them at will. Xaos Tool's TypeCaster (shown in Figure 8-9) was developed for Photoshop, but works well in After Effects and gives you the ability to create simple flying logos and network "bugs" (those little logos you see in the bottom left or right corners of the screen on nearly every cable channel these days) quickly and easily. You can create text with any installed font, extrude and bevel it, apply a wide range of colors, surface textures, and lighting to it, and animate any of its parameters with standard After Effects keyframe tools.

The integration of Apple's QuickDraw 3D with After Effects via third-party plug-ins opens up the possibility of creating professional-quality 3D animations in After Effects alone, with all of After Effects superior animation controls at hand. Drawing on the speed of the PowerPC chip, QuickDraw 3D provides applications with a standard for handling, displaying, and rendering 3D objects, much like QuickTime now allows any QuickTime-aware application to play movies with the standard Movie Controller and access any installed QuickTime code. The QuickDraw 3D spec also includes a standard 3D file format, called 3D MetaFile (3DMF). In theory, the 3DMF format will let any application read and process any other program's 3D files, which they definitely can't do now. The closest thing to a common 3D format is the DXF file, which doesn't support important 3D functions like texture mapping, object hierarchies, lighting, or animated models. If 3DMF is ultimately accepted as a cross-platform standard, it will support all these features and more, and it will finally allow 3D artists to freely exchange data among 3D programs on any platforms.

QD3D also supports plug-in third-party renderers and hardware acceleration for 3D display. This means that the 3D artist isn't limited to the simple Gouraud shading which is QD3D's default renderer; several developers are currently working on ray-tracing and radiosity renderers that will plug into QD3D and provide the highest quality rendered imagery. Hardware acceleration allows specialized display boards to speed up 3D screen redraw and rendering, so that a desktop machine with QD3D may be able to approach the performance of high-end SGI workstations, for a lot less money. And because any developer can easily support QuickDraw 3D, programs like After Effects will be able to access QuickDraw 3D's own plug-in render and display architecture.

The first of these, M.M.M. Software's HoloDozo, uses QD3D's basic renderer to map images and video to primitive shapes. Go to http://www.mmmsoft.com/holodozo /HoloDozo.html for more information on their special After Effects version. However, the really exciting news is that a major developer is preparing to release a full-blown 3D application as an After Effects plug-in. This plug-in will include sophisticated animation and lighting controls, the ability to import and texturize any 3DMF model, and best of all, a top-notch ray-trace renderer for QD3D that is said to be the equal of any in the business. The release of this plug-in will give After Effects the kind of 3D animation power that used to reside exclusively in 3D programs with steep learning curves and steeper prices, and that's good news for all After Effects artists.

A Taste of 3D Compositing

To give you a taste of working with a 3D image, we created a wheel from a piece of type in ElectricImage and rendered it as it executed a quarter-turn, using the "standard" metallic gold with an alpha channel. In this Studio Time, you are going to add colored highlights and a flared brightness to the wheel using the wheel itself as a mask. You will also use the mask to create a drop shadow. These actions—which are fairly easy in After Effects—would take a lot of computer render-time in a 3D program. One of the major benefits of using After Effects is the amount of time that can be saved in a production environment.

 ## Studio Time: Setting up the Comp

1.   Create a new Comp (Mac: Cmd-N, Windows: Ctrl-N). Name it "AE8 Comp 1." The length of the Comp should be 6 seconds. It is 30 fps.

2.   Select File → Import → Footage Files. Import the files Cross.mov, Backgrnd.psd, and Kairad.psd. When you are asked to Interpret the footage for the Cross.mov, select Straight as the alpha channel method.

3.   Set the Current Time to 00 (Mac: Cmd-G, Windows: Ctrl-G, then type 0).

4.   Drag the background image from the Project window into the Comp window. Let it snap to the center.

5. Press S to display the Scale property. Set the Scale to 35%.

6. While still at Time=00, drag Cross.mov into the Comp window. Let it snap to the center. Figure 8-10 shows the Comp window after the Project has been set up.

This is the basic layout for the final Comp. Next, we'll make the sub-comps that will be used to add the effect.

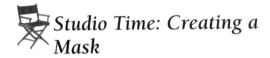 *Studio Time: Creating a Mask*

Figure 8-10: Comp window showing the background image and the wheel.

1. You need to make a mask for the gold wheel. Create a new Comp (Mac: Cmd-N, Windows: Ctrl-N). Name it "Mask W/Radial."

2. Set the Current Time to 00 (Mac: Cmd-G, Windows: Ctrl-G, then type 0).

3. Drag the Kairad.psd image into the Comp window. The image is a radial gradient created in Photoshop using the KPTGradient Explorer. Let it snap to the center of the Comp window.

4. Press S to display the Scale property. Set the Scale to 75%.

5. Press R to show the Rotation property. Click in the stop watch to make it keyframeable. Set the initial value at 0.

6. Got to the layer Out point (O). Add 1 full revolution to the Rotation.

7. Add a Fast Blur effect of 4 (Effect → Blur & Sharpen → Fast Blur).

8. Set the Current Time to 00 (Mac: Cmd-G, Windows: Ctrl-G, then type 0).

9. Drag Cross.mov into the Comp window. Make sure that it is centered at 160 x 120.

10. At the bottom of the Time Layout window is the Switches drop-down menu (seen in Figure 8-11). Change that to Transfer controls.

11. Highlight the Kairad.psd layer and specify the Cross.mov as its luma track matte, as shown in Figure 8-12. (You will learn about track mattes in Chapter 11. For now, just follow the instructions!) Figure 8-13 shows the mask and alpha as it should appear at this point. You can preview if you want. Notice that the radial gradient rotates along with the wheel and sheds different highlights as the wheel revolves. Close the Comp.

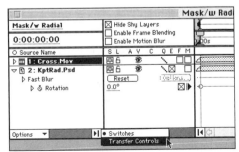

Figure 8-11: The Switches menu.

Studio Time: Adding a Color Balance Effect

1. Go back to the main Comp. Use the Home key on the numeric keypad to take you back to Time=00.

2. Duplicate the Cross.mov layer (Mac: Cmd-D, Windows: Ctrl-D). Rename the layer Color Cross.

3. Press T to bring up the Opacity property. Click in the stop watch to make it keyframeable. Set an Opacity keyframe of 0%.

4. Set the Current Time to 2:15 seconds (Mac: Cmd-G, Windows: Ctrl-G, and type 215, or just move the Playback Head until the Current Time reads 0:00:02:15).

5. Create an Opacity keyframe of 100%.

6. Go to Time=500, set the Opacity to 10%.

7. Set the Current Time to 00 (Mac: Cmd-G, Windows: Ctrl-G, then type 0).

8. Add the Color Balance HLS effect (Effect → Image Ctrl → Color Balance (HLS). Turn down the arrow on the effect name in the Time Layout window. Click in the stop watch to set a keyframe for Hue. Set it to -1 full revolution.

9. Change the Saturation to 33% but do not set a keyframe.

10. Go to the layer's Out point (o) and set the Hue to 0 (remove the -1 rotation on it). The dialog should be set as you see in Figure 8-14.

11. Set the Current Time to 00 (Mac: Cmd-G, Windows: Ctrl-G, then type 0).

12. Drag the Mask W/Radial Comp into the Comp window. Use this as the luma matte for the Cross Cross Layer (change to Transfer controls as you did in the earlier Studio Time) that is directly below it. Figure 8-15 shows the section of the Time Layout window.

Figure 8-12: Setting a track matte.

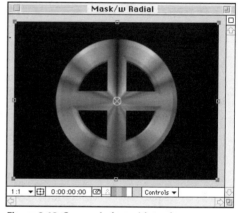

Figure 8-13: Comp window with track matte set.

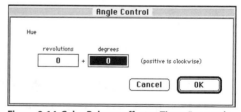

Figure 8-14: Color Balance effect at Time=5 seconds.

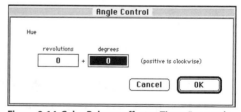

Figure 8-15: Mask W/Radial layer as luma matte for Color Cross.

Studio Time: Adding a Lens Flare Effect

Let's create a Lens Flare to add some shininess to the 3D wheel element. A Lens Flare simulates the effect of sunlight glaring onto a camera lens.

1. Set the Current Time to 00 (Mac: Cmd-G, Windows: Ctrl-G, then type 0).

2. Create a new solid (Mac: Cmd-Y, Windows: Ctrl-Y). Name it Lens Flare. It should be 320 x 240 pixels. The background color should be black.

3. Apply the PS+Lens Flare effect (Effect → Render → PS+Lens Flare). In the first dialog box, set the Brightness to 133 and the Lens Type is 50-300 Zoom. In the Effects Control box, you will need to set the Flare Center to the 160, 120 4. As a final step set the scale of the layer to 233%. (Press S to display the Scale property.)

5. Drag the Lens Flare layer above the Cross.mov. Set the Mode to Overlay (remember, you need to change the Switches to transfer Controls). This will make the whole image seem as if the color has been pumped up. You should see a change in the wheel element.

6. Now, you need to isolate the Lens Flare so that it only appears on the wheel itself. Duplicate the Cross.mov layer. Drag the copy on top of the Lens Flare layer. Click on the Lens Flare layer (you are already looking at the Transfer Controls). Specify it as the alpha matte for the Cross.mov layer. The background should appear normal again, but the wheel shows a delightful play of light (as you can see in Figure 8-16).

Save the project and take a short stretch. We're nearing the end. The only thing missing is the drop shadow.

Studio Time: Creating a Drop Shadow

1. Set the Current Time to 00 (Mac: Cmd-G, Windows: Ctrl-G, then type 0).

2. Create a new solid (Mac: Cmd-Y, Windows: Ctrl-Y). Name it "Gradation". The size should already be set to 320 x 240 and the background should be black.

3. Apply the Ramp effect (Effect → Synthesize → Ramp). Set the start of the ramp to 160,227. Set the start color to black. Set the end of the ramp to160,165. and set the end color to white. Figure 8-17 shows the Effects Ctrl window. This makes a nice gradation as seen in Figure 8-18.

4. Drag it right above the background layer.

Figure 8-16: Comp window after applying Lens Flare effect.

5. Temporarily turn off the other elements (click the eye icons to close them). All you want visible are the Background and the Gradation layers.

6. Duplicate the Cross.mov and rename it "Shadow Mask." Make it visible, and drag it above the Gradation layer.

7. Apply the Basic 3D effect (Effect → Perspective → Basic 3D). Set the Tilt to 73°. You should see the Cross in perspective as if it were a shadow.

8. Press P to display the Position property. Change the position of the Shadow Mask to 160, 203, so that it is in the correct position to be a shadow.

9. Highlight the Gradation layer. Make the Shadow Mask the alpha matte for the Gradation layer. The result will be clipping the gradation to the shape of the Cross. The result can be seen in Figure 8-19.

10. Click on the Shadow Mask layer to select it. Add a Fast Blur of 8 to soften it nicely (Effect → Blur & Sharpen → Fast Blur).

11. Select the Gradation layer, change Switches to Transfer Controls, and change the layer mode to Multiply. This makes the white in the Gradation layer transparent so that the shadow will seem more realistic.

12. Turn on the Color Cross, Lens Flare, and Cross.mov layers.

13. The shadow seems a bit dark. Highlight the Gradation layer. Press T to bring up the Opacity property. Set the Opacity to 75%.

14. Set the work area to end at 5 seconds.

15. Set the Quality switches to High.

16. Render the movie.

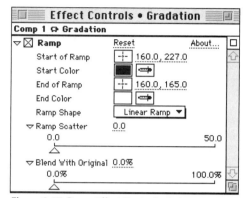

Figure 8-17: Ramp Effect Control window.

Figure 8-18: The ramp.

Figure 8-19: The shadow.

 Rewind

Figure 8-20: The finished Comp.

In this chapter, you learned a lot about 3D programs and 3D imaging. We covered such concepts as 3D models, polygonal geometry, spline geometry, Phong shading, ray tracing, Boolean modeling, deformations, particle systems, and inverse kinematics. We surveyed the most popular NT and Macintosh 3D programs. You also tried your hand at adding effects to a 3D element to make the rendering of that element much easier within the 3D program. After Effects is an excellent tool for the 3D artist, and 3D programs give the After Effects practitioner much wider scope for creativity.

 Coming Attractions

In Chapter 9, you will learn about another group of programs that work well with After Effects. You will see how Fractal Design's Expressions and Detailer can work with After Effects, and you will learn about some lesser-known products such as Tree and Bliss Paint. You will get a chance to try them out, or to work with footage created in them. You will also learn about DeBabelizer, Movie Cleaner, and some other important utilities to make your After Effects work easier.

Companion Programs

 Preview

There are many other programs that an After Effects artist needs in his or her toolbox. In this chapter, we will discuss of number of them.

These programs fall into three main categories:

- Programs that you use to prepare images and video for use in After Effects.

- Programs that utilize the video created in After Effects.

- Utility programs that do not create or use footage, but which help you to manage, compact, or otherwise handle video files efficiently, or prepare them for another venue (like the Web).

It is not terribly far-fetched to name these categories "Before," "After," and "During." We will use these labels even though some of these programs overlap our convenient categories. This chapter will concentrate on the programs used "before"—as input (since this chapter is in the section of the book that describes various types of input). However, we will also briefly cover the "during" and "after" programs as well.

Feature Presentation

Let's look at the list of "helper" applications that make up the toolbox of the practicing After Effects artist. You do not need them all, but each program adds a different capability.

1. Before
   - Photoshop
   - Illustrator
   - Premiere
   - Fractal Design Painter
   - Fractal Design Detailer
   - Fractal Design Expressions
   - Tree
   - Bliss Paint
   - Movie Flo
   - Strata Media Paint
2. After
   - Director/Authorware
   - ClickWorks
   - mTropolis
   - QuarkImmedia
   - Premiere
3. During
   - DeBabelizer
   - Movie Cleaner

Programs to Use "Before"

In many ways, After Effects is similar to a page layout program—it does not generally create content; it re-arranges, manipulates, and organizes it. Because of that, you need other programs to help create the content. Some of these programs—Photoshop, Illustrator, Premiere—are known to every graphic artist. Other programs which are very useful in creating content—Tree, Bliss Paint—are much less well known.

Photoshop

Adobe Photoshop is the most critical "other" application if you wish to use After Effects to animate still images such as textures and backgrounds. It is also the "other" program that you are most likely own—especially if you have entered the realm of digital video from the world of print design, as so many of us have.

Photoshop is a raster-(pixel) based program that allows you to create content and to edit, filter, and manipulate graphics. If you are not familiar with it, you probably should not be using After Effects either, as many of the concepts are shared between the programs and Photoshop is the most basic component of a professional graphic arts toolbox.

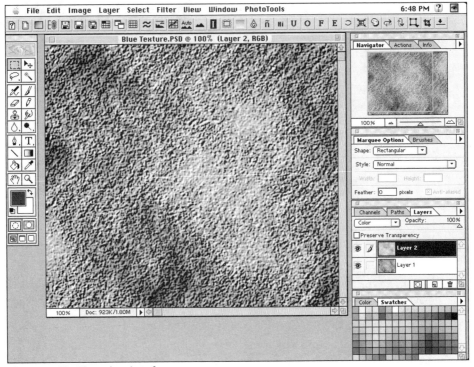

Figure 9-1: The Photoshop interface.

Figure 9-1 shows the Photoshop interface. Note that the image shown here—a texture used in the Chapter 1 movie—is composed of two layers. Layers are one of the basic elements that are shared between Photoshop and After Effects. Another common element is the *transfer mode* (typically called an Apply mode or Blending mode in Photoshop). In the Layers palette, you can see that the top layer is applied in Color mode.

A third, and very important common element is the *alpha* channel—an extra amount of information that defines the transparency of an image. You can use Photoshop to set up either alpha information for After Effects (information that uses the shape or outline of the

Figure 9-2a: Watering can image form KPT Power Photos.

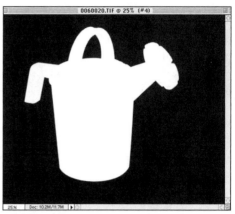

Figure 9-2b: Alpha channel with shape information.

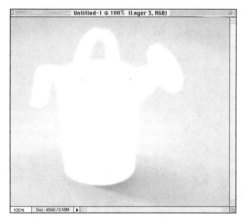

Figure 9-2c: Alpha channel with luminance information.

Figure 9-2d: Image using luminance alpha as a layer mask.

object), or luma information (which uses the shades of gray in the channel to determine transparency).

Figure 9-2a shows a watering can image from the KPT Power Photos collection. Figure 9-2b shows the alpha channel for that image. The alpha is in black and white, and would cause After Effects to keep the watering can and remove all of the background.

Figure 9-2c shows another alpha channel for the watering can. This one, however, has gray values in it. These gray values (i.e. not stark white or black) can be used as a luma matte in After Effects to allow for partial transparency in any area that is not 100% white. Figure 9-2d shows a patterned background in the layer below the watering can which uses the luminance values in the layer mask to calculate its transparency.

You would use Photoshop to create textures and backgrounds, scan and edit images, apply static filters, color correct images, and create transparency in images. The Photoshop format is the only major format that retains layers and transparency in the file (other formats may allow you to use an alpha channel for transparency). Therefore you can very easily produce images with built-in transparency without the need to physically draw or create alpha channels. Chapters 2, 6, and 12 give you a lot of practice using Photoshop images—both layered and flattened.

Illustrator

Adobe Illustrator is another essential production tool. One of the most common uses for After Effects is for titling and logo treatments. The original text is usually created in Adobe Illustrator.

Illustrator is a vector program. Figure 9-3 shows the interface for version 7.0 (the current version available for both Mac and Windows). Illustrator handles shapes and forms rather than pixels; it determines the area to manipulate because of PostScript commands written by the program rather than by discrete pixel locations on a "canvas." The advantage of a vector format is that it writes a file that is smaller than the corresponding raster image would be, and it can be infinitely resized without distortion or jaggedness.

After Effects is well integrated with Illustrator and can use the vector format without intermediate conversion. You can dynamically scale your text or shapes in After Effects and,

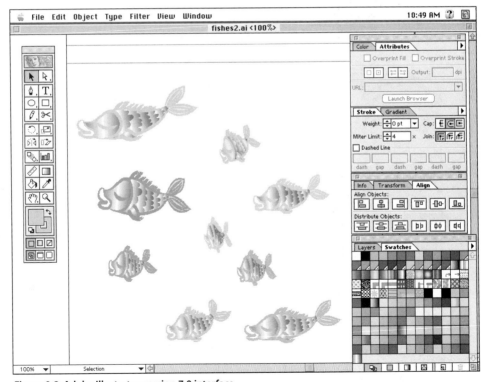

Figure 9-3: Adobe Illustrator version 7.0 interface.

by using the Continuously Rasterize switch, you can obtain exceptionally high quality text—sharp, clear, and not jagged. Chapter 5 showed you how to work with Illustrator text.

Illustrator is also handy for either rasterizing or resaving files that are in the Illustrator format but which were not written by Adobe Illustrator. After Effects can have a bit of trouble with these files—from Fractal Design Expression, Coral Draw, or Freehand—and the ability to resave them in Illustrator is valuable.

Premiere

Adobe Premiere provides the After Effects user with the most budget-conscious way to capture video—a function that is not available in After Effects itself. While a high-end user may not use Premiere for video capture (preferring hardware-specific programs to capture video), it is the most accessible means for the casual user or the small free-lance studio— especially if the final form for the video will be CD-ROM, screen, or Web output.

Premiere is a video editing program that works in a manner similar to that of a non-computerized video editing suite. It allows you to arrange video clips, splice and cut them, trim them, and write them out to a new roll of tape (either literally or digitally). It works by allowing you to place a clip in the A track and another one in the B track, and to set a transition between them (a place where the new film will be not-quite A and not-yet B). Figure 9-4 shows the Premiere interface, including a preview that shows the transition in process.

It is much more practical to sequence movie clips in Premiere than in After Effects, as Premiere is set up to perform that task much more quickly and efficiently.

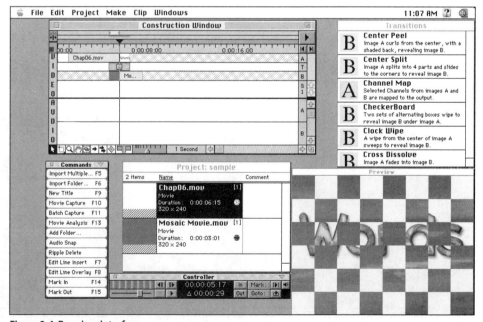

Figure 9-4: Premiere interface.

You might find that your workflow calls for you to acquire the video footage in Adobe Premiere, add effects in After Effects, and then move the footage back into Premiere for sequencing and final cuts. You could also capture and sequence in Premiere, and then move the footage into After Effects to composite it with a number of other moving and still footage items. Having both programs allows you full flexibility.

You can also use Premiere to prepare black and white transition movies that can be used as track mattes in After Effects. Chapter 11 shows you how to accomplish this task.

Fractal Design Painter

Even though it may seem as if Adobe is the only producer of mission-critical applications, that is not quite the case. Adobe certainly manufactures the basics, but there is more to life than basics. Fractal Design, now a partner with MetaTools in a new company named MetaCreations, also has an interesting variety of programs that can help your cause.

Fractal Design Painter is a raster-based program that is similar in many ways to Photoshop. However, it complements rather than competes with Photoshop. Fractal Design Painter specializes in creating Natural Media™ images—images that look as if they were actually done with pen and ink, or oils, chalk, or pastels. It also features a host of "Esoterica" effects such as marbling and mosaics that can be used in very interesting ways by After Effects.

Painter allows you to do onion-skinned animations as well. You can create a frame and then see where it was, in order to easily create the next frame. Using this technique, you can make animations that range in complexity from stick figures to anything that you have the patience to create. You can save the animation as a QuickTime movie and then import it into After Effects. Since it can be quite tedious to create a long animation in Painter, you might want to use the Time Remapping facility in After Effects—as we will do in a few paragraphs.

Another wonderful feature in Painter is its ability to create seamless patterns. By defining a file as a pattern file, you can use any of the painting tools within the file, and when your brush gets to the left edge of the file, the drawing continues along the right edge. This allows you to create a painterly seamless pattern that is quite effective— and very difficult to do in Photoshop.

In this Studio Time, you will use a seamless pattern that was created in Painter at 320 x 240 pixels, and a very simple animation also created in Painter. The animation was created in 10 frames using the Growth command from the Esoterica menu. It needs to be stretched to fit in After Effects.

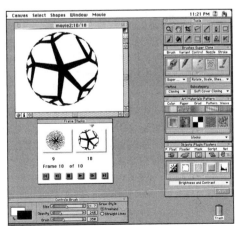

Figure 9-5: The Painter interface.

Studio Time: The Painter Animation

1. Create a new project (Mac: Cmd-Opt-N, Windows: Alt-Ctrl-N). Name it Painter.aep.

2. Import the Fractal3.mov and Pattern.psd files from the AE09Foot folder (Mac: Opt-Cmd-I, Windows: Alt-Ctrl-I). If you are asked to specify how to treat the unlabeled alpha channel in the Fractal3.mov, choose Ignore.

3. Create a new Comp (Mac: Cmd-N, Windows: Ctrl-N). Name it New Movie. Make it 10 seconds long, 30 frames per second, and 640 x 480 pixels. In the final movie, the image will rotate, so you need to increase the size of the background of the movie to make certain that it can rotate and cover the 320 x 240 pixel Comp at the same time.

4. Create a new solid (Mac: Cmd-Y, Windows: Ctrl-Y) and set its color to white. Make it 640 x 480 pixels. This will allow the image to rotate properly.

5. Drag the Fractal3.mov image into the Comp window and let it snap to the center.

6. Set the background color to white (Mac: Shift-Cmd-B, Windows: Shift-Ctrl-B).

7. Select Layer Enable Time Remapping. Turn down the arrow next to the Fractal3 layer to reveal the Time Remapping property, as shown in Figure 9-6.

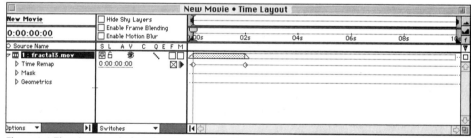

Figure 9-6: Time Layout window showing the Time Remapping property.

8. Place your cursor on the right turned-down corner of the time line. Drag the time line until it stretches to the 10-second mark. Click on the right-most keyframe indicator along the Time Remapping property, and drag it to the 10 second mark as well. Figure 9-7 shows the Time Layout window with the time line stretched to 10 seconds.

Figure 9-7: Time Layout window with time remapped.

9. Press the Opt key (Mac) or Alt key (Windows) to close the Comp and the Time Layout windows.

10. Create a new Comp (Mac: Cmd-N, Windows: Ctrl-N) named Painter Comp. Make it 320 x 240 and 10 seconds long at 30 frames per second.

11. Drag the Pattern.psd image into the center of the Comp window.

12. Set the Current Time to 00 (Mac: Cmd-G, Windows: Ctrl-G, then type 0).

13. Select Effect 'Distort 'Offset. Turn down the arrow on the layer in the Time Layout window to show the Mask, Effect, and Geometry properties. Turn down the Offset effect arrow and click in the stop watch next to the Shift Center To property to make it keyframeable.

14. Go to the Out Point of the layer (O). Make sure the crosshairs box is checked in the Effect Controls—Pattern.psd dialog. Drag the crosshairs in the Comp window to the bottom right corner of the image. Click the mouse to "set" the ending position for the Offset filter. Figure 9-8 shows the correctly-set dialog.

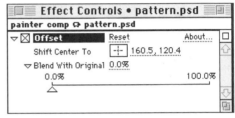

Figure 9-8: Offset Effect controls.

15. Set the Current Time to 00 (Mac: Cmd-G, Windows: Ctrl-G, then type 0). Preview the effect. Notice that the layer is seamless as it seems to move and wrap around—Figure 9-9 shows this at Time=4 seconds.

16. Set the Current Time to 00 (Mac: Cmd-G, Windows: Ctrl-G, then type 0).

17. Drag the New Movie Comp into the center of the Comp window.

18. Pull down the Switches menu at the bottom left of the Time Layout window, and change to the Transfer Controls as shown in Figure 9-10.

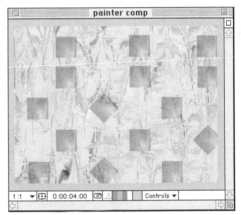

Figure 9-9: Seamless pattern wrapped and offset at 4 seconds.

19. Change the Transfer mode on the New Movie layer to Silhouette Luma (pull down the menu embedded in the Normal box next to the layer, and scroll to Silhouette Luma). This transfer mode uses the black pixels in the New Movie Comp to reveal the layer beneath (i.e. the pattern layer) and covers the rest of the image with black—the background color. Figure 9-11

Figure 9-10: Setting the Transfer Controls.

shows the Comp window after the transfer mode has been set.

20. Press S to display the Scale property and Shift-R to display the Rotation property. Click the stop watch next to each property to make them keyframeable.

21. Go to the Out point of the Comp (O).

22. Click to create a sustaining keyframe for Scale. Set the Rotation property to 3 full rotations.

23. Set the Current Time to 2:00 seconds.

24. Create a Scale keyframe of 110 %.

25. Go to 4 seconds. Make a Scale keyframe of 90%.

26. Go to 6 seconds and set a Scale keyframe of 100%.

27. At 8 seconds, make a Scale keyframe of 90%.

28. Return to the Switches menu and change the Quality settings to High.

29. Preview and render the Comp.

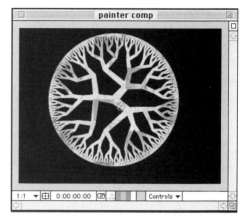

Figure 9-11: Comp window with transfer mode set to Silhouette Luma.

Fractal Design Detailer

Fractal Design Detailer is a 3D program that is based on Painter. It provides access to almost all of Painter's brushes and to many of the extra features of Painter. It also allows you to paint on 3D shapes and to create texture, bump, reflection, highlight, and glow maps for a 3D object. It does not allow you to create any 3D objects, however. Those must be imported from Ray Dream Designer or from another 3D program. You can render your objects or export them fully mapped to another 3D application for rendering. Figure 9-12 shows the Detailer interface.

The benefit of Detailer is that you can place elements and detail exactly where you want them on a 3D object—something that is hard to do in a traditional 3D program. If you look at the texture map in Figure 9-12, you can see the paint strokes that were drawn directly onto the model (they will be the areas in Blob.psd that you can see as yellow when you complete the Studio Time below). You can then render your image with an alpha channel for easy compositing. The "catch" for the After Effects artist, though, is that you cannot create an animation in After Effects as you can in many of the other 3D programs. So when you render your 3D object, it is a flat, 2D shape. You can animate this shape in After Effects—but you can only see one side of it. However, if you render more than one view of an object, you can obtain some very interesting results.

In this Studio Time, you will import and composite three images rendered from one model in Fractal Design Detailer and place them over a moving texture background.

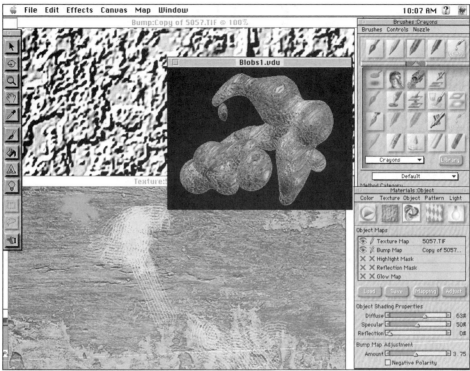

Figure 9-12: Detailer interface.

 Studio Time: Detailer Project

1. Create a new project (Mac: Cmd-Opt-N, Windows: Alt-Ctrl-N) named Detailer.aep.

2. Import the Painted.psd file from the AE09Foot folder as a Photoshop 3.0 Comp (File ' Import ' As Photoshop 3.0 Comp).

3. Open the Painted Comp. The layers from the Photoshop file are already in position and in the correct transfer mode (the top layer is in Hard Light mode).

4. Set the Current Time to 00 (Mac: Cmd-G, Windows: Ctrl-G, then type 0).

5. Select both layers and press P to show the Position property. Click in each stop watch to make the Position property in both layers keyframeable.

6. Change the Composition settings (Mac: Cmd-K, Windows: Ctrl-K) to make the Comp size 320 x 240 pixels. This positions both layers with their top-left corners in the top-left of the movie.

7. Select the Background layer (the bottom one). Press Shift and Option (Mac) or Alt (Windows) to snap the bottom-right corner of the layer to the bottom-right corner of the Comp window.

8.   Set the Current Time to 09:29 seconds (Mac: Cmd-G, Windows: Ctrl-G, and type 929, or just move the Playback Head until the Current Time reads 0:00:09:29).

9.   Select the Background layer (the bottom one). Press Shift and Option (Mac) or Alt (Windows) to snap the top-left corner of the layer to the top-left corner of the Comp window, so that the image moves diagonally over the 10-second duration of the movie.

10. Select the Background copy layer (the top layer). Change the position of the layer so that its bottom-right corner is in the bottom-right corner of the Comp window. The two layers trade places over the duration of the movie.

11. Press the Option key (Mac) or Alt key (Windows) to close both the Comp and the Time Layout windows.

12. Create a new Comp (Mac: Cmd-N, Windows: Ctrl-N), 10 seconds long, 30 frames per second, 320 x 240 pixels. You may leave the Comp 1 default name.

13. Import the Blob.psd, Blob2.psd, and Blob3.psd files from the AE09Foot folder (Mac: Opt-Cmd-I, Windows: Alt-Ctrl-I). When asked to specify the alpha treatment, select Straight and check the Inverted box. Detailer creates an alpha channel that is the reverse color of the one that After Effects expects.

14. While the three files are still selected, drag them into the center of the Comp window. Then deselect (Tab).

15. Move the Blob3.psd layer to the top of the list, and turn off the Eye icon in both the Blob and Blob 3 layers.

16. Select the Blob2.psd layer. Press S, Shift-R, Shift-T to show the Scale, Rotation, and Opacity properties. Click in each stop watch to make the properties keyframeable.

17. Set the Current Time to 4:00 seconds (Mac: Cmd-G, Windows: Ctrl-G, and type 400, or just move the Playback Head until the Current Time reads 0:00:04:00).

18. Set a keyframe for Scale of 40%, Opacity: 0%, and Rotation of 1 complete rotation.

19. Highlight the Blob.psd layer and turn on its Eye icon. Press P, Shift-S, and Shift-R to show the Position, Scale, and Rotation properties. Click in each stop watch to create an initial keyframe.

20. Set the Current Time to 00 (Mac: Cmd-G, Windows: Ctrl-G, then type 0).

21. Set a Scale keyframe of 10% and a Position keyframe of 25x, 218y. The Blob will start small and grow larger as it moves toward the center of the image. Figure 9-13 shows the Comp window.

22. Set the Current Time to 4:00 seconds (Mac: Cmd-G, Windows: Ctrl-G, and type 400, or just move the Playback Head until the Current Time reads 0:00:04:00).

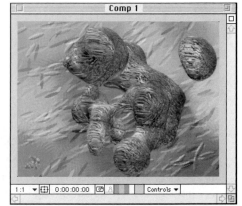

Figure 9-13: Comp window at Time=0.

23. Highlight the Blob3 layer and turn on its Eye icon to make the layer visible. Press Opt-[(Mac) or Alt-[(Windows) to trim the start of the footage to 4 seconds.

24. Go to the layer Out point (O).

25. Highlight the Blob layer. Set a keyframe for Scale at 30%. Set a Position keyframe at 367x, 276y. Set a Rotation keyframe for 3 full rotations.

26. Highlight the Blob3 layer. Press P, Shift-S, and Shift-R to show the Position, Scale, and Rotation properties. Click in each stop watch to leave initial keyframes. Set the Rotation property to -2 full rotations (so that it rotates in the opposite direction). Figure 9-14 shows the Comp window at 10 seconds.

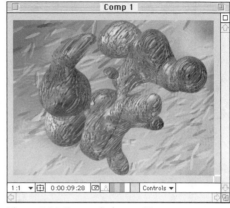

Figure 9-14: Comp window at 10.

27. Set the Current Time to 4:00 seconds (Mac: Cmd-G, Windows: Ctrl-G, and type 400, or just move the Playback Head until the Current Time reads 0:00:04:00).

28. Set a Position keyframe for the Blob3 to 48x, 36y. Set the Scale to 30% and set a Rotation keyframe of 0. Figure 9-15 shows the Comp window at 4 seconds.

30. Set the Current Time to 00.

31. From the project window, drag the Painted.psd comp into the Comp Window.

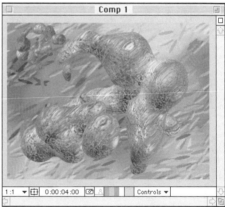

Figure 9-15: Comp window at 4 seconds.

32. Change the Quality settings for all layers to High.

33. Preview and render the movie.

Fractal Design Expression

Fractal Design Expression is a unique vector-based program created for Fractal Design by Creature House. It is the vector equivalent of Painter, as it gives you the never-before-possible ability to create natural media vector strokes. You can create vector paths that look and act like chalk, oil, water colors, etc. Since this is a vector program, each stroke remains editable and can be moved, resized, or changed into a totally different type of stroke with a mouse click.

One of the most intriguing capabilities, for the After Effects artist, is the program's ability to create compound brushstrokes (called *skeletal strokes*) that are fully realized

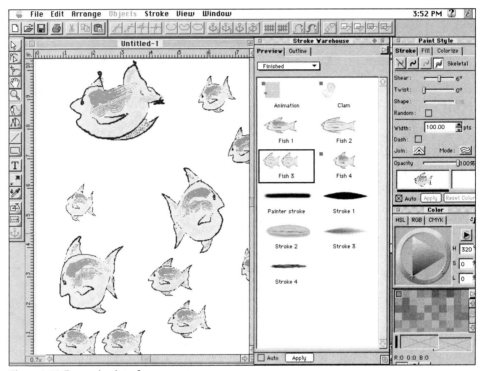

Figure 9-16: Expression interface.

drawings. These strokes can be applied to your canvas with a single click-and-drag action and can create a fish, a dog, a plant, or anything else that you are able to imagine. Since these strokes also create vector objects, you can reshape these strokes as you wish. Figure 9-16 shows the Expression environment with the brushstrokes window open and several fish in a document-in-progress.

You can also create a brush (called a multi-view brush) that contains variations of a single brush (a fish in slightly different positions, for example). An instance or view in the multi-view brush is the equivalent of a keyframe in an animation. In fact, you can create an animation of any length, frame rate, and resolution from this multi-view brush. Expression automatically tweens the views to create a smooth animation. Double-click on the Express.mov movie to see a tiny example of a multi-view brush saved as an animation.

In the Studio Time, you will use two fish brushes to create a tiny animation. The fish were created from a skeletal stroke brush in Expression and were saved in Adobe Illustrator format. The file was then opened and resaved in Illustrator, since After Effects did not recognize the AI format saved by Expression. In the exercise, you will animate the fish by changing its position, and by scaling it unevenly to make it contract and expand. In addition, you will use the auto-orient position feature to make one fish follow the motion path.

Studio Time: Expression Project

1. Create a new project (Mac: Cmd-Opt-N, Windows: Alt-Ctrl-N). Name it Express.aep.

2. Create a new Comp (Mac: Cmd-N, Windows: Ctrl-N). Name it Fish Comp and make it 320 x 240 pixels, 30 frames per second, and 4 seconds long.

3. Import the Fish3.ai and Fish4.ai files from the AE09Foot folder (Mac: Opt-Cmd-I, Windows: Alt-Ctrl-I).

4. Drag Fish3.ai into the Comp window and center it. Press P, Shift-S, and Shift-R to show the Position, Scale, and Rotation properties.

5. Click in the stop watches to make the three properties keyframeable. Click on the Scale property value to show the dialog box. Remove the checkmark in the Preserve Frame Aspect Ratio box as you need to scale the fish unevenly. Change the Scale to 80%, 100%. Set a keyframe for Position at 320x, 105.5y. Set an initial keyframe for Rotation of 0.

6. Set the Current Time to 1:00 seconds (Mac: Cmd-G, Windows: Ctrl-G, and type 100, or just move the Playback Head until the Current Time reads 0:00:01:00).

7. Change the Scale to 110, 100, and make a Position keyframe of 141x, 176.5y.

8. Set the Current Time to 2 seconds. Change the Scale to 120, 100, and make a Position keyframe of 176x, 137.5y. Create a keyframe for Rotation of 19°.

9. Set the Current Time to 3 seconds. Change the Scale to 70, 100, and make a Position keyframe of 85x, 60.5y. Create a keyframe of -1° for Rotation.

10. Set the Current Time to 4 seconds. Change the Scale to 50, 100, and make a Position keyframe of 18x, 183.5y. Create a keyframe for Rotation with a value of -43°. Figure 9-17 shows the Comp window.

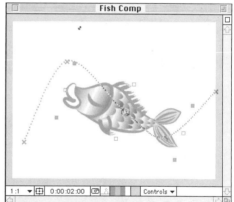

Figure 9-17: Comp window showing motion path for single fish.

11. Set the Current Time to 00 (Mac: Cmd-G, Windows: Ctrl-G, then type 0).

12. Drag the Fish4.ai image into the center of the Comp window.

13. Highlight the Fish3 layer name and drag a Marquee around all of the keyframe markers in the Fish3 layer (place the cursor at the upper-left above the keyframe markers, press the mouse button, and drag). The selected keyframes will turn solid black. Copy them to the clipboard.

14. Highlight the Fish4.ai layer. Press P, Shift-S, and Shift-R to show the Position, Scale, and Rotation properties.

15. Paste the keyframes from the clipboard.

16. Now we have a bit of a problem. The keyframes are in place, but Fish4 is swimming in the same path as Fish3, which results in a very boring movie. Let's reverse the keyframes so that the motion paths also reverse. Select Layer 'Time Stretch. In the resulting dialog, change the stretch factor to -100% and hold the Out point constant.

17. That's better—except now all of the action is taking place after the movie is over. Place your cursor on the still-selected time line ribbon and drag it back so that it starts at Time=0. Grab hold of a selected keyframe and position the group of keyframes so that the first one also starts at Time=0 as shown in Figure 9-18.

18. Preview the movie. Hmmm… It looks like we are not quite finished (unless you want the fish the swim backwards).

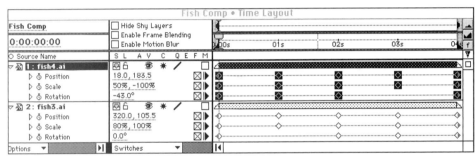

Figure 9-18: Time Layout window showing time reversal.

19. Set the Current Time to 00 (Mac: Cmd-G, Windows: Ctrl-G, then type 0).

20. Change the Scale keyframe on Fish4.ia from 100% height to 100 height. This flips the position of the fish. Use the keyframe navigation arrows to invert all of Fish4's Scale property heights to -100%.

21. Preview. Ooops! Now you have a dead fish swimming backwards. That definitely is not the "look" that is in! One more adjustment to make. In the Layer menu, under Geometrics, select Auto-Orient position. This makes the fish straighten out and swim right. Actually, he now follows the motion path with his nose and dives and rises based on curve of the path. Figure 9-19 shows the Comp window with both fish in it.

22. Set the Quality switches on both layers to High and turn on the Continuously Rasterize switch. Render.

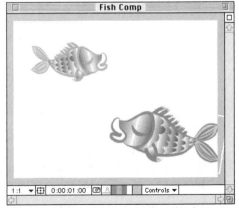

Figure 9-19: Comp window with two fish facing in the correct directions.

Tree

Tree Painter and Tree Professional, by Onyx Computing, are totally unique programs that accomplish only one task—they create trees. They are able to create trees that are either anatomically correct—conifers, palms, and broadleafs—or trees which exist only within your imagination. Tree allows you to model a tree from an existing parameter file or by specifying each parameter. You can save these parameters for later use or even use them, with a different random seed (pun not totally unintentional), to create a forest of the same species with the random characteristic of different members of the same tribe.

Tree Professional (but not the less-expensive Tree Painter) can export the models in .DXF format to a 3D program, for rendering or for inclusion in another scene. You can also render your models in Tree. You can change the viewpoint to see the tree from any angle, and you can cut off any branch of the tree with the chainsaw tool. You can even coax your tree into growing in Bonsai curves.

Tree allows you to render or export trees that have "placeholders" for leaves. You can scan actual leaves and place them on the trees, use leaves from the CD-ROM library that ships with the product, or substitute dollar bills or any other object you wish in place of the leaves (gee—a money tree; most starving free-lancers have often wished for that!).

Onyx Computing has allowed us to place a demo of their program on the CD-ROM. At the time that the CD-ROM was created, only the Mac version was available. If you are using a Windows-based computer, you can download a Windows demo from their Web site at http://onyxtree.com. This program is unique enough that it is worthy of a Studio Time demo to show you how it works.

 Studio Time: Using Tree

1. Load the Tree Pro demo from the CD-ROM.

2. Select Type ' Palms, and then choose File ' Load parameters. Load the Cocos.PALM file from the AE09Foot file.

3. Figure 9-20 shows the Tree interface. Notice the two series of controls along the bottom edge. The first set (the stick, wireframe cylinder, and shaded cylinder) control the view of the tree—stick, wireframe, or fully rendered. If you click on one of these, the screen will redraw.

4. Let the rendering view remain on Fully Rendered. Click on the Random Seed button on the right to select it, and then reduce the slider to 600 as shown in Figure 9-21. The new tree is of the same species, but much more curved.

Figure 9-20: Tree Professional interface.

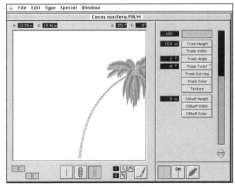

Figure 9-21: New random seed.

Figure 9-22: Leaf parameters.

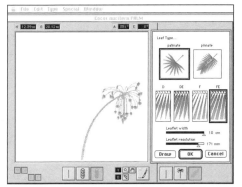

Figure 9-23: Changing the leaf type.

Figure 9-24: Changing the Petiole length.

5.   Notice that the leftmost button at the bottom of the right panel is selected (it looks like a straight line). This indicates that the trunk parameters are active. Click on the leaf icon to activate those parameters, shown in Figure 9-22.

6.   Click on the Leaf Type button and select Palmate, and FE, as shown in Figure 9-23. Increase the leaflet width to 10 and the leaflet resolution to 171. Click OK. As you can see in Figure 9-23, there is a huge change in the model.

7.   Change the Petiole Length to 50%. As you can see in Figure 9-24, this makes a big change.

8.   Play with the controls for the stems. You can magnify using the Zoom tool to see a close up view, as you can see by the leaves shown in Figure 9-25. You can also pan around the image in 3D space.

9.   The demo version does not render or save, so when you are finished experimenting, simply quit the program.

There is another version of Tree that works within ElectricImage (covered in the previous chapter). This is Tree EIAS Storm. Tree Storm is a plug-in that enables you to model trees in real-time from within an ElectricImage scene. You can animate the trees to simulate their behavior in wind, and set separate parameters for the trunks, branches, twigs, and leaves. You can even model the behavior of plants under water. We have included several of these animations for you to see.

One application of this program is to render the animation in ElectricImage and then composite the footage in After Effects to add visible rain or other particle effects— or to place it over a different animated background. Play the sample movies—you are sure to find them very impressive.

Figure 9-25: Close-up of the leaves.

Bliss Paint

Bliss Paint, by Imaja, is another very unique product. It is a color synthesizer that can be played as an instrument, but it produces a psychedelic color and light show rather than music. It allows you to place shapes and designs on the screen (scribblers and distributors in Bliss lingo). These shapes react to the colors, which are typed in as color "notes" on the keyboard. By using a midi instrument, or playing music into the program, you can record sequences for later playback, and you can render the screen animation to a QuickTime movie. The program is available for the Macintosh only.

Figure 9-26, which was taken from the Imaja Web site at http://www.imaja.com, shows the Bliss Paint interface. You can see the key elements: the scribbler list—which places specific types of shapes on the screen, and the distributor list—which determines the patterns that the shapes will take (for example, you can use a plaid scribbler with an odd grid rectangle distributor, and the plaid pattern will appear in a grid in alternate grid spaces). You can also see the Sequence window and the Paint window. The only missing main window is the Color Synthesizer, which holds the colors in use.

In its own way, Bliss Paint is as deep a program as After Effects. It can be used quite well by the casual user, but the musician or the person who is willing to make a serious study of it can find an enormous range of complexity and an unlimited amount of creative potential. Bliss Paint gives you the ability to see music as a series of moving colors that take shape and form. It takes a deep understanding of the subtleties of the program to fully control its results.

We have set up a short Studio Time using three movies that were generated and rendered in Bliss Paint. In this Studio Time, you will create a very simple movie that is the interaction of the three individual ones.

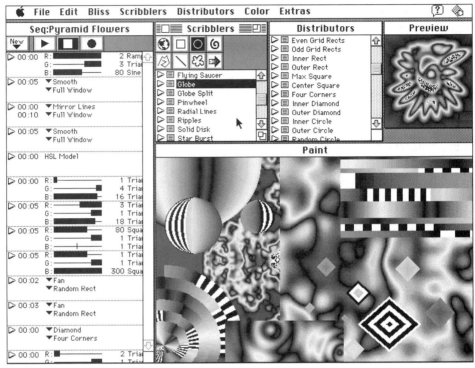

Figure 9-26: Bliss Paint interface.

 Studio Time: Bliss Paint

1. Create a new project (Mac: Cmd-Opt-N, Windows: Alt-Ctrl-N). Name it Bliss.aep.

2. Create a new Comp (Mac: Cmd-N, Windows: Ctrl-N). You can leave it at the default name of Comp 1. Make it 10 seconds long, 320 x 240, and 30 frames per second.

3. Import the Bliss1.mov, Bliss2.mov, and Bliss3.mov files from the AE09Foot folder (Mac: Opt-Cmd-I, Windows: Alt-Ctrl-I).

4. Set the Current Time to 00 (Mac: Cmd-G, Windows: Ctrl-G, then type 0).

5. Drag Bliss3.mov into the center of the Comp window. Figure 9-27 shows the first frame of the movie.

6. Drag Bliss1.mov into the center of the Comp window. Change the Switches to Transfer Controls and set the transfer mode

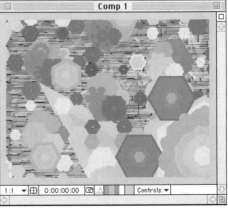

Figure 9-27: Bliss3.mov.

to Overlay. This makes the second movie show up in a modified form on top of Bliss3.mov. Figure 9-28 shows the first frame of the Bliss1.mov in Normal mode.

7. Drag Bliss2.mov into the center of the Comp window. Figure 9-29 shows the first frame of this movie. Change the transfer mode to Stencil Luma. This makes the bottom two movies show up only inside of the areas on the Bliss2.mov that are not solid black. Since the early part of the movie has a large area of black, this gives the footage an interesting look.

8. Press S to display the Scale property. Click in the stop watch to make it keyframeable. Set the initial Scale value to 200%.

9. Set the Current Time to 6:00 seconds (Mac: Cmd-G, Windows: Ctrl-G, and type 600, or just move the Playback Head until the Current Time reads 0:00:06:00).

10. Create a Scale value keyframe of 100%.

11. In the Switches area, set all of the Quality settings to High. Figure 9-30 shows the first frame of the combined movie in the Comp window.

12. Preview the movie and render it.

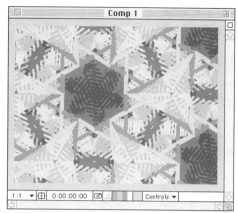

Figure 9-28: Bliss1.mov in Normal mode.

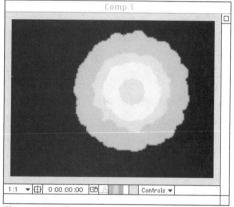

Figure 9-29: Bliss2.mov in Normal mode.

Movie Flo

Have you seen the recent commercials where the Mona Lisa smiles or the president on the dollars starts to talk? It is a very popular type of effect right now. While there are high-end programs that can do this, one of the very best tools is MovieFlo, from the Valis Group. MovieFlo is the top-of-the-line of the three Valis warping and morphing programs. Flo can only warp still images. MetaFlo is able to morph and warp. MovieFlo can layer images, warp and morph video footage, and create animations.

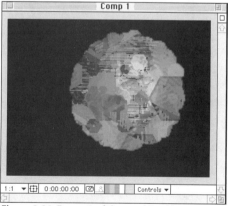

Figure 9-30: Frame 1 of the combined layers.

If you are not familiar with *morphing*, it is the ability to change one shape into another. It is a very popular effect in advertising and movies. An automobile turns into a tiger, a snowman turns into a little boy eating soup, people turn into superheros and robots. The earliest forms of desktop computer morphing of photographic images required that you identify specific points on an image and map each of those points to new locations on the target image. For example, you needed to select specific locations on the perimeter of a boy's face that correspond to the same locations on the monkey face that you want the boy to become.

MovieFlo has progressed far beyond that stage and is also capable of doing advanced warping—to allow George Washington to speak, the Statue of Liberty to bend, or a monkey to open its eyes much wider than it could ever do in real life. Figure 9-31 shows a

Figure 9-31: Warped computer by Jeff Schewe.

still image of a computer, created by artist Jeff Schewe, that has been totally warped and distorted, but which seems to flow seamlessly into its new shape. There are a number of

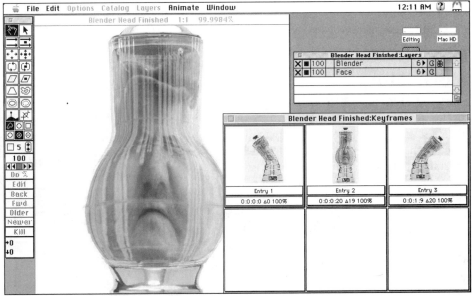

Figure 9-32: MovieFlo interface.

movies created by MovieFlo on the CD-ROM. Look at them, as the results are truly awesome.

MovieFlo also allows you to make one shape conform to another. In Figure 9-32, you can see three keyframes in an animation under construction. The image shows a man's head that has been warped to fit inside of a blender.

You can use MovieFlo to prepare footage to composite with other images in After Effects, or you can use MovieFlo to morph, warp, or integrate footage that you originally composited in After Effects. In either direction, it makes a very valuable addition to your toolbox.

Strata Media Paint

Strata Media Paint is a very interesting product. It is a video paint program. What, you ask, is that? A video paint program allows you to apply paint directly to a piece of digital video. However, there are some key differences between painting in Media Paint and taking your frames as a filmstrip into Photoshop. While you might be able to do the same things, painting frame-by-frame in Photoshop, it is unbelievably tedious, and you are actually painting over your footage. Taking the same movie into Media Paint is effortless and it does not actually touch your footage at all. Media Paint knows about video frames and timing. When you are finished with your painting and effects, you can output the new footage to a new movie.

Media Paint allows you to do simple things like change the color of a garment in the footage (not easy to do in After Effects at all), or more complex things like writing your name over a series of frames (which, of course, you can do in After Effects). Strata Media Paint is a full-featured paint program that was specifically designed to work with video footage.

Media Paint opens a QuickTime file as a read-only file. A transparent paint layer is placed above it. There is a third layer in Media Paint that holds the buffer information—it can store a PICT file or another QuickTime movie, and you can paint with the contents of this buffer layer as if it were a paint color. This allows you to composite movies together or to make it look as if a person is floating on top of another movie.

Many of the features and functions of Media Paint are irrelevant to the After Effects owner, but it is much easier to *rotoscope* in Media Paint than it is in After Effects. Rotoscoping is the process of painting something into a video image over a time line. Therefore, you can place flaring jolts of electricity into your image with relative ease. Look at the movie Arcs1.mov in the CH09Moves

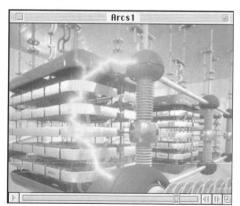

Figure 9-33: A frame from Arcs1.mov.

folder on the CD-ROM. Figure 9-33 shows a footage item with an arc of electricity totally created in Media Paint.

Figure 9-34: Lightning scribble.

There is a special effects add-on available for Media Paint that automates the process of creating a number of particle effects such as arcs, beams, lightning, fireworks, etc. Figure 9-34 shows one of the movies used in Chapter 13. It has been opened in Media Paint and the lightning tool is being used to scribble over the image. Figure 9-35 shows the Media Paint interface and the same image—this time with the scribble changed automatically into a lightning bolt.

You can use Media Paint as an adjunct to After Effects. Some of the special effects Media Paint modules are less expensive and yield similar results. You can take footage into Media Paint and then bring it back into After Effects, or use the program at any place in the process. Media Paint is available both for the Macintosh and for Windows/NT.

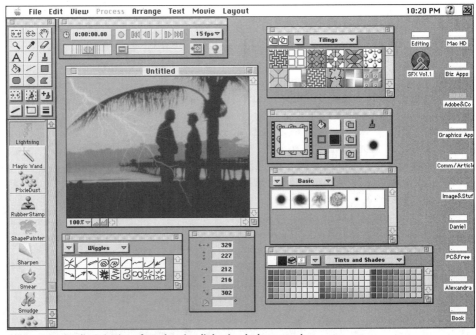

Figure 9-35: Media Paint interface showing lightning bolt on movie.

Real World After Effects Gallery

The After Effects Gallery contains movie sequences from the book as well as creations by other After Effects artists.

This skyline sequence is an example of compositing video on video as described in Chapter 4, *Video on Video*.

The following sequence is by After Effects artist Richard Lainhart, who used ElectricImage and After Effects.

"Haiku Setting

under the water

on the rocks resting

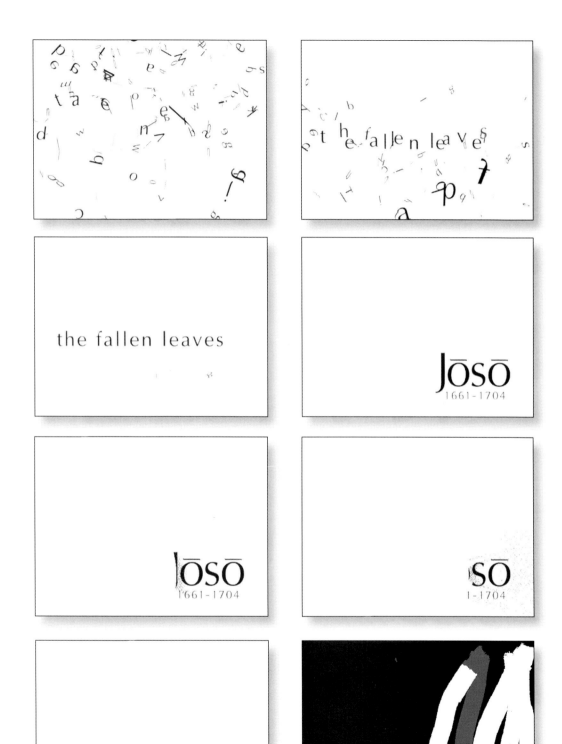

the fallen leaves

Jōsō
1661-1704

Dave Teich created this commercial using Illustrator, form•Z, Bryce and Photoshop. ©Dave Teich, Mind of the Machine.

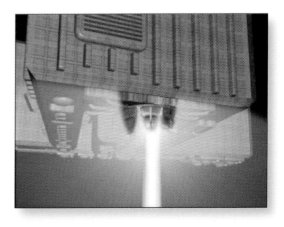

MCI Free Night at the Movies is a film resolution (2048 x 1536) animation created using the After Effects Motion Blur filter. ©Dave Teich, Mind of the Machine.

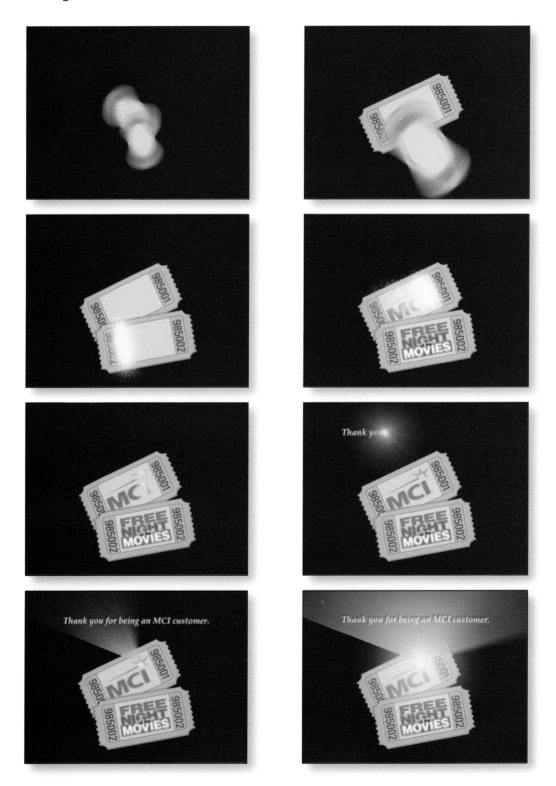

The H.O.R.D.E Concert Tour CD-ROM, produced by Fischer Multimedia Arts for Philips Media, was composited in After Effects to save rendering time.
©Dave Teich, Mind of the Machine.

The following sequence demonstrates working with Illustrator elements as found in Chapter 5, *Using Illustrator Files*.

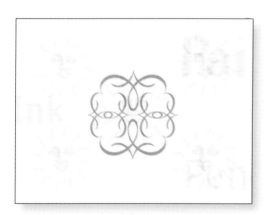

Lawrence Kaplan animated Dark Hearts in After Effects, using Final Effects, form•Z, Photoshop, and ElectricImage. ©1997 Lawrence Kaplan, Hot Tech Multimedia, Inc.

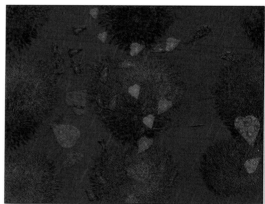

The Poems of Terezin by Dave Teich was created for The Roosevelt Arts Project. ©Dave Teich, Mind of the Machine.

The type for this sequence was created in Photoshop and modified in After Effects using Mr. Mercury and the FloMotion effects from MetaCreations (Chapter 14).

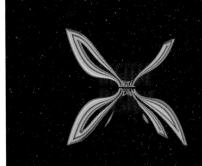

The type for this sequence was created in ElectricImage and composited in After Effects. Final Effects Pixel Poly was used to shatter the type and Studio Effects Time Blend was used to add the trail to the shatter.

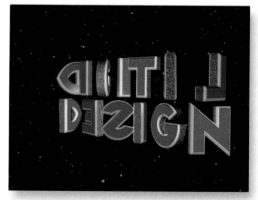

The model in the following sequence was shot on blue screen and composited using the Ultimatte effects. The background was modified with the Cyclonist effect from DigiEffects (Chapter 15, *Third-Party Effects*).

The following sequence was created by Jaime Beauchamp. The 3D work was rendered in Presenter Professional. ©1997 Jaime Beauchamp.

Dave Teich modeled and animated the following commercial for
The Health Rider exercise bike using ElectricImage and After Effects.

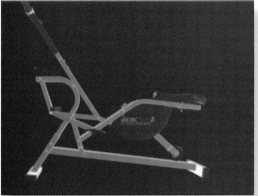

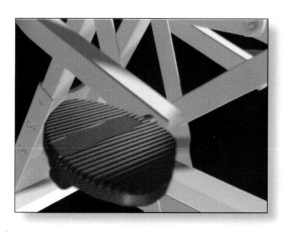

The following sequence is a television commercial created by Marc Steinberg. ©1997 Marc Steinberg.

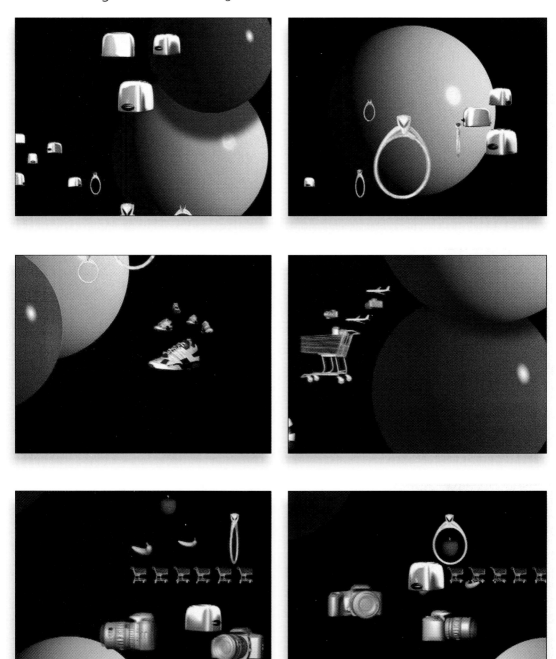

Another series from digital artist Marc Steinberg.

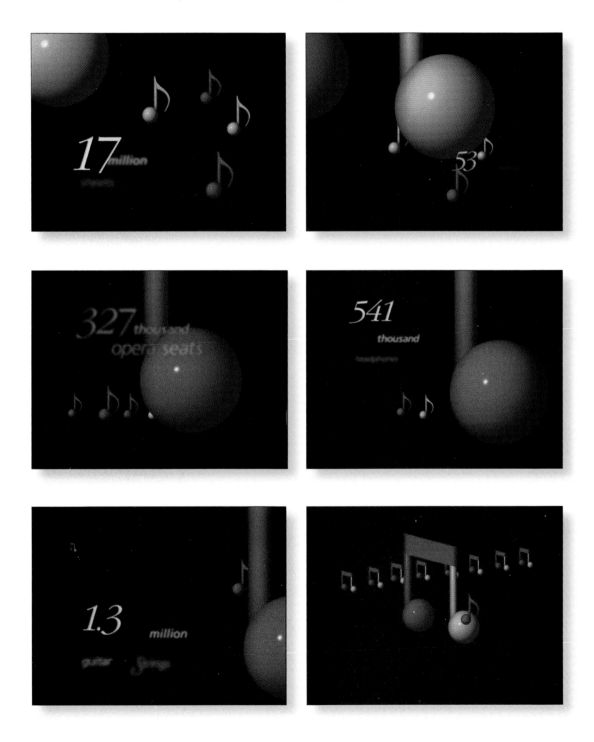

The *Fun in the Sun* sequence, which uses most of After Effects' masking techniques, is the example movie from Chapter 11, *Mattes.*

After

While this chapter is mainly concerned with input sources (the "before" you use After Effects), let's spend a few minutes discussing what happens "after." The programs listed below are common destinations for your After Effects images.

- Director/Authorware
- ClickWorks
- mTropolis
- QuarkImmedia
- Premiere

With the exception of Adobe Premiere (which is also listed in the "Before" section), all of these programs are geared towards multimedia and accept QuickTime movies as input. Macromedia Director is probably the most popular destination for movies that are to be part of a multimedia project. Director is the most widely used of any of the programs for developing interactive presentations, self-running kiosks, and many computer games. Authorware is the even-more-powerful big brother of Director—also from Macromedia.

The newcomers to the field are ClickWorks, mTropolis, and QuarkImmedia. They each take aim at a different facet of the Director market. For example, QuarkImmedia is aimed at the QuarkXPress user who needs to adapt material for multimedia or for the Web. It features an interface that is the same as the XPress interface—mostly because the program is a plug-in (XTension) to XPress and cannot operate without it. However, it uses commands and paradigms that are already familiar to the XPress user. It allows you to designate any XPress element as an Immedia interactive element. Boxes can contain movies; movies can be made into buttons or can be made to follow a path. There is a simple scripting language that is easy to learn and, while not nearly as powerful as Lingo, the full-featured programming language that allows you to script Director presentations, the scripting in Immedia does about 80% of anything that you are most likely to need.

mTropolis is the most widely discussed of the new programs and has some very powerful features. It is hoping to dislodge Director from its spot as number one.

During

There are two utility programs that are essential to the digital video artist. They are:

- DeBabelizer, from Equilibrium
- Movie Cleaner, from Terran International

DeBabelizer

DeBabelizer is the graphic artist Swiss army knife. It can translate from almost any raster format to almost any other raster format. It can perform a large number of functions on an image in batch mode—i.e. on a group of files at one time. For example, you can set it up to

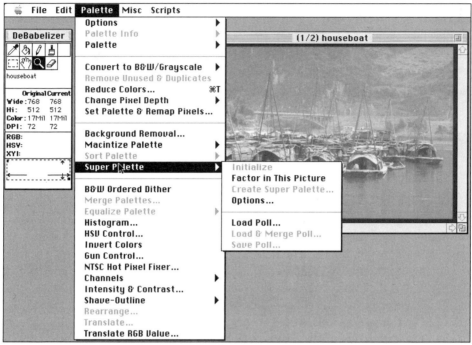

Figure 9-36: DeBabelizer interface showing SuperPalette menu.

read a group of files, change their mode to indexed color, reduce the size of the image, and output the image as a GIF file. This is less critical now that Photoshop 4.0 has Actions, but it is useful nevertheless.

DeBabelizer can accept almost all of the third-party plug-ins for Photoshop and use them in its batch processing. It can also automate third-party filters to create an animation of a filter over a given number of "frames." This is extremely useful for creating a QuickTime movie of a Photoshop filter that has controllable parameters, because a control can be automatically increased for each subsequent frame.

The feature that makes the program most valuable to a multimedia person, however, is its color reduction algorithms. It does a much better job of reducing an image to 256 colors than Photoshop, and it can create a SuperPalette—the one palette of 256 colors that best fits a number of different images. Figure 9-36 shows the DeBabelizer interface and the SuperPalette function. DeBabelizer is available for both the Mac and Windows/NT.

Media Cleaner

Media Cleaner, by Terran International, is a must-have program for the Macintosh digital video person. It allows you to prepare and compress movies for playback from CD-ROM, hard drive, or the Web. It is the program that used most heavily in the preparation of this book. Without it, we would not have been able to place as many examples on the CD-ROM.

Media Cleaner understands compression algorithms (called *codecs*), and it understands the various forms of digital video architecture (frequently called file formats—QuickTime, Video for Windows, and VDOLive). Using a simple question and answer format, Media Cleaner guides you through the process of selecting the right codec and the right settings for the intended use of the movie. Figure 9-37 shows the Media Cleaner interface.

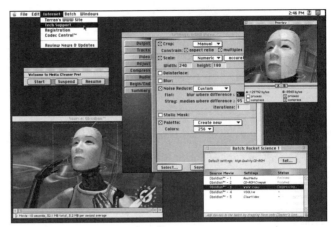

Figure 9-37: Media Cleaner interface

There are many wonderful features in this program. If you are not sure what the compression settings will do, you can compare the results of your decisions on a split "before and after" screen. You can correct for color or for the gamma difference between a PC and Mac monitor while you compress. Once you have found the optimum settings, you can batch process a group of movies. You can connect to the Internet at any time to get the latest updates, the latest codec information (from Codec Central) or find excellent quality tech support. The manual not only shows you how to use the program features, it teaches you *why* to use them. It provides an excellent introduction to the entire technical topic of multimedia and to the multimedia production cycle. It contains excellent tips on capturing video—things that would seem to be only tangential to the use of the program, but which are really essential for the best *intelligent* use of the program.

We will discuss some additional aspects of compression in Chapter 17, but you should make it a point, even if you work on a PC, to visit the Terran website. The URL is http://terran-int.com. They have some excellent tips and guidelines that are helpful throughout the entire production process.

 Rewind

This chapter took you on an extended tour of a number of different applications with input or output that interface with After Effects. You have had a chance to try out several different programs such as Tree, and to use the output from programs including Painter, Detailer, and Bliss Paint. You have also had a chance to play with time remapping and time reversal. We hope that you have also experienced a burst of creativity of the "gee-look-what-else-I-can-do-with-this-stuff" variety, and have had some fun with the chapter.

Coming Attractions

This chapter is the end of the Using a Variety of Input section. The next section discusses special effects. It is in the special effects department, of course, the After Effects excels. No other desktop program can provide so many effects for 2D footage. In the chapters in this next section, you will learn about creating smooth motion using velocity graphs, creating moving mattes, applying and using transfer modes, and using all of the built-in, and most of the available, third-party filters for After Effects.

Section 3
Special Effects

Keyframes and Animation

 **Preview**

The literal meaning of the word "animate" is "to bring to life." This chapter will give you a sense of the tools used in After Effects to give animations the illusion of life. Even though you have been making images move for nine chapters, you have not tried to "animate" them. You have merely moved them along as if they were weightless and in a vacuum. This chapter draws heavily on the experience of Josh Laurence, a talented animator, who works extensively with After Effects. You can read more about Josh in Chapter 19, After Effects Experts.

An animator starts by looking at life itself. Since anything that lives moves in its own particular way, careful observation of patterns of movement will give you a sense of the relationships between factors like speed, weight and gravity. You can move objects easily in After Effects, but the nuances of their movement portray different emotions or feelings that give your animation life.

You might want to stop and think about the walk of some person you know. Pay close attention to how their walk changes when they feel differently. You can sometimes tell a great deal about a person by the way they're walking. Some people walk quickly, some more slowly, some hop, some trip, scoot around, saunter, run, and some just amble. Everyone has a unique way of moving and everyone else has a fairly universal way of understanding what that motion means.

The same principle applies to objects that move although they aren't alive—like cars or jump ropes or salads. Heavy objects move differently than light objects. Heavy objects take a while to get moving if what's pushing them isn't very powerful, and feathers float when dropped because the air lifts and pushes the feather around. Even things that seem most rigid are sometimes very elastic. A taxi leans forward on its front wheels as if it's about to tumble over, when it screeches to a halt at a red light. As it finally stops, it rocks back and forth on its bad shocks a few times before coming to a rest, as if it's on a loose spring. You know that it weighs several tons and that if you kick it, you'll probably stub your toe, but it still moves with great agility.

The point is that how something moves tells the observer what it is. There aren't rigid rules of animation that apply to everything, but there are some general ideas that apply to many things. Once you have a good sense of some of these principles and can use the tools in After Effects, you can portray almost any kind of motion, and you can begin to develop your own style of animation.

Although you have been using keyframes for quite a while in this book, you have not yet met the advanced features of keyframes. It is these advanced features that allow you to create a convincing animation.

In this chapter, you will learn how to:

- Differentiate between the types of keyframes that After Effects can create.

- Create a variety of motion keyframes.

- Create Velocity and Spatial curves.

- Graph a variety of curves and change one type to another.

- Use the different types of curves to create smooth or convincing motion.

 # Feature Presentation

If you move an object from one side of the screen to the other, this is said to be animation. To move an object in After Effects, set the object where you want it at the beginning, set it where you want it to end, and voilá! The program "in-betweens" or "interpolates" the rest for you. Interpolating means that it figures out how much and in what direction to move the object in order for it to arrive at the end at the desired time. That's the easy part—and the part that you have already done. Making it get from one place to another in an interesting way is the challenge.

You have learned these basics of keyframes already:

- Whenever any aspect of an element changes over time, there are keyframes involved.

- When an object starts or stops changing, or when its change is significantly altered, a keyframe is needed.

- You can set keyframes for almost any attribute of an element that you can change.

- The position of the Current Time marker is important when you decide to add a keyframe.

    🐔 You need to make sure that you can see one of the attributes of the element you want to animate when you want to create a keyframe for it.

    🐔 Click once inside the stop watch next to the attribute and you've made an initial keyframe at that point in time.

    🐔 Move the Current Time marker to another point on the time line and change the value for the same attribute, and the program automatically adds an additional keyframe at that frame. It can now interpolate motion between the two.

    🐔 Once you've set keyframes, you can move them interactively in the Time Layout window. You can also copy and paste keyframes, singularly or in groups.

The Many Flavors of Keyframes

Keyframes in After Effects come in three colors: shaded, half shaded, or not shaded (for our purposes, we'll call them "hollow"). A fully shaded keyframe means that there is no other keyframe for that specific property of an element. Once you have two keyframes, the first one is shaded on its left half, and the second (last) one is shaded on the right half. If you make a change in between those two keyframes, then you'll get a hollow keyframe. The shading is just a way to let you know whether there are more keyframes and if they are before or after the one with which you are working.

Keyframes also come in four basic icon shapes: square, diamond, circle, and hourglass. The shapes describe the motion of the keyframe. Many times the keyframe consists of a different shape on each side. The shape on the left describes the motion as you come into the keyframe, and the shape on the right describes the motion as you exit from a keyframe.

The diamond, as shown in Figure 10-1, is a linear keyframe. The linear keyframe means that the rate of change is constant. If you have an object rotating with linear movement, then it rotates the same amount in every frame until it gets to the end, or the Current Time marker passes through a different kind of keyframe.

The square, shown in Figure 10-2, is a hold keyframe. The hold keyframe means that the value at the keyframe is held until

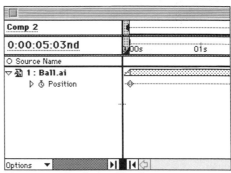

Figure 10-1: The diamond keyframe.

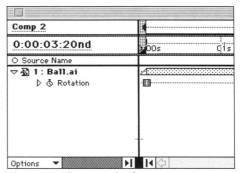

Figure 10-2: The square keyframe.

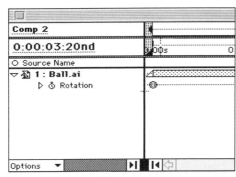

Figure 10-3: The circle keyframe.

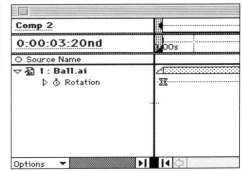

Figure 10-4: The Bezier (hourglass) keyframe.

the next keyframe. (We call these "sustaining" keyframes, but have not "formally" changed them into hold keyframes yet.)

The circle keyframe, shown in Figure 10-3, is an Auto Bezier Keyframe. An Auto Bezier keyframe automatically smooths the rate of change so that whatever is changing doesn't make any sharp or sudden adjustments to the values at that keyframe.

The hourglass, shown in Figure 10-4, is the *Bezier* or *Continuous Bezier* keyframe. The Bezier or Continuous Bezier keyframe is one where the rate of change for the property being animated is manually adjusted.

Often, when you change only the incoming or outgoing portion of the keyframe, you get a shape that looks like an arrowhead. The center keyframe in Figure 10-5 is a half-Bezier, half-linear keyframe. It shows that the motion graph (which we will discuss later in this chapter) has been manually adjusted coming into the

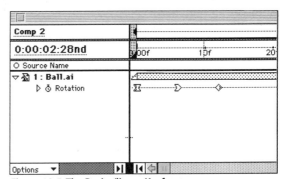

Figure 10-5: The Bezier/linear Keyframe.

specific point along the time line, but that the motion of the object is linear going out of the keyframe.

After Effects lets you add additional keyframes in either the Time Layout window or the Comp window. When you change the shape of a path by dragging an element or its Bezier handles around from within the Comp window, you're affecting the *Spatial Interpolation* of a keyframe. When you change a property over time from within the Time Layout window, you're affecting the *Temporal Interpolation*. Now that you've been given the formal definition of the difference, just know that *you can't change the shape of a path from the Time Layout window; you have to be in the Comp window.* If you want to change the type of keyframe in that path, you change it from the Layer → Keyframe Interpolation dialog box.

And when you want to change any other aspect of the keyframe, you change it in the Time Layout window.

Setting Up

So far, we've talked about some of the principles of animation and some of the tools After Effects provides to do the animating. In the following project, we're going to make an element—a ball—appear to bounce. First we need to make it move and then we'll animate it.

 Studio Time: Bouncing Ball Comp

1. Create a new Comp (Mac: Cmd-N, Windows: Ctrl-N), 320 x 240 pixels, 2 seconds long, 30 frames per second. Name it Bouncing Ball Comp and set the Background to white (Mac: Shift-Cmd-B, Windows: Shift-Ctrl-B).

2. Set the Current Time to 00 (Mac: Cmd-G, Windows: Ctrl-G, then type 0).

3. Import the Ball.ai file from the AE10Foot folder (Mac: Cmd-I, Windows: Ctrl-I).

4. Save the Project.

5. Select the Illustrator image (the Ball.ai file) and drag it to the center of the Composition window. (Hint: if you don't see the full circle of the ball, you have forgotten to change your background to white!) Press the Tab key to deselect.

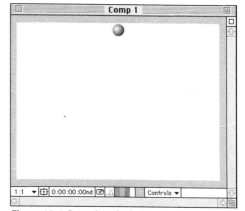

Figure 10-6: Dragging the ball to the top.

6. Drag the ball to the top of the image area, as shown in Figure 10-6. Keep the Shift key pressed after you start to drag, to constrain the movement vertically.

7. Press P to display the Position property. Click in the stop watch to make it keyframeable, as shown in Figure 10-7.

8. Set the Current Time to 1:00 seconds (Mac: Cmd-G, Windows: Ctrl-G, and type 100, or just move the Playback Head until the Current Time reads 0:00:01:00).

9. Drag the ball (using the Shift key to constrain its

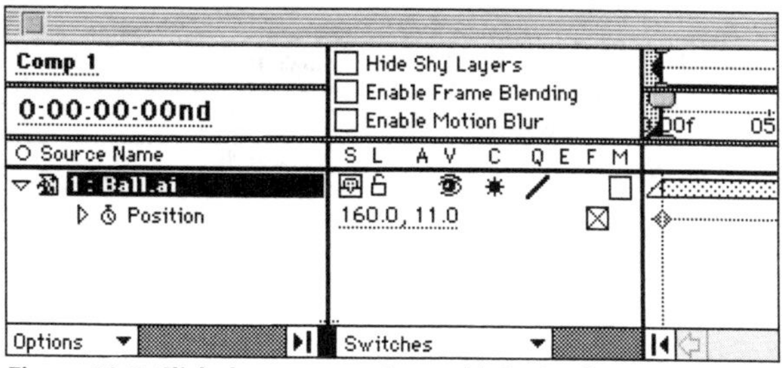

Figure 10-7: Click the stop watch to add the keyframe.

motion) to the bottom of the screen (see Figure 10-8).

10. Move the Current Time marker to the last frame by hitting the End key on the numeric keypad (or type the letter O).

11. Click on the keyframe that you created at Time=00 and copy it to the clipboard (Mac: Cmd-C, Windows: Ctrl-C). Paste in the selection from the clipboard (Mac: Cmd-V, Windows: Ctrl-V). A copy of the keyframe appears at the last frame of the layer— because that is where the Current Time marker is located.

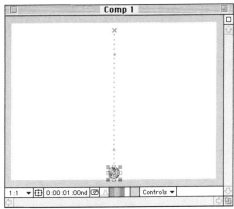

Figure 10-8: Dragging the ball to the bottom.

12. Press the "0" key on the numeric keypad to preview the motion in the alpha channel (or go to Composition → Preview → Motion (Work Area)).

The wireframe of the ball moves up and down, but it looks like it's in outer space— without any of the effects of gravity. If the bottom of the Comp window were the earth, then the ball would accelerate as it dropped and decelerate as the pull of gravity slowed its rise. Let's see what we can do about this.

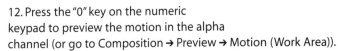

Figure 10-9: Revealing the Position velocity graph.

13. Turn the arrow down by the word "Position" and you'll see the velocity graph for the speed of the position change, as shown in Figure 10-9. If you highlight the first keyframe, you get a Bezier handle right below the Bezier keyframe.

14. Drag the handle to the bottom of the graph to signify that the ball does not move when the animation begins. (The handle is the tiny diamond. As you drag it toward the bottom of the graph, it changes into a larger circle.) Figure 10-10 shows the Bezier handle dragged to the bottom of the graph.

15. Select the last keyframe, and drag

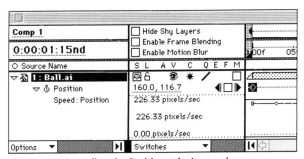

Figure 10-10: Dragging the Bezier to the bottom.

its outgoing handle to the bottom. Ideally, this slows it to a stop at the top of the rise. Preview the motion. The ball seems to exhibit better motion, but it doesn't stop when it gets to the top and it doesn't hit hard enough to be realistic when it gets to the bottom.

16. Grab the handle for the first keyframe (you need to click on the keyframe first in order to select it) and drag it to the right. (If you look in the Info palette, it will tell you how much influence you're giving the curve. Bring it to 100%.) Notice what happens to the curve. It seems to accelerate over time, but it dips just as it gets to the middle. Do the same to the final keyframe, pulling the outgoing handle to the left. Preview the motion.

17. Save the Comp.

The last change really makes a difference. You've given the motion a realistic quality by assigning it acceleration and deceleration with linear/Bezier keyframes. This looks more like something we would see every day since the pull of gravity affects everything on earth.

Smooshing the Ball

Now that you've created a realistic bounce to the ball, it's time to make the ball more lifelike. When you drop an object, it behaves differently upon impact. The difference is determined by the substance from which it is made. If it's an egg, it breaks upon impact. If it's a golf ball, it ricochets. If it's a rubber ball (which we're trying to simulate), then it squashes as it hits and regains its shape as it recovers.

To make it squash, we need to do two things. First, we'll move the Anchor point and then we'll scale it. The squash is going to demonstrate several very important rules about animation:

Rule 1: An object changes shape often, but it can never lose volume. This is important to remember because it will give your animations more life and character.

Rule 2: Almost all actions in animation should be exaggerated as much possible—without losing the sense of the action.

Rule 3: All objects have some elasticity in them and they squash and stretch as other forces act upon them.

 Studio Time: Impact

1. Set the Current Time to 00 (Mac: Cmd-G, Windows: Ctrl-G, then type 0).

2. Select the Ball.ai element in the Time Layout window.

3. Zoom into the Comp window to an 8:1 level. Scroll your window as needed so that you see the ball.

4. Select the Pan-behind tool (Y) from the Tool palette.

5. Click on the Anchor point for the ball and drag the Anchor point to the bottom center of the bounding box of the Ball.ai element, as shown in Figure 10-11.

6. Select the Pointer tool (Q).

7. Zoom out to 1:1

8. Set the Current Time to 1:00 seconds (Mac: Cmd-G, Windows: Ctrl-G, and type 100, or just move the Playback Head until the Current Time reads 0:00:01:00).

Notice that the ball is now slightly above the bottom of the Comp because we've moved the center of the element from where it was in step 5. Since the Position keyframes are based on the position of the Anchor point, the ball appears to have moved up at the hit point. We should change that.

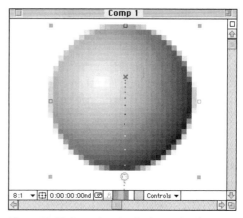

Figure 10-11: Dragging the Anchor point down.

9. Using the "Click, drag, then click the Shift key" method of constraining the movement on one axis, drag the ball to the bottom of the Comp (approximately position 160, 240).

Since we want to create a loop of the motion of the ball (I'm assuming you do, so go with it for now), it's going to be pretty difficult to get the exact position of the ball from the beginning to the end. If you paste the first keyframe here, it will not work the way that you expect it to. The first keyframe is a combination keyframe that goes from no motion into a Bezier and it would give you a less-than-desireable result at the end. It's better to get the numerical data from the first frame and enter that for the last frame.

10. Set the Current Time to 00 (Mac: Cmd-G, Windows: Ctrl-G, then type 0) or press the Home key on the numeric keypad.

11. Note the position for the first frame (it should be pretty close to 160, 30—if it isn't, change it to 160, 30).

12. Move the marker to the end of the time line (O) or press the End key.

13. Click once on the Position value in the Time Layout window. Enter 160, 30, as shown in Figure 10-12.

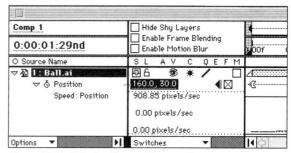

Figure 10-12: Entering the position numbers.

14. Preview the action.

It should look identical to where you had it before you moved the Anchor point. If it doesn't, then repeat the steps. If you're asking "So?" at this point, follow along for a few more steps as we're about to head into the next level.

15. Set the Current Time to 0.

16. Press Shift-S to display the Scale property, in addition to the displayed Position property.

17. Click in the stop watch to make Scale a keyframeable property.

18. Move the Current Time marker to the end of the Comp (O).

19. Click in the Keyframe Navigation box to add a Scale keyframe here as well. While it looks like it is a sustaining keyframe, it will not be by the time we finish with it!

20. Set the Current Time to 1 second.

21. With the Ball.ai element selected, grab the upper-right or left handle of the element and squash the ball down and pull it slightly out, as shown in Figure 10-13.

22. Preview the motion. Save your work.

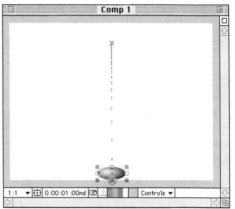

Figure 10-13: Squashing the ball element.

This looks interesting, but the ball seems to squash before it actually hits the bottom of the Comp. We need it to hold its shape until it hits, then squash upon impact. The next Studio Time shows you how to make the ball squash only after it hits the ground.

 Studio Time: Getting the Impact Right—Part 1

1. Select the Scale keyframe at 00:00 (because we want it to hold from the beginning to the next keyframe) and toggle it to a "hold keyframe" by choosing Layer →Toggle Hold Keyframe (Mac: Cmd-Opt-H, Windows: Ctrl-Alt-H).

2. Preview the motion.

3. The ball seems to hold the squash a little long. Drag the final scale keyframe to earlier and later positions along the Time Line until the motion and the feeling seem right to you.

4. For that matter, leave the Current Time marker at 1:00 and play with the squash of the object to see what different shapes do to the feeling of the bounce.

5. Save the project.

At this point, we're going to cover one more type of keyframe—the roving keyframe. It's called that because it moves around and is dependent on the influence of the non-roving keyframes before and after it. Let's see how that one works.

If you look at the velocity graph for the Position keyframes, you notice that the crest dips in the center, as shown in Figure 10-14.

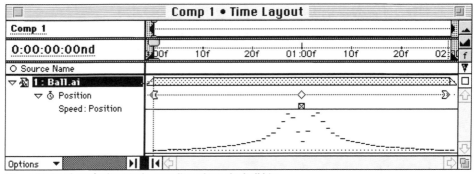

Figure 10-14: The velocity graph crest dips where the ball hits.

The dip is right at the hollow linear keyframe where the ball actually hits. The dip in the curve means that the change in position slows and stops at that point. This is not realistic, and if we played the animation slowly, we'd see that the ball slows before it hits bottom. We need a way to make the ball continue its acceleration through the hit, and start its deceleration as it rises back up.

 ## Studio Time: The Roving Keyframe

1. The checkbox below the middle keyframe controls turning the keyframe into a roving keyframe. Uncheck it by clicking once in the box.

2. Select the first keyframe.

3. Grab the Bezier handle in the velocity graph, and while watching the influence readout in the Info Palette, change the influence to 65% from 100%. See Figure 10-15.

4. Do the same for the last keyframe. You need to make sure that the Bezier handle is dragged to the bottom of the graph as well, or the roving keyframe gets too far from 1 second.

5. Preview the motion.

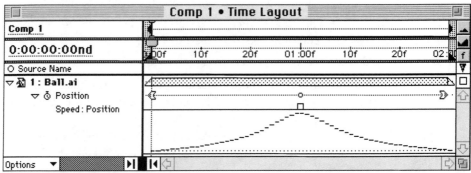

Figure 10-15: Changing the last Bezier handle.

6. You may need to reposition the ball at 1:00 so it hits the bottom of the frame. If you reposition it, you'll also need to uncheck the box below the middle keyframe again to restore the roving keyframe.

7. You'll notice the ball does exactly what it should.

8. Now that the ball is bouncing and squashing, we can make it bounce through the frame.

9. Set the Current Time to 00 (Mac: Cmd-G, Windows: Ctrl-G, then type 0).

10. Select the ball in the Comp window and drag it. Once it has started moving, hold down the Shift key to constrain its horizontal movement the same way you previously constrained its vertical movement. Move the ball offscreen to the left.

11. Move the Current Time marker to the layer Out point.

12. Select the ball again in the Comp window and drag it off screen to the right.

13. You'll notice that the motion path of the ball is shaped like the letter "U."

14. Preview the motion. This doesn't feel right at all. We need to affect the Spatial qualities of the keyframes. The only way to do that is from within the Comp window.

15. Set the Current Time to 00 (Mac: Cmd-G, Windows: Ctrl-G, then type 0).

16. Select the ball in the window (the actual ball is hidden because it doesn't get drawn when it's not onscreen—but the outline of the element is clear).

17. Just below and to the right of the element is the Bezier handle for that Position keyframe. Grab it and pull it parallel to the bottom of the screen (pull it directly to the right, as shown in Figure 10-16).

18. Move the marker to the keyframe at the end, find the Bezier handle, and do the same.

19. Preview the motion.

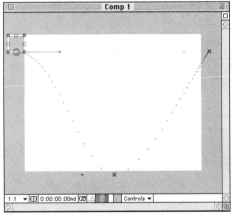

Figure 10-16: Moving the Bezier handle for the position keyframe.

There is still something wrong. The ball seems to slide through the middle keyframe at the bottom. This doesn't feel right because objects tend to move perpendicular or close to perpendicular to the ground when they hit. This is because gravity influences the object more than its momentum to travel horizontally. We need to change the roving Auto Bezier keyframe to a roving Bezier keyframe. But we need to do it from within the Comp window. There are two ways to accomplish this, which we will document in the next two—very short—Studio Times.

Studio Time: Roving Bezier Keyframes—Method 1

1. Select the keyframe in the middle.

2. Select Layer→Keyframe Interpolation (Mac: Shift-Cmd-Opt-K, Windows: Shift-Ctrl-Alt-K)).

3. For the Spatial interpolation, select Bezier, leaving the other two options untouched.

4. Press OK to exit the dialog.

 Studio Time: Roving Bezier Keyframes—Method 2

1. Select the keyframe in the middle

2. Holding down the Control key (on both Mac or Windows), drag the cursor over either Bezier handle until the cursor changes to an open arrow pointing towards the upper left corner.

3. Click and drag the Bezier handle a short distance.

4. Once the handle is dragged in this manner, the constraining link between each side of the Bezier handle is broken, and each half can be positioned separately. Let go of the Control key; you don't need to hold the it down any longer. If you do, it will change the Bezier keyframe back to an Auto Bezier keyframe and establish a continuous handle for the keyframe as before.

 Studio Time: Finishing the Motion

1. Change the middle keyframe to a Bezier keyframe using Method 1 or Method 2 (you may want to try it each way to see which is most comfortable to you).

2. Pull the Bezier handle perpendicular to the bottom of the screen (straight up, as shown in Figure 10-17).

3. Do the same for the handle on the other side of the keyframe.

4. Preview the motion. This looks a lot better!

Now you are ready to string together a bunch of these bouncing balls to make a composition.

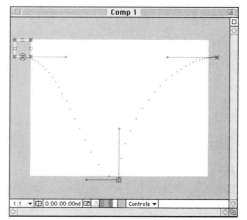

Figure 10-17: Making the Bezier perpendicular.

Studio Time: Adding More Bounce to Your Comp

1. Increase the length of your Composition to 3:18 seconds by selecting Composition→ Composition Settings (Mac: Cmd-K, Windows: Ctrl-K).

2. Make seven copies (Duplicate—Mac: Cmd-D, Windows: Ctrl-D) of this finished layer.

3. Set the Current Time to 5 frames (Mac: Cmd-G, Windows: Ctrl-G, and type 5, or just move the Playback Head until the Current Time reads 0:00:00:05). Place your cursor in the center of the time line ribbon for Layer 2, and start dragging toward the right, and just after you begin to drag, press the Shift key. The time line ribbon snaps to the Current Time marker. Since you need to repeat this for six more layers, let's call this motion "Shift-Drag." Remember, you can also set the position of the time line ribbon by pressing the Left bracket key ([) on either platform.

4. Set the Current Time to 12 and Shift-drag Layer 3 to that time, or press the Left bracket key ([).

5. Set the Current Time to 19 and Shift-drag Layer 4 to that time, or press the Left bracket key ([).

6. Set the Current Time to 25 and Shift-drag Layer 5 to that time, or press the Left bracket key ([).

7. Set the Current Time to 102 and Shift-drag Layer 6 to that time, or press the Left bracket key ([).

8. Set the Current Time to 110 and Shift-drag Layer 7 to that time, or press the Left bracket key ([).

9. Set the Current Time to 118 and Shift-drag Layer 8 to that time or press the Left bracket key ([).

10. Set the Quality switches to Best for all layers. Turn on the Continuously Rasterize switch for each layer, and click the M box to enable Motion Blur.

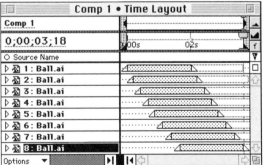

Figure 10-18: Showing the footage that has been offset.

Your results should look like Figure 10-18.

 **Rewind**

There you have it. You've just seen how to animate an object in the most realistic way possible. You can use what you've just learned in this lesson to animate anything in After Effects.

In this chapter, you have learned about the four different types of keyframe shapes (Linear, Hold, Auto Bezier, and Bezier) and how each of them works. You have seen and experienced the difference that the optimum use of these keyframe types can make. The ability to utilize these motion facilities separates the artist from the technician.

You have just begun to scratch the surface of the animation possibilities in After Effects, but you have all of the technical knowledge. What is missing is an appreciation for classical animation techniques that truly breathe life into an object. There are excellent sources in the library or in the bookstores about animation. Anything written about Disney animation is highly recommended.

One of the hottest areas in the animation and After Effects fields right now is for character animators—people who can create a ketchup bottle with an attitude or a bar of soap with a slippery personality. You have learned how to give a ball a bit of reality by squashing it as it hits the ground. By creating other deformations that are linked to motion, and other arrangements of the Hold, Bezier, and Auto Bezier keyframes, you could create a ball whose attitude says "Watch me…. I'm not going to be squashed when I hit the floor—I'll just roll over."

If you feel like you've missed something from this lesson, go back and retry it until you have a full understanding of the principles involved. Most of the remaining chapters tell you to go back and smooth the motion graphs as a final step. Now you know what that means.

 # Coming Attractions

Do you know how to simulate a searchlight moving across an object, or a ripple of color floating across a piece of text? How about creating a sun that sets, and type that circles the sun and sets with it? The next chapter will show you how to create mattes that let you accomplish these things. A matte is a mask, but unlike the stationery alphas with which you have worked so far, a matte is a traveling alpha; it can move while your footage either moves too, or sits around and is revealed by the action of the matte. You can create mattes based on shapes (alpha mattes) or mattes based on image density (luma mattes). The possibilities are endless.

Mattes

 **Preview**

If you have ever used masks or alpha channels in Photoshop, you know how much power these features can add to your ability to create an image. You have already used alpha channels in a number of the Studio Times in this book to hide or reveal image areas.

Just as After Effects sometimes seems like Photoshop on figure skates (i.e. you can make all your images move around and dance), so, too, can you make the alpha channels—by using them as track mattes—move around and skate. After Effects lets you create a *track matte*—basically an alpha channel that travels along with a footage item in a layer. To use another Photoshop analogy, it is somewhat like the clipping groups, where you can show only that portion of a layer that conforms to the opaque pixels beneath. In After Effects, however, it is the layer on top that becomes the track matte and determines what portions of the layer below it will be hidden or revealed.

Photoshop allows you to have alpha channels that are black and white or which contain grayscale values to partially hide or reveal areas; After Effects track mattes can be used as alphas (solid areas which hide or show the shape of item in the track matte), or as luma track mattes (think luminance), which hide or reveal areas based on the gray values in the track matte. You can also invert these track mattes to reverse their effects.

CHAPTER 11

The best part about track mattes is that they can be animated. You can change the shape, location, opacity, or any other property of the track matte just as if it were a regular layer. You can then use this layer to determine how much of the layer beneath it is visible. Awesome power is at your fingertips!

Preview the AECH11.mov movie. Don't panic! You *will* be able to create the effects you see! This movie uses almost every matting technique that can be crammed into one project. In this chapter you will learn how to:

- Create an alpha track matte.
- Create an alpha inverted track matte.
- Create a luma matte.
- Create a matte which causes a ripple to travel through text.
- Use the Mask properties of a layer.
- Create a rectangular mask.
- Create a see-saw mask to help control type.
- Create a Bezier mask matte that changes shape as the movie progresses.
- Create layer markers for ease in reading the Time Layout window.

 # Feature Presentation

The best way to learn about matting is to dive in and do it. Just to get you started, though, and to make sure that you understand the concept of matting, let's start with an author-set-up project that you just need to view.

 ## Studio Time: What Is a Track Matte?

1. Open the Project Simpmat.aep located in the AE11Done folder of the CD-ROM. Notice that the project has only three layers, a solid layer on top, and two movie layers.

2. Set the Current Time to 00 (Mac: Cmd-G, Windows: Ctrl-G, then type 0).

3. Press the spacebar to preview the Comp. Notice Beach.mov turns into Grandpa.mov as the project progresses, and then turns back into Beach.mov.

Why does this happen? What is causing the transition between the layers? The answer is that a *track matte* is causing the transition. A track matte is an image that resides in the layer above the "matted" layer and is used to control the opacity of the layer that it mattes. You can determine how the program "sees" the track matte in several different ways. In the example here, we used the shape of the solid layer (a rectangle the same size as the movie) as the track matte to determine the opacity of the Grandpa.mov below it.

At Time=0, the solid layer is physically positioned just outside the Comp window. As we said, the solid layer has been defined as an alpha track matte for Grandpa.mov, which means that you can see only the parts of Grandpa.mov that lie directly under the track matte. Since the track matte is off the screen when the movie starts, Grandpa.mov is hidden, and Beach.mov is revealed.

As the track matte enters the Comp window, Grandpa.mov begins to conceal Beach.mov; as the track matte leaves the Comp window, Grandpa.mov begins to reveal Beach.mov.

You can think of the track matte as being a light that illuminates Grandpa.mov. When the light is on, you can see Grandpa.mov; when the light is off, Grandpa.mov is hidden thus revealing the movie below it (Beach.mov).

The solid layer is filled with a Ramp effect—a black-to-white Gradient. If you were to change the matte type to luma matte, only areas of the track matte that were solid white would show 100% of the layer beneath. You will learn how to do that very soon. For now, close the project. Let's start on the "real thing."

Using the Mask Properties of a Layer

Let's first explore the topic of matting and masking by seeing how you can create a mask within a layer. One of the layer properties that we have ignored so far is the Mask. If, instead of selectively revealing properties such as Position, Scale, or Opacity, you simply turn down the arrow in front of a layer in the Time Layout window, you see that you have Mask properties and Geometry properties. The Geometry properties contain the Scale and Opacity, etc. that you have already used. The Mask properties allow you to hide and show areas of your image. You can also animate the mask.

 Studio Time: Setting Up the Beaches Comp

1. Create a new project (Mac: Cmd-Opt-N, Windows: Alt-Ctrl-N).

2. Create a new Comp (Mac: Cmd-N, Windows: Ctrl-N). Call it "Beaches." It should be 320 x 240, 30 fps, and 10 seconds long. Change the Background to white (Mac: Shift-Cmd-B, Windows: Shift-Ctrl-B).

3. Import the Beach.mov file from the AE11Foot folder (Mac: Cmd-I, Windows: Ctrl-I, and select the file in the dialog box). Drag it from the Project Window in to the center of the Comp Window. Duplicate it (Mac: Cmd-D, Windows: Ctrl-D) three times for a total of four movies in the Time Layout Window.

4. Select the top movie and rename it Low L (for lower left) by pressing the Return/Enter key. Press the M key to see the mask shape and click on the word "rectangle." The cursor in Figure 11-1 shows the location. Set the

Figure 11-1: Time Layout window showing mask type.

value of Top to 126, Left: 0, Right: 159, and Bottom: 240 as shown in Figure 11-2.

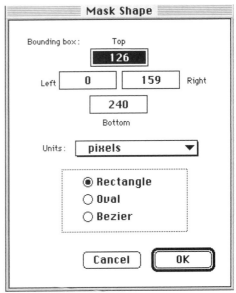

Figure 11-2: Mask Shape dialog box.

5. Double click on the movie title in the Layout window. You will see that there is a small rectangle there. The rectangle is the mask for which we just set values. Click on the Controls drop-down menu in the Movie Preview window. Scroll down to Mask Handles. This option allows you to adjust the mask parameters by hand. If you adjust the mask, the changes are reflected in the Comp window. If you scroll down to Mask Vertices and adjust the points, the points around the mask will change the actual shape of the mask instead of its size. If you have made any changes to the mask via your experiments, Undo them (Mac: Cmd-Z, Windows: Ctrl-Z) before continuing.

6. Select the next movie in the hierarchy (Layer 2). Rename it Up L. Set its mask points for Top: 0, Left: 0, Right: 159, and Bottom: 127.

7. Rename the movie copy in Layer 3 as Up R. It will mask out the upper-right portion of the video. Its mask values should be Top: 0, Left: 158, Right: 320, Bottom: 125.

8. The last movie will be named Low R. Set its mask values to Top: 120, Left: 158, Right: 320, Bottom: 241.

9. Now we will use the Color Balance HLS to colorize each movie. Select all of the layers (Mac: Cmd-A, Windows: Ctrl-A). Choose Effect→ Image Ctrlt→Color Balance (HSL). You can choose your own colors or use ours. Set a constant Hue value for each layer (no keyframe needed). The Hue values that we used are Low L layer: 70, Up L layer: 140, Up R layer: -110, for Low R: 141. Figure 11-3 shows the Color Balance Effect Controls window.

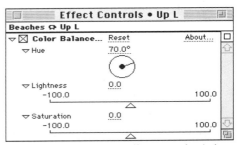

Figure 11-3: Color Balance Effect Controls window.

10. Preview the Comp. Notice how it plays the four colored movies as if they are one solid movie. Save the Project and close the Comp.

How did we decide on the mask values for each layer? As you might have guessed, the rectangular masks that we created were roughly each one-quarter of the total Comp size of 320 x 240. One would therefore expect the Up L portion, for example, to be set to Top: 0, Left: 0, and it was. The right edge of the mask was also predictable. With 320 pixels across, and the numbering of the pixels running from 0-319, the halfway point is 159, and that is exactly where we placed the mask. There is a natural break at the horizon line in the video, however, and that break is not at the exact halfway point in the Comp. Therefore, we used the horizon line measurement of 127 as the break point for the masks. In addition, we permitted a small overlap to make sure that no white edges appear in the final movie.

Preparing the Track Matte-to-be

In the final, everything-put-together Comp, The Beaches Comp appears as a single layer. It needs to be masked so that it can show just part of the movie. Let's set up a Comp to later act as a track matte.

Studio Time: The Square Comp

1. Import the Square.ai file from the AE11Foot folder (Mac: Cmd-I, Windows: Ctrl-I, and then select the correct file) into the Project. It is an Illustrator file.

2. Create a new Comp and name it "Square Comp." Make it 320 x 240, 10 seconds long, and 30 fps. Set the background color to white (Mac: Shift-Cmd-B, Windows: Shift-Ctrl-B).

3. Set the Current Time to 00 (Mac: Cmd-G, Windows: Ctrl-G, then type 0).

4. Drag the square element to the center of the Comp window. Press P to show the Position property. Set the position to 160, 110 as a constant as shown in Figure 11-04. Figure 11-05 shows the Comp window.

5. Set the Current Time to 1:00 seconds (Mac: Cmd-G, Windows: Ctrl-G, and type 100, or just move the Playback Head until the Current Time reads 0:00:01:00). Press S to show the Scale property and click in the stop watch to make it keyframeable. The Scale value should be set to 180%, 135%. You need to uncheck the Preserve Frame Aspect Ratio box in order to enter different percentages for the height and width. Figure 11-6 shows this dialog box.

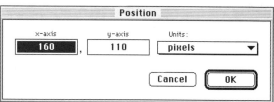

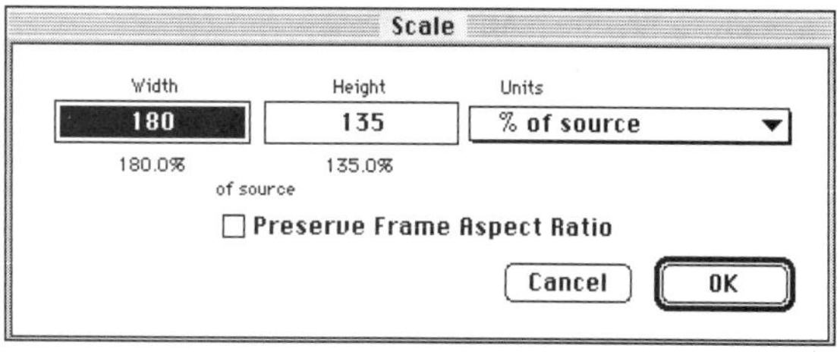

Figure 11-4: Position Dialog.

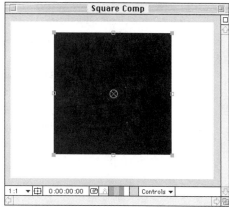

Figure 11-5: Square.ai correctly positioned in the Comp window.

Figure 11-6: Scale dialog showing asymmetric scale.

6. Go to 2 seconds. Make a Scale keyframe. The Scale value should be set to 130%, 95%. Set the layer to Continuously Rasterize and set the Quality to High. Close the Comp.

Consider for a moment what you have just done. You have taken a square and resized it asymmetrically over time. Should you have started with a rectangle? There is no reason to. In fact, the Square.ai file can and should become one of your library elements—a sort of After Effects "clip art" effect that you can move from project to project. Anytime you need a rectangular mask, you have one. Since you can resize to any percentage, and the Continuously Rasterize switch (re-read Chapter 5 if you don't remember) keeps all of your edges sharp and crisp, there is no need to create a new rectangle in any other project. The real fun starts when we use this rectangle as a track matte. First, however, we need another matte layer for the sun. This is a similar process, but the shape is circular rather than rectangular.

Studio Time: The Circle Matte

We need to build the animation in which the center circle will be the sun. The finished animation uses a track matte to produce that effect. Let's make the mask for that track matte.

1. Create a new Comp (Mac: Cmd-N, Windows: Ctrl-N). Name it Circle Matte. Make it 320 x 240, 10 seconds long, 30 fps, and set the background color to white (Mac: Shift-Cmd-B, Windows: Shift-Ctrl-B).

2. Import the circle.ai file from the footage folder.

3. Set the Current Time to 00 (Mac: Cmd-G, Windows: Ctrl-G, then type 0). Drag the Circle.ai file to the center of the Comp window. The circle is another Illustrator element, and just like the rectangle used in the Square Comp, it can be resized as needed to make a circular or elliptical matte.

4. Set the Current Time to 0:15 seconds (15 frames) (Mac: Cmd-G, Windows: Ctrl-G, and type 15, or just move the Playback Head until the Current Time reads 0:00:00:15). Press S to display the Scale property. Set a keyframe for Scale at 125%.

5. Set the Current Time to 1:25 seconds (Mac: Cmd-G, Windows: Ctrl-G, and type 125, or just move the Playback Head until the Current Time reads 0:00:01:25). Set an another keyframe for Scale at 35%.

6. Let's make the sun set. Set the Current Time to 8:20 seconds (Mac: Cmd-G, Windows: Ctrl-G, and type 820, or just move the Playback Head until the Current Time reads

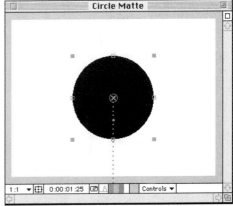

Figure 11-7: Circle Matte complete with motion path.

0:00:08:20). Press Shift-P to display the Position property. Click in the stop watch to make it keyframeable. Set the position to 160, 120.

7. Go to Time=9:20, and set the second keyframe with values of 160, 325. Set the layer to Continuously Rasterize with Quality set to High. Preview and close the Comp. Figure 11-7 shows the circle with the motion path that moves it off the screen.

Creating Track Mattes

Now that you have some Comps to use as track mattes, you need to create the Comp that will bring everything together. Your finished project is rendered from this "Container" Comp, and once you have created it, you can define your first track mattes.

 Studio Time: Building the Container Comp

The Container Comp acts as the container for the entire project. It is actually the movie that will be rendered. All the pieces that you have created come together here (though not quite yet).

1. Create a new Comp (Mac: Cmd-N, Windows: Ctrl-N). Name it Container Comp. It should 320 x 240, 30 fps, and 10 seconds long. Set the background color to white (Mac: Shift-Cmd-B, Windows: Shift-Ctrl-B).

2. Set the Current Time to 00 (Mac: Cmd-G, Windows: Ctrl-G, then type 0).

3. Drag in the Beaches Comp. Let it snap to the center. Place the Square Comp as well. Figure 11-8 shows the Comp Window. Make sure that the Square Comp is above the Beaches Comp in the Layer stack as shown in Figure 11-9. It's not very exciting, but we'll fix that problem.

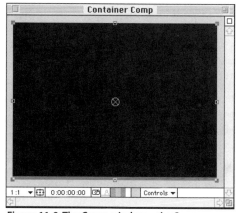

Figure 11-8: The Comp window—the Square Comp on top of the Beaches Comp.

Figure 11-9: Time Layout window—the Square Comp on top of the Beaches Comp.

4. In the Time Layout window, change the Switches pop-up to Transfer Controls. Figure 11-10 shows the location of this menu. The Transfer Controls window allows you to specify how you want a track matte created. Highlight the Beaches Comp layer under the TrkMat label. Click in the rectangle that says None and scroll to Alpha Matte "Square Comp" as shown in Figure 11-11. This turns off the Square Comp's video as you can see in Figure 11-12 (note the eye is closed). The layer is still active, but now it acts as the alpha channel for the layer below it. (That is what makes it a track matte). Notice that the solid line between the two layers is now a dotted line. This indicates that the two layers are linked together. The next two figures shows the effect of the track matte in the Comp window. Figure 11-13 shows the Comp window at Time=0, and Figure 11-14 shows the Comp window at Time=00:00:06:00.

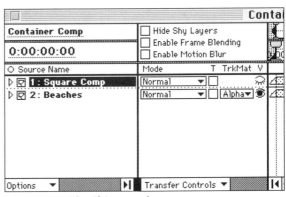

Figure 11-12: Identifying a track matte.

5. While still at Time=00, drag Beach.mov and Circle Matte into the center of the Comp window. Change the name of Beach.mov to Sun Comp.

6. Let's do the same thing as we did with the Beaches Comp. Make sure the Circle Matte is on top of Sun Comp. With Switches set to Transfer Controls, set the track matte of Sun Comp to Alpha Matte "[Circle Matte]."

7. Still at Time=00, drag Beaches.mov centered into the Comp window again. Make it the bottom layer (Mac: Cmd-B, Windows: Ctrl-B). Preview the movie. You will notice that there needs to be something done to add some separation and depth. We will change the brightness and contrast and create a shadow effect to achieve this.

Figure 11-13: The Comp window with track matte set at Time=0.

Figure 11-14: The Comp window with track matte set at Time=6.

8. Set the Current Time to 00 (Mac: Cmd-G, Windows: Ctrl-G, then type 0). Highlight the Beaches layer. Duplicate the layer (Mac: Cmd-D, Windows: Ctrl-D). Press Enter/Return and rename the layer as Beaches Shadow1. Duplicate the Square Comp as well. Name it Square Shadow1. Drag each of the duplicated layers below the Beaches layer (you can only drag one at a time). Make sure that Square Shadow1 is above Beaches Shadow1. Figure 11-15 shows the Time Layout palette's layer list at this point.

9. Check the status of the track mattes. Select the layer that you renamed Beaches Shadow1. This and its track matte layer should be below the Beaches. Figure 11-16 shows the Transfer Controls area of the Time Layout window.

10. Highlight Beaches Shadow1. Add a Gaussian blur effect (Effect → Blur & Sharpen → Gaussian Blur). Give it a value of 1. Do not set a keyframe.

11. We also need to change its color balance. Choose Effect → Image Control → Color Balance HLS. Change both the Lightness and Saturation to -100. This will make the shadow dark.

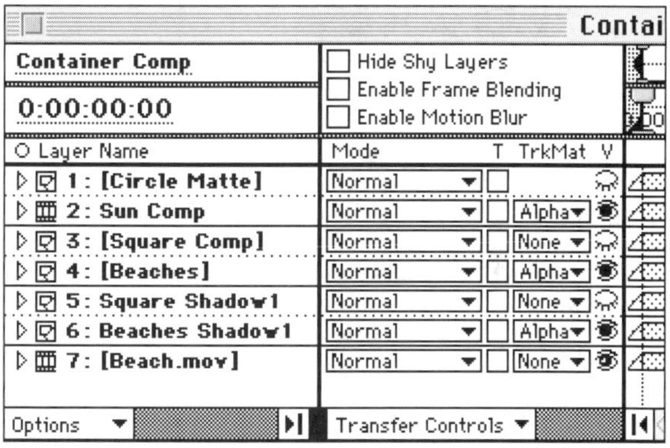

12. Now let's soften the shadow. Highlight the Square Shadow1 layer. Give it a Gaussian blur with the value set to 25. It can remain a constant value. Figure 11-17 shows these effects applied.

13. We need to repeat the same actions with the Sun Comp layer. Duplicate the Sun Comp and the Circle Matte layers. Rename the Sun Comp duplicate to Sun Shadow and the Circle Matte duplicate to Circle Shadow. Drag the duplicates below the Sun Comp layer. Re-link the track mattes if necessary. Figure 11-18 shows the Time Layout window.

14. Select the Sun Shadow layer. Choose Effect → Image Control → Color Balance HLS. Set Lightness to -75 and Saturation to -100.

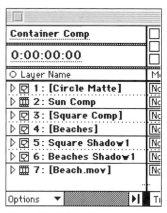

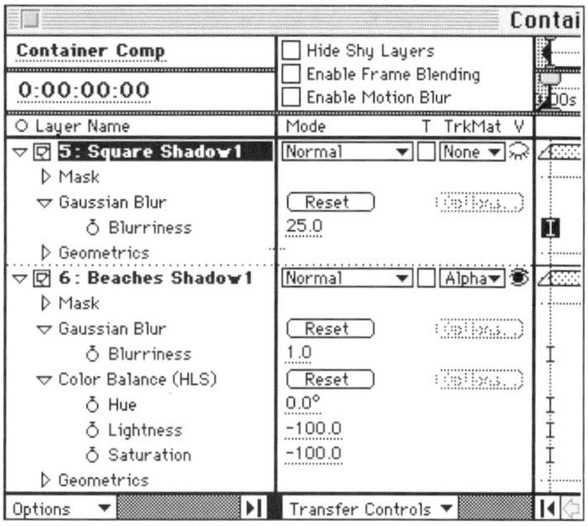

Figure 11-15: Time Layout window layer list.

Figure 11-16: Transfer Controls showing new layers.

Figure 11-17: Time Layout window with effects applied to Beaches Shadow1 and Square Shadow1 layers.

Highlight the Circle Shadow layer above it. Apply Effect → Blur & Sharpen → Gaussian blur with a value of 25.

15. To increase the separation between the items, we need to change the Brightness and Contrast of the Sun Comp layer. Apply Effect → image Control → Brightness & Contrast. Set the Brightness value to 6.5 and the Contrast value to 18. Figure 11-19 shows the Effect control.

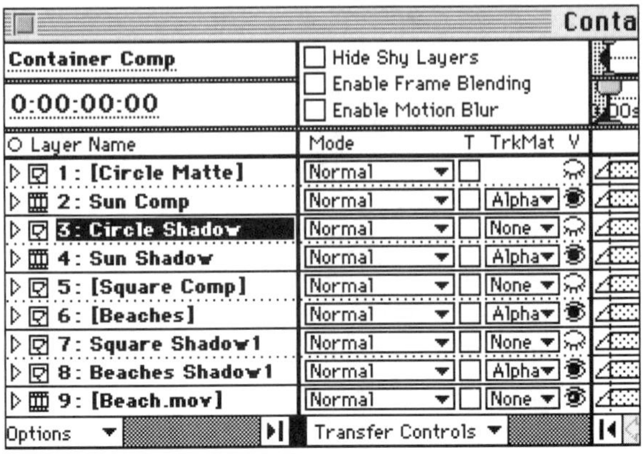

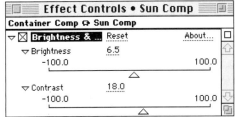

Figure 11-18: Time Layout window with Sun Shadow and Circle Shadow layers added.

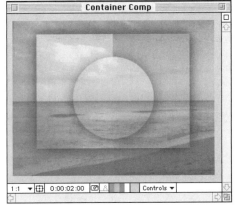

Figure 11-19: Brightness & Contrast Effect controls.

16. Collapse the layers and preview what you have done so far. Figure 11-20 shows the project at Time=2:00.

Figure 11-20: Container Comp at Time=00:00:02:00.

Adding Effects

Now, you can start with the second half of this project which contains the type effects and the sun element. This half of the project introduces you to some very exciting ways to use track mattes. First, though, let's turn our attention to creating the sun and its rays.

 Studio Time: Creating the Sun's Rays

1. You have already used the sun element in Chapter 5 of this book. Now, you need to bring that project into this project so that a piece of it can be used again. Go to the File menu and select Import Project. Locate AECH05.aep. It appears in the Project window as a folder, as you can see in Figure 11-21. Either double-click on the folder or turn down the arrow. This will allow you to see the contents of the folder.

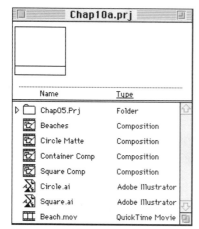

Figure 11-21: The Project window showing the imported AECH05.aep.

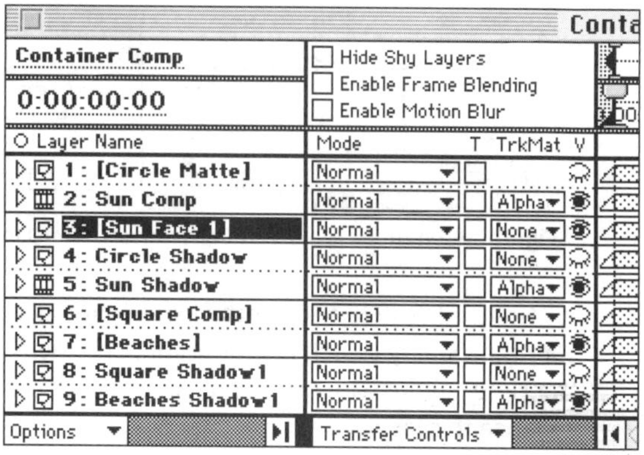

Figure 11-22: Positioning the Sun Face 1 Comp.

2. Set the Current Time to 00 (Mac: Cmd-G, Windows: Ctrl-G, then type 0). Select the Sun Face 1 Comp and place it centered into the Comp window. Drag it below the Sun Comp layer as shown in Figure 11-22.

3. Set the mask of the layer to 0 top, 0 left, 210 right, 106 bottom. This will keep the petals of the sun clipped to the horizon of the water.

4. Set the Current Time to 2:00 seconds (Mac: Cmd-G, Windows: Ctrl-G, and type 200, or just move the Playback Head until the Current Time reads 0:00:02:00).

5. Press T to bring up the Opacity property. Make an initial Opacity keyframe with the value set to 0%.

6. Go to Time=3 seconds. Set another Opacity keyframe with a value of 75%. Go to Time=820. Make a sustaining keyframe. Go to Time=920. Set the Opacity to 0%.

7. Go to Time=3 seconds. Press Shift-S to display the Scale property. Click in the stop watch to make it keyframeable. Set its value at 100%.

8. Set the Current Time to 2:15 seconds (Mac: Cmd-G, Windows: Ctrl-G, and type 215, or just move the Playback Head until the Current Time reads 0:00:02:15). Set another Scale keyframe with a value of 115%.

9. We need some Position keyframes in order to have the sun's rays set with the sun. Press Shift-P to display the Position property. Go to Time=820 and make an initial Position keyframe (just click in the stop watch). Leave the value at the current position. Figure 11-23 shows the Comp window.

Figure 11-23: Comp window at Time=820.

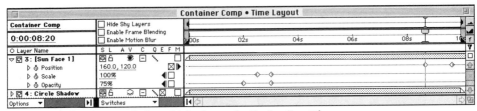

Figure 11-24: Time Layout window with keyframes for the Sun Face 1 layer.

9. Go to Time=920 and set the exit keyframe. The Position coordinates are 160, 325. Make sure the Quality switch is set to High. Change the Transfer mode to Color. Figure 11-24 shows the Time Layout window with all of the keyframes and the new Transfer mode set. You can collapse this layer.

That was fairly long! Take a breather if you want, and let's create the sun's face.

▶ *Studio Time: Creating the Sun Face*

1. Set the Current Time to 00 (Mac: Cmd-G, Windows: Ctrl-G, then type 0).

2. Duplicate the Sun Face 1 Comp (Mac: Cmd-D, Windows: Ctrl-D). This will be the sun's face. Bring it to the front (Mac: Cmd-F, Windows: Ctrl-F). Rename the version that is lower in the layer stack. Call it Sun Rays 1. Click on the Sun Face 1 layer to select it.

3. Press the M key to view the Sun Face 1 layer's Mask properties. Click on the word Rectangle. The Mask dialog box appears. Change Rectangle to Oval. Set the Top value to 54, Left: 56, Right: 154, and Bottom: 147. Figure 11-25 shows this dialog.

4. Do not change the keyframes for Opacity or Position.

5. Change the transfer function to Screen mode as shown in Figure 11-26.

6. Collapse the layer. Preview the movie if you have the patience (we suggest just positioning to various times to check out what's happening in the Comp). Figure 11-27 shows the Comp window at Time=9:03.

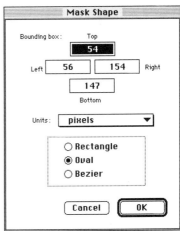

Figure 11-25: Mask position dialog box.

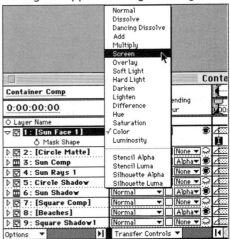

Figure 11-26: Selecting Screen mode.

Rippling Type

If you play the AECH11.aep again, you will see how much of the final project you have already created. You have managed to make a smaller, brightly colored version of the original movie, that coalesces to form a sun face, and that sun face sets just as does the real sun. Colors flicker in and out of the sun's rays.

Now, you need to create the two main type effects—the "Summer," type that shimmers in the wind, and the "Fun-in-the-Sun" type that runs around the sun. The type can take its colors from solid layers that use the alpha

Figure 11-27: The Comp window at Time=9:03.

mattes to get their shape. The type itself (i.e. the letterform) is in the alpha matte. In this next Studio Time, you will create the first part of the type treatment for the word "Summer." Here, you will color the type using a Ramp (Gradient) effect in a solid layer.

 Studio Time: Type Elements—the Summer Comp

1. Create a new Comp (Mac: Cmd-N, Windows: Ctrl-N). Name it "Summer 2 Comp." Make it 320 x 240, 10 seconds long, 30 fps.

2. Set the Current Time to 00 (Mac: Cmd-G, Windows: Ctrl-G, then type 0).

3. Create a new Solid layer (Mac: Cmd-Y, Windows: Ctrl-Y) and name it Solid 1. A Solid layer is simply an empty layer for which you can specify a solid color and a size. Set the size to be 320 x 240, and use the default color. Figure 11-28 shows this dialog.

4. Import the summer.ai into the project.

5. Drag in the Summer.ai file. Press P to display the Position property. Set the Position to 162, 193. You will see the coordinates, but the text is not visible because it is black text on a black background right now.

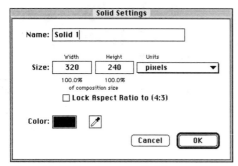

Figure 11-28: Creating a new Solid.   Figure 11-29: Initial Ramp Effect dialog.

6. Make sure that Summer.ai is on top of the solid layer. Select Transfer Controls from the Switches menu. Use the Summer layer as an alpha track matte.

7. Select the Solid 1 layer.

8. Apply the Ramp effect (Effect → Synthesize → Ramp). Figure 11-29 shows the Controls dialog when the Effect is first selected. It is an easy Effect to use, but a bit complex the first time that you see it.

9. Click on the Start Color swatch. The System Color Picker (Mac or Windows) appears as shown in Figure 11-30. Set the Lightness to about 50%. Then select a deep orange-red as the starting color. Click OK.

10. Click on the End Color swatch. The System Color Picker (Mac or Windows) appears as shown in Figure 11-31. Set the Lightness to about 50%. Then select a bright yellow as the starting color. Click OK.

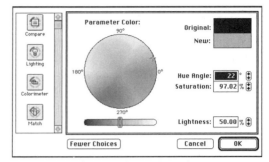

Figure 11-30: Choosing the starting color.

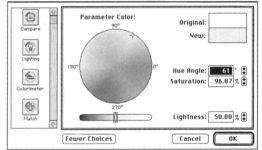

Figure 11-31: Choosing the ending color.

11. The colors that appear in the Comp window look very anemic compared to the colors selected. This is because the ramp (which is really a gradient) is actually starting at the top of the solid layer and ending at the bottom of the layer. Only a tiny range of colors shows through the alpha matte. You need to position the start and end points of the ramp tightly around the text as shown in Figures 11-32 and 11-33.

Figure 11-32: Positioning the Start of Ramp.

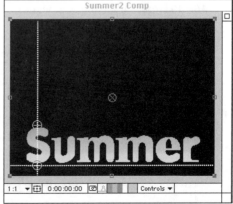

Figure 11-33: Positioning the End of Ramp.

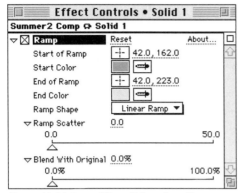

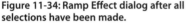

Figure 11-34: Ramp Effect dialog after all selections have been made.

Figure 11-35: The Summer Comp window.

12. Click on the End of Ramp cross-hair icon in the Ramp Effect Controls dialog. A dotted-line cross-hair cursor appears as shown in Figure 11-33. Position this cursor at the bottom of the letter "S" in Summer. Click once to set the position. Figure 11-34 shows the Ramp Effect Controls dialog after all choices have been made. Figure 11-35 shows the Comp window.

13. Set the Transfer Controls back to Switches. Select the Continuously Rasterize switch on the Summer layer and set both layer's Quality switches to High. Close up this Comp. Save your work.

You are going to need another mask for the word "Summer." This mask will hold the red highlight that travels through the text. This file is a white ripple against a black background. You are going to move this from left to right and back again, and then from bottom to top and back again. You will soften the footage with a blur and then matte it with the alpha channel of the summer.ai element. The trick produces a incredibly realistic flash of color as it moves through the type.

 Studio Time: Type Elements—Summer Ripple Mask

1. Create a new Comp (Mac: Cmd-N, Windows: Ctrl-N). Name it Summer Ripple Mask. Make it 320 x 240, 10 seconds long, and 30 frames per second. Leave the Background black.

2. Set the Current Time to 00 (Mac: Cmd-G, Windows: Ctrl-G, then type 0). Import the Ripple.ai file from the AE11Foot folder (Mac: Cmd-I, Windows: Ctrl-I and choose the Ripple file). Drag it into the Comp window, centered.

3. Open Summer2 Comp by double-clicking on it in the Project window. Select the Summer.ai layer and copy it (Mac: Cmd-C, Windows: Ctrl-C). Close the Summer2 Comp.

4. Paste the layer into the Summer Ripple Mask Comp (Mac: Cmd-V, Windows: Ctrl-V). This layer will become the track matte and help keep the type elements aligned. You may "turn on" the eye to reveal the layer if it helps you follow what is happening (it will turn off again automatically when you make this layer the track matte).

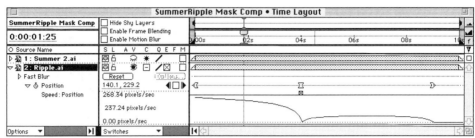

Figure 11-36: Motion graph for Summer Ripple Mask Comp.

5. Time is still at 00. Select the Ripple.ai layer. Press P to display the Position property. Set a Position keyframe with the coordinates of 603, 266.

6. Set the Current Time to 4:00 seconds (Mac: Cmd-G, Windows: Ctrl-G, and type 400, or just move the Playback Head until the Current Time reads 0:00:04:00).

7. Set a Position keyframe with the coordinates of -252, 179.

8. Set the Current Time to 9 seconds. Create another Position keyframe with the coordinates of 6, 287.

9. Smooth out the motion graph to make sure the motion is smooth. Figure 11-36 shows a smoothed motion graph.

10. Apply a fast blur of 15 (Effect → Blur & Sharpen → Fast Blur). This smooths out the edges of the ripple. Set the Quality level to High. Switch over to Transfer Controls and set the ripples track matte to the alpha of Summer.ai. Preview the movie. Notice how the Ripple flows through the shape of the Summer type.

11. Click on the Time Layout window close box with the Opt key (Mac) or Alt (Windows) key pressed to close the Comp window as well.

Tip:

If the type does not ripple through the text, then click on the Ripple.ai item in the Project window and select File'Replace Footage. Re-select the Ripple.ai element from the AE11Foot folder. There is a glitch that happens sometimes when you use an Illustrator file. After Effects either loses the link or fails to link the footage properly. It does not happen consistently, and replacing the item usually fixes it.

You might want to take a short break here before you tackle the remainder of the project. The next Studio Time shows you how to use the Ripple Mask that you created, and how to add a Bevel Alpha effect to the type.

Studio Time: Of Beveled Text and Ripple Masks

Let's use the Summer Ripple Mask Comp that you just created.

1. Set the Current Time to 00 (Mac: Cmd-G, Windows: Ctrl-G, then type 0).

2. Double-click on the Container Comp in the Project window. Drag the Summer2 Comp centered into the Comp window.

3. Drag the Summer Ripple Mask Comp centered into the Comp window. (It is above the Summer2 Comp.) Press T to bring up the Opacity property. Click in the stop watch to make the opacity keyframeable. Make an initial Opacity keyframe of 0%.

4. Set the Current Time to 20 frames (Mac: Cmd-G, Windows: Ctrl-G, and type 20, or just move the Playback Head until the Current Time reads 0:00:00:20). Set a keyframe value of 100%. Figure 11-37 shows the Comp window at 6 seconds.

Figure 11-37: Comp window with Summer Ripple Mask at 6 seconds.

5. Go to 8 seconds and make a sustaining keyframe (just click in the Keyframe Navigation box).

6. Go to 8:20 and make the last keyframe with a value of 0%.

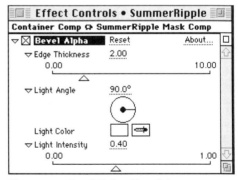

7. Set the Current Time to 00 (Mac: Cmd-G, Windows: Ctrl-G, then type 0).

8. Add a Bevel Alpha effect (Effects → Perspective → Bevel Alpha). This effect helps to add dimension to the type underneath. Set a keyframe for the light angle. Start with 90°. Figure 11-38 shows the effect dialog.

Figure 11-38: Bevel Alpha effect dialog.

9. Go to the end of the Comp. Make a new keyframe for light angle. Enter a value of 1 full rotation +90° as shown in Figure 11-39. Set the Quality switch to High. Figure 11-40 shows the image of the Comp window at 6 seconds, after that the Bevel Alpha effect has been added.

10. Set the Edge Thickness to 3.00.

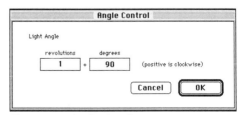

Figure 11-39: Setting rotations.

11. Go back to Time=00 and create a new solid (Mac: Cmd-Y, Windows: Ctrl-Y). Make it 320 x 240 and select a red as the color. Name it Ripple Solid and position it below the Summer Ripple Mask. Make the Summer Ripple Mask the Luma Matte for the solid layer.

12. While at 00, highlight the Summer2Comp layer. Add the bevel Alpha effect. Set the edge thickness to 2.95 and the Light Angle to -60. Set the Light Color to white, and the Light Intensity to 40.

Figure 11-40: Comp window with Bevel Alpha effect at 6 seconds.

13. Apply Effects → Blur & Sharpen → Fast Blur. Click in the stop watch to set an initial keyframe of 40. Go to Time=120, and set the value to 0. Go to Time=300 and set a sustaining keyframe. Go to Time=420, set the value to 15. Go to Time=800 and set the blurriness back to 0. Go to Time=900, set the blurriness to 40.

14. You need to add some Opacity keyframes as well. Set the Current Time to 00 (Mac: Cmd-G, Windows: Ctrl-G, then type 0). Press T to bring up the Opacity property. Click in the stop watch and set an initial Opacity keyframe of 0%. Go to Time=100 and set the Opacity to 100%. Go to Time=800. Set a sustaining keyframe. Go to Time=900. Set the Opacity to 0%.

Animating Type

In order to give the illusion that type is rising from the sea and circling around the sun, then setting, some very sophisticated masking is needed. Without it, the type simply rotates around the sun. With all of the masks in place, black type marches up over the sun and is joined by red type that seems to appear precisely on top of it. The two bands of type join forces, blur and circle off.

 Studio Time: Animating the Type—Part 1

We're almost there! It's time to animate the type that rotates around the sun. You are working still in the Container Comp.

1. Set the Current Time to 2:14 seconds (Mac: Cmd-G, Windows: Ctrl-G, and type 214, or just move the Playback Head until the Current Time reads 0:00:02:14).

2. Import the SunFun.ai file from the AE11Foot folder (Mac: Cmd-I, Windows: Ctrl-I). Drag it into the Comp window and let it snap to the center.

3. We need to change the point from which the element will be rotated. Press A to show the Anchor Point property. Change the anchor point to 86x, 87.5y. Do not set a keyframe.

4. Press Shift-P to show the Position property and change that to 160x, 121.5y. Do not set a keyframe.

Figure 11-41: Comp window with luma track matte at 6 seconds.

Figure 11-42: Comp window at 2 seconds.

5. Set a Rotation keyframe (press Shift-R to show the Rotation property, then click in the stop watch to make the property keyframable) with the value of -187°. Figure 11-42 shows the Comp window at this point.

6. Let's make some additional rotation keyframes. After all, if you want the type to rotate around the sun, it needs to know where to go. Go to 4 seconds and set a keyframe with a value of 0°. Go to Time=615 and make a sustaining keyframe. Go to Time=715 and make a final keyframe with a value of 185°.

7. Set the Current Time to 4:22 seconds (Mac: Cmd-G, Windows: Ctrl-G, and type 422, or just move the Playback Head until the Current Time reads 0:00:04:22).

8. Go to 7:15 and trim the end of the layer to this point (Mac: Opt-], Windows: Alt-]).

9. Set the Quality to High. Set your work area markers for the length of this layer and preview it.

You can no longer see the sun as it sets behind the horizon line into the ocean. As the type rotates into the ocean, you should not see it below the sea either. However, at the moment when the type rotates off to the right, it pops up at the beginning again, and you can see it even when you are not supposed to. You can fix that by making a simple track matte that will hide the text at the appropriate moments, which is what you will do in the next Studio Time.

 Studio Time: Animating the Type—Part II (the Mask)

1. Create a new Comp (Mac: Cmd-N, Windows: Ctrl-N) and name it Type Mask. Make it 320 x 240 pixels, 10 seconds long, and 30 fps. Set the background color to white (Mac: Shift-Cmd-B, Windows: Shift-Ctrl-B).

2. Set the Current Time to 00 (Mac: Cmd-G, Windows: Ctrl-G, then type 0).

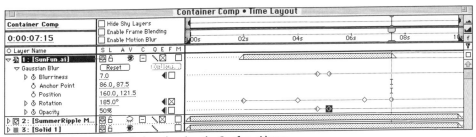

Figure 11-43: Time Layout window showing the Sunfun.ai layer.

3. Create a new Solid (Layer → New Solid) that is 320 x 116 pixels and colored black. Accept the default name of Solid 1. Line it up along the bottom of the comp as shown in Figure 11-44.

4. Make a new solid (it will be called Solid 2) that is black and 160 x 120 pixels. Press P to display the Position property. Set an initial Position keyframe of 240x, 120y.

5. Go to 15 frames and make another keyframe with the coordinates of 240x, 190y. Press ~ to hide the properties for this layer.

6. Set the Current Time to 1:00 seconds (Mac: Cmd-G, Windows: Ctrl-G, and type 100, or just move the Playback Head until the Current Time reads 0:00:01:00).

7. Create another solid the same size as the one you created in Step 4. It, too, is black. The default name of Solid 3 is fine.

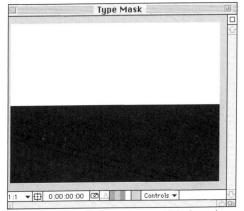

Figure 11-44: The first of three solid black mask shapes.

8. Press P to display the Position property. Create an initial keyframe at the coordinates 80x, 184.5y.

9. Go to Time=416 and make a sustaining Position keyframe.

10. At Time=501 make another Position keyframe with the coordinates of 80x, 140.5y. Close up this layer (~) and close the Comp (Mac: Opt-click, Windows: Alt-click).

Just what does this Comp do? It works like a see-saw or a set of pistons to hide and reveal the text as it revolves around the sun. At the beginning, the right side moves up and, at the end, the left side is up. In between, you create the illusion of the type actually dipping into the ocean.

In the next Studio Time, you place the mask that you just created and duplicate the entire "system" (type and mask) to create a layer of red type that follows in the path of the black type. You will also see how to create an inverted alpha mask.

Studio Time: More on the Container Comp

1. Double-click on the Container Comp in the Project window to open it again.

2. Set the Current Time to 2:14 seconds (Mac: Cmd-G, Windows: Ctrl-G, and type 214, or just move the Playback Head until the Current Time reads 0:00:02:14).

3. Drag the Type Mask Comp that you created in the last Studio Time into the Comp window and center it. Position it above the SunFun layer.

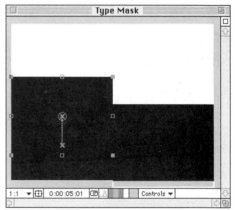

4. Add a Gaussian Blur effect (Effect → Blur & Sharpen → Gaussian Blur). Set the Bluriness to 5. Do not create a keyframe.

5. Click on the SunFun layer to select it. Change the Switches to Transfer Functions. Make the Type Mask Comp the alpha inverted track matte as shown in Figure 11-45.

6. Select the Type Mask layer.

7. Set the Current Time to 7:15. Trim the end of the Type Mask layer to this point (Mac: Opt-], Windows: Alt-]).

Figure 11-45: Setting an alpha inverted track matte.

8. Set the Current Time back to 2:14.

9. Duplicate the SunFun layer (Mac: Cmd-D, Windows: Ctrl-D). Name the duplicate "TypeFun" by pressing the Enter/Return key and entering the new name. Drag the duplicate above the Type Mask layer.

10. Create a new Solid (Mac: Cmd-Y, Windows: Ctrl-Y). Make it 320 x 240 pixels and select red (click on the color swatch and drag the resulting color slider about halfway; then select a red) as the color. Accept the default name of Solid 1. Position the layer right below the TypeFun layer.

11. Click on the Solid 1 layer to select it. Use the transfer functions to make the TypeFun layer the alpha track matte for the Solid 1 layer (this colors the type red).

O Layer Name	Track Matte		
▷ ☑ **1 : [Type Mask]**	Normal ▼ ☐	✦	⌁
▷ ⚒ 2 : [SunFun.ai]	Normal ▼	✓ No Track Matte	
▷ ☑ 3 : [SummerRipple M...	Normal ▼		
▷ ☑ 4 : [Solid 1]	Normal ▼	Alpha Matte "[Type Mask]"	
▷ ☑ 5 : [Sun Face 1]	Screen ▼	Alpha Inverted Matte "[Type Mask]"	
▷ ☑ 6 : [Circle Matte]	Normal ▼	Luma Matte "[Type Mask]"	
▷ ▦ 7 : Sun Comp	Normal ▼	Luma Inverted Matte "[Type Mask]"	
	Alpha ▼		

Figure 11-46: The Comp window with the new Solid and the duplicated SunFun layers.

12. Click on the Solid 1 layer and then Shift-click on its track matte layer (TypeFun) to select both. Compify the layers (Mac: Shift-Cmd-C, Windows: Ctrl-Cmd-C) together. The result will be a new Comp/layer called Pre-comp 1 (the default name). You have no other options when you compify multiple layers together.

13. Once the Pre-comp 1 Comp has been created, you need to delete it from the Container Comp. Don't worry, it will return as part of a new Comp. Just highlight the name in the Container Comp and press the Delete key. Pre-comp 1 is still listed in the Project window.

Let's finish creating the red type.

Studio Time: The Colored Type Comp

1. Create a new Comp (Mac: Cmd-N, Windows: Ctrl-N). Call it Color Type 1. It should be 320 x 240 pixels and 10 seconds long at 30 frames per second.

2. Set the Current Time to 00 (Mac: Cmd-G, Windows: Ctrl-G, then type 0).

3. Drag the Pre-comp 1 Comp from the Project window into the center of the Comp window. Set its Quality to High.

4. Set the Current Time to 2:14 seconds (Mac: Cmd-G, Windows: Ctrl-G, and type 214, or just move the Playback Head until the Current Time reads 0:00:02:14).

5. Drag the Type Mask Comp into the Comp window.

6. Select the Pre-comp 1 layer. Change the Switches to Transfer Controls. Make the Type Mask Comp into the alpha inverted track matte for the Pre-comp 1 layer.

Figure 11-47: Time=3:15 and the colored type shows up partway behind the mask.

7. Preview the Comp and then close it (Mac: Opt-click, Windows: Alt-click, on the close box). Figure 11-47 shows the Comp window at 3:15.

What did you just do? Basically, you built another Comp to hold the various pieces of the red type that circles the sun. You can see the Type Mask layer working to show only the appropriate portions of the type.

Okay, folks! This is it! This is the final Studio Time of the chapter, the place where it all comes together. This exercise contains two new skills—one practical and one with tremendous creative possibilities. The "practical" one shows you how to add layer markers to make it easy to either locate specific times on the time line or to leave notes for yourself (in this case, you will simply name the layers).

The "creative" skill involves the use of a layer mask that evolves and fans out over time. This is a very interesting technique, and one which you should easily be able to adapt to your own work.

 Studio Time: Finishing Up

1. Open the Container Comp again.

2. Make Sun Face 1 into Layer 1 (Mac: Cmd-F, Windows: Ctrl-F). Drag the Summer Ripple Mask below Layer 1, and bring the RippleSolid layer below that (to become Layer 3).

3. Position Summer2 Comp so that it is Layer 4.

4. Set the Current Time to 00 (Mac: Cmd-G, Windows: Ctrl-G, then type 0).

5. Drag the Color Type 1 Comp centered into the Comp window. (Remember, we told you that the Pre-comp 1 layer would still be used. Here it is—back again as part of the Color Type 1 Comp.) Drag it below the Summer2 Comp so that it becomes Layer 5.

6. You need to make a Bezier mask for the Color Type 1 layer so that it will continue to rotate after the black type is already there. Set the Current Time to 4 seconds.

7. Highlight the Color Type 1 layer and press the M key to expose its Mask property. Click in the stop watch to make it keyframeable.

8. Click on the word Rectangle. It will bring up the Mask Shape dialogue, choose Bezier and click OK. Double-click on the item in the Time Layout window. Figure 11-48 shows the Layer window at this point.

9. Choose Mask Handles from the Control menu.

Figure 11-48: Color Type 1 Layer window at 4 seconds.

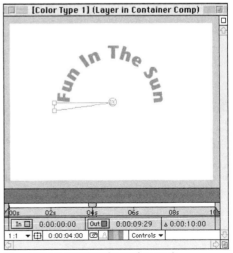

Figure 11-49: Starting the wedge mask.

Figure 11-50: Creating a new point on the wedge

Figure 11-51: Covering the letter "F."

10. Make the Pen tool active. The mask shape that you need to create is a wedge—as if it were a very thin piece of pie. Click with the Pen tool in the center of the window (where the center point of the mask controls is shown). This sets the first point (and removes the "center point" icon—the circle around the x). Place the Pen tool directly below and slightly to the left of the letter "F" and click to leave a second point. Make the third point directly under the second one. Click again on the first point to close the shape. Figure 11-49 shows this tiny wedge.

11. Move ahead two frames in time (Mac: Cmd-Right arrow—twice, Windows: Ctrl-Right arrow—twice). You need to enlarge the piece of pie. Figure 11-50 shows the Pen tool placed halfway between the center point and the letter "F" along to top mask line. As the Pen tool nears the line, its icon changes to the Pen+ tool so that you can add a point. Click to add a new point along that line. Hold down the Command key (Mac) or the Control key (Windows) while the pen is active. This turns the Pen tool into the Arrow (Selection) tool. Drag the newly-created point up and to the left so that the wedge now extends to cover the letter "F" as shown in Figure 11-51.

12. Move the time two frames forward (Time=4:04). Repeat Step 11. Continue to advance the clock two seconds and repeat Step 11 until all of the letters in the layer are enclosed in the wedge. Ignore the spaces as you increase the size of the wedge. Figure 11-52 shows the mask at 4:06 as it reaches between the words "Fun" and "In."

13. You should reach the end of the letters by Time=422. Figure 11-53 shows the finished wedge at Time=4:22. Close the Layer window and return to the Comp and Time Layout windows.

14. Set the mask feather to 3.

15. At 4:22, add a Fast Blur effect (Effect → Blur & Sharpen → Fast Blur). Turn down the arrow on the effect in the Time Layout window and click in the stop watch to make it keyframe-able. Set the value to 5.

16. Set the Current Time to 5:05 seconds (Mac: Cmd-G, Windows: Ctrl-G, and type 505, or just move the Playback Head until the Current Time reads 0:00:05:05).

17. Create another keyframe for blurriness with a value of 1. This will make the red type "pop" against the black type behind it.

18. Highlight the Sunfun layer. While you're still at Time=505, add a Gaussian Blur (Effects → Blur & Sharpen → Gaussian Blur). Click in the stop watch to make it keyframe-able, and create a keyframe with a value of 7. Go to Time=422. Set a keyframe with a value of 0.

Figure 11-52: Masking in between words

19. Go to Time=820. You need to make the Beach Comp and it's shadow fade out. Select the two layers, Beaches and Beaches Shadow, press the "T" key to show the Opacity settings. Make the initial Opacity keyframes for both items, with a value of 100%. Go to Time=920. Set the Opacity values of both items to 0.

20. Check to make sure that your layers are in the following order from top to bottom:

- Sun Face 1
- Summer Ripple Mask
- Ripple Solid
- Summer 2 Comp
- Color Type 1
- Type Mask
- Sunfun.ai
- Circle Matte
- Sun Comp
- Sun Rays 1
- Circle Shadow
- Sun Shadow
- Square Comp
- Beaches

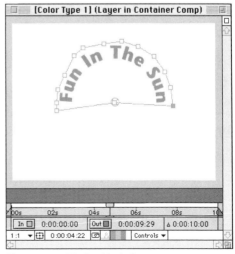

Figure 11-53: Wedge Mask done.

- Square Shadow

- Beaches Shadow

- Beach.mov

21. Label each layer or group of layers to make it easy to read the time line. To do this, highlight the layer that you want to mark. Go to the point in time where you want the mark to appear. Press the asterisk key on the numeric keypad (or select Layer → Add

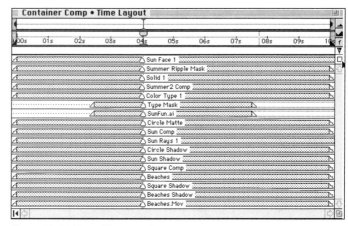

Figure 11-54: Named layer markers.

Marker). A layer marker appears. Double click the layer marker to name it. Figure 11-54 shows all the layers named.

22. Turn all of the Quality switches to High and render the movie. Take a deep breath and give yourself a pat on the back—you deserve it! This is a very complex project.

 # Rewind

There is a lot here to rewind. You have been introduced to many possibilities using masks and track mattes. We hope that you have thought of many more as you worked through this lesson. You have experimented with three of the four possible track matte settings: alpha, alpha inverted, and luma. You have also seen how to change a mask shape over time, and to create flickers by moving a mask through an image. You have also learned about manufacturing a mask that works like a piston to hide and show an image at the desired times.

 # Coming Attractions

The mattes that you have created can also be combined with layer apply modes—called Transfer modes in After Effects. These modes add to the range of effects that you can create. Chapter 12 shows how you can create wonderful moving textures and psychedelic effects using Transfer modes and track mattes. It also adds to your knowledge of track mattes by showing how you can create transitions in Adobe Premiere to use as track mattes.

Transfer Modes

 Preview

In Chapter 1, you were introduced to After Effects through an exercise that used a moving texture. That texture was contained in a movie, and you never got to see its component pieces—though you were promised the "secret" at a later time. The time is now, and your patience is about to be rewarded.

You've seen that After Effects can do amazing things with video. Many folks think that what it can do for still images is even more exciting. In this chapter, you will learn how to create moving textures—multiple images that rotate, grow, and interact within a Composition to produce an almost-organic form.

The magic is possible because After Effects is capable of using many of the Apply modes (transfer modes/blending modes—they are called by a variety of names) in Adobe Photoshop. It also has some transfer modes that Photoshop does not.

The transfer modes that After Effects shares with Photoshop are:

- Normal
- Dissolve
- Multiply
- Screen

- Overlay
- Soft Light
- Hard Light
- Darken
- Lighten
- Difference
- Hue
- Saturation
- Color
- Luminosity

Let's take a few minutes and look at the transfer modes. You may want to review them in the Adobe Photoshop manual as well. The transfer modes are based on color value—a number from 0 (black) to 255 (white). The program can perform mathematical calculations on these values to make layered images react to one another in new and exciting ways. A layer with a transfer mode needs to be on top of another layer for you see the effect.

Normal, is, of course the default transfer mode. It is completely opaque and uses 100% of the source image.

Dissolve mode shows up only if the opacity of the layer is less than 100%. The dissolved layer appears as tiny dots on top of the images below. The higher the opacity of the dissolved layer, the more dots are shown.

Multiply and *Screen* modes are opposites of one another. In Multiply mode, the image gets darker. Any areas of black in the Multiply layer create black in the result; areas of white show the layers below. In Screen mode, areas of black are transparent in the screened image, while areas of white stay white. The image makes what is under it much lighter.

Overlay, *Soft Light*, and *Hard Light* are the next group of transfer modes. They are similar in that they simulate the reaction of placing colored lights over a surface. The Overlay mode colors the surface below with the values of the overlaid layer. Black in the layer is lightened; white is colored by the image beneath. The effect is as if you placed a colored transparency over another image. None of the "transparency" colors are opaque. Soft Light is similar except that the effect is softer—as if the transparency were backlit and the colors on the top layer not as visible. Hard Light is the opposite—whites and blacks in the layer come through at full strength and only the midtones in the Hard Light layer pick up the colors below. It is as if a strong light were projected from the top layer.

Darken and *Lighten* modes are also opposites of one another. Within each color channel, the program compares the pixel in the top layer with the pixel visible below it and the pixel that is the darkest—in Darken mode—or lightest—in Lighten mode—is visible in the result.

Difference mode, which is discussed a bit later in more detail, can give your image wild color changes.

Hue uses the hue component of a pixel and applies that hue to the pixel below. *Saturation* mode uses only the saturation of the top layer, and *Luminosity* mode uses only the luminance. *Color* mode applies both the Hue and the Saturation of the top layer to the pixels below it.

In addition to these "in-common" modes, After Effects has a Dancing Dissolve mode—similar to Dissolve except that it vibrates randomly from frame to frame, and Add mode—a mode that is possible only by using Channel calculations in Photoshop. This adds the values in the "add" layer to the values visible below it, so that the image becomes generally lighter as it moves towards white.

After Effects also has another group of modes—Stencil Alpha, Stencil Luma, Silhouette Alpha, and Silhouette Luma. These allow you to use either the shape of the image in the layer (alpha), or the values of the image in the layer (luma), to keep the image below the layer inside (stencil) or outside (silhouette) of the layer shape.

The first part of this chapter discusses the creation of moving textures in After Effects and creates the project that you can preview as AECH12.mov or CH12PRD.mov. There are two versions of this movie because you have two ways in which you can create this project—depending upon whether you have purchased the Production bundle or the Non-Production version of After Effects. Preview the movies now. There is a slight difference between them.

The second part of this chapter shows you how to create transitions in Adobe Premiere and use them as track mattes inside of an After Effects project. These transitions also use the various transfer modes.

In this chapter, you will learn to:

- Select a transfer mode.
- Build a moving texture.
- Use a transition created in Premiere as a track matte.

Feature Presentation

Your mission in the first part of this chapter is to create a moving, changing, evolving texture. To do this, you will animate a few Photoshop textures. You will also use the Transfer Controls to apply math between the layers. Again, there are two versions of this project; one for the non-production bundle; the other for production bundle owners.

Creating a Moving Texture

A moving texture is a combination of several still images. These images can combine in a number of ways—they can rotate, change scale, change opacity, or change position, and they can employ one transfer mode that allows the changes to be visible. In the first Studio Time, you will create a new project and animate one of the layers—a layer formed in Photoshop using the Clouds filter.

Studio Time: Revolving Clouds

1. Create a new Project named Chap12a.

2. Import the footage files Clouds.psd, Graygoo.psd, and Sheen.psd from the AE12Foot folder (Mac: Cmd-I, Windows: Ctrl-I).

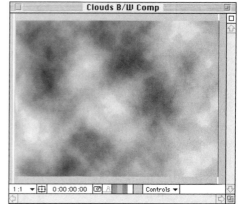

3. Create a new Comp (Mac: Cmd-N, Windows: Ctrl-N). Name it Clouds B/W Comp. Make it 320 x 240 pixels, 14 seconds long, at 30 Frames per second. This Comp will contain a clouds layer that will rotate and grow larger over time.

4. Set the Current Time to 00 (Mac: Cmd-G, Windows: Ctrl-G, then type 0).

5. Drag the Clouds file into the Comp window. Let it snap to the center.

Figure 12-1: Clouds Comp.

6. Click the Time Layout window and select the Clouds layer. Press the S key to show the Scale property. Press Shift-R to show the Rotation property. Click in the stop watch to create initial keyframes for Scale and Rotation. Set the Scale value to 43%. Set the Rotation value to 0.0 (the default value).

7. Press the End key on the extended keyboard to go to the end of the Comp (or type O). Set the Scale to 100% and set the Rotation value to -180. Adjust the velocity graphs so the motion is smooth and even. Set the Quality to High.

8. Close the Comp by clicking the close button on the Comp while pressing the Option (Mac) or Alt (Windows) key. Figure 12-1 shows the Comp window at Time=0.

The Displacement Map Effect

In this Studio Time, you will make a texture get "thicker" and change over time by applying the Displacement Map effect (found under the Distort category of effects). You will use the filter to give an embossed look to the texture. The Displacement Map effect, however, is available only if you have purchased the Production bundle. If you do not have this, just skip over those steps.

What is a displacement map? If you are familiar with Adobe Photoshop, you may already know, as there is a Displace filter under the Distort category in Photoshop that does the same thing. A displacement map is an image with values that are used to move or distort the image in the picture being filtered. This sounds complicated. Well, it is.

A displacement map uses only the gray values in the "map" image. The user (you) specifies to the filter the maximum amount (horizontally and/or vertically) that you will permit a pixel to move. When the filter is applied, it compares every pixel in the "map" to the corresponding pixel in the image being filtered. If the map pixel is white or black, the filter moves the image pixel the maximum amount (but in one direction for black and the opposite direction for white). If the map pixel is a gray of middle value (value 128), the image pixel is not moved at all. In between these extremes (maximum movement or no movement), every map pixel produces a specific amount of movement in the image. Aren't you glad that the computer does all of the calculations?

Studio Time: Adding a Displacement Map Effect

1. Create a new Comp named Gray Gooeys Comp 1. Make the Comp 320 x 240, 14 seconds long at 30 frames per second. Leave the background black.

2. Set the Current Time to 00 (Mac: Cmd-G, Windows: Ctrl-G, then type 0).

3. Drag Graygoo.psd into the Comp window. Let it snap to the center. Press S to display the Scale property. Press Shift-R to show the Rotation property. Make initial keyframes for Scale and Rotation. Set the Rotation to 0 (default). Set the Scale to 43%.

4. Press the End key to go to the end of the Comp (or press O). Change the Scale value to 100% and the Rotation to 180.

5. Press the Home key to return to Time= 00.

6. Note: You need the Production Bundle in order to complete this step. If you do not have it, just skip to Step 11. Click Effect → Distort → Displacement Map to apply the effect and open the "Effect Controls—Gooeys.psd" dialog box.

7. Select the Time Layout window. Turn down the Displacement Map arrow to display the Max Horizontal Displacement and Max Vertical Displacement properties (among others). Click on the stop watch next to Max Horizontal Displacement to make it keyframeable. Click on the stop watch next to Max Vertical Displacement to make it keyframeable. Set both values to 0%. Figure 12-2 shows the Time Layout window with initial values set for the two attributes.

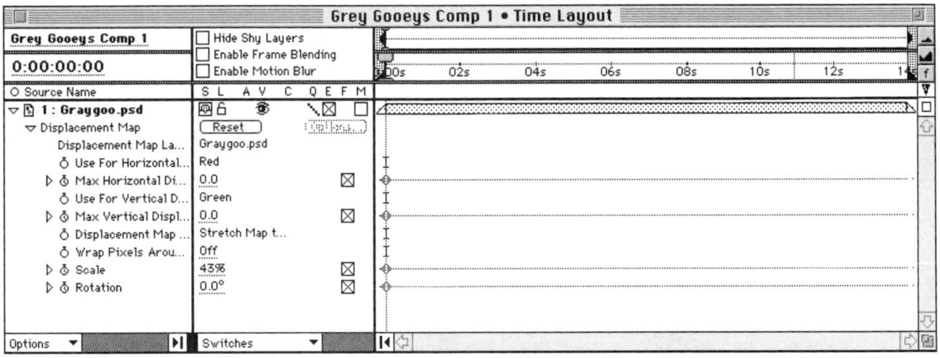

Figure 12-2: Time Layout window at Time=0 with Displacement Map options set.

8. At Time=4 seconds, set the Max Horizontal Displacement to 18 and the Max Vertical Displacement to 7.

9. At Time=715, set sustaining keyframes for both the horizontal and vertical displacements.

10. Press the End key to go to the end of the Comp (or press O). Set the Max Horizontal Displacement to 6 and the Max Vertical displacement to 2. Figure 12-3 shows the Comp window at 10 seconds.

11. Smooth the velocity graphs for all the keyframes in this Comp. Varying the settings will lead to new and different effects. Don't be afraid to experiment.

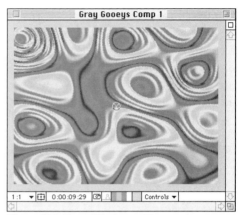

Figure 12-3: Comp Window at 10 seconds.

12. Apply a Fast Blur of 1 to complete the smoothing.

13. Set the Quality to High.

14. Preview the Comp if you wish. Close this Comp.

Choosing Transfer Modes

You are now going to build the final Comp for the texture animation. In this Comp, the various elements will fade up and vary in opacity. You will also add effects to the layers to make them react differently to one another.

 Studio Time: The Twirl Filter

1. Create a new Comp named Chapter 12A Comp 1. Make it 320 x 240, 15 seconds long, 30 fps, background black.

2. At Time=00 drag the Clouds.psd image into the center of the Comp window.

3. Set an initial Opacity keyframe by highlighting Clouds.psd in the Time Layout Window and pressing the T key. Click on the stop watch to create a keyframe. Set the Opacity to 0%.

4. At Time=1 second, set the Opacity to 100%.

5. At Time=12 seconds, make a sustaining Opacity keyframe.

6. At Time=14 seconds, make another Opacity keyframe with a value of 0%.

7. At Time=1 second, drag Sheen.psd into the Comp window and let it snap to the center. Press S, Shift-R, and Shift-T to show the Scale, Rotation, and Opacity properties. Set initial keyframes for Scale, Opacity, and Rotation by clicking the respective stop watches. Set Opacity to 0%, Rotation to 0, and Scale to 55%.

8. At Time=2 seconds, set an Opacity keyframe of 100%.

9. At Time=715, set a sustaining Opacity keyframe.

10. At Time=12 seconds, set the final Opacity keyframe at 0%.

11. While still at Time=12 seconds, create a keyframe for Scale and set it to 100%. Create a keyframe for Rotation and set it to 180. Adjust all the motion graphs to smooth the motion.

12. Now let's will add some effects. Go back to the In point of this layer by highlighting the layer and pressing the I key.

13. Select Effect → Image Control → Brightness and Contrast. Set the Brightness control to -5 and the Contrast to 15. These values will remain constant.

14. *Note: Users of the Non-Production Bundle need to select the PS+Twirl filter instead. Select 50 when prompted for Twirl Radius.* Choose Effect → Distort → Twirl. Make both items—Angle and Twirl Radius —keyframable items by clicking their stop watches under the Effect name in the Time Layout window. Set the Angle to 0° and the Twirl Radius to 50.

15. Go to Time=12 seconds. Set the Angle to 1 full rotation and the Twirl Radius to 15. Smooth out the motion graphs to make the motion smooth and consistent.

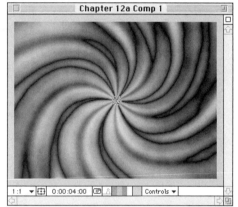

Figure 12-4: Comp window showing Gooeys and Sheen in Difference mode at 4 seconds.

16. Finally, switch over to Transfer Controls and change from Normal mode to Difference. You can collapse this layer (~). Set the Quality to High. Figure 12-4 shows the Comp window at 4 seconds, as it begins to twirl.

17. Set the Current Time to 100 (Mac: Cmd-G, Windows: Ctrl-G, then type 100).

18. Go to the Project window and highlight the Gray Gooeys Comp 1 and duplicate it. Change the duplicate's name to Gray Gooeys C1Rev, as shown in Figure 12-5. Drag it into the center of the Comp window.

19. Set the Current Time to 7:15 seconds (Mac: Cmd-G, Windows: Ctrl-G, and type 715, or just move the Playback Head until the Current Time reads 0:00:07:15). Press T

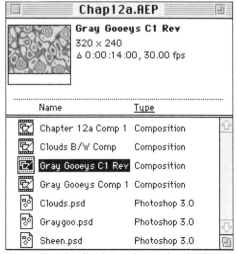

Figure 12-5: Duplicating and renaming the Gray Gooeys Comp.

to bring up the Opacity property. Click in the stop watch to make it keyframeable. Set an initial Opacity keyframe with the value of 0%.

20. Got to Time=13 seconds (1300) and set an additional keyframe with the value of 100%.

21. Go to Time=14:20 and make the last keyframe with a value set to 0%. Smooth out the motion graphs. Make the motion nice and smooth.

22. Press Shift-S to show the Scale property. Set the Scale at -100% to flip the image.

23. Go to Time=715. Trim the front end of this layer (Mac: Opt-[, Windows: Alt-[). Set the layer's Mode to Difference. Collapse the layer. Figure 12-6 shows the Time Layout window.

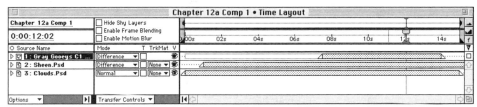

Figure 12-6: Time Layout window with Gray Gooeys C1 Rev set to Difference mode.

Difference mode is a very good way to make layers interact. This mode, like all of the transfer modes, is a math exercise. At the bottom of all of the transfer modes lives a set of relatively simple arithmetic moves. Every pixel in After Effects (or Photoshop) has a numeric value that ranges from 0 (for black) to 255 (white). If an image is in RGB mode, it has a set of gray values (0-255) for each of its three component channels (red, green, or blue). When you set something to Difference mode, After Effects takes the absolute value of the difference between the layer to which the transfer mode is applied, and the visible image beneath it. (For those of you whose math is shaky, you get the absolute value when you subtract item a from item b, and toss away the + or - sign in the result. Therefore if you want the absolute value of 300 and 1000, it will be 700 regardless of whether you subtract 300 from 1000, or 1000 from 300. The first example yields +700, the second one gives -700. Without the sign, the number is the same. This is interesting, but if you hate math, it is also irrelevant.) When you place layers in Difference mode and one of the layers is a grayscale image, you get a partial inversion of the color image, which is usually very interesting. It is the artistic effect that is important here—not the math.

 Studio Time: Adding the Gray Gooeys

1. Set the Current Time to 1:00 seconds (Mac: Cmd-G, Windows: Ctrl-G, and type 100, or just move the Playback Head until the Current Time reads 0:00:01:00).

2. Drag the Gray Gooeys Comp1 into the center of the Comp window.

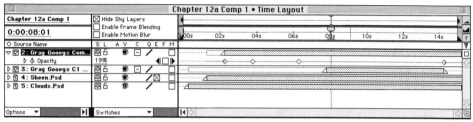

Figure 12-7: Time Layout window with trimmed Gray Gooeys Comp 1 footage.

3. Go to Time=2 seconds. Press T to bring up the Opacity property. Click in the stop watch to make it keyframeable. Set an initial Opacity frame of 0%.

4. Go to Time=315 and make an Opacity keyframe with a value of 100%.

5. Go to Time=6 seconds and make an Opacity keyframe with a value of 25%.

6. Go to Time=715 and set another Opacity keyframe with a value of 100%.

7. Go to Time=14 and set a final Opacity keyframe with a value of 0%.

8. Smooth out the motion graphs. Make the motion nice and smooth. Set the Quality to High.

9. Go back to Time=2 seconds.

10. Trim the front end of the footage (Mac: Opt-[, Windows: Alt-[).

11. Set the transfer mode to Difference. Figure 12-7 shows the Time Layout window and Figure 12-8 shows the Comp window at 8 seconds.

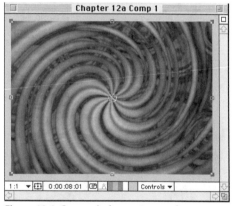

Figure 12-8: Comp window at 8 seconds.

Time now to finish up.

 Studio Time: Finishing the Texture

1. In the time layout window, duplicate the Gray Gooeys Comp.

2. Compify the layer (Mac: Shift-Cmd-C, Windows: Shift-Ctrl-C). Accept the default name. Select "Move all attributes into the new Composition." Click OK.

3. Compifying the layer lets you vary the Opacity. Set the layer's Opacity to 35%.

4. Set the transfer mode to Screen. This will lighten and brighten the overall movie.

5. Since we have compified the layer, it starts at Time=00. Set the Current Time to 2:00 seconds (Mac: Cmd-G, Windows: Ctrl-G, and type 200, or just move the Playback Head until

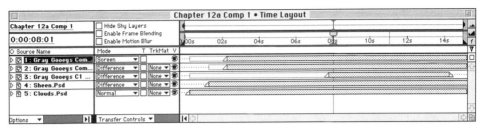

Figure 12-9: Time Layout window with footage trimmed and moved.

the Current Time reads 0:00:02:00). Trim the beginning of the footage at this point (Mac: Opt-[, Windows: Alt-[).

6. Collapse all of the layers.

7. Set the Current Time to 7 frames (Mac: Cmd-G, Windows: Ctrl-G, and type 7, or just move the Playback Head until the Current Time reads 0:00:00:07).

8. Select all of the layers (Mac: Cmd-A, Windows: Ctrl-A) and move the selected layers 7 frames towards the end of the Comp. The easiest way to do this is to grab the time ribbon on the Clouds.psd layer and let it snap to the Current Time marker. This will give you a few extra frames of black at the beginning of the movie. Figure 12-9 shows the Time Layout window with trimmed and moved footage. You can always trim these frames from the movie if you do not want them.

9. Render the movie.

Using the Texture

Here is a bonus for you. You may wonder what to do with this moving mass that you have created. You can certainly use it as a background. You can use it with a track matte above it so that only part of the texture is visible. You can also use it under a piece of text that is placed in Stencil Alpha mode so that it "clips" the texture. We'll do the latter.

Studio Time: Moving Text

1. In Illustrator, create a piece of type that you can use to have the texture "play through." (You can reuse any of the type in Chapter 5 as a Quick Start.)

2. Back in After Effects, create a new Comp.

3. Drag the Final Comp for the Project into the new Comp window.

4. Move the type over it.

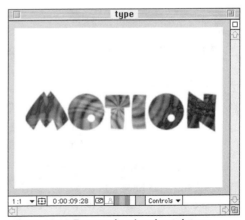

Figure 12-10: Texture showing through type.

5. Change the transfer mode for the type layer to Stencil Alpha. You might then want to set the background to white. Figure 12-10 shows the Comp window.

6. The type layer can be reimported to be used as a drop shadow. Put the "drop shadow" type below the texture layer. Offset it and blur it. Lower the opacity if you feel it's necessary.

Creating and Using Premiere Transitions

You can make very interesting textured transitions by using Adobe Premiere to create movies made from black and white stills (mattes, in the language of Premiere). By creating a "movie" that changes over time from all black to all white, you have an effect that can be used as a track matte (see Chapter 11 for review of track mattes if you need to).

If you are not familiar with Premiere, it is still easy to create the transition movie. Figure 12-11 shows the two mattes defined in Premiere (Project → Add Color Matte). Figure 12-12 shows the two mattes lined up in the A and B roll positions and a transition placed between them. Figure 12-13 shows the standard Multi-Spin transition settings dialog. Figure 12-14 shows one frame of the transition. The process is really as simple as that:

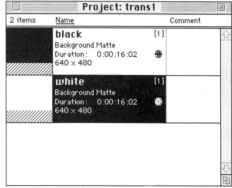

Figure 12-11: Defining mattes in Premiere.

- Define the two color mattes and place one in Video A and the other in Video B track.

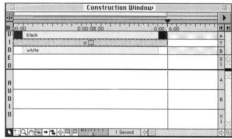

Figure 12-12: Mattes in the A and B tracks.

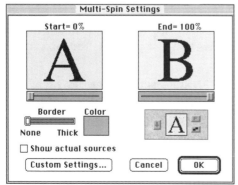

Figure 12-13: The Transition Control dialog.

Figure 12-14: Comp window showing Gooeys and Sheen in Difference mode at 4.

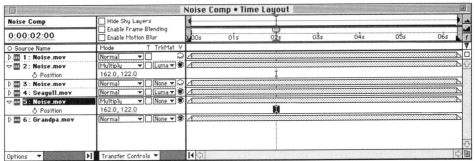

Figure 12-15: Time Layout window for Random Noise transition.

📋 Add a transition from any of the built-in or third-party effects available in Premiere.

📋 Make the movie.

We have pre-built two transitions for you in Premiere so that you can play with them in After Effects. You will use them as track mattes to apply the transition effect. You will also add some dimension to the elements using the elements themselves. These transitions can be used with moving footage, or with still images and textures. The instructions given here show them used with video footage. When you have finished the exercises, try using the transitions in a project that includes the texture files from this chapter.

 Studio Time: Using the Random Noise Transition

1. Create a new project (Mac: Cmd-Opt-N, Windows: Alt-Ctrl-N). Name it Trans.AEP. Import the footage files from the AE12Foot folder (Mac: Cmd-Opt-I, Windows: Alt-Ctrl-I). There are two source movie files: Grandpa.mov and Seagull.mov. The other two movies that you need to import are Slash.mov and Noise.mov. These are the pre-rendered Premiere files.

2. Create a new Comp (Mac: Cmd-N, Windows: Ctrl-N). Name it Random Noise Comp, and make it 6 seconds and 10 frames long, at 30 frames per second.

3. Set the Current Time to 00 (Mac: Cmd-G, Windows: Ctrl-G, then type 0).

4. Drag the Grandpa, Seagull, and Noise movies into the Comp window. Let them snap to the center of the window. Grandpa should be the bottom layer, Seagull on top of that, and Noise on the top.

5. Duplicate (Mac: Cmd-D, Windows: Ctrl-D) the Noise layer three times (for a total of four).

6. Drag one duplicate below the Seagull layer. Set its mode to Multiply. Invert this layer by applying the Invert effect found under the Channel submenu of the Effects menu. You do not need to specify any parameters for it—just select the effect.

7. Leave the other two duplicates where they are and turn them off visually for the moment (click on their Eye icons to turn them off).

8. Highlight the Seagull layer and make the Noise layer (directly above the Seagull layer) into a Luma Matte (remember that you need to change the Switches to Transfer Controls).

9. Turn on the Eye icons for the top two layers again.

10. Highlight the second Noise layer, make the Noise layer above it into its Luma Matte. Also change this layer's mode to Multiply and the Transparency to 50%.

11. Set the Current Time to 3:00 seconds (Mac: Cmd-G, Windows: Ctrl-G, and type 300, or just move the Playback Head until the Current Time reads 0:00:03:00).

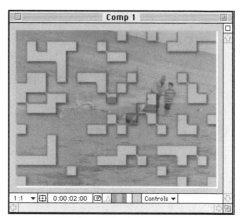

Figure 12-16: Random Noise transition movie at 3 seconds.

12. Select the layer below the Seagull. This is the Drop Shadow layer. Move this a pixel or two to the right and down. Add to this layer a Fast Blur of 4 (Effects'Blur & Sharpen'Fast Blur).

13. Highlight the second Noise layer and change its position 2 pixels right 2 pixels down (press P to show Position and change the position of the layer to 162, 122). This will add to the depth of the transition. Figure 12-15 shows the Time Layout window. Set the Quality to High for all of the layers.

14. Preview the effect and render the movie. Figure 12-16 shows the movie at 3 seconds.

Now that you have created one transition movie, the second one is even easier.

 ## Studio Time: The Slash Transition

1. In the Project window, highlight the Random Noise Comp. Duplicate it (Mac: Cmd-D, Windows: Ctrl-D). Rename the duplicate SlashTrans (press Enter/Return and type in the new name).

2. Delete all copies of the Noise.Mov in the SlashTrans Comp by selecting them and then pressing the Delete/Backspace key.

3. Drag the Slash.mov into the center of the Comp window.

4. Duplicate it three times and position the duplicates as you did in the Random Noise Comp.

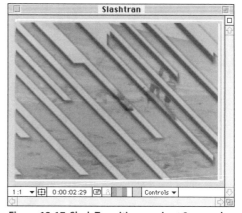

Figure 12-17: Slash Transition movie at 3 seconds.

5. Move the position of the lowest Slash.Mov layer to 162, 122.

6. Make the following changes: on the second Slash layer, set the Scale to 102%. Set the Position to 5 pixels to the right and 2 up (165, 118). Change the Opacity to 85 percent.

7. Preview the effect and render the movie. Figure 12-17 shows the movie at 3 seconds.

 Rewind

In this chapter, you learned how to layer textures and make them interact with each other by using layer transfer modes, changes in layer geometry, and a variety of effects. You also learned how to embed these moving textures inside of text. In addition, you learned how to create black and white transition effects in Adobe Premiere and how to use these transition movies as track mattes in After Effects.

Coming Attractions

In the next few chapters, you will learn about all of the filters supported by After Effects. It is from these filters and effects that After Effects gets much of its power. Conceptually, After Effects is fairly easy: you use the program to stack layers of images (moving or still) that react to each other in certain ways over time. You can create masks. You can change geometric properties—Scale, Position, Opacity, Rotation, or Anchor Point. These are the only things that you can do—except for applying effects. There are so many possible effects, however, both built-in or added by third parties, that the creative possibilities of After Effects become almost infinite.

Built-in Filters

 Preview

There was a TV commercial recently that showed a car being stirred like a bowl of pudding. Another commercial showed text swirling and changing. A third commercial showed a smiley face puffing its cheeks, whistling, and moving around the screen. While it is not certain that the creators of these spots used After Effects, they certainly *could* have, because After Effects can do all of these special tricks—and it is one of the few programs that can. One of the greatest strengths of After Effects is its ability to add special effects to your movies and animate those effects. After Effects' ability to create eye-catching animations with incredible special effects is probably why you brought the program in the first place.

The items that are listed in the Effect menu come from a variety of sources. Many third-party vendors offer add-ons for After Effects—this is one of the faster-growing markets at the moment. All of the effects in this chapter, however, are yours when you purchase Adobe After Effects—they come with the program.

In this chapter, you will:

- Explore the different Effect categories.
- Learn how to select options and set parameters for the various effects.
- Discover invaluable navigational shortcuts.

The exercises in this chapter provide the foundation you need to apply effects to your After Effects Projects. This is the longest and most detailed chapter in the book, so let's get started.

Feature Presentation

So far, we have used only a few filters to spice up our projects. This chapter introduces you to many of the effects shipping with the program and gives you an overview of how each can enhance your projects. Some of the effects that we will demonstrate in this chapter include: motion and radial blurs, mirror effects, drop shadow and bevel effects, embossing, creating mosaic tiles, adding a strobe light to your footage, and more.

Using Effects

You'll find the effects under—you guessed it—the Effects menu. Effects are divided into 14 subcategories: Blur, Blur & Sharpen, Channel, Distort, Image Control, Keying, Perspective, Render, Stylize, Synthesize, Text, Time Transition, and Video.

When you apply an effect to a layer, it appears inside of an Effects Control window. This window shows all of the effects added to a specific layer—and Effects can be stacked up like layers. If you add effects to more than one layer, you will have more than one Effects Control window in your image. Figure 13-1 shows the layout of the Effects Control window. Effects can also be toggled on/off individually by clicking on the box to the left of their name. Any parameters that can be adjusted are listed under the effect's name.

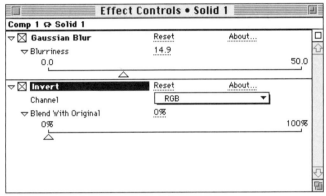

Figure 13-1: The Effects Control window.

You add and control keyframes to an effect in the Time Layout window, just as you would for any other property that you want to adjust. This means that you also need to click in the stop watch that appears when you turn down the arrow next to the effect name in the Layers palette. That is the only place where you can specify that a parameter be made keyframeable. If you only change the settings in the Effects Control window, you have created a constant—not a keyframeable property.

Any effect can be used in combination with any other. Filters can be stacked and rearranged just like any other layer within After Effects. The effects with a PS+ in front of their names are Photoshop effects. When you install After Effects for the first time, the installer will ask you to locate your copy of Adobe Photoshop. This will link After Effects to your Photoshop filters folder, making some of Photoshop's filters available to you. If you do not have the Photoshop filters installed, you will not see the PS+ effects as one of your Effect menu choices. Although these effects work just fine, they are not as reliably animated as their After Effects counterparts. Normally, the After Effects version offers more usable parameters. Plus, the After Effects version renders more quickly than its PS+ filter cousin.

Setting Up

In this chapter's project, you will see folders that correspond to different subcategories of effects. Each effect has a Comp, which should be used as a guide to the effect. To get the most out of this chapter, rebuild each effect when it's presented. Each effect has a corresponding finished movie folder. After you complete each Studio Time lesson, you have the option to render or preview the movie. If you do not wish to render the movie, simply select Preview (press the spacebar) and watch the Comp play on your screen. All the source footage provided for you in this chapter is 320 x 240 pixels—the size at which you would normally render anyway—and has been Cinepacked. This chapter includes many Comps that you are welcome to use for creating your own combinations of effects.

There are some keyboard shortcuts that will help you work with the Comps in this chapter. Typing the letter E reveals a layer's effects and works much like pressing the letter S for scale. Pressing Shift-E adds the Effects list to the properties already displayed on your screen. Highlighting a layer and pressing Cmd-T (Mac) or Ctrl-T (Windows) opens the layer's Effects window, which is where you can modify both the effects, as well as their order of application. To change an effect's position in the Rendering Queue, drag it above or below another effect.

Shortcuts

Command	Mac	Windows
Show a layer's effect	E	E
Show layer's Effect window	Cmd-T	Ctrl-T
Set Quality at Best	Cmd-U	Ctrl-U
Set Quality to Draft	Cmd-Shift-U	Ctrl-Shift-U
Set beginning of work area	B	B
Set the end of work area	N	N
Move ahead 10 frames	Cmd-Shift-Right arrow	Ctrl-Shift-Right arrow
Move back 10 frames	Cmd-Shift-Left arrow	Ctrl-Shift-Left arrow

Blur

There is only one effect in the Blur category. It is the Radial Blur filter that is "borrowed" from Photoshop.

PS+ Radial Blur

The PS+ Radial Blur blurs around a central point. There are two methods of blurring from which to choose: spin and zoom. Spin blurs around the center, mimicking a camera roll. Zoom also blurs around the center; however, it mimics a camera zooming in or out. The quality settings within this filter affect the output and rendering time. Figure 13-2 shows the PS+ Radial Blur dialog box that appears when you first add this effect.

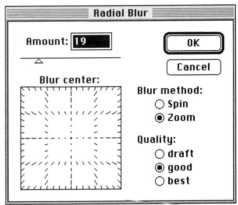

Figure 13-2: The PS+ Radial Blur dialog box.

The following project demonstrates the basics of using this filter. You will set up two Comps that illustrate the two methods of PS+ Radial Blur. The Comps are duplicates of each other, but with different parameters set.

 Studio Time: PS+ Radial Blur

1. Create a new Comp (Mac: Cmd-N, Windows: Ctrl-N). Make it 320 x 240, 6:15 seconds, at 30 fps. Name the Comp PS+ Radial Blur Spin.

2. Set the Current Time to 0.

3. Import the Girl.mov file from the AE13Foot folder (Mac: Cmd-I, Windows: Ctrl-I).

4. Drag the Girl.mov file into the center of the Comp window.

5. Apply Effects' Blur' PS+ Radial Blur. The first thing you will see is the effect's dialog box, as if you had applied it in Photoshop. You will need to specify the method, amount, and quality of blur. This filter tends to be slow so set the Quality to Good. Then we will set the method to Spin. Set a keyframe for the Blur Amount, which we will set at 1.

6. Set the Current Time to 3:00 seconds (Mac: Cmd-G, Windows: Ctrl-G, and type 3, or just move the Playback Head until the Current Time reads 0:00:03:00). Set the Blur Amount to 20.

7. Set the Current Time to 6:00 seconds. Set the blur back down to 1. The effect builds, then fades.

8. Save your work.

9. You've finished this Comp, so you can either preview or render it. Don't forget that there is still another Comp to create!

10. Go back to the Project window and duplicate the Comp.

11. Rename the Comp PS+ Radial Blur Zoom.

12. Open the Comp. Highlight the Girl.mov element. Use the "E" key to show the layers effects. Click on the Options button in the switch area of the Time Layout window. This brings up the options of the effect. Choose Zoom as the Blur method.

13. The zoom method is a little harder to see so let's go to the middle keyframe by setting the Current Time to 3:00 seconds. Next, let's increase the blur amount to 35.

14. Save your work.

15. Either preview the Comp by pressing the spacebar, or render it (Mac: Cmd-M, Windows: Ctrl-M).

Blur & Sharpen

There are a number of effects in the Blur & Sharpen category. This section describes them all. Blur and Sharpen effects are focus effects. The Blur-type filters all soften the focus in one way or another. The Sharpen effects increase the apparent focus of an image by accentuating the difference between neighboring pixels at the borders of a color "edge."

Channel Blur

Channel Blur enables you to blur specific channels independently of others. Equal amounts of this filter yield a result much like a Gaussian Blur. However, if you vary the amount used in each channel, you'll wind up with blurs that glow slightly.

Figure 13-3 shows the Channel Blur dialog box and the effect. Blurriness specifies the effect, in pixels, on each channel. The more you blur, the softer the image becomes. The repeat edge pixels prevent the edge from being affected. This filter is handy in reducing grain and noise on troubled footage.

The following example will create a colored glow.

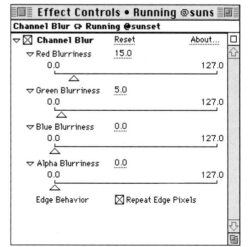

Figure 13-3: Channel Blur dialog box and the resulting effect.

Studio Time: Making the Runner Glow

We are going to blur two channels to create a glowing effect. You will notice a pattern in the keyframes: 1 second of parameter change, followed by 15 frames of sustain. Then the keyframes repeat with different parameters. Let's take a look.

1. Create a new Comp. Make it 320 x 240, 8:00 seconds, at 30 fps. Name it Glow Comp.

2. Set the Current Time to 0.

3. Import the Runsun.mov file from the AE13Foot folder (Mac: Cmd-I, Windows: Ctrl-I).

4. Drag the Runsun.mov file into the center of the Comp window.

5. Apply Effects → Blur → Channel Blur. Based on the colors of our footage, the blue channel doesn't really affect the image, so we won't use it.

6. Click in the stop watch to make Red Blurriness and Green Blurriness keyframeable. Set the Red to 0%, and the Green to 35.

7. Set the Current Time to 1:00 seconds (Mac: Cmd-G, Windows: Ctrl-G, and type 100). Set the Red to 20 and the Green to 5.

8. Set the Current Time to 1:15 seconds and make sustaining keyframes for Red Blurriness and Green Blurriness.

9. Set the Current Time to 2:15 seconds. Set the Red to 5 and the Green to 10.

10. Set the Current Time to 3:00 seconds. Make sustaining keyframes for Red Blurriness and Green Blurriness.

11. Set the Current Time to 4:00 seconds. Set the Red to 15 and the Green to 5.

12. Set the Current Time to 4:15 seconds. Make sustaining keyframes for Red Blurriness and Green Blurriness.

13. Set the Current Time to 5:15 seconds. Set the Red to 0 and the Green to 0.

14. Set the Current Time to 5:20 seconds. Set the end of your workspace (press N).

15. Make sure Repeat Edge Pixels is turned on.

16. Save the project.

We have successfully produced a slight glow.

Compound Blur

A Compound Blur allows us to blur one part of an image differently from another part. This blur is based on the luminance value of a grayscale image, its footage, or its Comp. We will refer to this as the Blur layer. Figure 13-4 shows the Compound Blur dialog and the effect. Note the pop-up menu enabling you to specify the Blur layer. By using a Comp, we can animate and control the blur over time. The principles of masking apply here: Black hides, white reveals. Quality settings affect the filter. Elements used as the Blur layer don't need to be visible in the Comp; they just need to appear in the Time Layout window.

Grayscale values are what make the Compound Blur work. We will use two Comps in this next example. In the first Comp, we will move a grayscale ramp from the bottom to the top, which will define the location of the Compound Blur. In the second Comp, we will use the grayscale Comp created in the first part of the exercise to create a blur across the entire image to gradually reveal the clean footage.

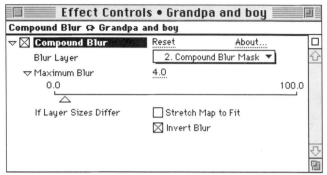

Figure 13-4: The Compound Blur dialog and the resulting effect.

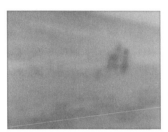

 Studio Time: Setting Up the Compound Blur Effect

1. Create a new Comp (Mac: Cmd-N, Windows: Ctrl-N) and name it Compound Blur Mask. Make it 320 x 240, 8:00 seconds, at 30 fps. Make the background black.

2. Set the Current Time to 0.

3. Import the GS320.psd file from the AE13Foot folder (Mac: Cmd-I, Windows: Ctrl-I).

4. Drag the GS320.psd file into the center of the Comp window.

5. Press P to display the Position property. Click in the stop watch to make Position keyframeable and set the Position to 160, 324.

6. Set the Current Time to 3:00 seconds (Mac: Cmd-G, Windows: Ctrl-G, and type 300).

7. Set a Position keyframe at 160,120.

8. The next keyframe will start moving "GS320.psd" out of the frame. As the ramp image moves out, the black background is revealed. Set the Current Time to 5:00 seconds. Set the final Position keyframe to 160, -34.

9. You will need a white solid to use as a background. Go back to 300, create a new solid (Mac: Cmd-Y, Windows: Ctrl-Y) that is 320 x 240 and white. Send it to the bottom (Mac: Cmd-B, Windows: Ctrl-B).

10. Set the Quality switch to Best.

11. Press the spacebar to preview the movie. You should see a black screen that reveals white.

12. Close the Comp (Mac: Opt-click, Windows: Alt-click, on the Time Layout window or Comp window close box). Both the Comp window and the Time Layout window close.

The Mask Comp is complete. Now it's time to apply the Mask to the effect.

 ## Studio Time: Applying the Compound Blur Effect

1. Create a new Comp (Mac: Cmd-N, Windows: Ctrl-N) and name it Compound Blur. Make it 320 x 240, 8:00 seconds, at 30 fps.

2. Set the Current Time to 0.

3. Import the Grandpa.mov from the AE13Foot folder (Mac: Cmd-I, Windows: Ctrl-I).

4. Drag the Grandpa.mov and Compound Blur Mask Comp files into the center of the Comp window.

5. Send the Blur Comp to the bottom and click on the Layer Visibility icon to hide it from view.

6. Highlight the Grandpa.mov layer.

7. Apply Effect → Blur & Sharpen → Compound Blur. The Blur layer is the Compound Blur Mask. You will only see two choices on the pop-up menu. Any element that is in the Comp will appear on the menu.

8. Set the Maximum Blur to 4.

9. Click the Stretch Map to Fit box off in the Effects Control window. The Map Comp is the correct size and does not need to be stretched.

10. Invert the blur, which is just like inverting the Mask Comp.

11. Set the layer's Quality to Best. Layer quality definitely affects this filter.

12. Press the spacebar to preview the movie, or Mac: Cmd-M, Windows: Ctrl-M, to render it.

Fast Blur

Fast Blur is similar to a Gaussian Blur, but not as accurate. Fast Blur is much faster than the Gaussian Blur, especially when applied to large areas. Use this filter when you want quick results and aren't concerned with accuracy. Fast Blur is ideal for smoothing textures. The higher you turn up the blur, the softer your image becomes. High resolution files require more blur to achieve the same effects as lower resolution files. As you blur the image, watch the edges of a solid layer. They often become softer and translucent. This effect is wonderful for creating drop shadows that move. Accuracy is not crucial with this effect; however, the speed in rendering is.

This next project demonstrates the effects of a Fast Blur that increases and then decreases over time.

 Studio Time: Fast Blur

1. Create a new Comp (Mac: Cmd-N, Windows: Ctrl-N) called Fast Blur. Make it 320 x 240, 06:15 seconds, at 30 fps. Set the Current Time to 0.

2. Drag the Girl.mov element into the center of the Comp window. Apply Effect → Blur & Sharpen → Fast Blur. Use the "E" key to show the layers effect. Click in the stop watch to make the Blurriness keyframeable. Set the Blurriness to a value of 0%.

3. Set the Current Time to 3:00 seconds. Set the Blurriness to a value of 20.

4. Set the Current Time to 6:00 seconds. Set the Blurriness to a value of 0.

5. This will increase and then decrease the effect.

6. Set the work area to the duration of the clip.

7. Save the project.

8. Preview or view the pre-rendered movie.

Gaussian Blur

The Gaussian Blur softens the image, making it look as if it were seen through a lens with Vaseline smeared on it. Gaussian Blur is a good way to eliminate the overall noise in an image, and it's a slower, more accurate filter than Fast Blur.

This next project demonstrates the effects of the Gaussian Blur, which will increase and then decrease over time.

 Studio Time: Gaussian Blur

1. Create a new Comp (Mac: Cmd-N, Windows: Ctrl-N). Make it 320 x 240, 6:15 seconds, at 30 fps. Name it Gaussian Blur.

2. Drag the Girl.mov file into the center of the Comp window.

3. Apply Effect → Blur & Sharpen → Gaussian Blur.

4. Use the "E" key to show the layers effects. Click in the stop watch to make the Blurriness keyframeable. Set the Blurriness to 0%.

6. Set the Current Time to 3:00 seconds (Mac: Cmd-G, Windows: Ctrl-G, and type 300). Set the Blurriness to a value of 12.

7. Set the Current Time to 6:00 seconds.

8. Make a final Blurriness keyframe, setting the value back to 0. This will increase the effect and then decrease it.

8. Set the work area to the duration of the clip.

9. Save the project.

10. Preview or view the pre-rendered movie.

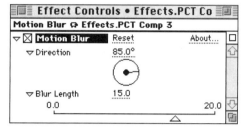

Figure 13-5: The Motion Blur dialog and the

Motion Blur

Motion Blur is another name for a Directional Blur. The Motion Blur filter mimics the real Motion Blur that After Effects applies to an image when rendering. Although the Motion Blur filter is not nearly as good as the real thing, it has a shorter rendering time. You should use the Motion Blur filter for animation requiring a quicker render. Usually, you will need to offset the image to make the blur more pronounced. Figure 13-5 shows the Motion Blur dialog and the effect.

In the dialog box, Direction specifies the direction of the blur and Blur Length refers to the amount of the blur. The Blur Length can be as high as 1000. To set the Blur Length above 20, click on the corresponding numerical value.

The next Studio Time moves a block of text across the window and uses this filter to simulate the Motion Blur effect.

 Studio Time: Motion Blur

1. Create a new Comp (Mac: Cmd-N, Windows: Ctrl-N). Make it 320 x 240, 3:00 seconds, at 30 fps. Name it Motion Blur. Set the background color to white (Mac: Shift-Cmd-B, Windows: Shift-Ctrl-B).

2. Set the Current Time to 0.

3. Import the Effects.psd file from the AE13Foot folder (Mac: Cmd-I, Windows: Ctrl-I).

4. Drag the Effects.psd element into the center of the Comp window.

5. Press S to bring up the Scale property. Set the Scale amount to 65%.

6. Press P to display the Position property. Click in the stop watch to make it keyframeable. Set the coordinates to 426,122.

7. Set the Current Time to 2:00 seconds (Mac: Cmd-G, Windows: Ctrl-G, and type 200). Set the keyframe coordinates to -110, 122.

8. Duplicate this layer.

9. Select the bottom layer.

10. Go to the first keyframe. Change the value of the X coordinate to 436. This will offset its position.

11. Go to the second keyframe and change its X coordinate to -102.

12. Compify the layer (Mac: Shift-Cmd-C, Windows: Shift-Ctrl- C). Let After Effects name the Comp. Accept the default name (Of.Ai Comp 1). Select "Move all attributes into the new Composition." Click OK. Compifying enables the Motion Blur to be applied to the entire frame, rather than just its size boundary.

13. Set the Current Time to 1:00 second.

14. Press T to bring up the Opacity property. Set the layer's Opacity to 75%. The image should start to make sense now.

15. Apply Effect → Blur & Sharpen → Motion Blur. Set the Direction to 85 degrees. The Blur length should be 15.

16. Set the Quality to Best.

17. Set your work area to end at 2:00 seconds.

18. Save the project.

19. Preview or view the pre-rendered movie.

Radial Blur

Radial Blurs are created around a specific point in a layer. As in the PS+ Radial Blur filter, the Radial Blur has two modes: spin and zoom. Spin simulates the effect of a zooming, rotating camera. Zoom simulates a camera zooming in. Radial Blur differs from the PS+ Radial Blur in the sense that its center position can be animated. If you own the Production Bundle, you can actually motion track a Radial Blur to an item. (See the Motion Tracking section in Chapter 16, Production Bundle, for more information on this topic.) With a Radial Blur, you can also specify the level of anti-aliasing. A Low setting renders faster than a High one. This filter is also affected by the layer's Quality settings, so you should beware of the grain at Draft quality. Figure 13-6 shows the Radial Blur dialog and the effect with the spin mode applied.

Below is the list of parameters that you can set in the Radial Blur filter.

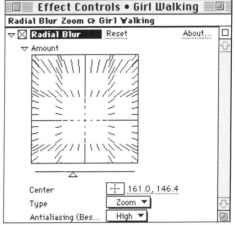

- *Spin* blurs in circles around the center point.

- *Zoom* blurs in lines that radiate from the center.

- *Center* enables you to set the blur's center point.

These properties are what makes Radial Blur different from the PS+ version. Also, Radial Blur's motion tracker information can be used to track a blur's center to a moving object.

Figure 13-6: The Radial Blur dialog and the resulting effect with the spin mode.

In the following exercise, we will experiment with both modes of the Radial Blur filter. You will have the chance to work with two Comps, which will be duplicates, but with different settings.

 Studio Time: Radial Blur

1. Create a new Comp (Mac: Cmd-N, Windows: Ctrl-N). Make it 320 x 240, 6:15 seconds, at 30 fps. Name it Radial Blur.

2. Set the Current Time to 0.

3. Drag the Girl.mov element into the center of the Comp window. Apply Effect → Blur & Sharpen → Radial Blur. Click in the stop watch to make the Amount and Center keyframeable.

4. It is easier to set this effect in the Layout window. In the Effects Control queue this item is controlled visually.

5. Grab the Center control from the effects queue. Click on the girl in the Comp window.

6. Set the Current Time to 6:00 seconds (Mac: Cmd-G, Windows: Ctrl-G, and type 600). Grab the Center control and click on the girl again. This will make the center of the blur move with the girl.

7. Set the Amount of blur to 20. As the center tracks the girl, the amount of blur increases.

8. Set the end of the work area to the length of the Comp.

9. Preview or view the pre-rendered movie. Close the Comp when done.

10. Now we will create the second Comp to illustrate the Zoom mode. Go to the project window and duplicate the Comp. Rename it Radial Blur Zoom.

11. Go to the first keyframe of the effect. Change Type to zoom instead of spin.

12. Go to the last keyframe and change the Amount to 75%. Zoom blurs need a higher setting to show the effect.

13. The center is already tracking the girl.

14. Save your work. Press the spacebar to preview the movie, or choose Composition → Make Movie to render it.

Sharpen

Sharpen increases the contrast where color changes occur. If over-applied, Sharpen can look grainy. Plus, it is not as accurate as the Unsharp Mask filter, which we'll discuss momentarily.

This next example uses the Sharpen filter on the Girl.mov footage. Notice how the increase in noise makes the movie seem jittery.

 Studio Time: Sharpen

1. Create a new Comp (Mac: Cmd-N, Windows: Ctrl-N). Make it 320 x 240, 6:15 seconds, at 30 fps. Name it Sharpen.

2. Set the Current Time to 0.

3. Drag the Girl.mov file into the center of the Comp window.

4. Apply Effect → Blur & Sharpen → Sharpen.

5. Use the "E" key to show the layers effects. Click in the stop watch to make the Sharpen Amount keyframeable. Set the keyframe value to 0%

6. Set the Current Time to 3:00 seconds. Set the Sharpen amount to 100.

7. Advance 15 frames and make a sustaining keyframe.

8. Set the Current Time back to 6:00 seconds and set the Sharpen amount to 0%.

9. Set the end of the work area to the length of the Comp.

10. Save your work. Press the spacebar to preview the movie, or choose Composition➔ Make Movie to render it.

Unsharp Mask

Unsharp Mask uses brightness and contrast to increase the sharpness of the image where colors meet other colors. Sharpness can be more fine-tuned using Unsharp Mask than by using Sharpen alone. Figure 13-7 shows the Unsharp Mask dialog and the effect. The Amount sets the amount of sharpness, the Radius counts how many pixels are being affected at a time, and the Threshold determines how many levels of high frequency colors the filter protects. The high-end colors can easily be over-sharpened. Threshold helps to control this.

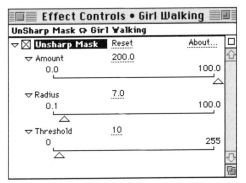

Figure 13-7: The Unsharp Mask dialog and the resulting effect.

Try playing with the Radius to achieve different results. This effect is very easy to over-apply, so you should use it accordingly. Over-applying this effect will yield images that look noisy and grainy.

In this next exercise, you will use Unsharp Mask to sharpen the Girl.mov footage. By using Threshold, you will protect random-noise pixels that are fairly close in value from being over-sharpened. When finished, you'll have footage that can be sharpened with greater control and depth.

 Studio Time: Unsharp Mask

1. Create a new Comp (Mac: Cmd-N, Windows: Ctrl-N). Make it 320 x 240, 6:00 seconds, at 30 fps. Name it Unsharp Mask.

2. Set the Current Time to 0.

3. Drag the Girl.mov file into the center of the Comp window.

4. Apply Effect ➔ Blur and Sharpen ➔ Unsharp Mask.

5. Show the layers effects. Click in the stop watch to make Amount, Radius, and Threshold keyframeable. Set the Amount to 300, the Radius to 1, and the Threshold to 0.

6. Set the Current Time to 2:00 seconds (Mac: Cmd-G, Windows: Ctrl-G, and type 200). Set the Amount to 200. Set a sustaining keyframe for Radius. Increase the Threshold to 5.

7. Set the Current Time to 2:15 seconds. Click in the Keyframe Navigation boxes of Amount, Radius, and Threshold to set sustaining keyframes.

8. The next process is to stabilize the Amount and change the Radius. As you increase Radius, also increase Threshold to prevent the footage from blowing out to white or black. Notice the color flicker on the horizon line.

9. Set the Current Time to 4:00 seconds. Set the Radius to 7 and the Threshold to 10.

10. Set the work area to end at 4:15 seconds.

11. Save the project.

12. Press the spacebar to preview the movie, or choose Composition → Make Movie to render it.

Channel

The Channel category of effects alters one of more of the channels in an image. The channels are either the Red, Green, or Blue color channels, a "virtual" channel calculated from Hue, Lightness, or Saturation, or an alpha (transparency) channel.

Arithmetic

The Arithmetic effect performs simple mathematical functions on specific channels of an image. Functions, such as multiplication, division, addition, and subtraction, can be performed on individual channels. Figure 13-8 shows the Arithmetic dialog.

The list below shows the parameters that can be changed in this effect.

- *Operator* allows you to choose the math function.

- *Red Value* allows you to set the value of the Red channel.

- *Green Value* allows you to set the value of the Green channel.

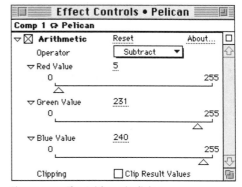

Figure 13-8: The Arithmetic dialog.

- *Blue Value* allows you to set the value of the Blue channel.

Blend

The Blend effect works by blending two images together using one of the following five methods: Crossfade, Color Only, Tint Only, Darken Only, or Lighten Only.

The next example demonstrates the Blend effect.

 ## Studio Time: Blend

1. Create a new Comp (Mac: Cmd-N, Windows: Ctrl-N). Make it 320 x 240, 6:15 seconds, at 30 fps. Name the it Blend.

2. Set the Current Time to 0.

3. Import the Lovers.mov and the Romance.mov from the AE13Foot folder (Mac: Cmd-I, Windows: Ctrl-I).

4. Drag the Lovers.mov and the Romance.mov files into the center of the Comp window.

5. Set the Current Time to 1:00 seconds (Mac: Cmd-G, Windows: Ctrl-G, and type 100). Apply Effect → Channel → Blend. Show the layers effects. Click in the stop watch to make the Blend With Original property keyframeable. Set the keyframe value to 0%. In the Effects Control, Blend With Layer will be the Romance.mov element, and the Mode will be Crossfade.

6. Set the Current Time to 3:00 seconds. Set Blend With Original to 100%.

7. The Romance element does not need to be visible.

8. Set the layers Quality switch to Best.

9. Set the work area to end at 315.

10. Save the project.

11. Press the spacebar to preview the movie, or choose Composition → Make Movie to render it.

Compound Arithmetic

This effect is obsolete in After Effects 3.0. However, it is included in this version so you can open and use files created in older versions of After Effects.

Invert

The Invert effect inverts the color information of an image.

Minimax

The Minimax effect assigns each pixel a minimum or maximum value based on a value located within a specified radius.

Remove Color Matting

The Remove Color Matting effect helps remove the color halo around images with an alpha channel. Removing or changing the color of the matte can help reduce halos.

Set Channels

The Set Channels effect enables you to set the channels of one image with channels from another. This effect provides you with an interesting way to combine images.

The following exercise combines two elements using this effect.

 Studio Time: Set Channels

1. Create a new Comp (Mac: Cmd-N, Windows: Ctrl-N). Make it 320 x 240, 7 seconds, at 30 fps.

2. Set the Current Time to 0.

3. Import the Runbirds.mov files from the AE13Foot folder (Mac: Cmd-I, Windows: Ctrl-I).

4. Drag the Romance.mov and Runbirds.mov files into the center of the Comp window.

5. Apply Effect → Channel → Set Channels. Figure 13-9 shows the Set Channels dialog and the effect.

6. Set the Source Layer 1 to Runbirds.mov.

7. Set Red to Source 1's Green.

8. Set the Source Layer 2 to Runbirds.mov.

9. Set Green to Source 2's Green.

10. Set the Source Layer 3 to None.

11. Set Blue to Source 3's Blue.

12. Set the Source Layer 4 to Romance.mov.

13. Set Alpha To Source 4's Luminance.

14. Leave the Stretch Layers to Fit, unchecked.

15. Save the project.

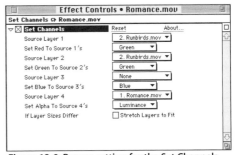

Figure 13-9: Proper setting for the Set Channels dialog and the resulting effect.

16. Press the spacebar to preview the movie, or choose Composition → Make Movie to render it.

Set Matte

The Set Matte effect allows you to assign an element's alpha channel to another element. The other element must be present in the Comp; however, it does not need to be visible. The problem with this filter is you really don't have any control over the element acting as the alpha channel. Transforming the alpha element doesn't give you any control either. You're better off choosing the Track Matte effect.

The Comp Set Matte A illustrates this effect's shortcoming, and the Comp Set Matte B shows why Track Matte works better.

 Studio Time: Set Matte

The Studio Time for the Set Matte effect differs from our normal Studio Times. In this instance, it demonstrates why this is not as effective as a Track Matte. The second Comp is provided as an example. For more information on matting, see Chapter 11, Mattes. Figure 13-10 shows the Set Matte dialog with settings that reflect the Comp below.

1. Create a new Comp (Mac: Cmd-N, Windows: Ctrl-N). Make it 320 x 240, at 30 fps. Name the Comp Set Matte A.

2. Set the Current Time to 0.

3. Import the Effects.psd file from the AE13Foot folder (Mac: Cmd-I, Windows: Ctrl-I).

4. Drag the Runsun.mov and the Effects.psd files into the center of the Comp window.

5. Highlight the Effects.psd layer. Press S to bring up the Scale property. Set the Scale amount to 75%. Notice how it appears. Send it to the bottom (Mac: Cmd-B, Windows: Ctrl-B) and click on the Layers Visibility icon to hide it from view.

6. Highlight the Runsun.mov layer. Add the Set Matte effect to it.

7. In the Effects Control, set Take Matte From to Effects.psd.

Figure 13-10: The Set Matte dialog and the resulting effect.

8. Set Use for Matte to the alpha channel.

9. Turn off the checkboxes for the next four items. Notice that your result is larger than your scaled type.

Avoid using this effect. Surprisingly enough, even compifying the type element has no bearing on the matte.

The Comp Set Matte B demonstrates the advantages of using the Track Matte to achieve the same result. You learned about Track Mattes in Chapter 11.

In order to put together this example, we created a Type Comp to use as a Track Matte. The type was scaled from 0 to 75%. A full rotation was also added. The layer was then specified as the Track Matte for the Runsun.mov element. The Type layer was duplicated and sent to the bottom. Next, the layer was offset 2 pixels (or two arrow keystrokes) right and 2 pixels down. The Opacity was set to 75%. A Fast Blur of 6 was then applied to soften the shadow.

Shift Channels

Shift Channels is very much like the Set Channels effect. It enables you to specify one channel as another. The major difference is that Shift Channels only works with one source: itself. Set Channels, however, lets you use additional sources. Figure 13-11 shows the Shift Channels dialog and the effect. The settings depicted are the ones used in the example that follows. Unfortunately, you cannot animate from one channel to another. The result of this effect is a re-coloration of the original footage.

We will shift the channels in this example to create a purple tint to the footage.

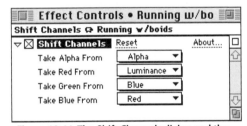

Figure 13-11: The Shift Channels dialog and the resulting effect.

Studio Time: Shift Channels

1. Create a new Comp (Mac: Cmd-N, Windows: Ctrl-N). Make it 320 x 240, at 30 fps. Name the Comp Channel Shift.

2. Set the Current Time to 0.

3. Drag the Runbirds.mov file into the center of the Comp window.

4. Apply Effect → Channel → Shift Channels.

5. Set the following parameters:

- Take Alpha From: Alpha.

- Take Red From: Luminance.

- Take Green From: Blue.

- Take Blue From: Red.

6. Save the project.

Press the spacebar to preview the movie, or choose Composition → Make Movie to render it.

Distort

The Distort category of effects—surprise!—distorts the geometry of the image. They warp, misshape, bend, stretch, and otherwise mistreat the pixels to create sometimes wild effects. There are a number of built-in effects in this category, and a number of effects borrowed from Photoshop.

Mirror

Mirror can be a wild, as well as useful, filter. It allows you to pick a point to act as the center of the mirrored reflection. You can also specify the angle of the reflection.

Figure 13-12 shows the Mirror dialog box. Note how it is used in conjunction with the Brightness & Contrast effect (which we will discuss later in this chapter). In a moment, we will create some Comps that explore using the Mirror effect.

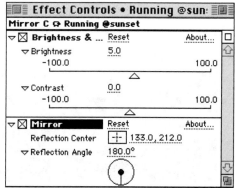

Figure 13-12: Mirror effect used with a second effect.

Studio Time: Mirror Effect

1. Create a new Comp (Mac: Cmd-N, Windows: Ctrl-N). Make it 320 x 240, 7:00 seconds, at 30 fps. Name it Mirror Comp A.

2. Set the Current Time to 0.

3. Drag the Runbird.mov file into the center of the Comp window. Apply Effect → Channel → Set Channels.

4. Set the Reflection Center coordinates to 160, 173. The Reflection Angle is 90 degrees. The Reflection Center and Reflection Angle make it look as though the man is running along the water. The Mirror effect provides the reflection in the water.

5. Add a Brightness & Contrast effect to the image. Set the Brightness to 4, and the Contrast to -4. This effect will brighten this movie a bit. It can be applied either before or after the Mirror effect. We are applying it first.

6. Save the project.

7. Press the spacebar to preview the movie, or Composition → Make Movie to render it. Close up this Comp when finished.

8. Now we'll make the second version of this effect. Duplicate the Mirror Comp A in the Project window. Rename it Mirror Comp B. Double click on the Comp to open it.

9. Highlight the Runbirds layer and Compify it. Name the new Comp Runbirds.mov. Move the attributes to the new Comp.

10. Apply the Mirror effect. The Reflection Center's position is 160, 120. The Reflection Angle is 90 degrees. The results are wonderful!

11. Save the project.

12. Press the spacebar to preview the movie, or choose Composition → Make Movie to render it. Close up this Comp when finished.

13. Let's use a different source file for Mirror Comp C. Create a new Comp. Make it 320 x 240, 6:15 seconds, at 30 fps. Name it Mirror C.

14. Drag the Runsun.mov into the Layout window.

15. Set the Current Time to 0. Highlight the Runsun.mov layer. Apply Effect → Image Control → Brightness & Contrast. Set the Brightness to 5, and the Contrast to 0.

16. Apply Effect → Distort → Mirror. We are going to change the Reflection Center over time. The object here is to try to keep the man from moving completely out of the Mirror effect.

17. Set the Reflection Angle to 180 degrees. This setting remains constant.

18. Click in the stop watch to make the Reflection Center keyframeable. Set the coordinates to 133, 212.

19. Set the Current Time to 4:00 seconds (Mac: Cmd-G, Windows: Ctrl-G, and type 400). Create a sustaining keyframe.

20. Set the Current Time to 6:00 seconds. Set the Reflection Center coordinates to 160, 212.

21. Set the work area to the outpoint of the Runsun.mov layer.

22. Save the Project.

23. Press the spacebar to preview the movie, or choose Composition → Make Movie to render it. Close up this Comp when finished.

Offset

The Offset filter moves the image within the layer. Images pushed off to the right and the bottom will return (wrap) around the left and top. It is very useful for creating seamless effects. If you create a seamless pattern and use the Offset filter, you can make it wrap continuously as the pattern scrolls across the movie.

Polar Coordinates

The Polar Coordinates effect takes an image and maps it to a polar space (as if you are going from a flat projection of the earth to one that shows the spherical shape of the earth). The following example will create a sparkling, glinting image that flies off screen. You will use a few other effects to help out; there will be four Comps in all.

 ## Studio Time: Polar Coordinates

1. Create a new Comp (Mac: Cmd-N, Windows: Ctrl-N). Make it 320 x 240, 6:50 seconds, at 30 fps. Name it Gray 4 sparkle 1.

2. Set the Current Time to 0.

3. Create a new solid (Mac: Cmd-Y, Windows: Ctrl-Y). Keep the default name. The size should be 80 x 1. Set the color to a middle gray. You can set the individual RGB values to 30583.

4. Apply the Effect → Stylize → Noise. Set the amount to 100. Turn off Use Color Noise and Clip Result Values. This will cycle through random values.

5. Press S to bring up the Scale property, and set the layer's Scale. Click on the Units pop-up menu, and choose % of Composition. Click off the Preserve Frame Aspect Ratio. Set the two values to 100%. The Gray noise now covers the whole Comp.

6. Create another new solid (Mac: Cmd-Y, Windows: Ctrl-Y). Use the default name for this solid too. The size should be 320 x 240, and the color should be the same as the other solid.

7. Apply Effect → Synthesize → Ramp. Ramp applies a gradient to the solid. Figure 13-13 shows the settings for the Ramp effect and its result. The coordinates for the black Start of Ramp should be set to 160, 184.5. The End of Ramp coordinates should be set to 160, 71.5. Set the color to white and the Ramp Shape to linear. Set Ramp Scatter and Blend With Original to 0.

 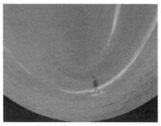 

8. Change the Layer mode to Multiply. You should see the gray stripes fading off to black at the bottom. Close the Comp (Mac: Opt-click, Windows: Alt-click, on the Time Layout window or Comp window close box). Both the Comp window and the Time Layout window close.

9. Create a new Comp (Mac: Cmd-N, Windows: Ctrl-N). Make it 320 x 240, 6:50 seconds, at 30 fps. Name it Sparkle Polar.

10. Drag the Gray for Sparkle 1 file element into the center of the Comp window.

Figure 13-13: Polar Coordinates effect dialog and the resulting effect.

11. Apply Effect → Distort → Polar Coordinates. Set the Interpolation to 100%. Set the Type of Conversion to Rect To Polar. You should see a rounded Sparkle image. You will need to smooth the hard line; here's how to do it.

12. Apply Effect → Blur & Sharpen → Fast Blur. Set the value to 2. Preview the file and notice how it changes at random. Close the Comp (Mac: Opt-click, Windows: Alt-click, on the Time Layout window or Comp window close box).

13. Create a new Comp (Mac: Cmd-N, Windows: Ctrl-N). Make it 320 x 240, 6:15 seconds, at 30 fps. Name it Sparkles Smoothed. The hard line was smoothed out, but not hidden in the previous example; this time, you will get rid of it.

14. Drag the Sparkle Polar Comp into the center of the Comp window.

15. Duplicate the Sparkle Polar Comp. Press R to show the Rotate property. Set the Rotation of one layer to 14 degrees and the other to 7. You have now covered up the hard edge.

16. Close up this Comp.

17. Create a new Comp (Mac: Cmd-N, Windows: Ctrl-N). Make it 320 x 240, 6:15 seconds, at 30 fps. Name it Polar Coordinates.

18. Set the Current Time to 0.

19. Drag the Sparkles Smooth Comp and the Grandpa.mov file into the center of the Comp window. Send Grandpa.mov to the bottom (Mac: Cmd-B, Windows: Ctrl-B).

20. The Sparkles element looks weird. Set its mode to Screen to make things look better.

21. Set the Current Time to 2:00 seconds (Mac: Cmd-G, Windows: Ctrl-G, and type 200. Click in the stop watch to make the Position keyframeable. Set the coordinates to 234, 95; the Sparkle element should be positioned over Grandpa's hands.

22. Set the Current Time to 4:15 seconds. Set the Position keyframe coordinates to -66, -34. This moves the Sparkle out of the frame and to the left.

23. Set the Current Time back to 0. Click in the stop watch to make the Scale keyframeable. Set the Scale amount to 0%.

24. Set the Current Time to 1:00 seconds (Mac: Cmd-G, Windows: Ctrl-G, and type 100). Set the Scale amount to 30%.

25. Set the Current Time to 2:00 seconds. Create a sustaining keyframe.

26. Set the Current Time to 4:15 seconds. Set the Scale amount to 55%. This makes the Sparkle element smaller as it exits.

27. The effect is complete! Set the Quality switches to Best.

28. Set the work area to end at 415.

29. Press the spacebar to preview the movie, or choose Composition → Make Movie to render it. Close up this Comp when finished.

PS+Pinch

In this next exercise, PS+Pinch is used to make part of the image seem smaller. Applying negative pinch makes that same part seem bigger.

Figure 13-14 shows this effect used in conjunction with the Tint effect.

You will animate an image of a pelican using PS+Pinch. You will make the pelican shrink and then grow.

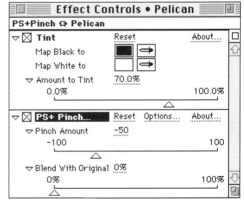

Figure 13-14: PS+Pinch used with the Tint effect.

 Studio Time: PS+Pinch

1. Create a new Comp (Mac: Cmd-N, Windows: Ctrl-N). Make it 320 x 240, 6:15 seconds, at 30 fps. Name it PS+Pinch.

2. Set the Current Time to 0.

3. Import the Pelican.mov file from the AE13Foot folder (Mac: Cmd-I, Windows: Ctrl-I).

4. Drag the Pelican.mov file into the center of the Comp window.

5. Apply Effect → Image Control → Tint. Set Map Black To: to Black and Map White To: to White. Set the Amount to Tint to 70%.

6. At frame 15, apply Effect → Distort → PS+Pinch. Click in the stop watch to make the Pinch Amount keyframeable. Set the value to 0.

7. Set the Current Time to 1:25 seconds (Mac: Cmd-G, Windows: Ctrl-G, and type 125). Set the Pinch Amount to 50. This will make the pelican seem smaller.

8. Set the Current Time to 4:00 seconds. Set the Pinch Amount to -50. The pelican will appear bloated now.

9. Set the Current Time to 4:25 seconds. Set the Pinch Amount to 0. This will return the Pelican back to its original state and finish the effect.

10. Set the work area to end at 4:25. Set the Quality switches to Best.

11. Save the project.

12. Press the spacebar to preview the movie, or choose Composition → Make Movie to render it. Close up this Comp when finished.

PS+Ripple

The PS+Ripple effect adds ripples to your footage. The results are pleasing when used to add a wiggle distortion to your image.

This next exercise turns up the PS+Ripple effect on an element, sustains it briefly, and then fades it back down.

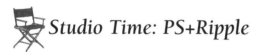 *Studio Time: PS+Ripple*

1. Create a new Comp (Mac: Cmd-N, Windows: Ctrl-N). Make it 320 x 240, 6:15 seconds, at 30 fps. Name it PS+Ripple.

2. Set the Current Time to 0.

3. Drag the Romance.mov file into the center of the Comp window.

4. Set the Current Time to 20 frames (Mac: Cmd-G, Windows: Ctrl-G, and type 20). Apply Effect → Distort → PS+Ripple.

5. Click in the stop watch to make the Amount keyframeable. Set the Amount value to 0%.

6. Set the Current Time to 3:00 seconds (Mac: Cmd-G, Windows: Ctrl-G, and type 300). Set the Amount to 200. This will build the effect up.

7. Set the Current Time to 3:15 seconds. Click in the Keyframe Navigation box to make a sustaining keyframe.

8. Set the Current Time to 5:00 seconds. Set the Amount to 0. This fades out the effect.

9. Set the work area to end at 5:00.

10. Save the project.

11. Press the spacebar to preview the movie, or choose Composition ➜ Make Movie to render it. Close up this Comp when finished.

PS+Spherize

PS+Spherize makes an image look spherical. The PS+Spherize example will makes the image look as if it is bulging in, then out.

 Studio Time: PS+Spherize

1. Create a new Comp (Mac: Cmd-N, Windows: Ctrl-N). Make it 320 x 240, 6:15 seconds, at 30 fps. Name the Comp PS+Spherize.

2. Set the Current Time to 0.

3. Drag the Romance.mov file into the center of the Comp window.

4. Set the Current Time to 0:15 seconds (Mac: Cmd-G, Windows: Ctrl-G, and type 015). Apply Effect ➜ Distort ➜ PS+Spherize.

5. Click in the stop watch to make the Amount keyframeable. Set the Amount to 0.

6. Set the Current Time to 2:15 seconds (Mac: Cmd-G, Windows: Ctrl-G, and type 215). Set the Amount to 100. This will make the image bulge out.

7. Set the Current Time to 3:00 seconds. Set a sustaining keyframe.

8. Set the Current Time to 4:15 seconds. Set the amount to 0. This will fade out the effect.

9. Set the work area to end at 4:15.

10. Save the project

11. Press the spacebar to preview the movie, or choose Composition ➜ Make Movie to render it. Close up this Comp when finished.

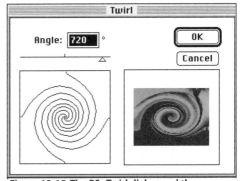

Figure 13-15: The PS+Twirl dialog and the resulting effect.

PS+Twirl

The PS+Twirl filter is a great effect that twists your image, somewhat like the spin art you can find at amusement parks. Figure 13-15 shows the PS+Twirl dialog and the effect. Note the preview's wireframe and picture.

This next Project will twirl an image and then restore it.

 Studio Time: PS+Twirl

1. Create a new Comp (Mac: Cmd-N, Windows: Ctrl-N). Make it 320 x 240, 6:15 seconds, at 30 fps. Name the it PS+Twirl.

2. Set the Current Time to 0.

3. Drag the Romance.mov file into the center of the Comp window.

4. Set the Current Time to 20 frames (Mac: Cmd-G, Windows: Ctrl-G, and type 20). Apply Effect → Distort → PS+Twirl.

5. Click in the stop watch to make the Twirl Angle keyframeable. Set the Twirl Angle to 0, 0.

6. Set the Current Time to 2:15 seconds. Set the Twirl Angle to 2 rotations. This will twirl the image.

7. Set the Current Time to 4:15 seconds. Set the Twirl Angle to 0, 0. This will reverse the direction of the twirl.

8. Set the work area to end at 4:15.

9. Save the project.

10. Press the spacebar to preview the movie, or choose Composition → Make Movie to render it. Close up this Comp when finished.

PS+Wave

The PS+Wave effect makes your image look like you applied a wave to it. This filter misbehaves and creates unpleasant artifacts when you change the number of generators used over time, so you should avoid animating it.

This next example demonstrates some of the PS+Wave effect settings.

 Studio Time: PS+Wave

1. Create a new Comp (Mac: Cmd-N, Windows: Ctrl-N). Make it 320 x 240, 615 seconds, at 30 fps. Name it PS+Wave.

2. Set the Current Time to 0.

3. Drag the Romance.mov file into the center of the Comp window.

4. Apply Effect → Distort → PS+Wave. Click at the following times to set keyframes for the following items. The number of Generators will remain constant at 5 (See Table 13-1).

5. Set the work area to end at 5:00.

6. Save the project.

7. Press the spacebar to preview the movie, or choose Composition → Make Movie to render it. Close up this Comp when finished.

At :00	At 2:15	At 5:00
Horizontal Scale-100	Horizontal Scale-75	Horizontal Scale-50
Vertical Scale-100	Vertical Scale-75	Vertical Scale-50
Min Amplitude-1	Min Amplitude-3	Min Amplitude-1
Max Amplitude-1	Max Amplitude-34	Max Amplitude-1
Min Wavelength-1	Min Wavelength-22	

Table 13-1: Setting up the keyframes for the PS+ Wave effect

PS+Zigzag

The PS+Zigzag effect gives the appearance of ripples in a pond. The next Comp creates a ripple that fades on and off.

 Studio Time: PS+Zigzag

1. Create a new Comp (Mac: Cmd-N, Windows: Ctrl-N). Make it 320 x 240, 6:15 seconds, at 30 fps. Name it PS+Zigzag.

2. Set the Current Time to 0.

3. Drag the Romance.mov file into the center of the Comp window.

4. Set the Current Time to 0:20 seconds (Mac: Cmd-G, Windows: Ctrl-G, and type 020). Apply Effect → Distort → PS+Zigzag.

5. Click in the stop watch to make the Amount keyframeable. Set the amount to 0.

6. Set the number of ridges to 8.

7. Set the Current Time to 3:00 seconds (Mac: Cmd-G, Windows: Ctrl-G, and type 300). Set the amount to 25. This will build up the effect.

8. Set the Current Time to 5:00 seconds. Set the amount to 0. This will fade the effect.

9. Set the work area to end at 5:15.

10. Save the project.

11. Press the spacebar to preview the movie, or choose Composition → Make Movie to render it. Close up this Comp when finished.

Spherize

The After Effects version of this effect gives you more control than the PS+ version. The Center of Sphere element, as well as the Radius, can be animated. Figure 13-16 shows the Spherize dialog and the effect.

This next Project demonstrates the effect that you obtain by moving the Center of Sphere.

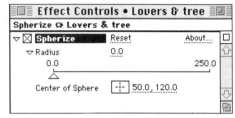

Figure 13-16: Spherize dialog and the resulting effect.

 Studio Time: Spherize

1. Create a new Comp (Mac: Cmd-N, Windows: Ctrl-N). Make it 320 x 240, 6:15 seconds, at 30 fps. Name it Spherize.

2. Set the Current Time to 0.

3. Drag the Romance.mov file into the center of the Comp window.

4. Apply Effect → Distort → Spherize. Click in the stop watch to make the Radius keyframeable. Set the keyframe value to 0, 0. Click in the stop watch to make the Center of Sphere keyframeable. Set the Center of Sphere coordinates to 160 x 120.

5. Set the Current Time to 1:00 seconds (Mac: Cmd-G, Windows: Ctrl-G, and type 100). Set the Radius to 100. Make a sustaining keyframe for Center of Sphere.

6. Set the Current Time to 2:00 seconds. Set the Radius to 125. Set new Center of Sphere coordinates at 257,120. This starts to move the sphere around.

7. Set the Current Time to 4:00 seconds. Set the Radius to 0 and the Center of Sphere to 50, 120.

8. Set the work area to end at 4:00.

9. Set Quality switches to Best.

10. Save the project.

11. Press the spacebar to preview the movie, or choose Composition → Make Movie to render it. Close up this Comp when finished.

Image Control

These effects will allow you to change the color value of your images.

Brightness & Contrast

Brightness & contrast adjusts the brightness and contrast of the entire layer. The layer's Quality switch does not affect the Brightness & Contrast filter.

Change Color

The Change Color effect adjusts the hue, saturation, and lightness for a range of colors. You can specify the criteria upon which the color change is based.

- *View* allows you to choose what you can see in the layer.

- *Hue Transform* enables you to set the hue in degrees. This will adjust the selected color.

- *Lightness Transform* controls the amount you can lighten or darken the selected color.

- *Saturation Transform* allows you to increase or decrease the saturation of the selected colors.

- *Color to Change* specifies the color you wish to change.

- *Matching Tolerance* specifies the degree of color matching, before the color is affected by the color change.

- *Matching Softness* specifies the softness of the color correction. The softness is based on the base color, not the affected color.

- *Match Color* specifies the criteria used to determine the similarity of two colors.

Color Balance

The Color Balance effect changes the amounts of Red, Green, and Blue in a layer. The control's center point is neutral. A -100 setting removes the color; a 100 setting intensifies the color.

Color Balance HLS

The Color Balance HLS effect alters an image's hue, lightness, and saturation. Hue adjusts the color. Lightness adjusts the lightness and darkness of an image. Saturation changes the intensity of the color.

Equalize

The Equalize effect alters the image's pixel values to create a more even brightness distribution. Using Equalize enables you to pick the method of equalization. *RGB* equalizes based on the individual channel components. *Brightness* uses the Brightness values of each pixel in the image. *Photoshop Style* equalizes based on redistributing the brightness values on a more even basis.

Layer Quality settings do not effect this filter.

Gamma/Pedestal/Gain

This effect adjusts the response curve for each channel independently. *Gamma* describes the shape of the curve, *Pedestal* specifies the lowest achievable output value for a channel, and *Gain* specifies the largest achievable output value for a channel.

Black Stretch remaps the low pixel values of all channels. Large Black Stretch values brighten dark areas. Black Stretch could be used to raise the black level of a video to broadcast quality; however, this technique is rarely used.

Layer Quality settings do not affect this filter.

Levels

The Levels effect allows you to remap a set of input values to a set of output values. You can also change the image gamma at the same time. Gamma can be set independently of low and high values. Figure 13-17 shows the Levels dialog applied to one element.

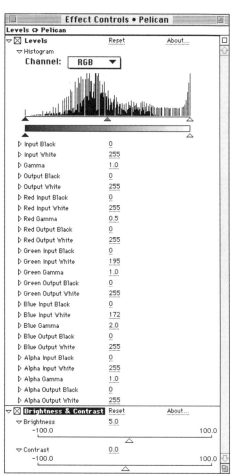

Figure 13-17: Levels dialog.

Median

The Median effect replaces each pixel with the median pixel value (the pixel in the middle) of neighboring pixels within a specified radius. Low value settings on this effect can reduce noise. High value settings produce painterly effects because the effect then removes so much of the variation in pixels that image starts to look as if it had been rendered in water colors.

Tint

The Tint effect changes the color of an image. You can select a color that replaces the black pixels in the image (the Map Black To color) and another color to replace the white pixels in the image (the Map White To color). The colors in between are assigned intermediate values that are a blend of the two tint colors. Figure 13-18 shows the Color Control for Tint and Levels.

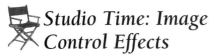 *Studio Time: Image Control Effects*

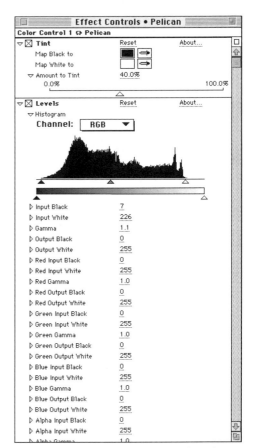

Figure 13-18: Color Control for Tint and Levels.

This next Studio Time consists of two Comps that use a combination of Image Control effects to color correct an image of a pelican. This footage was shot with a red filter to influence the image's color. We wouldn't want this to be easy would we?

1. Create a new Comp (Mac: Cmd-N, Windows: Ctrl-N). Make it 320 x 240, 0:10 seconds, at 30 fps. Name it Levels.

2. Set the Current Time to 0.

3. Drag the Pelican.mov file into the center of the Comp window.

4. Apply Effect → Image Control → Levels. Previous Figure 13-18 shows the Levels settings applied to the image. The individual channels have been tweaked to achieve a balance that works. Change the Green Input to 195, the Blue Input White to 172, and increase Blue Gamma to 2.

5. Apply Effect → Image Control → Brightness & Contrast to lighten the image. Set Lightness to 5.

6. Try playing with the settings and exploring on your own.

7. Set the work area to end at 2:00.

8. Press the spacebar to preview the movie, or choose Composition ➔ Make Movie to render it. Close up this Comp when finished.

9. Duplicate the Levels Comp in the Project window and rename it Color control 1. Double click the new Comp to open it.

10. Remove all effects.

11. Apply Effect ➔ Image Control ➔ Tint. Leave the Map settings as they are. Change Amount to Tint to 40%. This will neutralize the image a bit.

12. Apply Effect ➔ Image Control ➔ Levels. Simply change Input Black to 7 and Input White to 226. If it hasn't changed already, change the Gamma to 1, 1. This will add some life back into the image. The effect is complete.

13. Try playing with the setting and exploring on your own.

14. Set the work area to end at 2:00.

15. Press the spacebar to preview the movie, or choose Composition ➔ Make Movie to render it. Close up this Comp when finished.

Keying

Keying Effects are used to make areas of the image transparent based on a specific "key"—a color or a luminosity. The effects that come with After Effects are very basic. There are more sophisticated keying effects in the Production Bundle (discussed in Chapter 16).

Color Key

The Color Key filter affects all the pixels in an image that are similar to the specified key color. The result of this effect is to create transparency where the key color once was. Only the layer's alpha channel is affected. Figure 13-19 shows the Color Key settings and the effect. The *key color* is the color that will be made transparent.

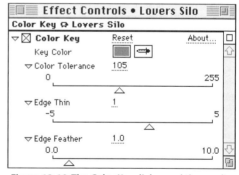

Figure 13-19: The Color Key dialog and the resulting effect.

■ *Color Tolerance* specifies how closely the color matches the key color. Higher values yield a broader range of the color.

■ *Edge Thin* specifies how the border matte is adjusted. Negative numbers make the mask smaller, eliminating the remains of the key color. Positive numbers make the mask bigger, allowing more key color to show.

■ *Edge Feather* specifies how much the mask's edge will be blurred or softened.

In this next exercise, you will use Color Key to composite the Lovers Silo on top of the Running w/boids footage.

 Studio Time: Color Key

1. Create a new Comp (Mac: Cmd-N, Windows: Ctrl-N). Make it 320 x 240, 6:15 seconds, at 30 fps. Name it Color Key.

2. Set the Current Time to 0.

3. Drag the Lovers.mov and Runbirds.mov files into the center of the Comp window. You don't need to make any keyframes because the effect will remain constant.

4. Apply Effect → Keying → Color Key to the Lovers.mov file.

5. Use the Eyedropper to select the orange background.

6. Set the Color Tolerance to 105.

7. Set Edge Thin to 1; this should set the edge nicely.

8. Set Edge Feather to 1; this should be smooth enough.

9. Set the work area end at 5:00. Set the Quality switches to Best.

10. Save the project.

11. Press the spacebar to preview the movie, or Composition → Make Movie to render it. Close up this Comp when finished.

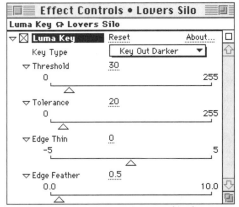

Figure 13-20: Luma Key settings used in the Studio Time and the resulting effect.

Luma Key

The Luma Key effect makes transparent all areas of an image with a specified luminance or brightness. Figure 13-20 shows the Luma Key dialog and the effect.

- *Key Type* replaces the image with transparency, based upon a set of criteria you establish.

- *Key Out Brighter* removes pixels with a greater Brightness than the Threshold.

- *Key Out Darker* does the opposite, removing pixels that are darker than the Threshold.

- *Key Out Similar* removes pixels within the Tolerance of the Threshold.

- *Key Out Dissimilar* moves pixels further away from the Threshold.

- *Threshold* sets the cutoff brightness value for Key Out Brighter and Key Out Darker.

- *Tolerance* sets the range of luminance levels you wish the effect to key out.

- *Edge Thin* specifies how the border matte should be adjusted. Negative numbers make the mask smaller, eliminating the remains of the key color. Positive numbers make the mask bigger, allowing more key color to show.

- *Edge Feather* specifies how much the edge of the mask will be blurred or softened.

The following Studio Time demonstrates using the Luma Key effect on Lovers.mov and filling it with the layer below it. You will see how to use the edge effects to create a shadow around the lovers.

 Studio Time: Luma Key

1. Create a new Comp (Mac: Cmd-N, Windows: Ctrl-N). Make it 320 x 240, 6:15 seconds, at 30 fps. Name it Luma Key.

2. Set the Current Time to 0.

3. Drag the Lovers.mov and Runbirds.mov files into the center of the Comp window. You will not need to set any keyframes because the effect will remain constant.

4. Apply Effect → Keying → Luma Key to the Lovers.mov file.

5. Set the Key Type to Key Out Darker.

6. Set the Threshold to 30.

7. Set the Tolerance to 20.

8. You do not need the Edge Thin property.

9. Set the Edge Feather to .5; this should be smooth enough.

10. Set the work area to end at 5:00. Set the Quality switches to Best.

11. Save the project.

12. Press the spacebar to preview the movie, or choose Composition → Make Movie to render it. Close up this Comp when finished.

Perspective

You can adjust an image's perspective using these controls.

Basic 3D

Basic 3D turns any element into a three-dimensional object. You can also add a specular highlight. Warning: Basic 3D is not a quick filter to execute.

■ *Swivel* controls the horizontal rotation

■ *Tilt* controls the vertical rotation.

■ *Distance to Image* sets the image's distance from the viewer, which helps keep your image from getting clipped by its boundaries.

■ *Specular Highlight* adds a highlight that moves across a rotating image.

This filter was also used in Chapter 5.

Bevel Alpha

The Bevel Alpha effect gives elements with alpha channels an embossed look. This effect is very popular on text-based elements. Figure 13-21 shows the Bevel Alpha dialog.

■ *Edge Thickness* specifies the thickness of the beveled edge in pixels.

■ *Light Angle* specifies the direction from which the emboss is coming.

■ *Light Color* allows you to set a color to the embossed edge.

■ *Light Intensity* sets the contrast from light to dark within the shape. If you set the light too high, the type will look as if it's been blown out. This will cause your image to lose detail and create pixel distortions.

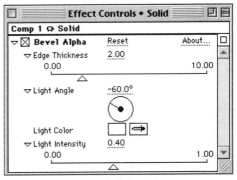

Figure 13-21: The Bevel Alpha dialog.

Bevel Edges

The Bevel Edges effect is similar to the Bevel Alpha effect. It is designed to work on square or rectangular images. The Bevel Edges effect is often referred to as "the button maker." Figure 13-22 shows the Bevel Edges dialog.

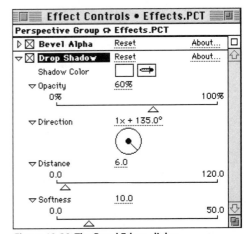

Figure 13-22: The Bevel Edges dialog.

- *Edge Thickness* specifies in pixels the thickness of the beveled edge.

- *Light Angle* specifies the direction from which the light is coming.

- *Light Color* allows you to set a color of the light affecting the edge.

- *Light Intensity* sets the contrast from light to dark within the shape. If you set the light intensity too high, the beveled edges can lose detail and look as if they have been blown out.

Drop Shadow

The Drop Shadow effect creates a drop shadow based on an element's alpha channel. It is one of the only filters that works outside its boundaries. When applying this effect to a layer that rotates, you should compify the layer first. This will enable the shadow to turn properly with the rotation. Figure 13-23 shows the Drop Shadow dialog.

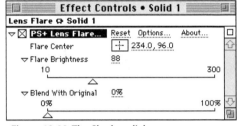

Figure 13-23: The Shadow dialog.

- *Shadow Color* allows you to set the color of the shadow.

- *Opacity* allows you to set the translucence of the shadow.

- *Direction* determines which way the shadow will fall from the element.

- *Distance* determines how far the shadow will fall from the element.

- *Softness* determines how soft and transparent an edge the shadow will have.

This next example uses three of the four Perspective effects. In the exercise, you will create type with an edge that changes. The type will sit on a button that has an edge which will be beveled.

 Studio Time: Perspective Effects

1. Create a new Comp (Mac: Cmd-N, Windows: Ctrl-N). Make it 320 x 240, 6:15 seconds, at 30 fps. Name it Perspective Group. Set the background color to white (Mac: Shift-Cmd-B, Windows: Shift-Ctrl-B).

2. Set the Current Time to 0.

3. Drag the Effects element into the center of the Comp window. Scale it to 60%.

4. Create a new solid (Mac: Cmd-Y, Windows: Ctrl-Y). Set it to 240 x 100 and color it blue. This element will be the Button. You will bevel the edges of this Button over time. The Button will also have a drop shadow that moves farther from it as time goes by.

5. Apply Effect → Perspective → Bevel Edges. Click in the stop watch to make the Edge Thickness keyframeable. Set the value to 0. Set the Light angle to -60°.

6. Set the Current Time to 1:00 seconds (Mac: Cmd-G, Windows: Ctrl-G, and type 100). Set the Edge Thickness to 0.10. This makes the edge's bevel build up.

7. Set the Current Time back to 0. Apply → Perspective → Drop Shadow. Set the color to black. Click in the stop watch to make the Opacity, Distance, and Softness keyframeable. Set the Opacity to 90%. Set the Distance and Softness to 0. Set the Direction to 135.

8. Set the Current Time to 3:00 seconds. Now set the Opacity to 60%. Set the Distance to 20 and the Softness to 35. The shadow gets lighter and softer as it recedes.

9. Set the Current Time to 0. Select the Effects layer. Now it's time to play with the type.

10. Apply Effect → Perspective → Bevel Alpha. Click in the stop watch to make the Light Angle keyframeable. Set the Light Angle to -60. Set the Edge Thickness to 6 and the Light Intensity to 0.48. Leave the color as is.

11. Set the Current Time to 3:00 seconds. Set the Light Angle to -1x+-60. This will give you one full rotation of the light in the type.

12. Set the Current Time to 0. Apply Effect → Perspective → Drop Shadow. Set the background color to white (Mac: Shift-Cmd-B, Windows: Shift-Ctrl-B). Click in the stop watch to make the Opacity, Distance, and Softness keyframeable. Set the Opacity to 90%. Set Distance and Softness to 0. Set the Direction to 135°.

13. Set the Current Time to 3:00 seconds. Now set the Opacity to 60%. Set the Distance to 6 and the Softness to 10. Set the Direction to 1x+135°. The shadow makes the type look like it's embossed.

14. Set the work area end at 3:10. Set Quality switches to Best.

15. Save the project.

16. Press the spacebar to preview the movie, or choose Composition → Make Movie to render it. Close up this Comp when finished.

Render

The Render category only contains one effect, and that effect is borrowed from Photoshop. If you do not have the Photoshop filters installed, you will not see "PS+Lens Flare" as one of your Effect menu choices.

PS+ Lens Flare

The PS+ Lens Flare effect adds a light source to an image. The flare mimics what happens when a bright light hits the lens of a camera. These flares are the direct result of reflections on and within the optics themselves, and are often added to digital imagery to enhance realism. Figure 13-24 shows the PS+ Lens Flare dialog and the effect.

■ *Flare Center* controls the center point of the flare. This property can be used with motion tracker information to map the center to a specific moving element.

■ *Flare Brightness* controls how bright the flare is. Think of this property as the size control of the flare.

■ *Blend with Original* blends the effect into the original. This allows for a fade up or fade out effect.

This next exercise demonstrates adding the Lens Flare to a solid black layer. It uses

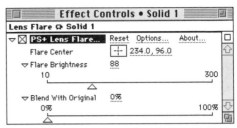

Figure 13-24: The PS+ Lens Flare dialog and the resulting effect.

the apply mode Screen to add the flare to the Grandpa footage. The result looks as if Grandpa is shining a really bright light towards you.

 Studio Time: PS+ Lens Flare

1. Create a new Comp (Mac: Cmd-N, Windows: Ctrl-N). Make it 320 x 240, 6:15 seconds, at 30 fps. Name it PS+ Lens Flare.

2. Set the Current Time to 0.

3. Drag the Grandpa.mov file into the center of the Comp window.

4. Create a new solid (Mac: Cmd-Y, Windows: Ctrl-Y). Set the solid to 320 x 240. Set the background color to black.

5. Bring the solid to the front (Mac: Cmd-F, Windows: Ctrl-F). Set the solid's layer mode to Screen. The black should appear transparent.

6. Apply Effect → Render → PS+ Lens Flare. Select the Flare Center tool and click on Grandpa's hands. Click in the stop watch to make the Flare Brightness keyframeable. Set the Flare Brightness to 10. Do not use the Blend with Original property.

7. Set the Current Time to 3:00 seconds (Mac: Cmd-G, Windows: Ctrl-G, and type 300). Increase the Flare Brightness to 150. This will make the light really bright.

8. Set the Current Time to 6:00 seconds. Reset the Flare Brightness to 10. This will fade out the effect.

9. Set the Quality switches to Best.

10. Set the work area to end at 6:00.

11. Save the project.

12. Press the spacebar to preview the movie, or choose Composition → Make Movie to render it. Close up this Comp when finished.

Stylize

The Stylize category of effects create a more painterly and less realistic look in the image. They make the image more abstract or impressionistic.

Brush Strokes

The Brush Strokes effect gives an image a hand-painted look. This effect alters the alpha channel, as well as the image. Figure 13-25 shows the Brush Strokes dialog and the effect.

- *Stroke Angle* sets the direction of the brush strokes.

- *Brush Size* indicates the size of the individual brush strokes.

- *Stroke Length* indicates the maximum size of each stroke.

- *Stroke Density* indicates how close the brush strokes are to each other.

- *Stroke Randomness* sets the random factor, which broadens the possibilities of the effect.

- *Paint Surface* enables you to choose where to apply the brush strokes. You can paint on the original or on a transparency. You can even alter the color between the strokes.

- *Blend with Original* blends the effect into the original, creating a fade up or out effect.

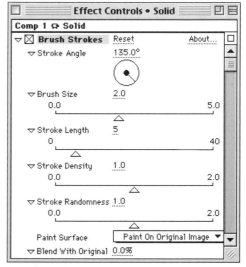

Figure 13-25: The Brush Stokes dialog used in this Studio Time and the resulting effect.

Studio Time: Brush Strokes

1. Create a new Comp (Mac: Cmd-N, Windows: Ctrl-N). Make it 320 x 240, 6:15 seconds, at 30 fps. Name it Brush Strokes.

2. Set the Current Time to 0.

3. Drag the Girl.mov file into the center of the Comp window.

4. Apply Effect → Stylize → Brush Strokes.

5. Set the Stroke Angle to 135 (Note: This is not a keyframe).

6. Click in the stop watch to make the Brush Size, Stroke Length, Stroke Density, and Stroke Randomness keyframeable. Set the Stroke Randomness to 1. Set the Brush Size, Stroke Length, and Stroke Density to 0.

7. Set the Current Time to 2:00 seconds (Mac: Cmd-G, Windows: Ctrl-G, and type 200). Set the Brush Size to 5 and the Stroke Length to 8. Set both the Stroke Density and the Stroke Randomness to 1.5. This builds up the effect.

8. Set the Current Time to 3:00 seconds. Make sustaining keyframes for all four keyframe properties.

9. Set the Current Time to 5:00 seconds. Reset the values back to the values in the keyframes in Step 6. This makes the effect fade out.

10. Set the work area to end at 5:05. Set Quality switches to Best.

11. Save the project.

12. Press the spacebar to preview the movie, or choose Composition → Make Movie to render it. Close up this Comp when finished.

Color Emboss

The Color Emboss effect works much like the Emboss effect. The major difference is that the Color Emboss effect keeps the embossed work in color. The Emboss effect tends to push images to a neutral gray, only using color around the edges. Figure 13-26 shows the Color Emboss dialog and the effect.

■ *Relief* is the height of the emboss. In the Color Emboss effect, large values tend to make the image look like it is out of registration and the color layers like they are misaligned.

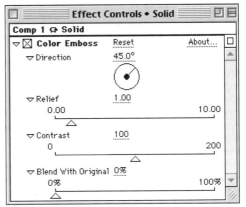

Figure 13-26: The Color Emboss dialog and the resulting effect.

- *Contrast* sets the contrast in the effect.

- *Blend with Original* blends the effect into the original. This allows for a fade up or fade out effect.

This next example applies the Color Emboss effect to add some dimension to the original footage. A transfer mode is used to control how this effect is applied.

 # Studio Time: Color Emboss

1. Create a new Comp (Mac: Cmd-N, Windows: Ctrl-N). Make it 320 x 240, 00:10 seconds, at 30 fps. Name it Color Emboss.

2. Set the Current Time to 0.

3. Drag the Girl.mov file into the center of the Comp window.

4. Duplicate the layer. Select the element on top.

5. Apply Effect → Stylize → Color Emboss. Click in the stop watch to make Direction and Relief keyframeable. Set the Direction to 70.

6. Set the Relief to 2. Set the Contrast Value to 100. Set Blend with Original to 0.

7. Set the Current Time to 2:00 seconds (Mac: Cmd-G, Windows: Ctrl-G, and type 200). Set the Direction to 80 and the Relief to 2.5.

8. Change the layer's mode to Hard Light. This will add a bit of color and dimension to the footage below it.

9. Press T to bring up the Opacity property. Set the Opacity of the layer to 50%. This will lessen the severity of the effect.

10. Set the Quality switches to Best.

11. Set the work area to end at 2:15.

12. Save the project.

13. Press the spacebar to preview the movie, or choose Composition → Make Movie to render it. Close up this Comp when finished.

Emboss

The Emboss filter makes images look as if they have an edge. This effect applies light at an angle that enhances the effect. The Emboss filter works better on images that are blurred first. Figure 13-27 shows the Emboss dialog box.

▪ *Direction* specifies the direction of the light. Think of this as controlling whether the emboss is an "innie" or an "outtie" (just like a belly button); an emboss can look either convex or concave.

▪ *Relief* specifies the height of the emboss.

▪ *Contrast* specifies light and darkness within the emboss. It is better to have more information than less. For instance, it is much easier to make gray whiter than it is to make white grayer.

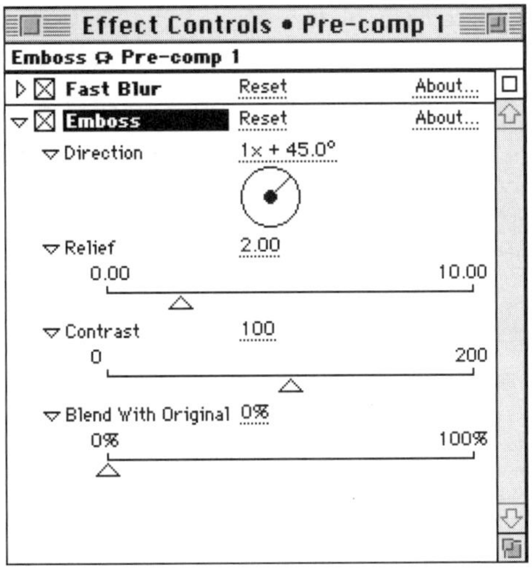

Figure 13-27: The Emboss and the Fast Blur effects used together.

▪ *Blend with Original* blends the effect into the original. This allows for a fade up or fade out effect.

This next example embosses type in an image. It animates the direction of the light, adding greater dimension to the type and more movement to the light source.

 Studio Time: Emboss

1. Create a new Comp (Mac: Cmd-N, Windows: Ctrl-N). Make it 320 x 240, 00:10 seconds, at 30 fps. Name it Emboss.

2. Set the Current Time to 0.

3. Create a new solid (Mac: Cmd-Y, Windows: Ctrl-Y). Make the solid 320 x 240. Set the color to white.

4. Drag the Effects Type file into the center of the Comp window.

5. Press S to bring up the Scale property. Set the Scale amount to 70%. Set the coordinates to 160, 120.

6. Duplicate the Effects Type file. The original should be on top. Click on the Layer Visibility icon to hide the original file from view.

7. Highlight the solid layer and the type element above it. Only two of the three elements should be selected.

8. Compify the layer (Mac: Shift-Cmd-C, Windows: Ctrl-Cmd-C). Accept the default name (Of.Pre- Comp 1). Select "Move all attributes into the new Composition." Click OK. It will

replace the two effects layers. This action marries the type to the white solid. Remember that setting a white background color would not have been a help in this case.

9. Highlight Pre-Comp 1. Apply Effect → Blur & Sharpen → Fast Blur. Set the Blur to 10.

10. Apply Effect → Stylize → Emboss. Click in the stop watch to make the Direction keyframeable. Set the value to 45 degrees. Set the Relief to 2 and the Contrast 100; these items remain constant.

11. Set the Current Time to 3:00 seconds (Mac: Cmd-G, Windows: Ctrl-G, and type 300). Add one full rotation to the Direction. This makes the Light Direction circle the type.

12. Switch to Transfer mode. Highlight Pre-Comp 1. Specify the Effects layer above it as the Track Matte for this item.

13. Go back to 0. Drag in the Girl.mov file, and send it to the bottom (Mac: Cmd-B, Windows: Ctrl-B). Now the effect is complete.

14. Set the Quality switches to Best.

15. Set the work area to end at 3:15.

16. Save the project.

17. Press the spacebar to preview the movie, or choose Composition → Make Movie to render it. Close up this Comp when finished.

Find Edges

Find Edges is an old effect from the early days of image processing, before anti-aliasing was possible. Back then, to smooth out the edge of an object, you would apply the Find Edges filter to it. You would turn the results of the Find Edges into a mask through which you'd apply a Blur to smooth the edges.

This next example uses Blend with Original to fade out the effect.

 Studio Time: Find Edges

1. Create a new Comp (Mac: Cmd-N, Windows: Ctrl-N). Make it 320 x 240, 6:15 seconds, at 30 fps. Name it Find Edges.

2. Set the Current Time to 0.

3. Drag the Girl.mov file into the center of the Comp window.

5. Apply Effect → Stylize → Find Edges. Click in the stop watch to make Blend with Original keyframeable. Set the value to 0.

6. Set the Current Time to 3:00 seconds (Mac: Cmd-G, Windows: Ctrl-G, and type 300). Set the Blend with Original to 100%. The effect is complete.

7. Set the Quality switch to Best.

8. Set the work area to end at 3:00.

9. Save the project.

10. Press the spacebar to preview the movie, or choose Composition → Make Movie to render it. Close up this Comp when finished.

Mosaic

The Mosaic effect gives your footage the appearance of a mosaic tile. Figure 13-28 shows the Mosaic dialog and the effect.

- *Horizontal Blocks* lets you specify the number of horizontal blocks.

- *Vertical Blocks* lets you specify the number of vertical blocks.

- *Sharp Colors* adds contrast to the image, which makes the footage jittery.

This next exercise animates the Mosaic effect to move from one square to many.

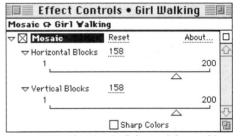

Figure 13-28: The Mosaic dialog and the resulting effect.

 Studio Time: Mosaic

1. Create a new Comp (Mac: Cmd-N, Windows: Ctrl-N). Make it 320 x 240, 6:15 seconds, at 30 fps. Name it Mosaic.

2. Set the Current Time to 0.

3. Drag the Girl.mov file into the center of the Comp window.

4. Apply Effect → Stylize → Mosaic. Click in the stop watch to make Horizontal Blocks and Vertical Blocks keyframeable. Set both values to 1. Keep Sharp Colors off.

5. Set the Current Time to 3:00 seconds (Mac: Cmd-G, Windows: Ctrl-G, and type 300). Set Horizontal Blocks and Vertical Blocks to 175. The effect is complete.

6. Set the Quality switches to Best.

7. Set the work area to end at 3:00.

8. Save the project.

9. Press the spacebar to preview the movie, or choose Composition → Make Movie to render it. Close up this Comp when finished.

Noise

Noise is a handy effect that simulates noise or static. It can help hide mistakes or obscure areas where you have edited an image. Use this effect when trying to match grain in film.

See the Polar Coordinates example; the Noise effect is used there.

PS+ Extrude

The PS+ Extrude effect turns an image into tiny pyramids or squares. This effect is weird at best, and its results are jittery. Figure 13-29 shows the PS+ Extrude dialog and the effect.

🖺 *Block Size* sets the size of the square or pyramid.

🖺 *Depth* sets the height of the square or pyramid.

🖺 *Blend with Original* allows you to fade the effect on or off.

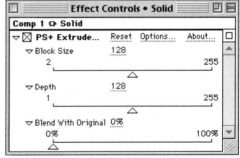

Figure 13-29: The PS+ Extrude dialog and the resulting effect.

In this next example, the PS+ Extrude effect creates a textured zooming effect.

 Studio Time: PS+ Extrude

1. Create a new Comp (Mac: Cmd-N, Windows: Ctrl-N). Make it 320 x 240, 6:15 seconds, at 30 fps. Name it PS+ Extrude.

2. Set the Current Time to 0.

3. Drag the Girl.mov file into the center of the Comp window.

4. Apply Effect → Stylize → PS+ Extrude.

5. In the dialog that appears, set the Type to Pyramids and click OK.

6. Click in the stop watch to make Block Size and Depth keyframeable. Set the Block Size to 4 and the Depth to 1.

7. Set the Current Time to 3:00 seconds. (Mac: Cmd-G, Windows: Ctrl-G, and type 300). Set the Block Size to 2 and the Depth to 50. This will make the shapes smaller and add depth to them. The edges will look as if they are zooming. Now the effect is complete.

8. Set the Quality switches to Best.

9. Set the work area end at 3:00.

10. Save the project.

11. Press the spacebar to preview the movie, or Composition → Make Movie to render it. Close up this Comp when finished.

PS+ Tiles

The PS+ Tiles effect turns your image into tiny square tiles. Like PS+ Extrude, this effect is rather weird, and the results are jittery. Figure 13-30 shows the PS+ Tiles dialog and the effect.

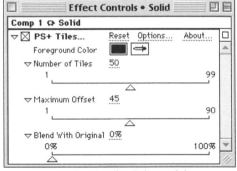

☙ *Block Size* sets the size of the square or pyramid.

☙ *Depth* sets the height of the square or pyramid.

☙ *Blend with Original* allows you to fade the effect on or off.

Figure 13-30: The PS+ Tiles dialog and the resulting effect.

  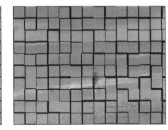

In the next exercise, the PS+ Tiles effect will create a textured zooming image.

Studio Time: PS+ Tiles

1. Create a new Comp (Mac: Cmd-N, Windows: Ctrl-N). Make it 320 x 240, 6:15 seconds, at 30 fps. Name it PS+ Tiles.

2. Set the Current Time to 0.

3. Drag the Girl.mov file into the center of the Comp window.

4. Apply Effect → Stylize → PS+ Tiles. Click in the stop watch to make Blend with Original keyframeable. Set the Blend with Original to 100. Set the Number of Tiles to 10,

5. Set the Current Time to 1:00 seconds (Mac: Cmd-G, Windows: Ctrl-G, and type 100). Set the Blend with Original to 0.

6. Go back to 1:00. Make Maximum Offset keyframeable. Set the value to 1.

7. Go to 3:00. Set the Maximum Offset to 12.

8. Set the Quality switches to Best.

9. Set the work area to end at 3:05.

10. Save the project.

11. Press the spacebar to preview the movie, or choose Composition → Make Movie to render it. Close up this Comp when finished.

Strobe Light

The Strobe Light effect mimics a real strobe light. This results in flashing of either color or transparency, depending on the operator. Figure 13-31 shows the Strobe Light dialog and the effect.

- *Strobe Color* indicates the color the strobe will use if the operator is *Copy*.

- *Blend with Original* specifies how much the effect will blend with the image.

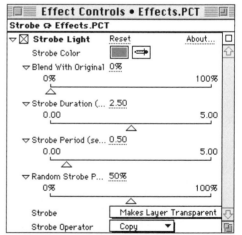

Figure 13-31: Strobe Light dialog and the resulting effect.

- *Strobe Duration* specifies how long the strobe effect lasts.

- *Strobe Period* specifies the duration of the strobe between blasts.

- *Random Strobe Probability* gives the appearance of randomness in the effect.

- *Strobe* (which is a pop-up) lets you select how the strobe reacts. The choices are transparency or color.

- *Strobe Operator* specifies the arithmetic method used to apply the effect.

The following example demonstrates applying the Strobe Light effect with both transparency and color.

 Studio Time: Strobe Light

1. Create a new Comp (Mac: Cmd-N, Windows: Ctrl-N). Make it 320 x 240, 6:15 seconds, at 30 fps. Name it Strobe.

2. Set the Current Time to 0.

3. Drag the Girl.mov and Effects.psd files into the center of the Comp window.

4. Select the Effects.psd file. Press S to bring up the Scale property. Click in the stop watch to make Scale keyframeable. Set the Scale amount to 0%.

5. Set the Current Time to 2:00 seconds (Mac: Cmd-G, Windows: Ctrl-G, and type 200). Set the Scale amount to 65%.

6. Set the Current Time to 3:00 seconds. Click in the Keyframe Navigation box to set a sustaining keyframe for Scale.

8. Set the Current Time to 5:00 seconds. Set the Scale amount to 0%.

9. Set the Current Time back to 0. Apply Effect → Stylize → Strobe Light. Click in the stop watch to make the Strobe Color keyframeable. Choose a red. (The finished example animates from magenta to black. Feel free to experiment with any color.) Set Strobe Duration to 2.5 and Strobe Period to .5. Set the Random Strobe probability to 50%. Choose Makes Layer Transparent from the Strobe pop-down. Set the Strobe Operator to Copy.

10. Set the Current Time to 5:00 seconds. Set the Color to blue (or any other different color). The effect is complete. Note: The color does not cycle in this Comp, but it will in the second Comp. This Comp is complete.

Preview the file or render out a movie. Then close up this Comp.

11. Now, duplicate the Strobe Comp in the Project window and rename it Strobe 2. Double click the Strobe 2 Comp to open it.

12. Change the Strobe to Operates on Color Only. This will create color flashes that cycle from red to blue.

13. Set the Quality switches to Best.

14. Set the work area to end at 5:00.

15. Save the Project.

16. Press the spacebar to preview the movie, or choose Composition → Make Movie to render it. Close up this Comp when finished.

Texturize

The Texturize effect applies a texture to an image. The texture is based on a grayscale image—any grayscale image—(known as a *texture map*). The layer used as the texture layer must be in the Comp. It does not need to be visible. Figure 13-32 shows the Texturize dialog and the effect.

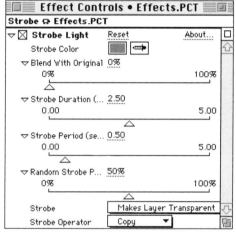

Figure 13-32: The Texturize dialog and the resulting effect.

☝ *Texture Layer* allows you to specify the layer to use as the texture.

☝ *Light Direction* allows you to choose the direction of the light applied to the texture. This helps to enhance the effect.

☝ *Texture Contrast* sets the contrast of the applied lighting.

☝ *Texture Placement* allows you to select a method for applying the texture, you can tile it, center it, or stretch it to fit.

This next example demonstrates using the Texturize effect to add texture to an image.

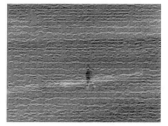

 Studio Time: Texturize

1. Create a new Comp (Mac: Cmd-N, Windows: Ctrl-N). Make it 320 x 240, 6:15 seconds, at 30 fps. Name it Texturize.

2. Set the Current Time to 0.

3. Drag the Girl.mov and Texture.psd files into the center of the Comp window.

4. Click on the Layer Visibility icon to hide the Texture layer from view.

5. Highlight the Girl.mov layer. Apply Effect → Stylize → Texturize. In the Effect Control window, select Texture.psd as the Texture Layer. Use the "E" key to show the layers effects. Click in the stop watch to make Light Direction and Texture Contrast keyframeable. Set the Light Direction to 0 degrees and the Texture Contrast to 0. Choose Center texture for Texture Placement because the source image and the target image are the same size.

7. Set the Current Time to 3:00 seconds (Mac: Cmd-G, Windows: Ctrl-G, and type 300). Set the Light Direction to 180 degrees and the Texture Contrast to 0.4.

8. Set the Current Time to 3:15 seconds. Click in the Keyframe Navigation box to make sustaining keyframes for Light Direction and Texture Contrast.

9. Set the Current Time to 5:00 seconds. Set Light Direction and Texture Contrast to 0. The effect is complete.

10. Set the Quality switches to Best.

11. Set the work area to end at 5:00.

12. Save the project.

13. Press the spacebar to preview the movie, or Composition → Make Movie to render it. Close up this Comp when finished.

Synthesize

The effects in this category are good for creating highlight elements or elements that can be used as masks.

Ramp

The Ramp effect creates a gradation from two source colors. The center point of each color can be specified and animated over time. Usually this effect is applied to a solid layer. See Figure 13-33, which shows the Ramp settings window.

The Ramp effect was used in the Polar Coordinates example earlier in this chapter.

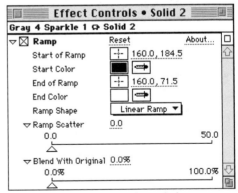

Figure 13-33: The Ramp settings window.

Text

The effects in this category create text and numbers.

Basic Text

The Basic Text effect gives you just that—basic text. You can animate the position of the text over time. Text can be applied to an image, or it can be applied in front of it. Quality settings alter the quality of the Basic Text.

Numbers

The Numbers effect can create sequential and non-sequential numbers and dates. You can use this effect to add time code or to simply date stamp your work.

Time

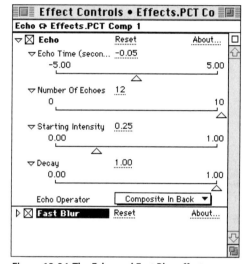

Time effects change the timing of the layer to which they are applied. Choosing a Time effect automatically negates any effect that was already applied to the layer, so you will need to compify the layer if you need to add additional effects.

Echo

The Echo effect combines frames from different times in a layer. Echo is most often used to create trails and smearing effects. Figure 13-34 shows the Echo dialog box.

Figure 13-34: The Echo and Fast Blur effects.

- *Echo Time* specifies the time in seconds between echoes. Negative numbers move backward in time; positive numbers move forward in time.

- *Number of Echoes* specifies the number of frames used to create the effect.

- *Starting Intensity* specifies the intensity of the first frame of the effect.

- *Decay* specifies the intensity of subsequent echoes.

- *Echo Operator* specifies the operation on which the echo will be placed.

The following example shows a technique that can be used to make a word bounce and leave a trail.

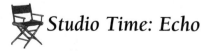 *Studio Time: Echo*

1. Create a new Comp (Mac: Cmd-N, Windows: Ctrl-N). Make it 320 x 240, 6:15 seconds, at 30 fps. Name it Echo.

2. Set the Current Time to 0.

3. Drag the Effects.psd file into the center of the Comp window.

4. Make the word "effects" bounce into and out of the frame as you did in Chapter 10. When you are done, Compify the layer.

5. Duplicate the layer. Select the bottom duplicate. This keeps a clean copy on top to enhance the effect.

6. Apply Effect → Time → Echo. Press E to show the layers effects. Click in the stop watch to make the Number of Echoes keyframeable. Set Number of Echoes to 12. Set the Echo Time to -.05 and the Starting Intensity to .25. Then set the Decay to 1 and select Composite in Back as the Echo Operator.

7. Set the Current Time to 2:00 seconds (Mac: Cmd-G, Windows: Ctrl-G, and type 200). Set the Number of Echoes to 8.

8. The effect is now complete.

9. Set the Quality switches to Best.

10. Set the work area to end at 2:10.

11. Save the project.

12. Preview or render.

Posterize Time

The Posterize Time effect locks an element into a specific frame rate. Comps can be generated at one frame rate and played back at another. This effect is sometimes referred to as a *hardware strobe*.

Transition

Transition effects allow you to create smooth transitions from one layer to another or between several others. The layer to which you apply the transition effect should be on top. When the Transition Completion reaches 100%, you will see the layers beneath.

Block Dissolve

The Block Dissolve effect makes a layer dissolve in random blocks. The size of the blocks can be set independently of one another. Layer Quality affects the output when using Block Dissolve.

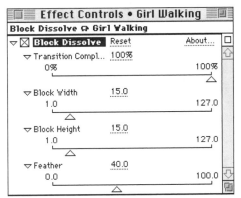

Figure 13-35: The Block Dissolve dialog and the resulting effect.

Figure 13-35 shows the Block Dissolve dialog and the effect.

- *Transition Complete* specifies the percentage of the transition that is complete.
- *Block Width* specifies the width of the block.
- *Block Height* specifies the height of the block.
- *Feather* specifies the softness around the edge of the block.

The following Studio Time demonstrates the Block Dissolve effect.

Studio Time: Block Dissolve

1. Create a new Comp (Mac: Cmd-N, Windows: Ctrl-N). Make it 320 x 240, 6:15 seconds, at 30 fps. Name it Block Dissolve.

2. Set the Current Time to 0.

3. Drag the Girl.mov and Grandpa.mov files into the center of the Comp window.

4. Highlight the Girl.mov layer. Set the Current Time to 0:15 seconds (Mac: Cmd-G, Windows: Ctrl-G, and type 015). Apply Effect → Transition → Block Dissolve.

5. Press E to show the layers effect. Click in the stop watch to make Transition Complete and Feather keyframeable. Set the Transition Complete to 0 and the Feather to 10. Set the Block Height and Block Width to 15.

6. Set the Current Time to 2:15 seconds. Set the Transition Complete to 100% and the Feather to 40. The transition is now complete.

7. Set the Quality switches to Best.

8. Set the work area to end at 3:00.

9. Save the project.

10. Preview or render.

Gradient Wipe

The Gradient Wipe effect creates a wipe based on the luminance value of a grayscale image. The source of the grayscale image is referred to as the *Gradient Layer*. Although the Gradient

Layer must be present in the Comp, it does not need to be visible. Figure 13-36 shows the Gradient Wipe dialog and the effect.

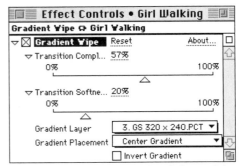

- 🎞 *Transition Complete* specifies the percentage of the transition that is complete.

- 🎞 *Transition Softness* adds softness to the transition.

- 🎞 *Gradient Layer* is the element providing the luminance values.

- 🎞 *Gradient Placement* allows you to specify where the gradient is positioned in the frame.

Figure 13-36: The Gradient Wipe dialog and the resulting effect.

- 🎞 *Invert Gradient* reverses the direction of the wipe.

This next example demonstrates the Gradient Wipe effect.

 Studio Time: Gradient Wipe

1. Create a new Comp (Mac: Cmd-N, Windows: Ctrl-N). Make it 320 x 240, 6:15 seconds, at 30 fps. Name it Gradient Wipe.

2. Set the Current Time to 0.

3. Drag the Girl.mov, GS320.psd, and Grandpa.mov files into the center of the Comp window.

4. Send the GS320.psd file to the bottom (Mac: Cmd-B, Windows: Ctrl-B) and click on the Layer Visibility icon to hide the layer from view.

5. Apply Effect → Transitions → Gradient Wipe to the Girl.mov layer. Show the layers effects. Click in the stop watch to make Transition Complete keyframeable. Set Transition Complete to 0. Set the Transition Softness to 20. Choose the GS 320 x 240 element as the Gradient Layer.

6. Set the Current Time to 2:15 seconds (Mac: Cmd-G, Windows: Ctrl-G, and type 215). Set the Transition Complete to 100%.

7. The transition is now complete. Set the Quality switches to Best.

8. Set the work area to end at 2:25.

9. Save the project.

10. Preview or render.

Linear Wipe

The Linear Wipe effect makes a layer dissolve in a specific direction. Figure 13-37 shows the Linear Wipe dialog and the effect.

■ *Transition Complete* specifies the percentage of the transition that is complete.

■ *Wipe Angle* specifies the angle of the wipe.

■ *Feather* specifies the softness around the edge of the effect.

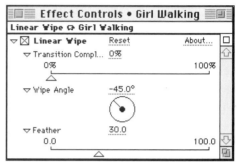

Figure 13-37: The Linear Wipe dialog and the resulting effect.

This next example demonstrates the Linear Wipe effect.

 Studio Time: Linear Wipe

1. Create a new Comp (Mac: Cmd-N, Windows: Ctrl-N). Make it 320 x 240, 6:15 seconds, at 30 fps. Name it Linear Wipe.

2. Set the Current Time to 0.

3. Drag the Girl.mov and Grandpa.mov files into the center of the Comp window.

4. Set the Current Time to 0:15 seconds (Mac: Cmd-G, Windows: Ctrl-G, and type 015). Apply Effect → Transitions → Linear Wipe to the Girl.mov layer.

5. Press E to show the layers effects. Click in the stop watch to make Transition Complete, Wipe Angle, and Feather keyframeable. Set the Transition Complete to 0, the Wipe Angle to -45 degrees, and the Feather to 30.

6. Set the Current Time to 3:00 seconds. Set the Transition Complete to 100%, the Wipe Angle to -180 degrees, and the Feather to 10.

7. The transition is now complete. Set the Quality switches to Best.

8. Set the work area to end at 3:15.

9. Save the project.

10. Preview or render.

Radial Wipe

The Radial Wipe effect makes a layer dissolve in a circular wipe around a specific point. Figure 13-38 shows the Radial Wipe dialog and the effect.

- *Transition Complete* specifies the percentage of the transition that is complete.

- *Start Angle* specifies the angle at which the effect begins.

- *Wipe Center* allows you to specify the center point of the effect.

- *Feather* specifies the softness around the edge of the effect.

Figure 13-38: The Radial Wipe dialog and the resulting effect.

The following example demonstrates the Radial Wipe effect.

 Studio Time: Radial Wipe

1. Create a new Comp (Mac: Cmd-N, Windows: Ctrl-N). Make it 320 x 240, 6:15 seconds, at 30 fps. Name it Radial Wipe.

2. Set the Current Time to 0.

3. Drag the Girl.mov and Grandpa.mov files into the center of the Comp window.

4. Set the Current Time to 0:15 seconds (Mac: Cmd-G, Windows: Ctrl-G, and type 015). Select the Girl.mov. Apply Effect → Transitions → Radial Wipe.

5. Press E to see the layers effects. Click in the stop watch to make Transition Complete keyframeable. Set Transition Complete to 0. The coordinates of the wipe center are 160, 120. Set the wipe to move clockwise, and set Feather to 10.

6. Set the Current Time to 3:00 seconds Set Transition Complete to 100%. The transition is now complete.

7. Set the Quality switches to Best.

8. Set the work area to end at 3:15.

9. Save the project.

10. Preview or render.

Venetian Blinds

The Venetian Blinds effect makes a layer dissolve using stripes of specific width and direction. The Layer Quality of this filter affects anti-aliasing. Figure 13-39 shows the Venetian Blinds dialog and the effect.

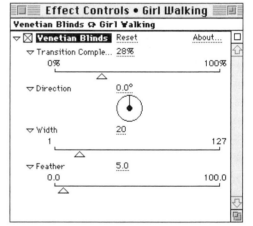

- *Transition Complete* specifies the percentage of the transition that is complete.

- *Direction* specifies the angle of the stripes.

- *Width* specifies the width of the stripes.

- *Feather* specifies the softness around the edge of the stripe.

Figure 13-39: The Venetian Blinds dialog and the resulting effect.

The following Studio Time demonstrates the Venetian Blinds effect.

Studio Time: Venetian Blinds

1. Create a new Comp (Mac: Cmd-N, Windows: Ctrl-N). Make it 320 x 240, 6:15 seconds, at 30 fps. Name it Venetian Blinds.

2. Set the Current Time to 0.

3. Drag the Girl.mov and Grandpa.mov files into the center of the Comp window.

4. Set the Current Time to 0:15 seconds (Mac: Cmd-G, Windows: Ctrl-G, and type 015). Apply Effect → Transitions → Venetian Blinds.

5. Press E to show the layers effects. Click in the stop watch to make the Transition Complete keyframeable. Set the Transition Complete to 0. Set the Direction to 0, the Width to 20, and the Feather to 5.

6. Set the Current Time to 3:00 seconds. Set the Transition Complete to 100%. The transition is now complete.

7. Set the Quality switches to Best.

8. Set the work area to end at 3:15.

9. Save the project.

10. Preview or render.

Video

Video effects are most useful when your final output medium is video tape.

Broadcast Colors

The Broadcast Colors effect changes an image's pixel color so that it will be more accurately represented on television.

Reduce Interlace Flicker

The Reduce Interlace Flicker effect reduces high frequencies so that images flicker less when transferred to an interlaced medium. This effect should not be used to de-interlace footage destined for videotape. Rather, Reduce Interlace Flicker cleans up captured footage that will be used onscreen, in order to lessen the effects of interlaced video.

Timecode

The Timecode effect displays a timecode or frame number for use within After Effects. The time is embedded along the bottom edge of the Blue channel pixels of an image. Filters that distort the color of an image or change the size, position, rotation, etc. of the image render this effect useless, unless you applied this filter last—after any other such filters have done their damage.

# Rewind

You certainly have gone through a lot of Comps in this chapter! You now should have a better grasp of using the filters that ship with After Effects. Try combining different filters to make your own effects. Some of the most ingenious effects are achieved by using many effects on one image. Experiment with the footage provided on the disk.

Coming Attractions

If you thought that was fun, just wait till you get through the next few chapters. They cover third-party effects. The first company discussed is MetaCreations. MetaCreations has two effects packages on the market at this writing: Final Effects and Studio Effects. At least one more is in the planning stages, as are Windows versions of the filters. These packages are loaded with imaginative and invaluable effects.

MetaCreations Effects

 ## Preview

Although there are a number of third-party filters and effects for After Effects, the two sets available from MetaCreations (formerly MetaTools), are outstanding. These two MetaCreations packages for After Effects, Final Effects and Studio Effects, are loaded with exciting, invaluable add-ons that bring your projects to life. Because the sets are so useful, we are devoting an entire chapter to them.

In this chapter, you will:

- Explore the different Final Effects and Studio Effects filters.
- Learn how to select options and set parameters for the various effects.

 ## Feature Presentation

So far this book has examined the built-in filters. Now it's time to explore the MetaCreations effects packages, Final Effects and Studio Effects. Some of the effects we'll cover include breaking your footage into stars that fly through space, making your images turn like a book page or swirl like a kaleidoscope, and creating molten metal with Mr. Mercury!

Using Final and Studio Effects

These two packages run the gamut of the different effects categories. The Studio Effects set lists all of its effects in one category whereas Final Effects scatters them throughout the Effects menu.

There are demo versions of the software on the CD-ROM included with this book. Feel free to try them out. They do not render, but you can preview the effects. You can also take a look at the pre-rendered movies provided. At press time, the NT versions of these filters were not ready. Check the MetaCreations Web site for availability.

Any of the effects can be used in combinations with any others. Filters can be stacked and rearranged just like any other effects within After Effects.

One thing to keep in mind is that, while the MetaCreations packages can perform resolution independent work, many other packages cannot. The MetaCreations products offer creators of large artwork the necessary resolution independence and quality. However, as you will see in Chapter 17, when you work with a 2000 x 2000 pixel project, all filters do not behave the same way on large canvases, and the effect as you see it applied to a proxy may not look the same as the final high-resolution replacement file.

It is important to test for these issues. Not all the results of these effects work as well for video output as they might on a computer screen or for print, so it is important to know the implications of their results. The MetaCreations filter products all work quite nicely at any resolution. Other company's filter effects might not work as well. Keep this in mind.

Setting Up

This chapter's projects offer a sampling of Comps that represent some of the best effects from each of the MetaCreations packages. The packages are broken down into two projects. Comps are not supplied for each filter, and not every Comp is discussed. Use the Comps as a guide to the effect; rebuild each one to get the full benefit of this chapter.

A finished movie folder shows what the effects look like after they are applied and rendered. If you don't actually own the effects, this will come in handy. Each movie is rendered from its corresponding project.

The last step of each Studio Time asks you to render or preview the movie. This choice is up to you. All source footage provided is 320 x 240 and Cinepacked. The size for all Comps that will be created is 320 x 240. Feel free to use whatever footage is included to invent new own combinations of effect uses.

Shortcuts		
Command	**Mac**	**Windows**
Move 1 Frame Ahead	Page Down	Ctrl-T
Move 1 Frame Back	Page Up	Ctrl-U

Final Effects

The group of effects that follows are all part of the Final Effects set of filters. There are 28 effects in this package.

Ball Action

The Ball Action effect turns an element or footage into balls. The balls can be rotated and twisted around a specific axis or a combination of axes. Only completely opaque pixels will become balls. This means that you have to watch out for semi-transparent edges. Figure 14-1 shows the Ball Action dialog and the effect.

- *Scatter* uses a process that applies a dispersion effect. The higher the scatter value, the further the balls disperse.

- *Rotation Axis* specifies the axis or combination of axes used to rotate the balls. There are nine different settings from which to choose. Some are single axis settings, and some are multiple. The XYZ axis rotates the balls around all three axes. The X15Z axis rotates the balls 15 times around the Z axis for every 1 time the balls are rotated around the X axis. The XY15Z setting rotates the balls 15 times around the Z axis for every 1 rotation around the X and Y axes.

- *Rotation* uses these settings to set up the number of times the balls rotate around the specified axis.

- *The Twist Property* contains 11 types of twists:

- The X and Y choices allow you to select the axis for the effect.

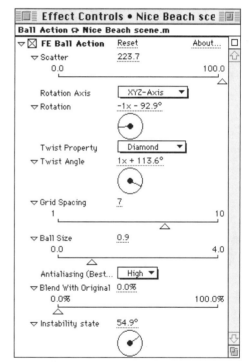

Figure 14-1: The Ball Action dialog and the resulting effect.

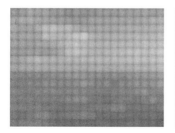

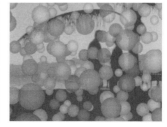

- Center-X, Center-Y starts the effect in the center of the axis.

- Radius focuses the intensity of the twisting effect towards the center or edge of the image. The effect then diminishes towards the edges.

- The Random twist creates a random, chaotic effect.

- The Red, Green, and Blue twist is based on the intensity of the color channel of the image.

- The Brightness twist is based on the brightness values in an image. Darker parts of the image receive more twist.

- Diamond and Rectangle produce twists in shapes.

- Fast Top twists on the X and Y axes with the Y axis twisting faster, producing a topped shape.

- *Twist Angle* sets the angle of the twist property selected from the above list.

- *Grid spacing* controls how many balls are involved in the effect. As strange as it may sound, lower numbers produce higher quantities of balls. Higher numbers produce fewer balls.

- *Ball Size* controls the size of the balls.

- As with all *Anti-Aliasing*, lower settings render faster and do not look as nice. Higher settings render slowly but look better.

- *Blend with Original* blends the effect with the original in the specified amount.

- *Instability State* introduces some randomness to the twist.

The following example applies the Ball Action effect to a clip and makes it reveal the layer below.

 Studio Time: Ball Action

1. Create a new Comp (Mac: Cmd-N, Windows: Ctrl-N). Make it 320 x 240, 9:00 seconds, at 30 fps. Name it Ball Action.

2. Set the Current Time to 0.

3. Import the Beach.mov and the Romance.mov files from the AE14Foot folder (Mac: Cmd-I, Windows: Ctrl-I).

4. Drag the Beach.mov and the Romance.mov files into the center of the Comp window.

5. Bring the Beach.mov file to the front (Mac: Cmd-F, Windows: Ctrl-F).

6. Apply Effect → Particle → FE Ball Action. Make Scatter, Rotation, Twist Angle, and Instability State keyframeable.

7. Set the following properties to the following values: Scatter=0, Rotation Axis=XYZ Axis, Rotation=0°, Twist Property=Diamond, Twist Angle=0°, Grid Spacing=7, Ball Size=0.9, Anti-aliasing=High, Blend with Original=0, Instability State=40°.

8.   Set the Current Time to 7:25 seconds. (Mac: Cmd-G, Windows: Ctrl-G, and type 725). Set the following property values: Scatter=225, Rotation=-1 and -95.0°, Instability State=55°. Now the ball setup is complete. Next, you'll make the balls a bit translucent while they spin. To finish the effect, you'll fade the balls into the element below.

9.   While at 7:25, press T to bring up the Opacity property. Click in the stop watch to make the Opacity keyframeable. Set the Opacity to 0%.

10. Set the Current Time to 6:25 seconds. Set the Opacity to 70%.

11. Set the Current Time to 0. Set the Opacity to 100%. As a final step, adjust the velocity graphs to smooth out the effect.

12. Set the work area to render the desired time span.

13. Set the Quality to Best.

14. Save your work.

15. Press the spacebar to preview the movie, or choose Composition → Make Movie to render it.

Page Turn

The Page Turn effect is the animated version of the KPT Page Curl filter. Use this effect to turn a page, as if it were a book page, to reveal the footage below it. Figure 14-2 shows the Page Turn effect dialog and the effect.

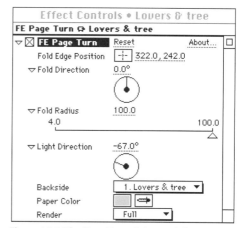

- *Fold Edge Position* sets where the effect will start and end.

- *Fold Direction* designates the direction the turn will follow. The following Studio Time starts at 0 and goes to -90°. This will turn the page from right to left.

- *Fold Radius* determines how wide the turn is.

- *Light Direction* determines the direction from which the light highlights the page curl.

Figure 14-2: The Page Turn dialog and the r esulting effect.

☙ *Backside* offers a choice of what will appear on the reverse side of the turning page—a solid color or the footage.

☙ *Render* specifies what parts to render. Full renders the entire effect. Backside renders only the back. Frontside renders only the front of the effect.

This next example uses the Page Turn effect to reveal the footage below it.

Studio Time: Page Turn

1. Create a new Comp (Mac: Cmd-N, Windows: Ctrl-N). Make it 320 x 240, 9:00 seconds, at 30 fps. Name it Page Turn.

2. Set the Current Time to 0.

3. Import the SEGirl.mov and the Romance.mov files from the AE14Foot folder (Mac: Cmd-I, Windows: Ctrl-I).

4. Drag the SEGirl.mov and the Romance.mov files into the center of the Comp window.

5. Bring the Romance.mov element to the front (Mac: Cmd-F, Windows: Ctrl-F).

6. Apply Effect → Stylize → FE Page Turn. Set initial keyframes for Fold Edge Position, Fold Direction, Fold Radius to keyframeable. Set the Fold Edge Position coordinates to 322 x 242. Set Fold Direction to 0°. Set the Fold Radius to 100. Set the Light Direction to -67°.

7. Set the Current Time to 3:10 seconds (Mac: Cmd-G, Windows: Ctrl-G, and type 3:10). Set the Fold Edge Position coordinates to -75 x 119. Set the Fold Direction to -90°. Set the Fold Radius to 50.

8. Set the Current Time to 2:10 seconds. You should see the effect nicely. Choose the type of Backside you want; this will remain constant.

9. Choose which setting to render. Toggle through to see the results of each selection. We chose to Render the full Comp for this example.

10. Set the work area accordingly.

11. Set Quality to Best.

12. Save your work.

13. Preview or view the pre-rendered movie.

FloMotion

The FloMotion effect works like a vortex that sucks things into the center of an image. This effect can be applied to foreground as well as background elements. Figure 14-3 shows the FloMotion effect dialog and the resulting effect. The effect is generated from knots, which look like vortexes that move in and out and around. Setting a zero value will make a knot inactive. Values set numerically range from -16 to 16. The further the setting is from zero, the longer it takes to render.

◙ *Fine Control* increases the sensitivity of all of the other settings by a factor of 20.

◙ *Edge Behavior* determines how the edges are handled. Selecting Wrap Edges pins the corners of the effect to the edges of the image.

◙ *Anti-aliasing* smooths the edges of the effect. The higher the setting, the longer it takes to render.

In this next example, the FloMotion effect will make the footage shrink up, move around, and wrap itself back into a complete image again. Adding a drop shadow, which will be demonstrated, gives the image a bit of dimension as it rolls around atop another clip.

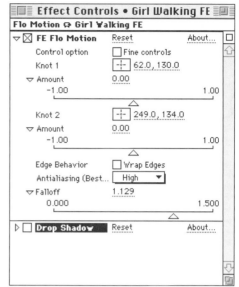

Figure 14-3: The FloMotion dialog and the resulting effect.

  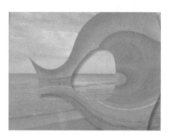

 Studio Time: FloMotion

1. Create a new Comp (Mac: Cmd-N, Windows: Ctrl-N). Make it 320 x 240, 9:00 seconds, at 30 fps. Name it FloMotion.

2. Set the Current Time to 0.

3. Drag the SEGirl.mov into the center of the Comp window.

4. Set the Current Time to 1:00 seconds (Mac: Cmd-G, Windows: Ctrl-G, and type 100). Drag the Beach.mov into the Comp window. Center it, and send it to the back

5. Set the Current Time to 0. Highlight the SE girl.mov element. Apply Effect → Distort → SE FloMotion. Make the two knot Positions and their Amounts keyframeable. Set the Position of Knot 1 to 80 x 60. Set the Amount of Knot 1 to 0. Set the Position of Knot 2 to 240 x 180 and the Amount to 0.

6. Set the Current Time to 3:00 seconds. Set the Position of Knot 1 to 138.5 x 120.7 and its Amount to .99. Set the Position of Knot 2 to 185 x 120.8 and its Amount to 1.

7. Set the Current Time to 5:00 seconds. Set the Position of Knot 1 to 160 x 184 and its Amount to 1. Set the Position of Knot 2 to 160 x 50 and its Amount to -0.6.

8. Set the Current Time to 8:00 seconds. Set the Position of Knot 1 to 62 x 130 and its Amount to 0. Set the Position of Knot 2 to 249 x 134 and its Amount to 0.

9. Apply Effect → Perspective → Drop Shadow. Set the shadow color to black. Set the Opacity to 60% and the Direction 135°. Set the Distance to 8.2 and the Softness to 8.4.

10. Set the work area to render the desired portion of the Comp.

11. Set Quality to Best.

12. Save your work.

13. Preview or render.

Griddler

The Griddler effect cuts an image into squares or tiles. The tiles can be scaled and rotated over time. Selecting a smaller size produces more squares; selecting a larger size produces less squares. Figure 14-4 shows the Griddler effect dialog and the effect.

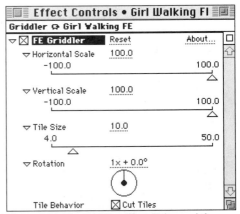

- *Horizontal and Vertical Scale* sets the scale of the image within the tile.

- *Tile Size* sets the size of the actual tile.

- *Rotation* controls the rotation of the tiles.

- *Cut Tiles* introduces transparent spacing between the tiles.

In this next exercise, the Griddler effect is wiped in the image.

Figure 14-4: The Griddler effect dialog and the resulting effect.

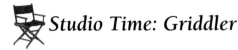

Studio Time: Griddler

1. Create a new Comp (Mac: Cmd-N, Windows: Ctrl-N). Make it 320 x 240, 9:00 seconds, at 30 fps. Name it Griddler.

2. Set the Current Time to 0.

3. Drag the Romance.mov file into the center of the Comp window.

4. Set the Current Time to 0:05 seconds. Drag the SEGirl.mov file into the center of the Comp window. The SEGirl.mov element should be in front of the Romance.mov file.

5. While at 0:05 seconds, apply Effect → Distort → FE Griddler. Set the Current Time to 0. Make Horizontal and Vertical Scale, Tile Size, and Rotation keyframeable. Set the Horizontal and Vertical Scale to 0, the Tile Size to 10, and the Rotation to 0. Turn on Cut Tiles.

6. Set the Current Time to 3:05 seconds. Set the Horizontal and Vertical Scale to 88. Set the Tile Size to 23.5 and the Rotation to 1 full rotation. This will rotate the squares as they scale up.

7. Set the Current Time to 5:05 seconds. Make sustaining keyframes for Horizontal and Vertical Scale, Tile Size, and Rotation.

8. Set the Current Time to 7:05 seconds. Set the Horizontal and Vertical Scale to 80, the Tile Size to 10, and the Rotation to 1 full rotation +45°.

9. Set the Current Time to 8:05 seconds. Change the Horizontal and Vertical Scale to 100%. Change the Rotation back to 1 full rotation. This will turn the footage back into a solid layer.

10. Set the work area to render the desired portion of the Comp.

11. Set Quality switches to Best.

12. Save your work.

13. Preview or view the pre-rendered movie.

Kaleida

The Kaleida effect makes footage look like it is being seen through a kaleidoscope. This effect is fun, although it does not have as many choices as Terrazzo2. Kaleida is by far faster than Terrazzo, which is not really set up for After Effects. Figure 14-5 shows the Kaleida effects dialog and the effect.

■ *Size* sets the size of the tile only, not the movie within it.

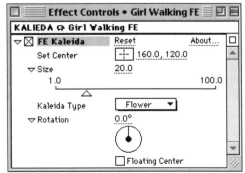

Figure 14-5: The Kaleida effects dialog and the resulting effect.

 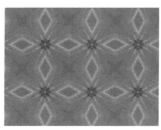 

- *Kaleida Type* sets the flavor of the effect. Try experimenting with the different settings.

- *Rotation* turns the tiles.

- *Floating Centers* locks the center of the effect to the center of the layer when unchecked.

The next example demonstrates the Kaleida effect.

 Studio Time: Kaleida

1.   Create a new Comp (Mac: Cmd-N, Windows: Ctrl-N). Make it 320 x 240, 9:00 seconds, at 30 fps. Name it Kaleida.

2.   Drag the SEGirl.mov file into the center of the Comp window.

3.   Apply Effect → Stylize → FE Kaleida.

4.   Make Set Center, Size, and Rotation keyframeable. Make the Set Center coordinates 111, 119. Set the Size to 20 and the Rotation to 1 rotation. Select flower as the Kaleida type. Turn on the Floating Center.

5.   Set the Current Time to 3:00 seconds (Mac: Cmd-G, Windows: Ctrl-G, and type 300). Make the Set Center coordinates 229, 123. Set the size to 30 and the Rotation to 1x+150.0°. This will center the effect. Next you're going to vary the rotation to change the effect.

6.   Set the Current Time to 4:25 seconds. Set the Rotation to 1x+175°.

7.   Set the Current Time to 7:00 seconds. Set the Rotation to 1x+140°

8.   Set the Current Time to 7:15 seconds. Change the Size to 40.

9.   Set the Current Time to 8:25 seconds. Set the Rotation to 1x+175°.

10. Smooth out the velocity graphs to enhance the effect.

11. Set the work area to render the desired portion of the Comp.

12. Set Quality to Best.

13. Save your work.

14. Preview or view the pre-rendered movie.

Scatterize

Scatterize scatters your image into a cloud of swarming bees—or into a cloud of dust, or whatever you prefer. Figure 14-6 shows the Scatterize effect dialog and the effect.

- *Amount* controls the degree to which the pixels scatter.

- *Right and Left Twist* apply a twist to the element. Use this to put an element into perspective as it scatters.

The following example demonstrates scattering stylized type as it moves into perspective. It also shows how to make the scattered type fade off.

 *Studio Time: Scatterize*

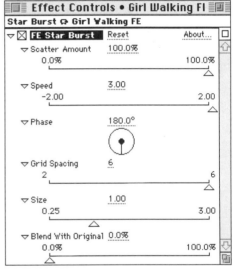

1. Create a new Comp (Mac: Cmd-N, Windows: Ctrl-N). Make it 320 x 240, 9:00 seconds, at 30 fps. Name it Scatterize.

2. Import the Ddtype.psd files from the AE14Foot folder (Mac: Cmd-I, Windows: Ctrl-I).

3. Drag the SEGirl.mov and Ddtype.psd files into the center of the Comp window.

4. Set the Current Time to 0:20 seconds (Mac: Cmd-G, Windows: Ctrl-G, and type 020). Highlight the Ddtype.psd layer. Apply Effect → Stylize → FE Scatterize.

5. Make Amount, as well as the Right and Left Twist, keyframeable. Set the three values to 0.

Figure 14-6: The Scatterize effect dialog and the resulting effect.

6. Set the Current Time to 1:20 seconds. Set the Amount to 1.5. Set the Left and Right Twist to -64. This will tilt the type back into perspective while it scatters slightly. Next, you will see how to fade the type on and off as it scatters.

7. Set the current time to 4:10. Set the amount to 35.

8. Set the Current Time back to 0. Press T to bring up the Opacity property. Make Opacity keyframeable. Set the Opacity to 0%.

9. Set the Current Time to 1:00 seconds. Set the Opacity to 100%.

10. Set the Current Time to 3:15 seconds. Set a sustaining keyframe for the Opacity.

11. Set the Current Time to 4:10 seconds. Set the Opacity to 0%. This will fade off the scatter.

12. Set the work area to end at 4:20 seconds.

13. Set Quality to Best.

14. Save your work.

15. Preview or view the pre-rendered movie.

Star Burst

The FE Star Burst effect takes footage and breaks it into stars that it spreads out into space. This effect can be animated to simulate flying through a star field. Figure 14-7 shows the StarBurst dialog and the effect.

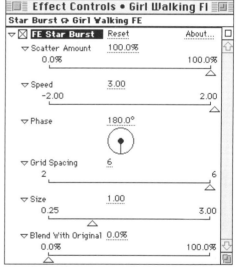

Figure 14-7: The Star Burst effects dialog and the resulting effect.

- *Scatter Amount* controls the space between stars.

- *Speed* controls how fast you travel through the star field. Negative values give the appearance of moving into the image.

- *Phase* returns the effect back to the original position of the layer.

- *Grid Spacing* controls how densely the stars are packed.

- *Size* controls the size of the stars.

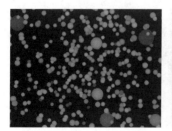
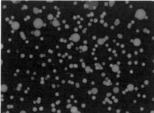
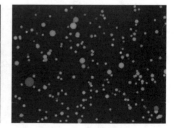

The following example demonstrates turning a clip into a star field.

Studio Time: FE Star Burst

1. Create a new Comp (Mac: Cmd-N, Windows: Ctrl-N). Make it 320 x 240, 9:00 seconds, at 30 fps. Name it Star Burst.

2. Set the Current Time to 0.

3. Drag the SEGirl.mov file into the center of the Comp window.

4. Apply Effect → Particle → FE Star Burst. Make the Scatter Amount, Speed, Phase, and Size keyframeable. Set the values as follows: Scatter Amount=50.4, Speed=0.35, Phase=0°, Size=1.73.

5. Set the Current Time to 8:00 seconds (Mac: Cmd-G, Windows: Ctrl-G, and type 800). Set the Scatter Amount to 50.5 and the Speed to 3. Set the Phase to 180° and the Size to 1.

6. Set the Grid Spacing to 6. Do not use Blend with Background.

7. Set the work area to end at 8:03 seconds.

8. Set Quality to Best.

9. Save your work.

10. Preview or view the pre-rendered movie.

Studio Effects

The next section looks at the nineteen effects that are part of MetaCreations Studio Effects. All of these effects are located in the Studio Effects submenu of the Effect menu.

Glass Wipe

The Glass Wipe effect creates a nice glossy transition between two elements. This effect is based on displacement and light values. Glass Wipe requires that elements used as source material be present in the Comp, but not necessarily visible. Figure 14-8 shows the Glass Wipe dialog and the effect.

- *Layer to Reveal* allows you to select the layer that will be revealed.

- *Gradient Layer* allows you to choose what source to use as the displacement map.

- *Transition Completion* sets the completion percentage of the effect.

- *Displacement Amount* allows you to set the amount of glass displacement the effect uses.

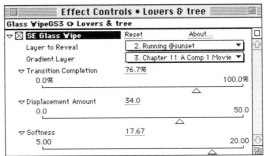

Figure 14-8: The Glass Wipe dialog and the resulting effect.

🎬 *Softness* allows you to soften this displacement.

The following example creates a transition using a grayscale movie as the gradient layer in the Glass Wipe effect.

 ## Studio Time: SE Glass Wipe

1. Create a new Comp (Mac: Cmd-N, Windows: Ctrl-N). Make it 320 x 240, 9:00 seconds, at 30 fps. Name it Glass Wipe.

2. Set the Current Time to 0.

3. Import the Runsun.mov, Romance.mov, and Ch11.mov files from the AE14Foot folder (Mac: Cmd-I, Windows: Ctrl-I).

4. Drag the Runsun.mov and Romance.mov files into the center of the Comp window.

5. Set the Current Time to 0:10 seconds. Drag the Ch11.mov file into the center of the Comp window. Send it to the bottom. Click on the Layer Visibility icon to hide it from view.

6. Make the Romance.mov file the first layer in the stack. Highlight it.

7. Set the Current Time to 1:00 seconds.

8. Apply Effect → Studio Effects → SE Glass Wipe.

9. Select Runsun.mov as the Layer to Reveal, and select Ch11.mov as the Gradient Layer.

10. Make Transition Completion, Displacement Amount, and Softness keyframeable. Set Transition Completeness to 0, Displacement Amount to 15, and Softness to 10.

11. Set the Current Time to 2:15 seconds. Set the Displacement Amount to 50.

12. Set the Current Time to 4:00 seconds. Set the Transition Completeness to 100, the Displacement Amount to 20, and the Softness to 20.

13. Set the work area to end at 4:14 seconds.

14. Set Quality switches to Best.

15. Save your work.

16. Preview or view the pre-rendered movie.

Glue Gun

The SE Glue Gun effect is like painting with movies. The effect can be shiny, dull, or reflective. A writing effect can be achieved by setting keyframes. Production bundle users can take advantage of Motion Math to animate their brushes. Figure 14-9 shows the SE Glue Gun dialog and the effect.

- *Brush Position* controls where the brush is at any point in time.

- *Stroke Width* determines the width of the stroke.

- *Density* determines the height of the stroke.

- *Time Span* sets the life span of the brush-stroke.

- *Reflection Amount* sets the amount of reflection in the paint.

- *Blob Influence* controls the thickness of the paint and how it spreads.

- *Paint Action* allows you to choose between wobbly, liquid-like action or dryer, glue-like action.

- *Wobble Width* and *Wobble Height* allow you to set the width and height of the paint.

- *Wobble Speed* determines the speed of the wobbles.

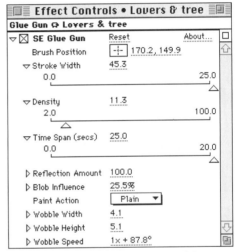

Figure 14-9: The SE Glue Gun dialog and the resulting effect.

This next example demonstrates painting footage with the Glue Gun effect.

 Studio Time: SE Glue Action

1. Create a new Comp (Mac: Cmd-N, Windows: Ctrl-N). Make it 320 x 240, 9:00 seconds, at 30 fps. Name it Glue Gun.

2. Set the Current Time to 0.

3. Drag the Runsun.mov file into the center of the Comp window.

4. Set the Current Time to 0:15. Drag the Romance.mov file into the center of the Comp window.

5. Apply Effect → Studio Effects → SEGlue Gun to the Romance.mov.

6. Make the Brush Position keyframeable. Set the Brush Position to the coordinates 26, 76.

7. Set the Current Time to 0:25 seconds. Set the Brush Position to the coordinates 127, 83.

8. Set the Current Time to 1:05 seconds. Set the Brush Position to the coordinates 42, 171.

9. Set the Current Time to 1:15 seconds. Set the Brush Position to the coordinates 142, 179.

10. Set the Current Time to 1:25 seconds. Set the Brush Position to the coordinates 181, 105.

11. Set the Current Time to 2:05 seconds. Set the Brush Position to the coordinates 76, 100.

12. Set the Current Time to 2:15 seconds. Set the Brush Position to the coordinates 163, 60.

13. Set the Current Time to 2:25 seconds. Set the Brush Position to the coordinates 224, 70.

14. Set the Current Time to 3:05 seconds. Set the Brush Position to the coordinates 321, 151.

15. Set the Current Time to 3:15 seconds. Set the Brush Position to the coordinates 9, 235.

16. Set the Current Time to 3:25 seconds. Set the Brush Position to the coordinates 311, 2.

17. Set the Current Time to 4:05 seconds. Set the Brush Position to the coordinates 3, 4.

18. Set the Current Time to 4:15 seconds. Set the Brush Position to the coordinates 6, 137.

19. Set the Current Time back to 0:15 seconds. Click in the stop watch to make the Stroke Width, Density, Time Span, Blob Influence, Wobble Width, Wobble Height, and Wobble Speed keyframeable. Set the following values: Stroke Width=4.0, Density=25, Time Span=0, Blob Influence=0, Wobble Width=2.5, Wobble Height=2.5, Wobble Speed=1x+0.0°.

20. Set the Current Time to 1:13 seconds. Set Wobble Width to 4.0 and Wobble Height to 5.0.

21. Set the Current Time to 1:24 seconds. Set the Density to 10.

22. Set the Current Time to 2:15 seconds. Set Blob Influence to 50%.

23. Set the Current Time to 3:04 seconds. Set the Stroke Width to 100, the Density to 5.0, and the Time Span to 50.

24. Set the Current Time to 4:15 seconds. Set the Stroke Width to 200 and the Blob Influence to 100%. Set the Wobble Width to 6, Wobble Height to 7, and Wobble Speed to 2x+0.0°.

25. Now we'll set the constant values. Set Reflection Amount to 100. Select Plain as the Paint Action.

26. Set the work area to end at 4:24 seconds.

27. Set Quality to Best.

28. Save your work.

29. Preview or view the pre-rendered movie.

Time Blend FX

The SE Time Blend FX effect is a great way to add trails to images. This effect works best with items that move. The next Studio Time demonstrates applying Time Blend FX twice, as the filter's manual suggests. The effect copies and pastes frames from the image buffer back into the image, making delayed or advance copies. One duplicate will copy into the image buffer, the other will paste from it. The image buffer stores previous frames. The result is similar to that of the Echo effect, only Time Blend FX's is far better. Figure 14-10 shows the SE Time Blend FX dialog and the effect.

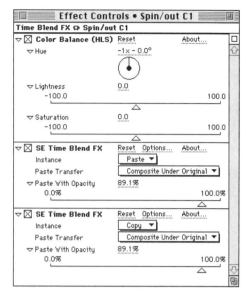

Figure 14-10: SE Time Blend FX dialog and the resulting effect.

■ *Buffer Instance* allows you to select whether to copy to the buffer or paste from the buffer.

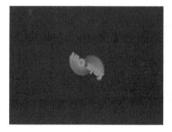  

■ *Paste Transfer* allows you to select how the buffer will be composited with the previous frame.

■ *Blend with Original* blends the next frame with the previous frames.

■ *Composite Under Original* composites the next frame on top of the previous frames.

■ *Composite Over Original* composites the next frame under the previous frames.

■ *Paste with Opacity* allows you to set the Opacity of the pasted frames.

The following example animates type that will spin and scale into and out of the image. SE Time Blend FX is then applied to add trails to the image.

The first Comp animates the words "Spin Out." The type will spin up and scale at the same time. The type will sustain for a few frames, then spin and scale out. In the second Comp, you'll add Time Blend FX to the image and colorize it.

Studio Time: Time Blend FX

1. Create a new Comp (Mac: Cmd-N, Windows: Ctrl-N). Make it 320 x 240, 9:00 seconds, at 30 fps. Name it Spin/Out C1.

2. Import the Spinout.ai file from the AE14Foot folder (Mac: Cmd-I, Windows: Ctrl-I).

3. Drag the Spinout.ai file into the center of the Comp window.

4. Set the Current Time to 2:15 seconds. Press S to bring up the Scale property and Shift +R to show the Rotate property. Click in the stop watch to make the Scale and Rotation keyframeable. Set the Scale amount to 100% and the Rotation to 2x+0.0.

5. Set the Current Time to 2:25 seconds. Set sustaining keyframes.

6. Set the Current Time to 5:10 seconds. Set the Scale amount to 0% and the Rotation to –2x+0.0°. This will spin and scale out the effect.

7. Set the Current Time back to 0. Set the Scale and Rotation to 0. This will complete the spin and scale up effect.

8. Select the Motion Blur effect (the M column toggle) and the Enable Motion Blur toggle in the Time Layout window. See Figure 14-11. The Motion Blur makes the image seem like it is moving.

9. Set the Spinout.ai file to Continuously Rasterize. See Chapter 5 for an explanation of what this does.

10. Press the spacebar to preview the movie. Close the Comp.

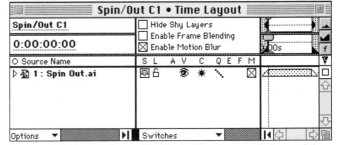

Figure 14-11: Motion Blur enabled in the Time Layout window and the resulting effect.

11. Create a second Comp (Mac: Cmd-N, Windows: Ctrl-N). Make it 320 x 240, 9:00 seconds, at 30 fps. Name it Time Blend FX.

12. Drag the Spin Out C1 Comp into the center of the Comp window.

13. Duplicate it. Turn off the Comp on the top. Select the bottom-most of the two. Apply Effect → Image Control → Color Balance HLS.

14. Set the Current Time to 0. Make the Hue keyframeable. Set the Hue to -45°.

15. Set the Current Time to 2:15 seconds. Set the Hue to 0.

16. Set the Current Time to 2:25 seconds. Set a sustaining keyframe.

17. Set the Current Time to 5:10 seconds. Set the Hue to -1x + 0.0.

18. Apply Effect → Studio Effects → SE Time Blend FX. Figure 14-12 shows a dialog that warns of the dangers of using Time Blend FX. If you encounter any screen drawing

mistakes, try correcting them by requesting the effect-setting window a second time after closing it. If you don't encounter any other problems, you should then be able to proceed as follows.

19. Set the Instance to Paste. Set the Paste Transfer to Composite Under Original. Set the Paste with Opacity to 89.1%

20. Highlight the effect in the effects window and duplicate it.

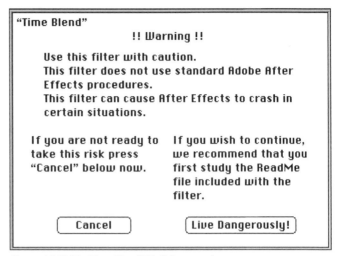

Figure 14-12: The Time Blend FX dialog warning.

21. Set Instance to Copy, and set Paste Transfer to Composite Under Original. Set the Paste with Opacity to 89.1%

22. Set the work area to end at 6:00. This will allow the trails to fade out when previewed or rendered.

23. Turn on the top layer again. This element will be used as the clean copy on top of the effect, and will be brighter and more defined than the element with the effect. As the type spins out, it will change to a color different from the effect.

24. Set the Current Time to 2:25 seconds. Apply Effect → Image Control → Color Balance HLS. Make Hue keyframeable. Set the Hue to $0.0°$.

25. Set the Current Time to 5:10 seconds. Set the Hue to $-1 x + 0.0°$. The effect is complete.

26. Set Quality switches to Best.

27. Save your work.

28. Preview or view the pre-rendered movie.

Mr. Mercury

The SE Mr. Mercury effect is a very cool way to make your footage look as if it were made of molten metal or liquid. Mr. Mercury uses one of the two types of particle systems found within Studio Effects. Mr. Mercury's particles resemble blobs of liquid. This effect is very realistic and can be used on images with alpha channels, as well as straight footage items. Figure 14-13 shows the SE Mr. Mercury dialog; there are many settings.

* The *X and Y Radius* allow you to set the radius of the producers.

* *Producer* allows you to set the position of the blob maker.

■ *Direction* allows you to set the direction of the blobs.

■ *Velocity* allows you to set how fast the blobs come out of the blob maker.

■ *Birth Rate* allows you to set the number of blobs born at that time.

■ *Longevity* allows you to set how long the blobs live.

■ *Gravity* allows you to control the gravitational force applied to the blobs.

■ *Extra* is an "extra" factor according to the manual. It is a surprise factor with a value undefined in the manual, but we are assured that it varies based on the particle used.

■ *Animation system* allows you to set the type of animation to apply to the blobs. There are many to choose from. Try experimenting with them all.

■ *Blob Influence* allows you to control how fast and how much the blobs attract each other.

■ *Influence Map* allows you to specify the behavior of the blobs as they appear and disappear. Experiment with the settings.

■ *Blob Birth and Death Size* allows you to set the starting size and the ending size of the blobs.

The first Comp applies the Mr. Mercury effect to an image.

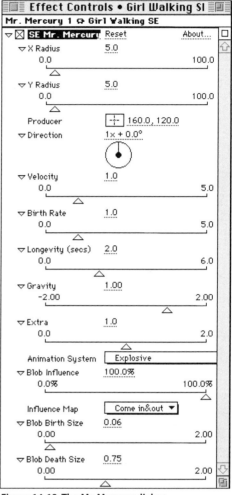

Figure 14-13: The Mr. Mercury dialog.

 Studio Time: SE Mr. Mercury

1. Create a new Comp (Mac: Cmd-N, Windows: Ctrl-N). Make it 320 x 240, 10:00 seconds, at 30 fps. Name it Mr. Mercury 1.

2. Import the Grandpa.mov file from the AE14Foot folder (Mac: Cmd-I, Windows: Ctrl-I).

3. Drag the Grandpa.mov file into the center of the Comp window.

4. Set the Current Time to 1:00 seconds. Drag the SEGirl.mov file into the center of the Comp window.

5. Apply Effect → Studio Effects → Mr. Mercury. Follow table 14-1 to set up the keyframes:

6. Now set the constant values:

Producer=160, 120.
Direction=1x+0.0.
Velocity=1.0
Birth Rate=1.0
Longevity=2.0
Gravity=1.0
Animation System=Explosive
Influence Map=Come In and Out

7. The effect is complete. Figure 14-14 shows the keyframes in the Time Layout window and the resulting effect.

8. Set the Current Time to 5:15 seconds, and set the end of the work area there.

9. Set Quality switches to Best.

10. Save your work.

11. Preview or view the pre-rendered movie.

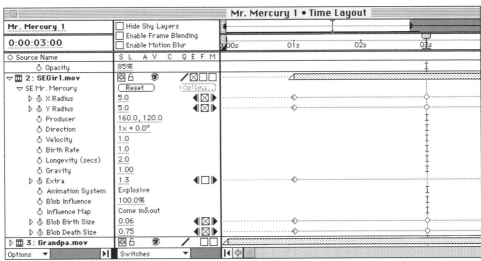

Figure 14-14: The Mr. Mercury keyframes in the Time Layout window and the resulting effect.

Function	@100	@300	@415
X Radius	5	5	80
Y Radius	5	5	100
Extra	1.00		1.6
Blob Birth Size	0.06	0.06	2.00
Blob Death Size	0.75	0.75	2.00

Table 14-1: Setting up the keyframes for the SE Mr. Mercury effect.

That's one way to use the effect. The following sequence demonstrates another. This next example applies Mr. Mercury to a white solid layer. In this exercise, two things will be created: an alpha mask cut into the shape of the blob, and a grayscale version of the blob to overlay back onto the footage.

1. Create a new Comp (Mac: Cmd-N, Windows: Ctrl-N). Make it 320 x 240, 10:00 seconds, at 30 fps. Name it Merc Mask.

2. Create a new solid (Mac: Cmd-Y, Windows: Ctrl-Y). Name it Solid 1, make it 320 x 240, and make its color white.

3. Apply Effect → Studio Effect → Mr. Mercury. Follow table 14-2 below to set up the keyframes:

4. Now set the constant values:
Producer=160, 120.
Direction=1x+0.0°.
Velocity=1.0
Birth Rate=1.0
Longevity=2.0
Gravity=1.0
Animation System=Explosive
Influence Map=Come In and Out

5. Set the Quality switch to Best. Press the spacebar to preview the movie if you want.

6. Close the Comp.

7. Create a new Comp (Mac: Cmd-N, Windows: Ctrl-N). Make it 320 x 240, 10:00 seconds, at 30 fps. Name it Mr. Mercury 2.

8. Drag the Grandpa.mov file into the center of the Comp window.

9. Set the Current Time to 1:10 seconds.

10. Drag the SEGirl.mov file into the center of the Comp window.

11. Drag the Merc Mask Comp into the center of the Comp window.

12. Duplicate the Merc Mask Comp twice. There should be three copies of it in total.

13. Highlight the SEGirl.mov file. Switch to Transfer Controls and select the Merc Mask on top of it as the Alpha Track Matte.

14. Highlight Layer 2. Specify the Merc Mask above it as the Alpha Track Matte. Set the Layers mode to Overlay. Overlay will add shape to the layer and brighten it up.

15. Turn off Layer 2. Set the Current Time to 4:00 seconds. Notice how the movie looks cut out and non-dimensional. Turn Layer 2 back on and look at the effect.

16. Set the Current Time to 6:15 seconds, and set the work area to end. The effect is complete.

17. Set Quality switches to Best.

18. Save your work.

19. Preview or view the pre-rendered movie.

Function	@00	@200	@315
X Radius	5	5	80
Y Radius	5	5	100
Extra	1.00		1.6
Blob Birth Size	0.06	0.06	2.00
Blob Death Size	0.75	0.75	2.00

Table 14-1: Setting up the keyframes for the SE Mr. Mercury effect applied to a solid white layer.

 # Rewind

Wasn't that fun? The MetaCreations people sure know what they're doing! Don't forget to try combining the effects. Also, try adding an effect a number times to the same element. The possible combinations are endless.

 # Coming Attractions

The upcoming chapter explores some of the other third-party filters available for After Effects. The effects packages discussed include The Aurorix 2 Effects, The DigiEffects' Berserk Effects, The Knoll Lens Flare package, and the Auto F/X Video Edges. Clean off those hard drives, there's more fun ahead!

Third-Party Effects

 Preview

There are a number of third-party companies that produce effects packages for After Effects. These companies, DigiEffects, Auto F/X, and Ultimatte, to name a few, will be joined by others in the coming months. Now that After Effects has been released for Windows/NT, many more companies are planning to release companion products. This chapter:

- Explores the Aurorix 2 package.

- Explores the Berserk package.

- Explores the Cyclone package.

- Takes a look at the Knoll Lens Flare Pack, as well as the Ultimatte Keying Effects and Video Edges packages.

 Feature Presentation

So far this book has explored the built-in filters. Chapter 14 discussed the MetaCreations effects packages Final Effects and Studio Effects. In this chapter, we will investigate the various packages from DigiEffects, Aurorix, Berserk, and Cyclonist. We will also examine the Knoll Lens Flare package, as well as the Auto F/X's Video Edges and Ultimatte. These third-party packages offer users powerful effects that just a few years ago cost thousands of dollars to produce. Many of the effects you see on television today are produced using effects from the products discussed in this chapter.

Setting Up

This chapter's projects offer a sampling that represents some of the best effects from each of the packages mentioned above. Not every effect contained in each package is discussed. We have provided Comps that use the various effects for you to further your exploration.

Use the Comps as a guide to the effect. You should rebuild each one to get the full benefit of this chapter. There is a finished movie folder that shows what the effects look like after being applied and rendered. This will come in handy if you don't actually own the effects. Each movie is rendered from its corresponding project. The last step of each Studio Time asks you to render or preview the movie. This choice depends on whether you have the effects package.

All the source footage provided for you is 320 x 240 and Cinepacked. The size for all Comps that will be created is 320 x 240. Feel free to use whatever footage is included to invent new combinations of effect uses. When using these effects on high-resolution footage, test out the effect first. It may not look the same when applied to a proxy (see Chapter 17, which discusses the creation of high-resolution images). When preparing an image for video, be sure to test render the effect first to see that it interlaces properly. Effects that produce thin lines will be a problem. Some of the effects in the DigiEffects package produce results that might work better with multimedia and QuickTime presentations. Such effects are not fast, they only install on Power Macs, and they benefit from the PowerPC's performance.

Shortcuts

Command	Mac	Windows
Open a Project Window	Cmd-O	Ctrl-O
Render Queue	Cmd-Opt-O	Ctrl-Opt-O
Move 1 Frame Back	Page Up	Ctrl-U

Cyclonist

Cyclonist is an amazing effect that creates natural textures which look hand-painted. The Cyclonist effect is actually an organic particle generator. Think of it as a super-set of Xaos Tools' Paint Alchemy filter. Cyclonist is ideal for creating images that are made up of particles such as fire, rain clouds, and smoke. This effect can be used on elements like the Video Edges to create interesting framing effects.

How does Cyclonist work? Cyclonist creates its effect by simulating the way people paint. People paint by dabbing the brush against the canvas; Cyclonist sees these dabs as particles. Each particle has six parameters:

- *Coating* determines the location and blending.

- *Stroke* determines the image used as the particle.

- *Translucency* determines the opacity of the particle.

- *Chroma* defines the color of the particle.

- *Direction* determines the angle of the particle.

- *Magnitude* sets the size of the particle.

These parameters are controlled by the values sampled from the source footage. These values exist at any point in the time line. The source footage can be any footage within the Comp. The effect can even be applied to the image used as the Source.

The Cyclonist interface is broken down into different sections: Presets, Stroke, Coating, Chroma, Magnitude, Direction, and Translucency.

The program ships with at least 100 Presets, some of which are very interesting, such as Route 66, which is demonstrated in one of the examples. Presets are a good place to begin exploring. As you find Presets you like, modify them and change them to make them your own. Presets can be saved and used again. There should never be an idle machine in a home equipped with Cyclonist. Whenever the computer is free, have it crank out some of these textures. Build up a library; textures are always good to have.

The dialog box for Cyclonist is huge since the number of animatable parameters is staggering. Figure 15-1 shows some of Cyclonist's parameters. Figure 15-2 shows the middle part of the Cyclonist dialog. Even

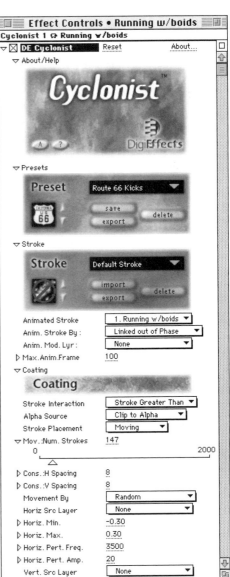

Figure 15-1: Some of Cyclonist's parameters.

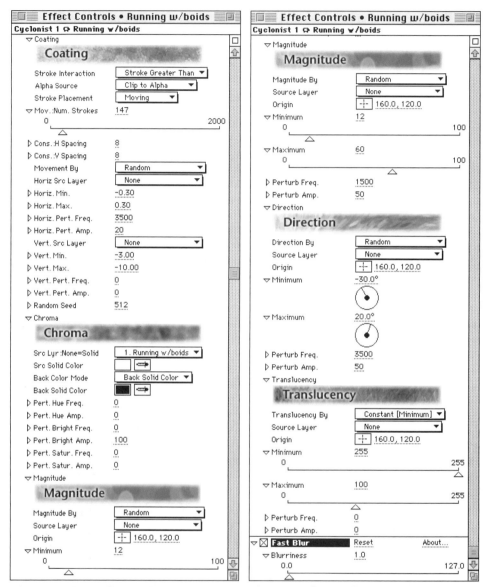

Figure 15-2: The middle part of the Cyclonist dialog.

Figure 15-3: The rest of the Cyclonist dialog.

with a 20-inch monitor, it still doesn't fit in the window completely. Figure 15-3 shows the rest of the Cyclonist dialog.

In the following examples, we will apply a few different Presets to the same source footage, creating four Comps in all. This will illustrate the kind of results Cyclonist can produce.

Studio Time: Cyclonist 1

1. Create a new Comp (Mac: Cmd-N, Windows: Ctrl-N). Make it 320 x 240, 8:00 seconds, at 30 fps. Name it Cyclonist 1.

2. Import the Runbirds.mov file from the AE15Foot folder (Mac: Cmd-I, Windows: Ctrl-I).

3. Drag the Runbirds.mov file into the center of the Comp window.

4. Apply Effect → DigiEffects Cyclonist → DE Cyclonist. Scroll through the Presets to Route 66 Kicks. Isn't the Route 66 sign great?

5. Directly below the Preset section lies the Stroke section. Set the Animated Stroke to Runbirds.mov. Also set the Anim Stroke By to Linked Out of Phase. This will make the stroke animated by the source itself. The frames that travel through the Comp are randomly scattered from the source footage. This combination of settings will slow the machine down to a crawl; however, the results justify the wait.

6. Set the work area to end at 7:00 seconds. You may want to set it for a shorter time.

7. Set Quality switch to Best.

8. Preview or view the pre-rendered movie.

9. As a variation, bring the source footage in again and send that layer to the bottom (Mac: Cmd-B, Windows: Ctrl-B).

10. Highlight the layer with the effect. Change the Layer mode to Screen. This produces an interesting effect of the two sources combined. The Comp is named Cyclonist 1B. The Comp and the movie are provided on the CD-ROM.

This next example applies a different Preset.

 Studio Time: Cyclonist 2

1. Create a new Comp (Mac: Cmd-N, Windows: Ctrl-N). Make it 320 x 240, 8:00 seconds, at 30 fps. Name it Cyclonist 2.

2. Drag the Runbirds.mov file into the center of the Comp window.

3. Apply Effect → DigiEffects Cyclonist → DE Cyclonist. Scroll through the Presets until you see Pool Caustics. Notice the fiery effect when it finishes rendering.

4. Set the work area to end at 7:00 seconds. You may want to set it for a shorter time.

5. Set Quality to Best.

6. Preview or view the pre-rendered movie.

7. As a variation, follow the same step as in the previous Comp. Bring the source footage in again and send it to the bottom.

8. Highlight the layer with the effect. Change the Layer mode to Screen. This produces another interesting effect of the two sources combined. The Comp is named Cyclonist 2B. Both the Comp and the movie are provided on the CD-ROM.

 Studio Time: Cyclonist 3

1. Create a new Comp (Mac: Cmd-N, Windows: Ctrl-N). Make it 320 x 240, 8:00 seconds, at 30 fps. Name it Cyclonist 3.

2. Drag the Runbirds.mov file into the center of the Comp window.

3. Apply Effect → DigiEffects Cyclonist → DE Cyclonist. Scroll through the Presets to Smoky Steam SL=None. Notice the steamy, smoky, fiery effect when it finishes rendering.

4. Set the work area to end at 7:00 seconds. You may want to set it for a shorter time.

5. Set Quality to Best.

6. Preview or view the pre-rendered movie.

7. There is no variation for this Comp. Feel free to try any changes on your own.

 Studio Time: Cyclonist 4

1. Create a new Comp (Mac: Cmd-N, Windows: Ctrl-N). Make it 320 x 240, 8:00 seconds, at 30 fps. Name it Cyclonist 4.

2. Drag the Runbirds.mov file into the center of the Comp window.

3. Apply Effect → DigiEffects Cyclonist → DE Cyclonist. Scroll through the Presets to Egg Zone. Notice the organic tentacle effect when it finishes rendering.

4. Set the Animate Stroke By to Linked Out of Phase.

5. Set the work area to end at 7:00 seconds. You may want to set it for a shorter time.

6. Set Quality to Best.

7. Preview or view the pre-rendered movie. The last Comp is perhaps the best of the four. It looks like a collection of sea anemones in an aquarium.

8. As a variation, follow the alternate step as in the previous Comps. Bring the source footage in again and send it to the bottom.

11. Highlight the layer with the effect. Change the Layer mode to Screen. This Comp is named Cyclonist 4B. The Comp and the movie are provided on the CD-ROM.

Aurorix

The Aurorix filters are another set of filters from DigiEffects. We'll look at four of the most handy ones.

Aged Film

The Aged Film effect makes any footage look old, adding dust, scratches, and even hair! You can colorize the footage, as well as make it jittery. The results of this one effect easily justify the purchase of the entire package. There are many settings here to explain; Figure 15-4 Shows the Aged Film dialog box and the effect.

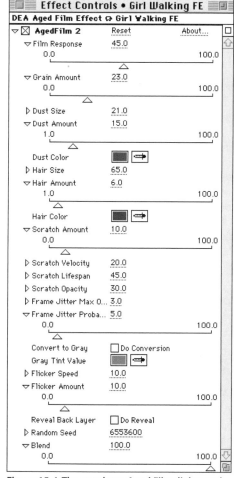

- *Film Response* allows you to control the Gain of the footage. Old film gets lighter or less saturated with age.

- *Grain Amount* controls the amount of grain added to the footage.

- *Dust Size* sets the size of the dust particles.

- *Dust Amount* sets the amount of dust.

- *Dust Color* allows you to set the color of the dust.

- *Hair Size* sets the length of the hairs.

- *Hair Amount* sets the amount of hair.

- *Hair Color* allows you to set the color of the hair.

- *Scratch Amount* sets the number of scratches applied to the film.

- *Scratch Velocity* controls the horizontal speed at which your scratches travel.

Figure 15-4: The very large Aged Film dialog and

- *Scratch Lifespan* controls how long the scratches appear.

- *Scratch Opacity* sets the opacity of the scratches.

- *Frame Jitter Max Offset* sets how far the frame jumps when it simulates slipping sprockets.

- *Frame Jitter Probability* sets the probability that a frame will jump.

- *Convert to Gray* changes the film into grayscale for the purpose of colorizing.

- *Gray Tint Value* allows you to set the color to tint the film.

- *Flicker Speed* sets the amount of flickers in the footage. Flickers mimic the way old projectors have trouble steadying the film frames.

- *Flicker Amount* sets the brightness differences for the flicker.

- *Reveal Back Layer* shows the back when the sprockets are skipped.

- *Blend* is the standard blend with image.

This next example adds the Aged Film effect to some footage and demonstrates animating the amount of scratches and hair that affects the film.

 ## Studio Time: Aurorix Aged Film

1. Create a new Comp (Mac: Cmd-N, Windows: Ctrl-N). Make it 320 x 240, 9:00 seconds, at 30 fps. Name it Aged Film.

2. Import the FEGirl.mov file from the AE15Foot folder (Mac: Cmd-I, Windows: Ctrl-I).

3. Drag the FEGirl.mov file into the center of the Comp window.

4. While at 00, apply Effect → DigiEffects Aurorix2 → Aged Film 2. There are only two items that will be keyframed. Show the layers effects. Click in the stop watch to make the Hair Amount and Scratch Amount keyframeable. Set the Hair Amount to 6 and the Scratch Amount to 10.

5. Set the Current Time to 4:00 seconds (Mac: Cmd-G, Windows: Ctrl-G, and type 400, or just move the Playback Head until the Current Time reads 0:00:04:00). Set the Hair Amount to 12 and the Scratch Amount to 20.

6. Set the Current Time to 5:00. Set the Hair Amount to 20 and set a sustaining keyframe for Scratch Amount.

7. Set the Current Time to 7:00. Reset the Hair Amount to 6 and the Scratch Amount to 10.

8. Set the rest of the constant values:

Film Response	45
Grain Amount	23
Dust Size	21
Dust Amount	15
Dust Color	Black
Hair Size	65

Hair Color	Black
Scratch Velocity	20
Scratch Lifespan	45
Scratch Opacity	30
Frame Jitter Max	3
Frame Jitter Probability	5
Do Conversion	Off
Gray Tint Value	N/A
Flicker Speed	10
Flicker Amount	10
Do Reveal	Off
Random Seed	6553600
Blend	100

9. Set the Quality to Best.

10. Preview or render.

What we have just done is taken a film of a girl walking, and made it look like an old film clip. Did you notice the amount of dust we applied, and how the hair gives this a human touch? It's very much like watching old news reel footage.

Earthquake2

Earthquake is a handy effect that simulates a shaky camera and looks like what an earthquake would do to a camera and its subject. Figure 15-5 shows the Earthquake dialog and the effect.

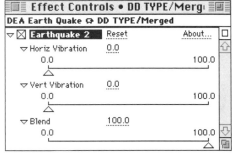

Figure 15-5: The Earthquake2 dialog and the resulting effect.

- *Horizontal Vibration* allows you to set the amount of horizontal vibrations.

- *Vertical Vibrations* allows you to set the amount of vertical vibrations.

- *Blend* is the standard blend with image.

This next example shakes a logo as if it were in an earthquake.

Studio Time: Earthquake2

1. Create a new Comp (Mac: Cmd-N, Windows: Ctrl-N). Make it 320 x 240, 9:00 seconds, at 30 fps. Name it Earthquake.

2. Import the DDType.psd file from the AE15Foot folder (Mac: Cmd-I, Windows: Ctrl-I).

3. Drag the DDType.psd file into the center of the Comp window.

4. Press S to bring up the Scale property. Set the Scale amount to 40%.

5. Apply Effect → DigiEffects Aurorix → Earthquake 2. Show the layers effects. Click in the stop watch to make the Horizontal and Vertical Vibrations keyframeable. Set both values to 0%.

6. Set the Current Time to 2:00 seconds (Mac: Cmd-G, Windows: Ctrl-G, and type 200, or just move the Playback Head until the Current Time reads 0:00:02:00). Set the Horizontal Vibration to 50 and the Vertical Vibration to 25. This will shake the element quite a bit.

7. Set the Current Time to 4:00 seconds. Set the Horizontal Vibration and the Vertical Vibration back to 0. This will close out the effect.

8. Set the work area to end around 4:00 seconds.

9. Set Quality to Best.

10. Save your work.

11. Preview or view the pre-rendered movie

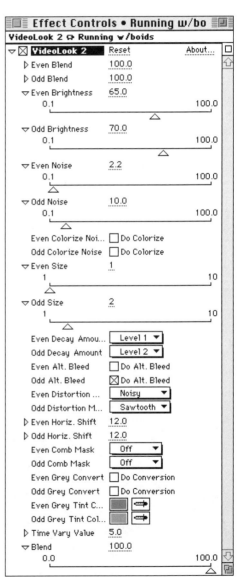

Figure 15-6: The many settings of the VideoLook effect and the resulting effect.

Video Look

The Video Look effect allows you to re-create cheap-looking, grungy video, complete with video screen noise and television scan lines. This effect is great for simulating a television screen image. Video Look works in even and odd frames, so does the effect. Even and odd

parameters must be set separately. Figure 15-6 shows the densely packed Video Look dialog and the effect.

- *Blend* is a fine-tune control for reducing the effect. The effect works by blending back the even or odd lines with original footage.

- *Brightness* allows you to set the brightness of the line.

- *Noise* allows you to add snow to the line.

- *Colorize Noise* creates colored snow.

- *Size* allows you to set the size of the line.

- *Decay Amount* allows you to set the amount of decay. Experiment with these settings; many interesting combinations are possible.

- *Alt. Bleed* when checked bleeds the image.

- *Distortion Method* allows you to choose how the lines will be distorted. Experiment with the different settings and the even/odd combinations.

- *Horizontal Shift* sets the amount of horizontal shift based on the distortion method.

- *Comb Mask* allows you to set the horizontal skipping. Play with the settings and experiment. There are many interesting combinations to discover. For example, select on one of the presets and compare the results with the other settings. The Comb masks set a distinct pattern in the video, such as the refresh lines moving from left to right or right to left.

- *Gray Convert* converts the line to gray.

- *Gray Tint Color* allows you to set the color of the line when converted to gray.

- *Time Vary Parameter* allows you to set the phase of the distortion method.

- *Blend* is the standard blend with image.

This next Studio Time makes the footage look like a cheap video. Since the settings are dense, you are not asked to place any keyframes into the Comp.

 Studio Time: Video Look

1. Create a new Comp (Mac: Cmd-N, Windows: Ctrl-N). Make it 320 x 240, 9:00 seconds, at 30 fps. Name it Video Look.

2. Drag the Runbirds.mov file into the center of the Comp window.

3. Apply Effect → DigiEffects Aurorix 2 → VideoLook 2. Just set the parameters and let the effect play out. Play with the settings after setting it up.

4. Now set the rest of the constant values:

Even Blend	100
Odd Blend	100
Even Brightness	65
Odd Brightness	70
Even Noise	2.2
Odd Noise	10
Even/Odd Colorize	Off
Even Size	1
Odd Size	2
Even Decay	Level 1
Odd Decay	Level 2
Even Alt. Bleed	Off
Odd Alt. Bleed	On
Even Distortion	Noisy
Odd Distortion	Sawtooth
Even/Odd Horiz. Shift	12
Even/Odd Comb Mask	Off
Even/Odd Gray Convert	Off
Even/Odd Color	NA
Time Vary	5.0
Blend	100

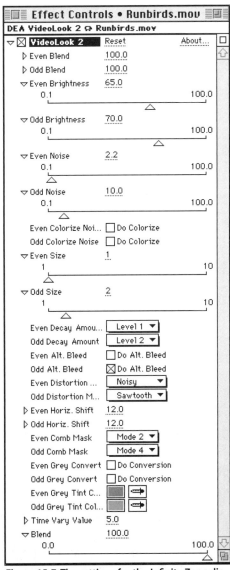

5. This effect certainly has enough parameters to define! Play with the pop-up menus to vary and modify the effect.

6. Set the work area to end at 4:00 seconds.

7. Set Quality switch to Best.

8. Save your work.

9. Preview or view the pre-rendered movie.

Infinity Zone

The Infinity Zone effect is an animated KPT Vortex Tiling filter. This is a great effect, since now things can move through the tiling. In the KPT Vortex Tiling filter, the image is repeated many times around a specific point within the image. In Infinity Zone, you can affect the

Figure 15-7: The settings for the Infinity Zone dialog and the resulting effect.

image as a single channel effect (RGB). Or you can treat the image as separate channels and animate the effect's center on the individual channels. Not only can you tile the image, but you can also tile it out of registration, which would make the image look as if you were seeing it cross-eyed. This effect looks utterly 60s psychedelic. Figure 15-7 shows the Infinity Zone effect dialog and the effect.

This next example creates two Comps: one will animate the effect as a single channel, and the other will animate it as a separate channel effect. Both produce fantastic results.

 Studio Time: Infinity Zone

1. Create a new Comp (Mac: Cmd-N, Windows: Ctrl-N). Make it 320 x 240, 7:00 seconds, at 30 fps. Name it Infinity Zone 1. This will be the single channel effect Comp.

2. Drag the Runbirds.mov file into the center of the Comp window.

3. Apply Effect → DigiEffects Aurorix 2 → Infinity Zone 2. Set the Current Time to 0. Click in the stop watch to make the Red Strength and Red Centroid keyframeable. Set the Red Strength to 0.1. Set the Red Centroid coordinates to 162.2, 122.4. The Red Channel controls the RGB in a single channel mode.

4. Set the Current Time to 6:00 seconds (Mac: Cmd-G, Windows: Ctrl-G, and type 600, or just move the Playback Head until the Current Time reads 0:00:06:00). Set the Red Strength to 90. Set the Red Centroid coordinates to 160, 120.

5. The rest of the effects have no bearing on a single channel effect. They will be adjusted in the next Comp.

6. Set the work area to end at 4:00 seconds.

7. Set Quality switch to Best.

8. Save your work.

9. Preview or view the pre-rendered movie

It's time to move onto the second Comp. This Comp will be different because the Centroids are animated as a multi-channel effect.

Studio Time: Infinity Zone #2

1. Create a new Comp (Mac: Cmd-N, Windows: Ctrl-N). Make it 320 x 240, 7:00 seconds, at 30 fps. Name it Infinity Zone 2. This Comp will be the multi-channel effect.

2. Drag the Runbirds.mov file into the center of the Comp window.

3. Apply Effect → DigiEffects Aurorix 2 → Infinity Zone 2. Show the layers effects properties. Click in the stop watch to make the : Red and Green Strength keyframeable. Set both the Red and Green Strength to 0.1.

4. Set the Current Time to 1:00 seconds (Mac: Cmd-G, Windows: Ctrl-G, and type 100, or just move the Playback Head until the Current Time reads 0:00:01:00). Set the Red and Green Centroids to the coordinates 160, 120.

5. Set the Current Time to 3:00 seconds. Set the Red and Green Strength to 75. Change the Red Centroid to 160, 100. Change the Green Centroid to 160, 140. This will move the red channel closer to the top and the green channel closer to the bottom.

6. Set the Current Time to 5:00 seconds. Return the Centroids back to their original positions of 160, 120.

7. Set the Current Time to 6:00 seconds. Set both the Red and Green Strength back to .1.

8. Set the work area to end at 6:00 seconds.

9. Set Quality switch to Best.

10. Save your work.

11. Preview or view the pre-rendered movie

Berserk

Berserk is the third special effects package we'll look at. It contains a large number of separate effects for you to try.

Blizzard

The Blizzard effect turns any scene into a winter storm. The snow is generated by a particle system. The particle system controls the flake size and speed. Try applying the snow to a solid black layer. The layer can then be screened onto the footage to create the effect. The Blizzard effect's snowflake edges need to be softer and more translucent for the footage.

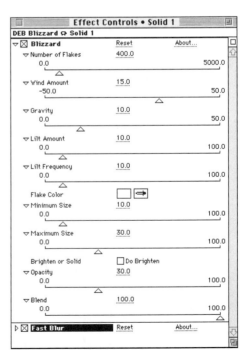

Figure 15-8: The Blizzard dialog and the resulting effect.

When they are applied to the solid layer, the layer can be blurred and the transparency can be controlled independently from the effect. Figure 15-8 shows the Blizzard dialog and the effect.

- *Number of Flakes* sets the amount of flakes in the effect.

- *Wind Amount* sets the velocity of the horizontal offset.

- *Gravity* controls the speed of the falling snow.

- *Lilt Amount* sets the amount of left-to-right sway.

- *Lilt Frequency* sets the speed of the sway.

- *Minimum Size* sets the minimum size for any flake.

- *Maximum Size* sets the maximum size for any flake.

- *Brighten or Solid Brighten* causes the flake to make the underlying image brighter. Solid renders without regard to the underlying image.

- *Opacity* controls the transparency of all flakes.

Studio Time: Blizzard2

1. Create a new Comp (Mac: Cmd-N, Windows: Ctrl-N). Make it 320 x 240, 9:00 seconds, at 30 fps. Name it Blizzard.

2. Set the Current Time to 0.

3. Import the Runbirds.mov file from the AE15Foot folder (Mac: Cmd-I, Windows: Ctrl-I).

4. Drag the Runbirds.mov file into the center of the Comp window.

5. Create a new solid (Mac: Cmd-Y, Windows: Ctrl-Y). Set it to 320 x 240, and select black as its color. Set the Layer mode to Screen.

6. Apply Effect → DigiEffects Berserk → Blizzard. Set the Current Time to 0. Click in the stop watch to make the Number of Flakes, Wind Amount, and Gravity keyframeable. Set the Number of Flakes to 0; set the Wind Amount and Gravity to 2.

7. Set the Current Time to 3:00 seconds (Mac: Cmd-G, Windows: Ctrl-G, and type 300, or just move the Playback Head until the Current Time reads 0:00:03:00). Set the Number of Flakes to 200; increase the Wind Amount to 4 and the Gravity to 6.

8. Set the Current Time to 5:00 seconds. Set the Number of Flakes to 400. Set the Wind Amount to 15 and the Gravity to 10.

9. The Flake Color is white. Set the Lilt Amount and Lilt Frequency to 10. Set the Minimum Size to 10 and the Maximum Size to 30. Leave Brighten off, and set the Opacity to 30. These settings will remain constant.

10. Apply Effect → Blur → Fast Blur to the solid. Set the effect to 2. Applying it blurs the flakes, not the image.

11. Set the work area to end at 5:10 seconds.

12. Set Quality switch to Best.

13. Save your work.

14. Preview or view the pre-rendered movie.

Ripploid

The Ripploid effect is a super-Ripple. It is much stronger that the Ripple effect that comes with the After Effects. These Ripples are very fluid. Figure 15-9 shows the Ripploid dialog and the effect.

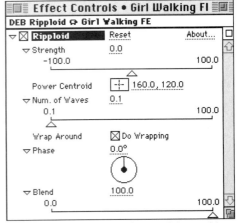

- *Strength* allows you to set how strong the warp will be.

- *Power Centroid* allows you to specify the center of the effect.

- *Number of Waves* allows you to define the quantity of waves in the ripple.

Figure 15-9: The Ripploid dialog and the resulting effect.

- *Wrap Around* allows the effect to wrap around the opposite side to fill in the source layer.

- *Phase* allows you to control the phase of the waves.

- *Blend* allows you to fade the effect into the underlying layer.

This next Studio Time applies the Ripploid effect to the footage and spins it up, then back.

Studio Time: Ripploid

1. Create a new Comp (Mac: Cmd-N, Windows: Ctrl-N). Make it 320 x 240, 10:00 seconds, at 30 fps. Name it Ripploid.

2. Set the Current Time to 0.

3. Import the FEGirl.mov file from the AE15Foot folder (Mac: Cmd-I, Windows: Ctrl-I).

4. Drag the FEGirl.mov file into the center of the Comp window.

5. Apply Effect → Berserk → Ripploid. Set the Current Time to 0. Click in the stop watch to make the Strength, Number of Waves, and Phase keyframeable. Set the Strength and Phase to 0. Set the Number of Waves to 0.1 (which is actually invalid and will be reset to 0.1000061).

6. Set the Current Time to 6:00 seconds (Mac: Cmd-G, Windows: Ctrl-G, and type 600, or just move the Playback Head until the Current Time reads 0:00:06:00). Set the Strength to 20, the Number of Waves to 12.2, and the Phase to 56°.

7. Set the Current Time to 8:00 seconds. Reset the values back to the values set at the first keyframe.

8. Turn on Do Wrapping.

9. Set the work area to end at 8:15 seconds.

10. Save your work.

11. Set Quality switch to Best.

12. Preview or view the pre-rendered movie.

Spintron

The Spintron effect looks like a Twirl effect that gets sucked into the center of the twirl. Spintron works well with images that have alpha channels. This effect needs to be

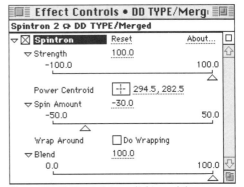

Figure 15-10: The Spintron dialog and the resulting effect.

performed with the Quality switches set to Best. Figure 15-10 shows the Spintron dialog and the effect.

- *Strength* allows you to set how strong the effect is.

- *Power Centroid* allows you to control the center of the effect.

- *Spin Amount* allows you to control the amount and direction of the rotation.

- *Do Wrapping* makes the image wrap around the other side of the effect.

- *Blend* allows you to set the blend of the effect with the original image.

The following exercises build two Comps. In the first Comp, you will apply the Spintron effect to a logo. In the second, you will modify the parameters further.

 ## *Studio Time: Spintron*

1. Create a new Comp (Mac: Cmd-N, Windows: Ctrl-N). Make it 320 x 240, 9:00 seconds, at 30 fps. Name it Spintron.

2. Set the Current Time to 0.

3. Import the DDType.psd file from the AE15Foot folder (Mac: Cmd-I, Windows: Ctrl-I).

4. Drag the FEGirl.mov file into the center of the Comp window. Press S to bring up the Scale effect. Set the Scale amount to 40%.

5. Apply Effect → DigiEffects Berserk → Spintron. Set the Current Time to 0. Click in the stop watch to make the Strength and Spin Amount keyframeable. Set the Strength to 0 and the Spin Amount to 12.

6. Set the Current Time to 2:15 seconds (Mac: Cmd-G, Windows: Ctrl-G, and type 215, or just move the Playback Head until the Current Time reads 0:00:02:15). Set the Strength to 125 and the Spin Amount to 18.

7. Set the Current Time to 4:00 seconds. Set the Spin Amount to 0; this will return the logo to normal.

8. Set the Power Centroid to 294.5, 282.5. Make sure Wrapping is not selected (it should be off).

9. Set the work area to end at 4:00 seconds.

10. Save your work.

11. Set Quality switch to Best.

12. Preview or view the pre-rendered movie.

Now it's time to complete the second Comp. In this Comp, you will use the logo at full size and make it spin completely into the center. The logo will then rise from the effect, at a smaller size, spinning in the opposite direction.

Studio Time: Spintron2

1. Start by duplicating the Spintron effect layer (Mac: Cmd-D Windows: Ctrl-D).

2. Set the Current Time to 0. Press S to bring up the Scale property. Click in the stop watch to make the Scale keyframeable. Set the Scale amount of the DDType.psd file to 150%.

3. Now modify the Spintron effect: Set the Strength and the Spin Amount to 0.

4. Set the Current Time to 2:00 seconds (Mac: Cmd-G, Windows: Ctrl-G, and type 200, or just move the Playback Head until the Current Time reads 0:00:02:00). Set the Strength to 100 and the Spin Amount to 30. Change the Scale amount to 100%.

5. Set the Current Time to 2:01 seconds. Set the Spin Amount to -30, and change the Scale amount to 40%. At this point, the logo is invisible so you can change the values radically. The logo will spin out from the other direction and it will be the specified size when it spins out.

6. Leave the Power Centroid and the Wrapping values as they are.

7. Set the Current Time to 3:15 seconds. Change the Spin Amount to 0. This closes out the effect.

8. Set the work area to end at 4:00 seconds.

9. Save your work.

10. Set Quality switch to Best.

11. Preview or view the pre-rendered movie.

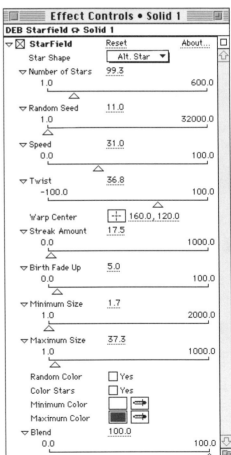

Figure 15-11: The many settings of the Starfield dialog and the resulting effect.

Starfield

The Starfield effect is a Star Wars-type starfield generator. The effect animates the number of stars, their size, and their speed, to name a few settings. Try combining layers with the effect; set the Layer modes to Screen for the best results. Use Starfield to make the layers jump to lightspeed. Figure 15-11 shows the many settings of the Starfield dialog and the effect.

■ *Star Shape* allows you to chose the type of star you to use from a pop-up menu. Experiment with these settings.

 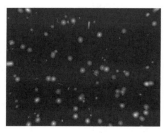 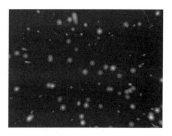

- *Speed* allows you to control how fast the image travels through space.

- *Twist* allows you to set the circular rotational speed.

- *Warp Center* allows you to set the point from which the stars emanate.

- *Streak Amount* allows you to set the length of the stars' streak.

- *Birth Fade Up* allows you to set the how many frames it takes to fade up a star. Lower numbers are faster; higher numbers are slower.

- *Minimum* allows you to set the minimum size of any star.

- *Maximum* allows you to set the maximum size of any star.

- *Random Color* allows the colors to be generated randomly.

- *Color Stars* is enabled when Random Color is enabled.

- *Minimum/Maximum Color* allows you to set the minimum and maximum color range used when creating stars. Note that these settings can only be active when Random Color is *not* turned on.

The following example applies the Starfield effect to a solid layer, animating the number of stars, their size, and their speed.

 ## Studio Time: Starfield

1. Create a new Comp (Mac: Cmd-N, Windows: Ctrl-N). Make it 320 x 240, 9:00 seconds, at 30 fps. Name it Starfield.

2. Set the Current Time to 0. Create a new solid (Mac: Cmd-Y, Windows: Ctrl-Y). Name it Solid 1, and set its size to 320 x 240 and its color to black.

3. Apply Effect → DigiEffects Berserk → Starfield. Set keyframes for

Number of Stars=70
Speed=20.0
Twist=25.3
Streak Amount=5.0
Minimum Size=1.0
Maximum Size=30.0

4. Set the Current Time to 3:15 seconds (Mac: Cmd-G, Windows: Ctrl-G, and type 315, or just move the Playback Head until the Current Time reads 0:00:03:15). Set the following values:
Number of Stars=110
Speed=35.0
Streak Amount=22.0
Minimum Size=2.0
Maximum Size=40.0

5. Set the Current Time to 5:15 seconds. Set following values:
Number of Stars=150
Speed=55.0
Twist=50.0
Streak Amount=4.0

6. Set the Random Seed to 11; animating this setting will yield unpredictable results. Let the Warp Center remain constant at 160, 120. Set Birth Fade Up to 5. Turn off both Random Color and Color Stars. Select white as the Minimum Color and blue as the Maximum color.

7. The effect is complete. Save your work.

8. Set Quality switch to Best.

9. Preview or view the pre-rendered movie.

Knoll Software

The Knoll Lens Flare creates realistic lens flare effects to compositions within After Effects. You can fully animate the Lens Flare effects. You can also control size, color, position, and the type of flare. There are two types of flare effects. One is the normal Lens Flare that reproduces the glare and multiple internal reflections occurring when a bright light source is viewed through a lens. The other is called Scratch. Scratch reproduces the spikish, glowy look a light source has when viewed through scratched acetate or plastic. The Knoll Lens Flare package also includes an additional effect called Unmult, which creates an alpha channel for the flare effects. Unmult only works with After Effects 3.0; the other Knoll Lens Flare effects ship with the 2.0 compatible versions. This package is truly worth the price.

Usually, these effect are applied to a solid black layer and the Layer mode is set to screen. In the Screen mode, black is a neutral color. Figure 15-12 shows the Scratch effect applied to a solid layer.

The first Studio Time adds the Lens Flare effect to an image through a movie that

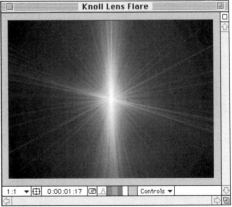

Figure 15-12: The Knoll Scratch effect applied to a solid layer.

contains the effect applied to a solid layer. This movie contains three types of Lens Flare effects: Rock Concert, Sun Flare, and 35 mm Lens.

 ## Studio Time: Lens Flare

1. Create a new Comp (Mac: Cmd-N, Windows: Ctrl-N). Make it 320 x 240, 8:00 seconds, at 30 fps. Name it Knoll Lens Flare.

2. Import the Romance.mov and the KnollFlr.mov files from the AE15Foot folder (Mac: Cmd-I, Windows: Ctrl-I).

3. Drag the Romance.mov and the KnollFlr.mov files into the center of the Comp window.

4. Send the Romance.mov layer to the bottom.

5. Set the KnollFlr.mov Layer mode to Screen.

6. Set the work area to end at 7:15 seconds.

7. The effect is complete. Save your work.

8. Set Quality switch to Best.

9. Preview or view the pre-rendered movie.

Ultimatte

The Ultimatte effects package is excellent for performing blue/green screen extraction of mattes, as well as compositing. The software is set up to yield optimum results from little effort. For anyone who wants to get under the hood, the Ultimatte effects provide amazing control of all parameters.

How do these effects work? Basically the Ultimatte effects are producing a composite. The composite is made up of a foreground image and a background image. The Ultimatte system produces a matte that is applied to the foreground, as well as the background. The results of the two functions are then combined to complete the composite. There are three basic effects in the Ultimatte package: Screen Correction, Grain Killer, and Ultimatte.

It is can be very difficult to maintain a perfectly lit background. There are often hot spots and darker areas. Screen Correction evens out the blue backing to provide a better key. Figure 15-13 shows the Screen Correction dialog.

Grain Killer is used to remove grain. Grain comes from many sources, such as noise on video cameras and the resulting transfer of

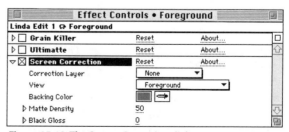

Figure 15-13: The Screen Correction dialog.

data. Grain is also present when scanning or converting film footage. The Ultimatte system is very sensitive and therefore could composite the grain. Using Grain Killer removes this grain by softening the backing color. There are powerful algorithms that help separate subjects from the backing in the softening process. These settings can also be performed manually for any under-the-hood types out there. Figure 15-14 shows the Grain Killer dialog.

Ultimatte is used to perform the final composite. Ultimatte uses something its

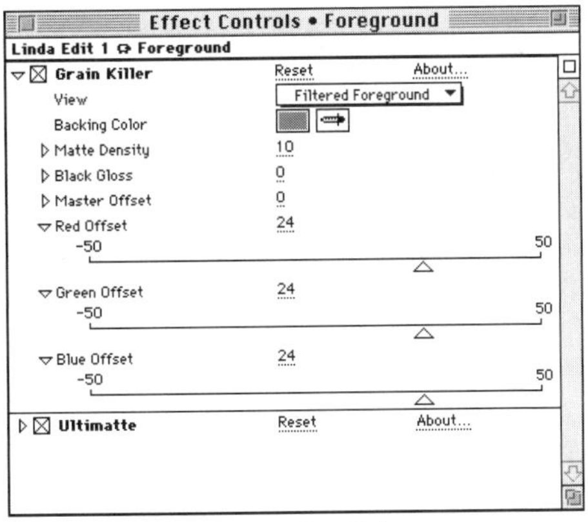

Figure 15-14: The Grain Killer dialog.

makers referred to as Ultimatte Intelligence, which is a system of setting various color selections of foreground and background images to gather measurements. Such measurements are used to automatically adjust the parameters of the effect (usually) to give you the best result. The settings are based upon the experience of the Ultimatte engineers. Of course,

you can modify the parameters to fine-tune the results. Figure 15-15 shows the many control settings of the Ultimatte effect and the effect.

The following example consists of a movie created using the Ultimatte effects. The model was shot on Hi-8 video, in front of Ultimatte Blue material. The shoot was made a bit more difficult by a fan that was pointed at our model (she was warm because tungsten lights are hot). It is very difficult to key out fine detail like moving hair (after all, the intent was to make a good test). The footage was digitized using a Targa 2000 Pro video capture card. The Grain Killer was used to smooth out the grain. The Ultimatte effect was then added. What you will see are the results of Ultimatte Intelligence, at the automatic setting. In our opinion, if you do a good amount of work that involves color keying, this effect is a definite must to add to your arsenal. It takes all the guesswork out of the picture.

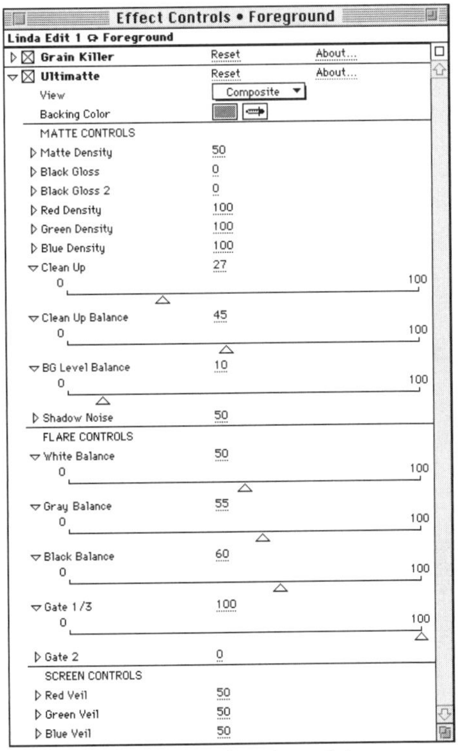

Figure 15-15: The control settings of the Ultimatte effect and the resulting effect.

Auto F/X Video Edges

The Auto F/X Video Edges package doesn't really contain any effects. Rather, it contains an invaluable set of masks that can be used as track mattes in After Effects. The Auto F/X Video Edges package can also be used in Premiere. The masks provide edges as well as shadow masks. There are also some special images that can be used as split screen masks. The package houses hundreds of these masks, in all kinds of shapes and sizes, with varying edges. It's one resource that's definitely worth having. The edges are easy to work with. Simply use them as track mattes. They can be sized and scaled to order.

Setup

There are two Studio Times for these add-ons. The first example uses one of the Video Edges to play video within video. It also demonstrates using the Video Edge to create the drop shadow for the element.

Studio Time: Video Edges A

1. Create a new Comp (Mac: Cmd-N, Windows: Ctrl-N). Make it 320 x 240, 7:00 seconds, at 30 fps. Name it Video Edges A.

2. Set the Current Time to 0.

3. Import the Beach.mov, Romance.mov, and VidEdge1.psd files from the AE15Foot folder (Mac: Cmd-I, Windows: Ctrl-I).

4. Drag the Beach.mov, Romance.mov, and VidEdge1.psd files into the center of the Comp window.

5. Bring the VidEdge1.psd. Send the Beach.mov to the bottom.

6. Select the Romance.mov. Press S to bring up the Scale property. Set the Scale amount to 85%. Set the layer's track matte to the VidEdge1.psd layer above it. Now the Romance.mov layer should be visible.

7. Set the Current Time to 2:00 seconds (Mac: Cmd-G, Windows: Ctrl-G, and type 200, or just move the Playback Head until the Current Time reads 0:00:02:00). Select the Video Edge element. Turn off the preserve aspect ratio checkbox. Click in the stop watch to make the

Scale Width and Scale Height keyframeable. Set its Scale Width to 50% and its Scale Height to 35%.

8. Set the Current Time to 0. Set both the Scale Width and Height to 0.

9. Duplicate the VidEdge1.psd layer. Rename it Video Shadow.

Video Edge 1A • Time Layout

| Video Edge 1A | ☐ Hide Shy Layers ☐ Enable Frame Blending ☐ Enable Motion Blur |
| 0:00:02:00 | |

○ Layer Name	S L A V C Q E F M
▽ 📄 1 : [Videdge1.PSD]	🔲🔒 ⚌ / ☐
▷ ⏱ Scale	50%, 35% ◀☒ ◇
▽ 🎬 2 : [Romance.mov]	🔲🔒 👁 / ☐☐
⏱ Scale	85%
▽ 📄 3 : Video Shadow	🔲🔒 👁 /☒ ☐
▷ Fast Blur	(Reset)
▷ 🎬 4 : [Beach.mov]	🔲🔒 👁 / ☐☐

| Options ▼ | ▶┃ | Switches ▼ | ┃◀ |

Figure 15-16: Video Edges 1 shows the proper ordering of the layers with their track mattes.

10. Drag it below the Lovers layer. Make it visible again. Press T to bring up the Opacity property. Set the Opacity to 75%.

11. Apply Effect → Blur → Fast Blur. Set the effect to 11.

12. The effect is complete. Figure 15-16, Video Edges 1, shows the proper order of the layers with the track mattes specified.

13. Set the work area to end at 3:00 seconds.

14. Save your work.

15. Preview or view the rendered movie.

Next you will duplicate the first Comp and modify it. To start, you will use the effect to zoom on the entire frame. You will also animate the drop shadow to add some depth to the effect.

 Studio Time: Video Edges B

1. Duplicate the Video Edges A Comp. Rename it Video Edges B.

2. Set the Current Time to 0. Highlight the Video Shadow layer. Click in the stop watch to make the Scale, Position, Opacity, and Fast Blur keyframeable. Press P to show the Position property, S to bring up the Scale property, and T to bring up the Opacity property. Keep Position at the same value. Set the Scale amount to 100% and the Fast Blur to 11.

3. Set the Current Time to 3:00 seconds (Mac: Cmd-G, Windows: Ctrl-G, and type 300, or just move the Playback Head until the Current Time reads 0:00:03:00). Set the Opacity to 45%; the Position to 170, 136; and the Fast Blur to 16. The drop shadow has moved away, and gotten lighter and softer over time.

4. Select the Romance.mov element. Press S to bring up the Scale property. Set the Scale amount to 100%.

5. Highlight the top VidEdges 1.psd layer used as the track matte. Duplicate the layer.

6. Select the layer below the duplicate. It should still be the track matte.

7. Set the Current Time to 3:00 seconds., Click in the stop watch to make the Scale keyframeable. Leave the Scale Height set to 50% and the Scale Width set to 35%.

8. Set the Current Time to 4:00 seconds. Set the Scale Width to 78% and the Scale Height to 58%.

9. Add some depth to the shape: Highlight the top layer and copy it.

10. Create a Create a new Comp (Mac: Cmd-N, Windows: Ctrl-N). Make it 320 x 240, 10:00 seconds, at 30 fps. Name it Video Edge Depth.

11. Paste the element. Make layer visible again.

12. Create a new solid (Mac: Cmd-Y, Windows: Ctrl-Y) the size of the Comp. Select the color as white.

13. Send the solid to the back.

14. Close the Composition (Mac: Opt-click, Windows: Alt-click on the Time Layout window or Comp window close box). Both the Comp window and the Time Layout window close.

15. Set the Current Time to 0. Drag in the Video Edge Depth Comp. This layer will be a variable effect layer, depending upon the Layer mode chosen.

16. Drag Video Edge Depth Comp below the first VidEdge1.psd element.

17. Specify the VidEdge1.psd layer as the Video Edge Depth's track matte.

18. Apply Effect→ Invert and Effect→ Blur→ Fast Blur. Set the Fast Blur to 8.

19. Set the Current Time to 110 seconds; it is easier to see the effect from this point in time. Change the Layer mode to Multiply. Notice how it adds some depth to the edges. Now change the mode to Luminosity. Notice how there's color on the edges and white in the center. You will use this as an effect.

20. Set the Current Time to 200 seconds. Press T bring up the Opacity property. Click in the stop watch to make the Opacity keyframeable. Set the Opacity to 13.

21. Set the Current Time to 300 seconds. Set the Opacity to 0.

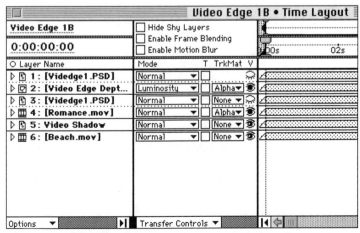

Figure 15-17: Video Edges 2 shows the proper order of layers.

22. Set the Current Time back to 0. Set the Opacity to 100%.

23. Figure 15-17 Video Edges 2 shows the proper order of the layers. The effect is complete.

24. Set the work area to end at 4:15 seconds.

25. Save your work.

26. Preview or view the rendered movie.

 # Rewind

There are many creative effects available to After Effects users other than those that ship with the program. This chapter has explored some of the premier effects from the folks at DigiEffects, Aurorix, Berserk, and Cyclonist. You had a chance in this chapter to play with one of the Auto F/X Video Edges files, as well as the results of the Knoll Lens Flare package.

 # Coming Attractions

The next chapter takes a look at the After Effects Production Bundle effects. Even if you don't have the Production Bundle, you can follow along and view the results.

Production Bundle

Preview

Adobe After Effects is sold in two versions—a retail product, which we have covered throughout this book, and a Production Bundle, which has a number of features not available in the retail product. The Production Bundle includes features that are aimed at the high-end user. Owning the retail product gives you the ability to upgrade to the Production Bundle for only the cost difference between the two products. This chapter examines the benefits of upgrading to the Production Bundle. It will:

- 🎬 Explore the Keyframe Assistants.
- 🎬 Explore the Keying Effects.
- 🎬 Explore the Matting Tools.
- 🎬 Explore the Distort & Stylize effects.

Feature Presentation

So far, this book has explored the built-in filters and the vast amount of third-party effects available for After Effects. This chapter looks at the some of the features of After Effects that are only available in the Production Bundle. These features, such as the Keyframe Assistants, make the Production Bundle a necessary purchase for many video professionals.

Setting Up

This chapter's project contains Comps that correspond to some of the Production Bundle effects and demonstrate some basic uses for them. Unfortunately, we cannot provide samples of these effects for you on the accompanying CD-ROM, as we did with some of the third-party effects. The Production Bundle is dongle-protected and Adobe has not provided any "no save" evaluation-only versions of them. If you own the Production Bundle, please follow along and perform each step as you go. If you do not own the Production Bundle, see the results provided for each step of each effect.

All the source footage provided is 320 x 240 and has been Cinepacked. The Blue Example has not been compressed. Blue screen keying can be difficult enough without the introduction of noise resulting from compression. The size for any Comp that will be created is also 320 x 240. Feel free to use whatever footage is included to invent new combinations of effects.

It is especially important to use the project files provided when going through the examples in this chapter, as many of them are dependent on preset selections and options.

Using Production Bundle Effects

The Production Bundle was designed with the professional in mind. The effects in this package are certainly worth the added cost. The keying effects are exceptional. The Keyframe Assistants are indispensable animation tools. The distortion effects are tools worthy of using on a daily basis. This is a priceless package if you are serious about After Effects. It's best to have as many tools as possible to help tackle any problems that may arise. In this chapter, the effects are broken down into the sections in which they are found.

Keyframe Assistants

The Keyframe Assistants in the Motion Pack perform functions that add, delete, and modify keyframes. Keyframe Assistants help control motion and animation. The Keyframe Assistants are found in their own category under the Layer menu (Layer ➜ Keyframe Assistants).

Exponential Scale

The Exponential Scale Keyframe Assistant operates on Scale only. This effect re-creates the way a zoom lens zooms in on a subject, and it processes the entire time length with the Scale operation. The existing keyframes are redistributed to resemble the zooming lens. There are no settings for this effect, since it processes all selected keyframes at once.

The following example applies the Exponential Scale Keyframe Assistant to a scaling type.

Studio Time: Exponential Scale

1. Start a new project and save it as AECH16.aep. You will be using this project for all the Studio Times in this chapter

2. Create a new Comp (Mac: Cmd-N, Windows: Ctrl-N). Make it 320 x 240, 3:00 seconds, at 30 fps. Name it Exponential Scale.

3. Set the Current Time to 0.

4. Import Ddtype.psd from the AE16Foot folder (Mac: Cmd-I, Windows: Ctrl-I). When prompted, select layer1.

5. Drag Ddtype.psd into the center of the Comp window. Press S to bring up the Scale property. Click in the stop watch to make the Scale keyframeable. Set the Scale amount to keyframe 0 %.

6. Set the Current Time to 2:00 seconds (Mac: Cmd-G, Windows: Ctrl-G, and type 200, or just move the Playback Head until the Current Time reads 0:00:02:00). Set the Scale amount to 40%.

7. Highlight both keyframes. Choose Exponential Scale from the Keyframe Assistant menu.

8. Notice the increase in the number of keyframes. The effect will remap the Scale over time, making it more pronounced and drastic.

9. To better enhance this effect, turn on the Motion Blur effect by clicking on the box under the "M" in the Time Layout window. Remember to turn on the Enable Motion Blur button to see the effect in preview.

10. The effect is complete. Set the work area to end at 4:00 seconds.

11. Set layers' Quality to Best.

12. Save your work.

13. Preview or view the rendered movie.

Motion Math

Motion Math is one of the most sophisticated tools in the Production Bundle. It enables you to change the properties of a layer by linking one set of parameters to another and creating dependencies. In its simplest form, it copies the relative values from one parameter into the values of another. In a more sophisticated example, it makes one layer point to another, or it allows you to automatically change the values of one parameter based on the state of another. For example, it allows you to change opacity in response to the changing volume of a sound file. This type of example was shown in Chapter 7.

By reviewing the default equation that appears in the program text field, you can quickly get a sense for the flow of these manipulations with the Easy Equation pop-up menus used to build the math equations. The Channel pop-up menus are just as important to this understanding. They offer a way to work with a property that has more than one value and is easy to visualize.

For the really daring, the Motion Math scripting environment is a language that permits you to write small programs for creating and manipulating parameters or layer properties. It is based on the C language, but it is easier to use.

In the program text field, you can enter a long string of these equations to be executed each time the plug-in is activated. These strings are the small program that organizes and executes a series of the intended operations.

So rich are the rewards it promises, this exciting capability should keep you up for days. Refer to the Production Bundle documentation, which details these capabilities far better than this book can in the available space. The examples provided here stand as a fast and effective overview designed to spark enough excitement to carry you the rest of the way.

Motion Sketch

The Motion Sketch effect captures a path that you draw directly in the Comp window. This enables you to draw a motion by hand for your graphic to follow.

Motion Sketch also records the timing of a path as you draw it. Hesitations in drawing the path will be reflected in the results. Very often, you will need to re-draw the path a few times to get the timing and the shape of the path correct. You can capture motion in real-time or at a number of different rates. In most cases, you will want to apply the Smoother effect to remove excess keyframes and smooth the motion. Figure 16-1 shows the Motion Sketch dialog and the effect.

▣ Start indicates the beginning of the work area.

▣ Duration shows you the length of the capture. This is dependent upon setting the end of the work area.

▣ As you capture motion, select (click on) Show Wireframe of Layer During Sketch to turn an element into a wireframe.

▣ When clicked on, Don't Erase Contents of Window shows the rest of the Comp.

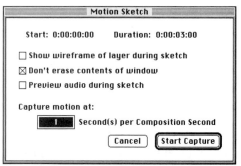

Figure 16-1: The Motion Sketch dialog and the resulting effect.

▪ When clicked on, Preview Audio plays the audio while you sketch.

▪ Capture Motion At allows you to capture motion in real time or at a different speed. A setting of 1, known as the number of Seconds per Composition Second, is real time. A setting of 2 captures twice as fast. A setting of .5 captures half as fast.

The following Studio Time uses Motion Sketch to define a path for a sparkling element. You will see the results without the Smoother applied.

 Studio Time: Motion Sketch

1. In the same AECH16.aep project that you started in the previous Studio Time, create a new Comp (Mac: Cmd-N, Windows: Ctrl-N). Make it 320 x 240, 7:00 seconds, at 30 fps. Name it Motion Sketch.

2. Set the Current Time to 0.

3. Import the Grandpa.mov file from the AE16Foot folder (Mac: Cmd-I, Windows: Ctrl-I).

4. Drag the Grandpa.mov file into the center of the Comp window.

5. Import the Sparkles.aep project from the AE16Foot folder (File → Import → Project).

6. Drag the Sparkles Smoothed Comp into the center of the Comp window. Set the Layer mode to Screen. Press S to bring up the Scale property. Set the Scale amount to 30%.

7. Set the work area to end at 3:00 seconds.

8. Select the Motion Sketch Keyframe Assistant (Layer → Keyframe Assistants → Motion Sketch). Click off Show Wire Frame View. Click on Don't Erase Contents of Window to see what you're doing. Set the Capture Motion to 1. This will make the frame rate equal to time. Click on Start Capture.

9. The Motion Sketch will not begin recording your path until you click on Grandpa's hands. The motion will be recorded within the boundaries of the work area.

10. Press Cmd-Z if you need to undo the recording. Sometimes it takes a few tries until you get just what you want.

11. The effect is complete.

12. Set layers' Quality to Best.

13. Save your work.

14. Preview or view the rendered movie.

The Motion Tracker

The Motion Tracker contains some cutting-edge technology and is one of the most sought-after features in the Production Bundle. This gem observes the movement of your content.

With a little practice, you will be able to match the movement of any element in your footage and attach your graphics to follow it.

However, do not be misled by that last statement. The Motion Tracker is a sophisticated tool; like all powerful tools, it has a definite learning curve, and complete coverage of its capabilities is beyond the scope of this book.

The footage used in the following example has been pre-selected for its ability to track a subject predictably. Some subjects in your footage may be difficult to track, and although the tool has the ability to track obscured objects, no object that is obscured indefinitely can be tracked.

You must become familiar with the tracker's options to be consistently effective at extracting motion from most footage. The Production Bundle documentation describes the

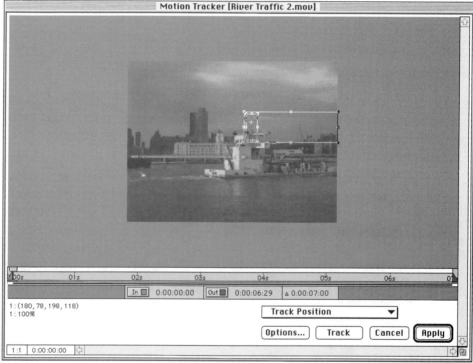

Figure 16-2: The Motion Tracker's dialog and the resulting effect.

options well and should be required reading before doing serious work with the Motion Tracker.

Nonetheless, the first project below will familiarize you with the concept of motion tracking and help you gain confidence in mastering the tool. You will be using the Motion Tracker to isolate the flagpole of a tugboat in the River Traffic file. You will then attach a logo to the flagpole.

Figure 16-2 shows the Motion Tracker dialog and the effect. It contains two boxes enclosing a cross. The boxes and cross define the location of the tracking operation. The inside box isolates the subject to be tracked (the flagpole). The higher the contrast selected, the better the track. The outer box defines the area of expected movement and activity. Finally, the cross provides a Position for the placement of the logo that will match movement with the pole. (The cross can, in fact, be placed anywhere on the canvas of the footage.)

The menu below can be changed from Track Position to Track Rotation, Track Position and Rotation, or Corner Pin.

This exercise uses only the Track Position option. The Track Rotation choice works similarly, only it provides two sets of boxes. The first box tracks the center of the subject's Rotation, and the second one tracks an outer extremity.

The Track Position and Rotation choice combines the features of the first and second choices. This gives you two sets of boxes that operate as before, only this time, the first set can track Position as well. So now you will be able to track something that moves while it spins.

The Corner Pin tracker provides four sets of boxes, each capable of tracking the four corners of any subject with perspective. This tracker can, for example, insert a full frame animation into footage of a passing billboard. It can also track the perspective in a scene, to help match computer graphic elements to raw footage of all kinds.

 Studio Time: Motion Tracker

1. While still in AECH16.aep, create a new Comp (Mac: Cmd-N, Windows: Ctrl-N). Make it 320 x 240, 10:00 seconds, at 30 fps. Name it Motion Tracker.

2. Set the Current Time to 0.

3. Drag Ddtype.psd into the center of the Comp window. Import Riverprd.mov from the AE16Foot folder (Mac: Cmd-I, Windows: Ctrl-I) and drag it into the center of the Comp window.

4. Send the Riverprd file to the bottom (Mac: Cmd-B, Windows: Ctrl-B).

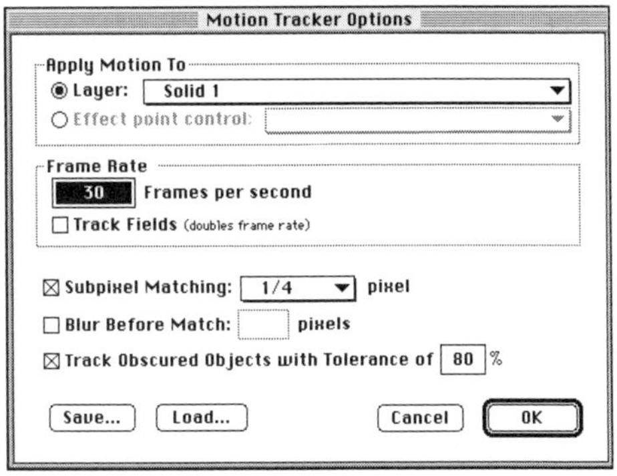

Figure 16-3: The Motion Tracker Options dialog.

5. Highlight the Ddtype layer, which will become the flag on the boat. Press S to bring up the Scale property. Set the Scale amount to 5%.

6. Set the Anchor Point to 486, 236. This moves the Natural Position and Rotation Axis for the element to the right edge. The right edge is the leading edge of the flag as it relates to the motion of the boat.

7. Set the Quality to Best and the Window zoom factor to 4:1. This makes it easier to see where you're positioning the subject. Reset the zoom factor to 1:1.

8. Select the Riverprd layer.

9. Now select the Motion Tracker (Layer → Keyframe Assistants → Motion tracker). Expand the window as needed to view the tracking dialog clearly.

10. Click the Options button to open the tracking options settings and refer to Figure 16-3, which shows the Options dialog settings.

11. Click the Load button, select the Track Settings file in the chapter folder, and click OK. Click OK in the Motion Options window.

12. Click Track to preview the tracking operation.

13. When the preview is complete, click the Apply button.

14. Don't set an end to the work area because you want to preview/render the full length of the Comp. The effect is complete.

15. Set layers' Quality to Best.

16. Save your work.

17. Preview or view the rendered movie.

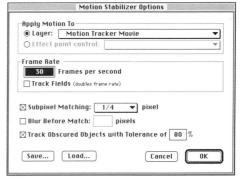

Figure 16-4: The Motion Stabilizer Options Dialog

Motion Stabilizer

The Motion Stabilizer is an "inverse" of the Motion Tracker. Instead of wiggling your footage to match something else, the Motion Stabilizer tries to remove the jittering and shaking.

The purpose of this should be obvious. It will, in many cases, remove the vibration from footage shot in a shaky situation such as a moving car or a hand held camera.

The Motion Stabilizer uses the same metaphor as the Motion Tracker, providing a control box with just two rectangles to select a high-contrast area of the shaky material. See the Motion Tracker for steps on operating this effect. The details of the steps are very similar, and you should recognize the method immediately. If you have trouble, review the steps. See Figure 16-4 for the Motion Stabilizer dialog.

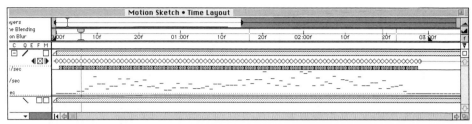

Figure 16-5: Keyframes from a Motion Sketch.

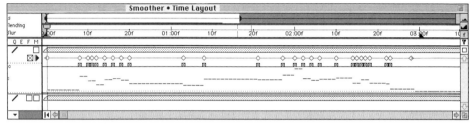

Figure 16-6: The results of applying the Smoother.

The Smoother

The Smoother smooths out any property to which it is applied. You can use it to smooth out as well as scale motion. This is perfect for smoothing out Motion Sketch paths. A Motion Sketch path has many more keyframes than actually needed. This causes motion that is uneven and jerky. The Smoother will remove the unnecessary keyframes, smoothing the motion and timing. The motion and timing will be very close to the original curve. Figure 16-5 shows the keyframes from a Motion Sketch. Figure 16-6 shows the results of applying the Smoother to the same motion path.

This next example applies the Smoother to a Motion Sketched path. There will be a difference in the number of keyframes.

 Studio Time: Smoother

1. Duplicate the Motion Sketch Comp. Name it Smoother.

2. Highlight the Sparkles element.

3. Show its Position properties. Command-click on the word "Position" to select all the keyframes.

4. Apply Layer → Keyframe Assistant → The Smoother. Approve the defaults in the Smoother dialog. Notice that many of the keyframes are removed. The effect will remove unnecessary keyframes, keeping the motion and timing the same.

5. The effect is complete.

6. Set layers' Quality to Best.

7. Save your work.

8. Preview or view the rendered movie.

The Wiggler

The Wiggler allows you to add randomness to properties. Use it to make an item shake as it moves from position A to position B. The effect of the Wiggler can vary depending upon the properties applied to it. Figure 16-7 shows the Wiggler dialog and the effect.

📑 *Apply To* allows you to select between time or physical properties.

📑 *Dimension* allows you to set the axis of the disturbance.

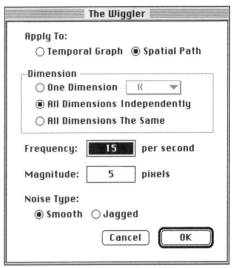

Figure 16-7: The Wiggler dialog and the resulting effect.

📑 *Frequency* allows you to specify the period of the wiggle.

📑 *Magnitude* allows you to set the intensity of the disturbance.

📑 *Noise Type* allows you to select either Smooth or Jagged noise.

The following Studio Time applies the Wiggler to a Motion Sketched path. It will make the Sparkle shake and jitter as it travels along its path.

 Studio Time: Wiggler

1. Duplicate the Motion Sketch Comp. Name it Wiggler.

2. Highlight the Sparkles element.

3. Show its Position properties. Command-click on the word Position to select all the keyframes.

4. Apply Layer → Keyframe Assistant → The Wiggler. Change the Apply to Spatial. Set the Frequency to 15 and the Magnitude to 5 pixels. Keep the Noise Type set to Smooth.

5. Finally, enable Motion Blur to enhance the effect (click on the M box and the Enable Motion Blur box).

6. The effect is complete.

7. Set layers' Quality to Best.

8. Save your work.

9. Preview or view the rendered movie.

Channel

Alpha Levels

The Alpha Levels effect provides you with a method of fine tuning images that contain alpha channels. You can expand or contract the alpha channel by adjusting the number of black and white pixels in the channel. This effect works just like the normal levels found within Photoshop. The only thing missing is the histogram. Alpha Levels is perfect for use on type imported from Photoshop. Sometimes such type has a slight halo around it. If this is the case, use the Alpha Levels effect to tighten the alpha up a bit. Figure 16-8 shows the settings of the Alpha Levels dialog and the effect.

- *Input Black* allows you to adjust the amount of black in the alpha channel.

- *Input White* allows you to set the amount of white in the alpha channel.

- *Gamma* allows you to control the overall brightness of the alpha channel.

- *Output Black Level* allows you to change the output value of black in the alpha channel.

- *Output White Level* allows you to set the level of white in the alpha channel.

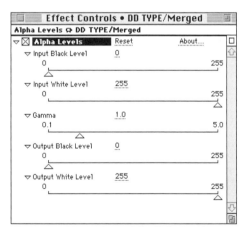

Figure 16-8: The settings of the Alpha Levels dialog and the resulting effect.

The next example uses the Alpha Levels effect to expand and contract the edges of a masked item.

 Studio Time: Alpha Levels

1. Create a new Comp (Mac: Cmd-N, Windows: Ctrl-N). Make it 320 x 240, 7:00 seconds, at 30 fps. Name it Alpha Levels. Set the background color to white (Mac: Shift-Cmd-B, Windows: Shift-Ctrl-B).

2. Set the Current Time to 0.

3. Drag Ddtype.psd into the center of the Comp window. Position it so you can see any edge of a letter.

4. Apply Effect → Channel → Alpha Levels. There are no keyframes in this exercise. Just observe what the different effects do.

5. Drag the Black Input slider toward the right and notice that the mask starts to be choked and the type gets smaller.

6. Slide the Input White Level down from 255, and notice how the type starts to spread out a bit.

7. Play around with the Gamma and look at the overall adjustment that it makes. Gamma works well controlling soft faded edges.

8. Slide up on the Output Black Level, and notice how the edge becomes blacker.

9. Slide the Output White Level down from 255, and notice how the image starts to fade.

10. These settings allow you to fine-tune the alpha channel of an image, even if the image is animated.

11. There is no rendered movie for this example.

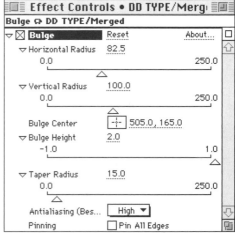

Figure 16-9: The Bulge dialog and its settings and the resulting effect.

Distort

The Distortion Pack contains a group of interesting advanced effects to alter your images.

Bulge

The Bulge effect is similar to the familiar image of a mouse running underneath a carpet in a cartoon. This effect can produce amusing and happy results. Figure 16-9 shows the Bulge dialog settings and the effect.

- *Horizontal Radius* allows you to set the horizontal width of the distortion. This can be set in the Comp window itself.

- *Vertical Radius* allows you to set the vertical height of the distortion, which can also be set in the Comp window. Figure 16-10 shows the handles defining the Horizontal and Vertical Radius, which set the two values independently.

- *Bulge Center* allows you to specify the location of the effect, which allows the center of the effect to be animated over time.

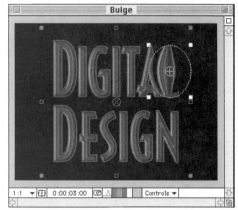

Figure 16-10: The Horizontal and Vertical Radius handles.

- *Bulge Height* sets the altitude of the effect. Positive numbers give the appearance of pulling pixels towards you, while negative numbers give the appearance of pushing pixels away from you.

- *Taper Radius* allows you to set the smoothness of the area on the edge of the effect. Smaller numbers are lower settings and can cause abrupt edges around the effect. Higher numbers produce smoother areas around the effect.

- *Anti-aliasing* allows you to select High or Low Smoothness for the effect. This control works in Best Quality only. Experiment with the settings. The Best Quality setting will dramatically increase the rendering time. Make sure the results are worth the increased time. Often, lower settings that take less time to render may work just as well.

- *Pin All Edges* keeps the edges of the element from being distorted by the effect.

This next example applies the Bulge effect to a logo and makes it look as if there is something running underneath it.

Studio Time: Bulge

1. Create a new Comp (Mac: Cmd-N, Windows: Ctrl-N). Make it 320 x 240, 7:00 seconds, at 30 fps. Name it Bulge.

2. Set the Current Time to 0.

3. Drag Ddtype.psd into the center of the Comp window. Press S to bring up the Scale property. Set the Scale amount to 40%.

4. Apply Effect → Distort → Bulge. Set the Current Time to 0. Click in the stop watch to make the Horizontal Radius, Vertical Radius, and Bulge Center keyframeable. Set the Horizontal Radius and Vertical Radius to 50.0. Set the position of the Bulge Center to -23, 530.

5. Set the Current Time to 1:00 seconds (Mac: Cmd-G, Windows: Ctrl-G, and type 100, or just move the Playback Head until the Current Time reads 0:00:01:00). Set the Bulge Center to 552, 430.

6. Set the Current Time to 2:00 seconds. Set the Horizontal Radius to 100 and the Vertical Radius to 125. Set the Bulge Center coordinates to 70, 153.

7. Set the Current Time to 3:00 seconds. Set the Bulge Center coordinates to 505, 165.

8. Set the Current Time to 4:00 seconds. Set the Horizontal Radius to 65 and the Vertical Radius to 75. Set the coordinates of the Bulge Center to -23, 525.

9. Set the Bulge Height to 2 and the Taper Radius to 15. Set the Anti-aliasing to high, and leave the Pinning off.

10. The effect is complete. Set the work area to end at 4:00 seconds.

11. Set layers' Quality to best.

12. Save your work.

13. Preview or view the rendered movie.

Corner Pin

The Corner Pin effect distorts images by repositioning their corners. This enables you to put an image into perspective. Imagine an image with a billboard in it. You could use Corner Pin to map a piece of footage into the proper perspective of that billboard. This effect is easy to use and its controls are self-explanatory.

Displacement Map

The Displacement Map effect uses one layer to displace another. The layer selected to perform the displacing is called the *displacement map*. The Displacement Map effect often looks glassy and smooth. This effect can vary

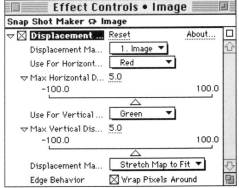

Figure 16-10: The Horizontal and Vertical Radius handles.

from subtle to stark. Figure 16-11 shows the Displacement Map dialog.

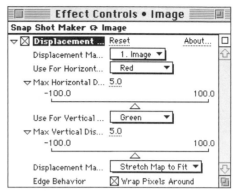

Figure 16-11: The Displacement dialog.

- *Displacement Map Layer* allows you to specify the layer in the Comp to perform the displacing. Although the layer used as the displacement map must be present within the Comp, it does not need to be visible.

- *Horizontal Displacement* allows you to select the channel that shifts horizontally.

- *Vertical Displacement* allows you to select the channel that shifts vertically.

- *Maximum Horizontal Displacement* allows you to set the upper limit of both the vertical and horizontal shift. Negative numbers will reverse the direction of this shift.

- *Displacement Map Behavior* allows you set how the map is applied to the image. If the map is smaller than the image, you can stretch it to fit. You can center the map if it is the same size. You can also tile the map repeatedly.

- *Edge Behavior* allows you to set how the edges behave. Use Wrap Pixels to bring around to the opposite side the pixels that have moved off the screen. This prevents an offset edge from revealing the transparency that lies below.

Ripple

The Ripple effect gives the appearance of water ripples moving through an image from a chosen spot. The movement of the effect can be animated over time. Remember that with watery effects, waves weaken as they move away from the center. Figure 16-12 shows the settings of the Ripple dialog and the effect.

- *Radius* allows you to set the distance from the center that is influenced by the

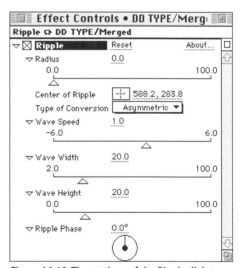

Figure 16-12: The settings of the Ripple dialog and the resulting effect.

effect. The result is based on the content of the image. Any transparent areas will not be manipulated by the effect.

- *Center of Ripple* allows you to set the location of the ripple's origin.

- *Type of Conversion* allows you to choose between symmetric or asymmetric ripples.

- *Wave Speed* allows you to specify the speed of wave travel. Positive numbers move ripples outward from the center, while negative numbers reverse the ripples inward. The value should remain constant with this setting, or you will have to deal with wave timing issues. Basically, a wave speed that matches your frame rate will produce a wave that appears to not move at all, or to spin in reverse, the way a car wheel looks on television. Animating the Wave Speed works best when small changes are applied. Large shifts in value create unpredictable results. If all else fails, do not animate the Wave Speed at all.

- *Wave Width* allows you to specify the distance in pixels between horizontal wave crests.

- *Wave Height* allows you to specify the distance in pixels between vertical wave crests.

- *Ripple Phase* allows you to specify the origin level of the wave center. Webster's defines *phase* as "the point or stage in the period of a circular motion to which the rotation has advanced, considered in its relation to an assumed starting point." If the Phase is 0 degrees, then the center is stationery. However, if it is at 90 degrees it will be at its crest, and if it rises to 180 degrees, it will again be at rest. Finally, if the setting climbs to 270 degrees, then the center will be a trough.

Animating the Ripple Phase setting can be confusing since a moving wave can obscure the effects of this parameter. A wave that travels from the center outward appears to have the full, up and down crests and troughs as the same wave at a 90 degree phase, but it is running exactly one-quarter of a cycle later than the wave at a phase of 0 degrees.

Put more simply, if you set a ripple for 0 speed and 0 phase, and apply another ripple also set to 0 speed but 180 phase, they will cancel each other out. A wave is a physics property, and wave theory subjects you to such thinking. Don't animate anything that seems unfamiliar, and you will always get good results.

The following Studio Time applies the Ripple effect to a logo and makes part of the logo look as if it has turned to liquid.

 Studio Time: Ripple

1. Create a new Comp (Mac: Cmd-N, Windows: Ctrl-N). Make it 320 x 240, 7:00 seconds, at 30 fps. Name it Ripple.

2. Set the Current Time to 0.

3. Drag Ddtype.psd into the center of the Comp window. Press S to bring up the Scale property. Set the Scale amount to 40%.

4. Apply Effect → Distort → Ripple. Set the Current Time to 0. Click in the stop watch to make the Radius and the Center of Ripple keyframeable. Set the Radius to 0.0 and the Center of Ripple coordinates to -1.8, 281.

5. Set the Current Time to 2:00 seconds (Mac: Cmd-G, Windows: Ctrl-G, and type 200, or just move the Playback Head until the Current Time reads 0:00:02:00). Set the Radius to 30.

6. Set the Current Time to 4:00 seconds. Set the Radius to 0 and the Center of Ripple to 588, 283.

7. Set the Wave Speed to 1. Set both the Wave Width and Wave Height to 20. Set the Ripple Phase to 0.

8. The effect is complete. Set the work area to end at 4:00 seconds.

9. Set layers' Quality to Best.

10. Save your work.

11. Preview or view the rendered movie.

Twirl

The Twirl effect allows you to twist pixels around a specific point. The pixels closer to the center of the effect get twisted more than the pixels further away from the center. The effect can be rather slow on big images so beware. Figure 16-13 shows the Twirl dialog and the effect.

Figure 16-13: The Twirl dialog and the resulting effect.

🖋 *Angle* allows you to specify how far to twist the image. Positive numbers twist clockwise. Negative numbers twist counterclockwise.

🖋 *Twirl Radius* allows you to specify how much of the image will be affected. This amount is relative to the size of the image.

🖋 *Twirl Center* allows you to specify the center of the effect.

This next example applies the Twirl effect to a logo and twists it up, then returns it to the original condition.

Studio Time: Twirl

1. Create a new Comp (Mac: Cmd-N, Windows: Ctrl-N). Make it 320 x 240, 7:00 seconds, at 30 fps. Name it Twirl.

2. Set the Current Time to 0.

3. Drag Ddtype.psd into the center of the Comp window. Press S to bring up the Scale property. Set the Scale amount to 40%.

4. Apply Effect → Distort → Twirl. Set the Current Time to 0. Click in the stop watch to make the Angle keyframeable. Set the Angle to 0.0°.

5. Set the Current Time to 2:00 seconds (Mac: Cmd-G, Windows: Ctrl-G, and type 200, or just move the Playback Head until the Current Time reads 0:00:02:00). Set the Angle to 2 full rotations.

6. Set the Current Time to 4:00 seconds. Set the Angle back to 0.0°.

7. Set the Twirl Radius to 50.

8. Set the Twirl Center to 294, 283.

9. The effect is complete. Set the work area to end at 4:00 seconds.

10. Set layers' Quality to Best.

11. Save your work.

12. Preview or view the rendered movie.

Wave Warp

The Wave Warp effect sends a wave traveling through the image. Wave Warp can be used to create the effect of a flag waving in the breeze.

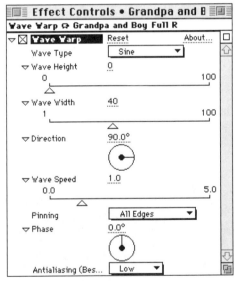

Figure 16-14: The settings of the Wave Warp dialog and the resulting effect.

It can be applied to images with or without alpha channels. Figure 16-14 shows the settings of the Wave Warp dialog and the effect.

- *Wave Type* allows you to choose the type of wave applied to the image. Click on the pop-up menu to see your choices. Experiment with the different types of waves.

- *Wave Height* allows you to set the height of the wave.

- *Wave Width* allows you to set distance between the waves. Low values give you short waves. High values give you long, slow waves.

- *Direction* allows you to set the direction the wave will travel.

- *Wave Speed* allows you to set the speed the wave travels through the image.

- *Pinning* allows you to specify which edges of the image won't be affected by the wave. The example that follows pins the edges of the image so the wave doesn't affect them.

- *Phase* allows you to specify at what point a wave begins a wave cycle. Animating this gives the appearance of speed.

- *Anti-Aliasing* allows you to set the smoothing of the distortion. Test the results. Lower settings often yield similar results to the higher settings. The better settings take longer to render.

This next exercise applies the Wave Warp to the Grandpa footage and uses the Pinning feature to keep the effect away from the edges of the image.

Studio Time: Wave Warp

1. Create a new Comp (Mac: Cmd-N, Windows: Ctrl-N). Make it 320 x 240, 7:00 seconds, at 30 fps. Name it Wave Warp.

2. Set the Current Time to 0.

3. Drag Grandpa.mov into the center of the Comp window.

4. Apply Effect → Distort → Wave Warp. Set the Current Time to 0. Click in the stop watch to make the Wave Height keyframeable. Set the Wave Height to 0.

5. Set the Current Time to 3:00 seconds (Mac: Cmd-G, Windows: Ctrl-G, and type 300, or just move the Playback Head until the Current Time reads 0:00:03:00). Set the Wave Height to 10.

6. Set the Current Time to 5:00 seconds. Set the Wave Height back to 0.

7. Set the constant values. Select Sine as the Wave Type. Feel free to try some of the other settings.

8. Set the Wave Width to 40. Set the direction to 90° and the Wave Speed to 1.

9. Choose All Edges from the Pinning pop-up menu. Set the phase to 0. Anti-aliasing can be set to low since there are no masked edges to worry about.

10. The effect is complete. Set the work area to end at 5:00 seconds.

11. Set layers' Quality to Best.

12. Save your work.

13. Preview or view the rendered movie.

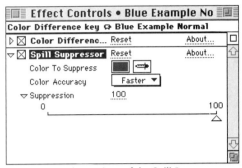

Figure 16-15: The settings of the Spill Suppressor.

Keying

Keying effects allow you to make specific colors transparent. The classic example of this effect is the television weather broadcast. A weather person is shot against a blue screen so that the weather maps appear to be behind her when, in reality, she is pointing to a blank wall. There are different ways to perform such operations. After Effects provides different tools for different keying problems. This section explores how to use each of these effects. If masking in Photoshop is not your favorite occupation, you might want to move your image into After Effects and use the Keying features from the Production Bundle to make an easier composite.

Spill Suppressor

Spill Suppressor is used to remove the halo around a keyed element. The Spill Suppressor effect neutralizes the color on the edges for a more aesthetically pleasing composite. Figure 16-15 shows the settings of the Spill Suppressor.

▪ *Color to Suppress* allows you to select the color to suppress.

▪ *Color Accuracy* allows you to set the accuracy. When keying to commonly used colors, select Faster. Use Better when keying with uncommon colors.

▪ *Suppression* allows you to specify the amount of color suppression.

Figure 16-16: The Color Difference Key settings and the resulting effect.

The Spill Suppressor is used in all the keying examples that follow.

Color Difference Key

The Color Difference Key works differently from other methods of linear keying; it works more like traditional optical keying. The principle of the Color Difference Key is that the selected layer is broken down into two grayscale images: matte partial B, which represents the amount of the key color found within the pixels; and matte partial A, which is based on a color very different from the key color. The final matte is a combination of the two.

The Color Difference Key is used to create a better quality key. It is also used on more difficult keys that involve things like smoke and shadows. Figure 16-16 shows the settings of the Color Difference Key and the effect.

The next Studio Time uses the Color Difference Key to add a woman to the Grandpa footage.

Studio Time: Color Difference Key

1. Create a new Comp (Mac: Cmd-N, Windows: Ctrl-N). Make it 320 x 240, 7:00 seconds, at 30 fps. Name it Color Difference Key.

2. Set the Current Time to 0.

3. Import Bluex.mov from the AE16Foot folder (Mac: Cmd-I, Windows: Ctrl-I).

4. Drag Grandpa.mov and Bluex.mov into the center of the Comp window.

5. Send the Grandpa.mov layer to the bottom (Mac: Cmd-B, Windows: Ctrl-B).

6. Highlight the Bluex.mov layer. Apply Effect → Keying → Color Difference Key.

7. Expand the dialog so you can see it completely. Click on the A button under the thumbnail on the right.

8. Choose the eyedropper with the black tip. Use it to select the background from the thumbnail on the right.

9. Click on the B button. Select the eyedropper with the white tip.

10. Use the white-tipped eyedropper to select the woman. Click on the woman and move the eyedropper around until you've made as much of her white as possible. You should see a fairly decent key.

11. Set the Matte in Black to 128. This will improve the quality a bit.

12. The values of the other settings are listed below. They can vary depending upon the areas sampled or the footage used. Try and match the settings to these amounts:
    Partial A In Black=128
    Partial A In White=255
    Partial A Gamma=1.0
    Partial A Out Black=0

Partial A Out White=255
Partial B In Black=0
Partial B In White=175
Partial B Gamma=1.0
Partial B Out Black=0
Partial B Out White=255
Matte In Black=128
Matte In White=255
Matte Gamma=1.0

13. Add Effect → Keying → Spill Suppressor. This will neutralize the blue halo so the woman fits more naturally into the scene. Set the amount to 100%.

14. The effect is complete. Set the work area to end at 5:00 seconds.

15. Set the layers' Quality to Best.

16. Save your work.

17. Preview or view the rendered movie.

Color Range

The Color Range effect keys out color the same way the color range in Photoshop does. Color Range works best when the background has many variations of the key color. This method is not as accurate as the Color Difference Key. Figure 16-17 shows the Color Range dialog and the effect.

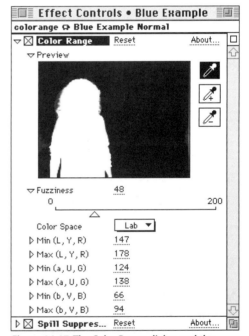

Figure 16-17: The Color Range dialog and the resulting effect.

🖮 *The + eyedropper* chooses the color to key out.

🖮 *The - eyedropper* chooses the colors not to key.

🖮 *Fuzziness* allows you to fine-tune the balance of the mask.

🖮 *Color Space* allows you to specify the color space the key is done in.

🎞 *The Min./Max. settings* allow you to spread and choke the matte.

The following example uses the Color Range effect to key out the background color.

 Studio Time: Color Range

1. Create a new Comp (Mac: Cmd-N, Windows: Ctrl-N). Make it 320 x 240, 7:00 seconds, at 30 fps. Name it Color Range.

2. Set the Current Time to 0.

3. Drag Grandpa.mov and Bluex.mov into the center of the Comp window.

4. Send the Grandpa.mov layer to the bottom (Mac: Cmd-B, Windows: Ctrl-B).

5. Highlight the Bluex.mov layer. Apply Effect → Keying → Color Range.

6. Set the Color Space to Lab.

7. Expand the dialog so you can see it completely. Click on the + eyedropper, and use it to select the range of blues in the background. Hold the mouse button down and drag it around the background.

8. Choose the - eyedropper to select the colors not to be included in the key. These would be the colors inside the shape of the woman.

9. Set the Fuzziness to 48.

10. Leave the other settings as the program has set them.

11. Apply Effect → Keying → Spill Suppressor. This will neutralize the blue halo so the composited element fits more naturally into the scene. Set the amount to 100%.

12. The effect is complete. Set the work area to end at 5:00 seconds.

13. Set layers' Quality to Best.

14. Save your work.

15. Preview or view the rendered movie.

16. Compare the results to the Color Difference Key results.

Figure 16-18: The settings of the Difference Matte dialog and the resulting effect.

Difference Matte

The Difference Matte creates a matte based on the difference between one layer and another. Pixels in the source layer that resemble pixels in the difference layer become transparent. Figure 16-18 shows the Difference Matte settings and the effect.

- *View* allows you to specify what you are seeing.

- *Difference Layer* allows you to choose the layer to compare with the source layer.

- *If Layer Sizes Differ* allows you to use images that are not the same size as the source.

- *Stretch to Fit* will scale the image to the size of the source.

- *Matching Tolerance* acts as a fine-tuner that eliminates the blue.

- *Matching Softness* helps control the edge of the matte.

- *Blur Before Difference* blurs the background to help remove grain. This helps neutralize the key color background.

This next example will composite the image into a background and use the Difference Matte to key out the source layer's background color. It will also create a new Comp to produce the difference matte.

 # Studio Time: Difference Matte

1. Create a new Comp (Mac: Cmd-N, Windows: Ctrl-N). Make it 320 x 240, 7:00 seconds, at 30 fps. Name it Difference Matte.

2. Set the Current Time to 0.

3. Drag Grandpa.mov and Bluex.mov into the center of the Comp window.

4. Send the Grandpa element to the bottom (Mac: Cmd-B, Windows: Ctrl-B).

5. Create a new Comp (Mac: Cmd-N, Windows: Ctrl-N). Make it 160 x 120, 2:00 seconds, at 30 fps. Name it Comp 1.

6. Set the Current Time to 0.

7. Drag Bluex.mov into the center of the Comp window. Position it so only blue is visible.

8. Select Comp → Save Frame As → File. Let the program name the file. Import it into the Project when it is finished rendering.

9. Close up Comp 1 and delete it from the Project. It won't be needed any longer.

10. Drag the newly created blue image into the Difference Matte Comp. Send it to the bottom (Mac: Cmd-B, Windows: Ctrl-B). The pixels in this image are a representation of the pixels in the background of the source image. In other words, they create a good source to key against.

11. Highlight the Bluex.mov layer. Apply Effect → Keying → Difference Matte. View the final output. Set the Difference layer to the Comp 1 file that you created in Step 10. Select Stretch to Fit. Notice the Grandpa layer starting to appear.

12. Set the Matching Tolerance to 35%. Set Matching Softness to 15%. Set Blur Before to 1. These settings do a nice job of keying out the background of this footage.

12. Add Effect → Keying → Spill Suppressor. This will neutralize the blue halo so it fits more naturally into the scene. Set the amount to 100%.

14. The effect is complete. Set the work area to end at 5:00 seconds.

15. Set layers' Quality to Best.

16. Save your work.

17. Preview or view the rendered movie.

18. Compare the results to the Color Difference Key results.

Extract

The Extract effect produces a matte based on any channel within the image. This effect is not as sensitive as Difference Matte or Color Difference. Figure 16-19 shows the settings of the Extract dialog and the effect.

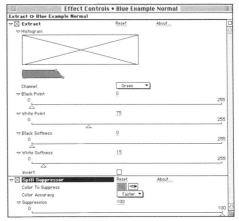

- The *Histogram* shows you where the pixels are in the selected channel. The histogram can be adjusted by the various slider controls below or by adjusting the gray bar itself.

- *Channel* allows you to specify the channel used to extract a matte.

Play with the black and white settings to fine-tune the choke and spread of the matte.

Figure 16-19: The settings of the Extract dialog and the resulting effect.

The following Studio Time uses the Extract effect to composite the source footage into the background element.

 ## Studio Time: Extract

1.   Create a new Comp (Mac: Cmd-N, Windows: Ctrl-N). Make it 320 x 240, 7:00 seconds, at 30 fps. Name it Extract.

2.   Set the Current Time to 0.

3.   Drag Grandpa.mov and Bluex.mov into the center of the Comp window.

4.   Send the Grandpa.mov layer to the bottom (Mac: Cmd-B, Windows: Ctrl-B).

5.   Select the Bluex.mov layer. Apply Effect → Keying → Extract. Open the effect's window wide enough to see the entire dialog.

6.   Set the channel to Blue. Set the White Point to 128 and the White Softness to 25.

7.   Apply Effect → Keying → Spill Suppressor. Disable both effects by clicking on both check-boxes in the Effects Control palette. Using the eyedropper in the Spill Suppressor, click on the blue outside the subject. Turn the effects back on. This will neutralize the blue halo so it fits more naturally into the scene. Set the amount to 100%.

8.   The effect is complete. Set the work area to end at 5:00 seconds.

9.   Set layers' Quality to Best.

10. Save your work.

11. Preview or view the rendered movie.

12. Compare the results to the results of the other keying effects.

Linear Color Key

The Linear Color Key effect works by comparing each pixel within the image to a specific key color. This effect works best with solid areas that do not contain translucency, such as hair or smoke. Figure 16-20 shows the settings of the Linear Color Key dialog and the effect.

- The *Preview* allows you to see the source. You can also use the eyedropper to specify the color to key.

- *View* allows you to choose what you see: the final output, the source, or the matte.

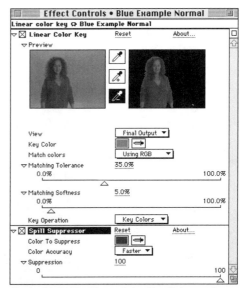

Figure 16-20: The Linear Color Key dialog settings and the resulting effect.

- *Key Color* allows you to sample the color to be used as the key.

- *Matching Tolerance and Matching Softness* allow you to fine-tune the matte. Use the two settings to balance each other out.

This next example will use the Linear Color Key to composite the source material into the background footage.

 Studio Time: Linear Color Key

1. Create a new Comp (Mac: Cmd-N, Windows: Ctrl-N). Make it 320 x 240, 7:00 seconds, at 30 fps. Name it Linear Color Key.

2. Set the Current Time to 0.

3. Drag Grandpa.mov and Bluex.mov into the center of the Comp window.

4. Send the Grandpa.mov layer to the bottom (Mac: Cmd-B, Windows: Ctrl-B).

5. Select the Bluex.mov layer. Apply Effect → Keying → Linear Color Key. Open the effect's window wide enough to see the entire dialog.

6. Using the key color eyedropper, click in the left preview's blue background.

7. Set the View to Final Output. Match colors using RGB.

8. Set the Matching Tolerance to 35% and the Matching Softness to 5.0%.

9. Apply Effect → Keying → Spill Suppressor. This will neutralize the blue halo so it fits more naturally into the scene. Set the amount to 100%.

10. The effect is complete. Set the work area to end at 5:00 seconds.

11. Set layers' Quality to Best.

12. Save your work.

13. Preview or view the rendered movie.

14. Compare the results to the other keying effects' results.

Matte Tools

The Keying Pack of the Production Bundle includes several Matte Tools to refine the mattes of images you've created. You can set different amounts of transparency for professional results.

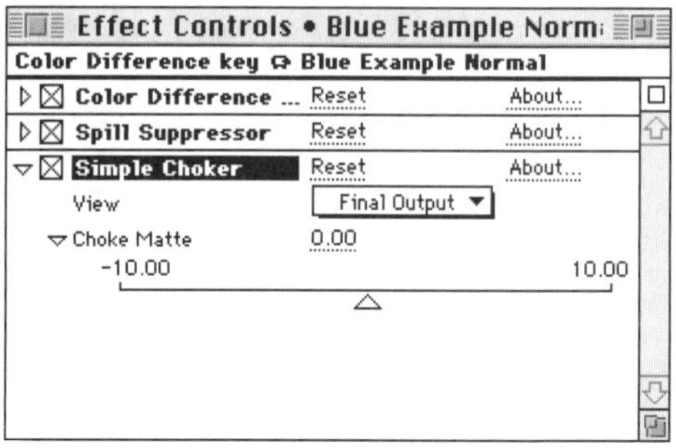

Simple Choker

Simple Choker shrinks or expands the edges of mattes. The tool can be applied as an overall spread or choke effect. Figure 16-21 shows the settings of the Simple Choker.

The *View* parameter allows you to see either the final output or the matte itself.

Figure 16-21: The settings of the Simple Choker.

Matte Choker

The Matte Choker is used to create more demanding chokes and spreads. The Matte Choker uses a technique of choking and spreading to evenly affect large areas without changing the shape. Figure 16-22 shows the settings of the Matte Choker dialog. You apply Choke 1 first, then Choke 2. Choke 1 works from one side of the matte while Choke 2 works from the other. The two settings balance each other out. Adjust the chokes as needed to fix the problem.

- *Geometric Softness* allows you to soften the edge spread or choke.

- *Choke* allows you to specify the value of your choke or spread. Positive numbers choke the matte. Negative numbers spread the matte.

- *Gray Level Softness* allows you to specify the softness of the edges of the matte.

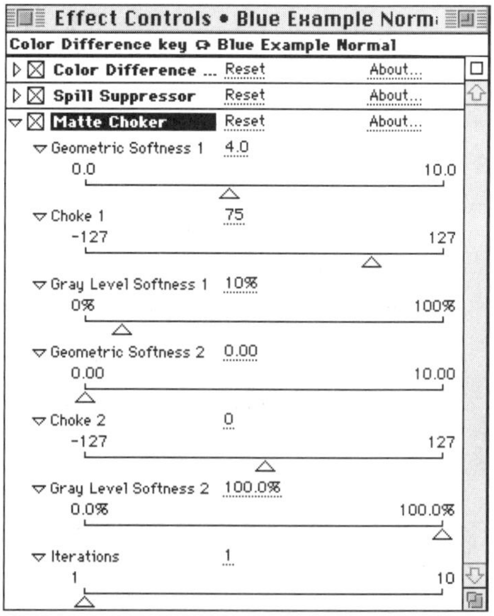

Figure 16-22: The settings of the Matte Choker dialog.

Stylize

The Stylize effects are found in the Distortion Pack.

Glow

Glow simulates the way a brightly lit object scatters illumination. The effect can be used to subtly add a healthy glow to items that contain transparency. Figure 16-23 shows the settings of the Glow dialog and the effect.

- *Glow Based On* allows you to choose the source of the glow. The glow can be based on either the alpha channel of the image or the actual color channels themselves.

- *Glow Threshold* allows you to set the pixel value of the threshold. This means that pixels greater than the value you set will glow, while pixels lower than the value will not be touched.

- *Glow Radius* allows you to set the distance of the glow.

- *Glow Intensity* allows you to set the strength of the glow. Note that the strength is also determined by the Glow Operation.

- *Composite Glow* allows you to specify that the glow be placed in front or behind the element.

- *Glow Operation* allows you to determine how the glow will be combined with the image. The pop-up menu enables you to choose from a list of Math Methods, which are similar to the layer transfer modes within After Effects. Experiment with the settings.

- *Glow Colors* allows you to specify the colors of the illumination used, and Original Colors samples them from the image. A & B Colors use the eyedropper. Arbitrary Map allows you to apply a saved Adobe Photoshop map.

- *Color Looping* allows you to specify the method used to create the glow. Play with the various settings under the pop-up menu.

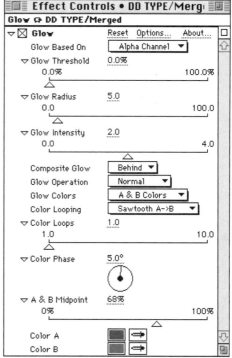

Figure 16-23: The settings of the Glow dialog and the resulting effect.

- *Color Loops* allows you to specify the number of times the color loop will repeat.

- *Color Phase* allows you to cycle through the color gradient.

- *A&B Midpoint* allows you to control the balance of color between A and B.

The following exercise will create a richer look to a logo by applying the Glow effect. This will make the logo stand out against other footage.

 # Studio Time: Glow

1. Create a new Comp (Mac: Cmd-N, Windows: Ctrl-N). Make it 320 x 240, 7:00 seconds, at 30 fps. Name it Glow.

2. Set the Current Time to 0.

3. Drag Ddtype.psd into the center of the Comp window. Press S to bring up the Scale property. Set the Scale amount to 40%.

4. Apply Effect → Stylize → Glow. Set the Current Time to 0. Click in the stop watch to make Glow Threshold and Glow Radius keyframeable. Set the Glow Radius to 5.0 and the Glow Threshold to 0.

5. Set the Current Time to 2:00 seconds (Mac: Cmd-G, Windows: Ctrl-G, and type 200, or just move the Playback Head until the Current Time reads 0:00:02:00). Set the Glow Threshold to 80% and the Glow Radius to 40.

6. Set the Current Time to 4:00 seconds. Set the Glow Threshold to 0.0% and the Glow Radius to 10.

7. Set the Glow Intensity to 2. The Composite Glow setting is Behind. Set the Glow Operation to Normal. Set Glow Colors to A & B Colors. Set the Color Looping to Sawtooth A→B. Set the Color Loops to 1 and the Color Phase to 5.0°. Set the A&B Midpoint to 68%. Pick the colors from the type itself. The ones used here are blue for A and a brownish orange for B.

8. Set the Current Time to 0. Drag Grandpa.mov into the center of the Comp window and send it to the bottom (Mac: Cmd-B, Windows: Ctrl-B).

9. Apply Effect → Blur → Fast Blur to Grandpa.mov. Set the fast Blur to 5. This will make it seem further away from the type.

10. The effect is complete. Set the work area to end at 4:00 seconds.

11. Set layers' Quality to Best.

12. Save your work.

13. Preview or view the rendered movie.

Scatter

The Scatter effect randomly redistributes pixels within the image area and softens the image. Scatter closely resembles the glass distortion effect in Painter. It is also a good alternative to a particle system.

You can use this effect to create a softer, non-textured glass distortion that can be

Figure 16-24: The settings for the Scatter dialog and the resulting effect.

used to resolve banding problems. Add noise to the problem footage, then apply the Scatter effect. The effect scatters the pixels, thereby reducing banding. Figure 16-24 shows the settings for the Scatter dialog and the effect.

- *Scatter Amount* allows you to set the amount of scatter applied to the image.

- *Grain* allows you to specify the direction of the scatter. *None* scatters the pixels uniformly throughout the image.

- *Scatter Randomness* allows you to chose whether the randomness will be applied frame by frame, or whether a single setting will be used for the entire work area.

The following example applies the Scatter effect to some footage in an attempt to achieve a Painter-esque glass distortion look. The Scatter effect will be scaled on, then off.

 Studio Time: Scatter

1. Create a new Comp (Mac: Cmd-N, Windows: Ctrl-N). Make it 320 x 240, 7:00 seconds, at 30 fps. Name it Scatter.

2. Set the Current Time to 0.

3. Drag Grandpa.mov into the center of the Comp window.

4. Apply Effect → Stylize → Scatter. Set the Current Time to 0. Click in the stop watch to make Scatter Amount keyframeable. Set the Scatter Amount to 0.

5. Set the Current Time to 3:00 seconds (Mac: Cmd-G, Windows: Ctrl-G, and type 300, or just move the Playback Head until the Current Time reads 0:00:03:00). Set the Scatter Amount to 127.

6. Set the Current Time to 5:00 seconds. Close out the effect by setting the Scatter Amount back to 0.

7. Set the Grain to none to give it an overall glassy look.

8. Keep Randomizing off to prevent a jumpy look.

9. The effect is complete. Set the work area to end at 5:00 seconds.

10. Set layers' Quality to Best.

11. Save your work.

12. Preview or view the rendered movie.

Synthesize

Lightning

The Lightning effect produces synthetic lightning. It can also be used it to produce a tesla coil effect. Figure 16-25 shows the settings of the Lightning dialog and the effect.

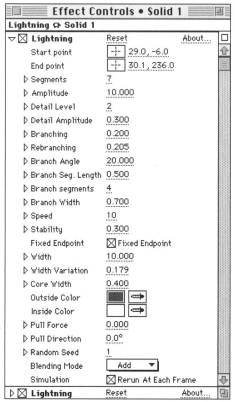

Figure 16-25: The Lightning effect dialog settings and the resulting effect.

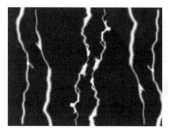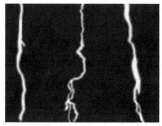

Play with the settings to vary the bolts of lightning. Try applying the effect a number of times.

This next Studio Time shows you how to apply the Lightning effect to a solid and then duplicate and flip the layer. To finish, we add the Strobe effect to provide random flashes to a logo that has a strobe of its own.

Studio Time: Lightning

1. Create a new Comp (Mac: Cmd-N, Windows: Ctrl-N). Make it 320 x 240, 7:00 seconds, at 30 fps. Name it Lightning.

2. Set the Current Time to 0.

3. Drag Ddtype.psd into the center of the Comp window. Press S to bring up the Scale property. Set the Scale amount to 40%.

4. Create a new solid (Mac: Cmd-Y, Windows: Ctrl-Y) that is 320 x 240. Make the color black.

5. Apply Effect → Synthesize → Lightning.

6. Set the start point to 29, -6. Set the end point to 30.1, 236. This creates a bolt that goes from the top to the bottom.

7. Apply Effect → Synthesize → Lightning again. This time move the position to the middle of the Comp. Vary some of the settings so the bolt is different. Don't worry; you can't mess up too badly here.

8. Apply Effect → Synthesize → Lightning one more time. The bolt should be towards the right side of the image. Again, vary the settings to change the bolt.

9. Now, to add some variation, apply Effect → Stylize → Strobe Light. Set the parameters for the strobe: The Strobe Color doesn't matter; the Strobe Duration should be 2.0; the Strobe Period 2.55; and the Random Strobe Probability 81%. Set the Strobe to Makes Layer Transparent and the Operator to Screen.

10. Highlight the layer and duplicate it. Press S to bring up the Scale property. Set the Scale amount to -100. This will flip the layer. Set the Layers mode to Screen. Go into one of the Lightning effects in this layer and modify it a bit.

11. Change the settings of the Strobe effect: Set the Strobe Period to 2 and the Probability to 72. The other settings can remain the same.

12. Select the Type layer. Bring it to the front (Mac: Cmd-F, Windows: Ctrl-F). Apply Effect → Stylize → Strobe Lighting to this element

13. Set the following settings for the Strobe effect: Strobe Duration to 1.05, Strobe Period to 3.0, and Random Probability to 26%. Select Makes Layer Transparent. Select Copy as the Operator.

14. The effect is complete. Set the work area to end at 3:00 seconds.

15. Set layers' Quality to Best.

16. Save your work.

17. Preview or view the rendered movie.

Time

If you'd like to displace the time of pixels, use the Time Displacement effect found in the Distortion Pack.

Time Displacement

Time Displacement allows you to displace the time of pixels in one image using the luminance values of another image as the displacement map. Figure 16-26 shows the Time Displacement dialog and the effect.

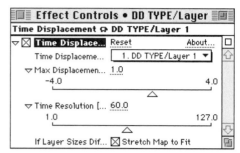

Figure 16-26: The Time Displacement dialog and the resulting effect.

- Time Displacement Layer allows you to specify the layer used to displace time.
- Max Displacement Time allows you to set the maximum difference in seconds and controls how long an element will be displaced over time.
- Time Resolution allows you to set the number of times per second the effect is applied.
- Stretch Map to Fit scales the displacement element to match the size of the source footage.

Rewind

In this chapter, you have seen a variety of effects that can only be applied if you own the Production Bundle. It is well worth the cost of the upgrade to obtain these extremely valuable additions. You have seen how you can make an element cling to a piece of moving video footage using the Motion Tracker. You have also seen a variety of Keying effects to make unwanted colors drop out of a layer and allow for undetectable compositing. In addition, you have seen a variety of distortion and stylizing effects. You have also learned to create lightning and distort time. It's a shame that After Effects can't be used to create a 30 hour day!

Coming Attractions

This chapter marks the end of our coverage of Effects. The next chapter discusses Output. You will learn how to create single-frame high-resolution images for those times when all you want to do is to hijack an After Effects effect and place it into Photoshop.

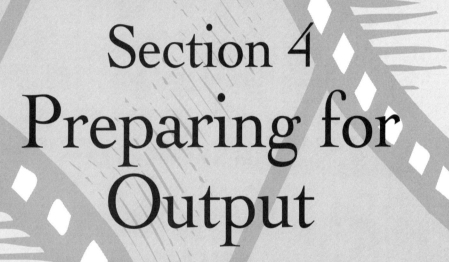

Section 4
Preparing for
Output

Big Images are not Just for Print

 ## Preview

What is it like to work with huge images? Up until now, you have worked with small 320 x 240 Comps. In this chapter, you will get the feel of working with high resolution images. The time needed to render these images may well surprise you. In addition, we will also discuss how to use After Effects to create still images.

In this chapter, you will learn how to:

- 🎬 Work with high resolution art.
- 🎬 Set and use proxies.
- 🎬 Create and replace placeholders.
- 🎬 Save frames as files.
- 🎬 Save frames as Photoshop comps.
- 🎬 Create art for print.

Feature Presentation

After Effects limits the size for any image or sequence to 4000 pixels by 4000 pixels. This rule is absolute.

In the print world, a 4000 x 4000 pixel image is 55.556 x 55.556 inches at 72 dpi or 13.33 x 13.33 inches at 300 dpi. For the TV and movie world, the size of an image can be as high as 2048 x 1536 pixels per frame (for Film Academy standard film resolution.) You need to use a frame size that is appropriate for your final output. There are tricks and techniques to help you work more comfortably at these large sizes. If you work with more pixels than necessary, you spend more time calculating and less time actually working. Those of you who work in print will easily understand this—it's like working on a 600 dpi image that will be used in a newspaper that is output at 100 dpi (in other words—a major waste of time).

Proxies

Understand that the larger the image size used in After Effects, the slower After Effects becomes. When you add filters for special effects, slow becomes even slower. There are some things you can do to help this. One way is to use a *proxy*. Proxies are low-resolution representations of the original file. A proxy can be a single frame or it can be a movie. Whichever it is, it needs to be in the same ratio as the size of the file for which it substitutes. (Chapter 18 has more information on aspect ratio.) In this chapter's example, you will composite high-resolution images using proxies.

The proxies used in the project were made by using the Image Size command in Photoshop to reduce the high resolution image to 25% of its original size, as shown in Figure 17-1. It was then saved as a new file. If you want to make a proxy from an existing movie, you could create the proxy by rendering out the movie at a reduced size. The duration of the clip or image is not important. When you specify a proxy for an item, After Effects scales the proxy to the size and duration of the actual footage. Any effects, masking, and geometry that are applied to the proxy are automatically applied to the original when you replace the proxy with the "real thing" at the end.

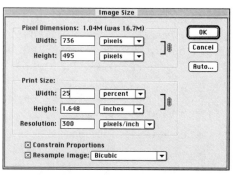

Figure 17-1: Reducing the size of an image in Photoshop.

When you are finished editing, you can have After Effects use the proxy to preview your movie. You can also have After Effects use the original footage to preview your work if you prefer. You can specify which footage item is used to render your movie—the proxy or the original. This gives you added flexibility. If you're rendering only to check timing issues and you really don't need to see the movie at high resolution, a low-resolution movie will surely save time. Save the high resolution for the final render, not for the tests.

The file that is used as the proxy is not actually a part of the project, nor is it listed in the Project window. It is just linked to the actual footage through After Effects. To assign a proxy to an item, you must first highlight the item to be replaced in the Project window. Choose "Set Proxy" from the File menu, or use the shortcut of Cmd-Opt-P (Mac) or Ctrl-Alt-P (Windows). Your proxy choices are File or None. Choose File. You are then asked to locate the file to be used as a proxy. You can remove a proxy by choosing None from the same menu.

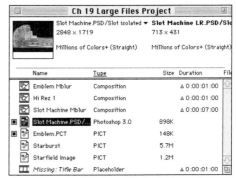

Figure 17-2: Proxies shown in the Project window.

You can switch between the proxy and the actual footage by clicking on the proxy indicator, which you can see in Figure 17-2. The proxy indicator is the box to the left of the elements icon in the Project window. When the box is filled with solid black, the proxy is in use; when the indicator box is filled with white, the original footage is being used. Elements without these indicators do not have proxies. Proxies also make it easier to work at a lower resolution (which we will discuss shortly).

In this Studio Time, you will composite two hi-res images. You will set proxies for these items, and add some effects to them. You will also experiment with the resolution settings. You may want to increase the memory allocation for After Effects. Files this size can quickly exceed the normal memory allocation. We have found that After Effects on the Mac failed to draw the imported images because the Minimum RAM was set to 7,151 K, and the Maximum, 40,000 K. The program complained that it was short about 3,700 K. We increased the memory allocation to 75,000 to alleviate the problem and restarted After Effects.

Studio Time: Setting Proxies for the Hi-Rez Comp

1. Create a new project (Mac: Cmd-Opt-N, Windows: Alt-Ctrl-N). Name it AE17Lrg.AEP. There will be two files in this project—both of which have a high-res and a low-res version.

2. Create a new Comp (Mac: Cmd-N, Windows: Ctrl-N). Make it 2000 x 2000 pixels, 1 second long, 30 frames per second. Name the Comp Hi Rez 1 and set the background color to black (Mac: Shift-Cmd-B, Windows: Shift-Ctrl-B).

3. Import the Slothr.psd file from the AE17Foot folder (Mac: Cmd-I, Windows: Ctrl-I). You are asked to choose a layer. Choose Slot isolated.

4. Highlight the Slothr.psd file. Select Set Proxy File from the File menu, or type Cmd-Opt-P (Mac), Ctrl-Alt-P (Windows). In the Open dialog box choose Slothr.psd. You will be asked to

specify a layer. Choose Slot isolated (the same layer as the hi-res image). Figure 17-3 shows the dialog. You have just selected this file to be used as the proxy. Notice the black square next to the element in the Project window, as you saw in Figure 17-2.

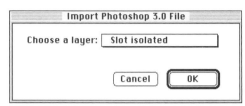

Figure 17-3: Picking a layer in the Photoshop file.

5.   Import the Emblemhr.pct file from the AE17Foot folder (Mac: Cmd-I, Windows: Ctrl-I, then select the correct file). The emblem has an alpha channel which should be treated as straight. Figure 17-4 shows the Interpret Footage dialog.

6.   Select a proxy file for the emblem by clicking on the Emblem file in the Project window. The proxy's file name is Emblemlr.pct. You will need to specify its alpha treatment as straight, too.

Figure 17-4: Interpret Footage dialog.

7.   Set the Current Time to 00 (Mac: Cmd-G, Windows: Ctrl-G, then type 0). Drag both elements into the Comp window.

8.   Press S to display the Scale property. Set the scale of the Slot Machine to 73.

9.   Press Shift-P to display the Position property. The position coordinates are 1004, 1404.

10. Figure 17-5a shows that the Emblem needs to be flipped the other way. Press S to display the Scale property. You can flip the image over by giving it a Scale value of -100 wide. Click off the Preserve Aspect Ratio box or both settings will be set to the same scale factor. Figure 17-5b shows the Time Layout window with the Scale set and the Comp window with the element properly oriented.

11. Press P to display the Position property. The position coordinates are 1636, 1172. Drag the Emblem layer below the Slot Machine layer.

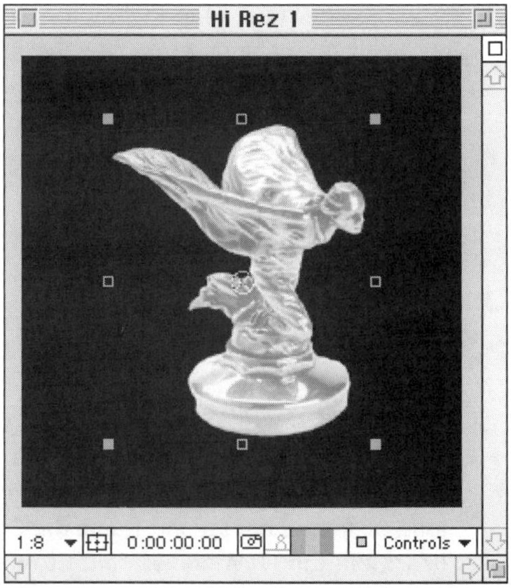

Resolution

Another way to work more easily with a huge file is to work at a smaller resolution. You can set a Comp's resolution by accessing it under the Composition menu. By working at smaller resolutions, less time is spent recalculating the elements (since there are fewer pixels to

Figure 17-5a: Image facing the wrong direction.

move around). When you are working on a 640 x 480 comp at full resolution, your output is the same size as what you see on the screen. However, if you are working on a 640 x 480 Comp and you set the resolution to half, your output will be 320 x 240. At one-quarter resolution the final output would be 160 x 120. This adds up to serious savings in rendering time. This is very useful to you as you are developing your hi-res projects. When you are done, you can set the resolution back to your needed size (since you did not change the resolution of the source footage, you can always re-render the movie at its original resolution, once you are satisfied with the smaller results).

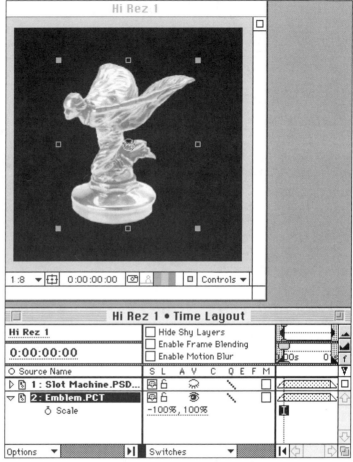

Figure 17-5b: Notice the scale factor and the correctly flipped image.

When you set the resolution for a 640 x 480 comp to half, the display becomes very pixelated. You can make that display sharper by reducing your view. The Comp for this chapter was created at 2000 x 2000. To make life easier, it was worked at a third of the resolution, and with a view of 1:4. It was adequately sharp at this setting and there was elbow room on the screen as well. If you are "only" using a 17" screen size, you will probably have to work at 1:8.

The next Studio Time lets you change the resolution of the Comp and add some effects to the Composition.

Figure 17-6a: Starburst image.

Figure 17-6b: Starfield image.

 Studio Time: Reducing Resolution

1.   Select the Composition menu and set the resolution to one-third. Change the view on the Comp window to something appropriate for your monitor. On a 17″ monitor, 1:8 worked well.

2.   Import the files Starbrst.pct and Starfld.pct. Both of these files were created using third-party filters. The Starburst image shown in Figure 17-6a was created using Knoll Software's Scratch filter. The Starburst was created by first using the ramp filter on a solid layer (to give the star filter colors with which to create an effect.) Then the FE Starburst filter from MetaCreations was applied. Figure 17-6b shows the Starfield image. Since you might not have copies of these filters, we have provided the hi-res files for you.

3.   Set the Current Time to 00 (Mac: Cmd-G, Windows: Ctrl-G, then type 0).

4.   Drag the two new items centered into the Comp window. Send the Starfield image to the bottom (Mac: Cmd-B, Windows: Ctrl-B).

5.   Click on the Switches menu to show the Transfer Controls as shown in Figure 17-7. (For a refresher on transfer modes see Chapter 12.) Select the Starburst layer and change its mode to Screen. In the Screen mode, black is a neutral color, and so it becomes transparent. Use your arrow keys to nudge the Starburst into place. It should be placed over the hole in the coin slot of the slot machine.

Figure 17-7: Transfer Controls/Switches menu.

Effects

We need to digress for a moment to point out another reason for you to build additional Comps inside of your Projects. In Chapter 6, we introduced the concept of compifying— building Comps within Comps for convenience, faster processing, or to change the order of the rendering pipeline.

In the Studio Time segment that follows, you will need to compify a layer so that the Motion Blur effect applied to it is not clipped or cut off by the Bounding Box of the element.

 Studio Time: Applying Motion Blur Effects

1. Select the Slot Machine layer. Figure 17-8 shows the control points on the Bounding Box that surrounds the image in the Comp window. If you were to apply a Motion Blur to this image, these boundaries would clip the image. Figure 17-9 the top edge where the blur attempted to extend beyond the bounding box and was cut off in a very unnatural hard line. To avoid this, you need to compify the layer.

2. Before you do that, however, you will first duplicate (Mac: Cmd-D, Windows: Ctrl-D) the layer.

3. Select the bottom duplicate. Compify this layer (Mac: Shift-Cmd-C, Windows: Shift-Ctrl-C). In the resulting dialog, move all of the layer attributes into the new Composition. Name the new Composition "Slot Machine Mblur."

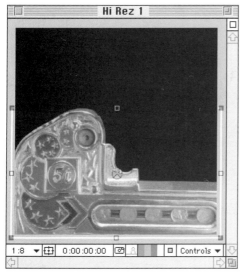

Figure 17-8: Layer showing Bounding Box.

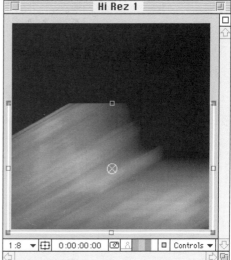

Figure 17-9: Layer showing clipping of Motion Blur filter along top edge.

4.   Now we will apply the Motion Blur to this layer (Effect → Blur & Sharpen → Motion Blur). The direction should be set to 61°, and the blur length to 100.

5.   Press P to show the Position attribute. You need to reposition this layer to make the Motion Blur more pronounced. Set the Position coordinates to 1100, 936. Press Shift-T to show the Opacity property. Set the Opacity to 75%. Both of these values are constants (do not set a keyframe).

6.   Repeat this process with the Emblem layer. Duplicate it. Select the bottom layer and duplicate it. Compify it, moving the attributes to the new Comp. Name the Comp "Emblem Mblur."

7.   Apply a Motion Blur to the Emblem Mblur layer. The direction should be 72°. The Blur Length should be 150. The position will also need to change to extend the blur. Press P to show the Position property. The position coordinates should be 1140, 932. Press Shift-T to show the Opacity property. The Opacity of this layer should be set to 65%.

8.   At this point, display the Comp at 1:1. Notice that it is pixelated and hard to see. Click on the boxes in the Project window to let the "proxied" items preview from the originals. The file takes even longer to render. Imagine what it must be like to have to render out a few minutes worth of footage!

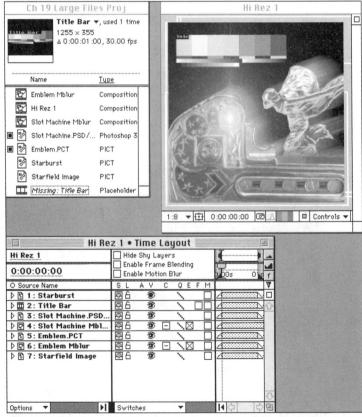

Figure 17-10: Placebar identified by color bars in Project, Time Layout, and Comp windows.

Placeholders

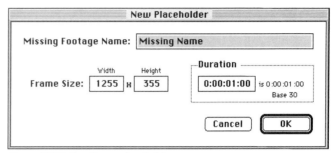

Figure 17-11: Creating a placeholder.

Another way of dealing with large high-resolution files is to use a placeholder. As with a proxy, any effects, geometry, or masks that are applied to the placeholder are also applied to the image it represents. To use a place-holder, choose "Import Placeholder" from the File menu. In the dialog box, specify the name, size, and duration of the placeholder. The placeholder is shown as a set of color bars as you can see (in glorious grayscale) in Figure 17-10. Any missing footage in After Effects is shown as the same place-holder color bars.

You can replace the placeholder with the "real" footage by double-clicking on the placeholder in the Project window. You can also highlight the placeholder in the Project window and choose Replace Footage from the File menu. The shortcut for the Replace Footage command is Cmd-H (Mac) or Ctrl-H (Windows).

1. Choose File → Import → Placeholder. The dialog shown in Figure 17-11 appears. Name the placeholder "Title Bar." Set the size to 1255 x 355 and the Duration to 1 second. You will replace the footage before you render the image.

2. Set the Current Time to 00 (Mac: Cmd-G, Windows: Ctrl-G, then type 0).

3. Drag the placeholder into the Comp.

4. Press P to display the Position property. Change the Position property of the placeholder to 720x, 312y. Drag this layer below the Starburst layer.

5. Let's replace the missing footage. Double-click on the "Missing: Title Bar" element in the project window. Figure 17-12 shows the element high-lighted in the Project window. (You could also use the keyboard shortcut Cmd-H for Mac, or Ctrl-H for Windows.) Choose the file that will replace the missing footage. For this exercise, the file name is Barcomp.pct.

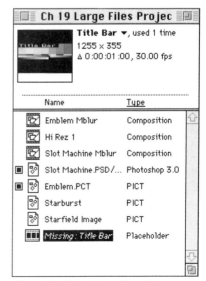

Figure 17-12: Replacing the missing footage.

The Barcomp image was created entirely in After Effects using just a few solids. The Bevel Edges filter was applied to a red solid. A solid was made to sit in the center of the "button." A ramp was applied to add shape to the button. Small thin solids were applied as highlights on the edge of the bevel. A small Gaussian Blur was added to soften the edges.

The type was added with a copy below it acting as the drop shadow. The drop shadow was de-saturated using the Color Balance HLS effect and then Gaussian Blurred. We have included the Barcomp project in the Chapter 17 footage folder so that you may examine it. Of course this could have been created completely in Photoshop, but knowing that you can also do it in After Effects may spark your creativity and help you think of ways to build a complex image like this through animation.

Shortcuts

Command	Mac	Windows
Suspend Redraw	Caps-Lock	Caps-Lock
Full Resolution	Cmd-J	Ctrl-J
Half Resolution	Cmd-Shift-J	Ctrl-Shift-J
Third Resolution	Cmd-Opt-Shift-J	Ctrl-Alt-Shift-J
Set Proxy	Cmd-Opt-P	Ctrl-Alt-P
Replace Footage	Cmd-H	Ctrl-H

Saving as Frames, and Photoshop Comps that Use Proxies

Now that you have experienced the increase/decrease of rendering times based on resolution settings, we will explore methods of saving frames as images and as Photoshop Comps. We will also talk about the proper proxy usage.

It is possible to keep the resolution of a Comp at one setting, while rendering the file using at a different resolution. For example, set your resolution to one-third and still render a single frame at full resolution (which you will do in the Studio Time that follows). Clicking on the proxy indicator toggles between the proxy and the original.

When saving a frame as a Photoshop Comp, keep in mind that you are rendering only a moment in time. A file saved as a Photoshop Comp can be opened in either Photoshop 3 or 4 (or in Fractal Design Painter or any other program that reads Photoshop layers). The layer order in the After Effects project is preserved as well. Layers used as mattes are also rendered.

In this Studio Time, you will keep the Comp resolution at one-third, and render a frame as a PICT (or PCX) file at full resolution. You will then save the same frame as a Photoshop Comp.

Studio Time: Render that Frame

1. Continue working the same Project as you have been using.

2. Set the Current Time to 10 frames (Mac: Cmd-G, Windows: Ctrl-G, then type 10). When you render a single frame, you need to first decide which frame to render. In this Comp, no time-based changes have been applied, so every frame is the same. Therefore, it really does not matter which frame you select.

3. Choose Save Frame As-File from the Composition menu. You are prompted to save the frame, name it, and choose its destination, using the standard Mac or Windows File Save dialog.

4. The next window you see is the Render Queue. At the bottom of the window you see the file(s) that you have lined up for output. Your file already should be highlighted at the bottom, as shown in Figure 17-13. If not, click to highlight it.

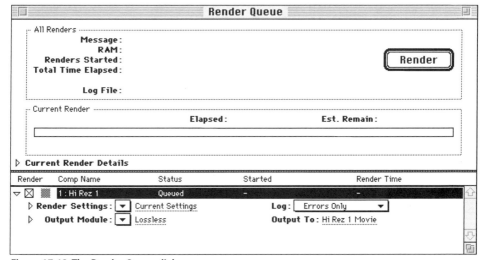

Figure 17-13: The Render Queue dialog.

5. Click on the underlined Current Settings next to the Render Settings triangle at the bottom of the Render Queue dialog, change the Quality to Best as shown in Figure 17-14. Set the resolution to Full.

6. Repeat Steps 1-5, saving the frame at a lower Quality level (name the files differently) and compare the output. Set the resolution to Full.

7. You can also specify proxy use. First, try saving the file using the proxy. Then retry it specifying "use no proxies."

8. Click on the underlined Millions+PICT next to the Output Module. In the dialog box click on the Import into project when done button. This imports the completed file into the

program for viewing or using.

9. Save the same frame as a Photoshop Comp. You will need to make the same decisions as you did in the previous steps. Proxies, resolution, and quality always need to be determined when you prepare a frame for output.

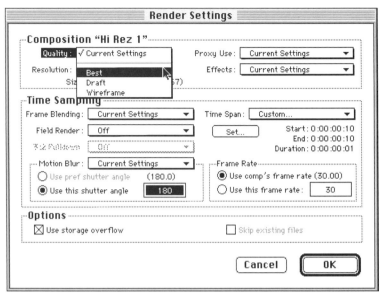

Figure 17-14: Change the Render Quality to Best.

Rewind

Those rendering times can really get crazy. Proxies and placeholders go a long way toward helping the "greater cause." When you are wrestling with large files, taking advantage of every little speed trick helps.

Using After Effects to prepare single images or elements for Photoshop is a good technique to master. Filters like MetaCreations' Final Effects and Studio Effects and the Knoll Software's Lens Flare Pak are great tools to add to a Photoshop toolbox.

Coming Attractions

In the next chapter, we will take a good hard look at the technical information associated with After Effects. We will look at aspect ratio, exact video specifications, and a variety of Interpret Footage concerns.

Section 5
After Thoughts

After Effects Technical Esoterica

 Preview

As you continue to work with After Effects, it is inevitable that you will come across technical issues that have not been covered in previous chapters. Many of these technical issues are addressed here. You will find information relating to NTSC standard video, rendering for film, and other technical esoterica to help bolster your knowledge of After Effects. In this chapter, you will:

- Determine and set frame rate.
- Establish Title Safe and Action Safe areas.
- Determine and set NTSC compliance.
- Determine and set video aspect ratios.
- Determine and set interlace.
- Address video transfer issues.
- Learn how to render for film.

Feature Presentation

If you are producing computer-based multimedia, your output options are quite limited—they are confined to computer display. However, you may want to output your work in any or all of the various media delivery formats, including print, CD-ROM, the Web, and videotape. This section will provide the information you need to know about After Effects output, and it will give you the basic understanding to achieve your goals, regardless of the format.

After Effects has become the great equalizer. It is well suited to many kinds of output, including print, animation, special effects, and sound. The ability to read and write to most of the popular video formats is integrated into the software. You need to know how to access these capabilities, however, before you can make them work for you.

A quick re-examination of Chapter 6 and Chapter 7 may be helpful before you begin this chapter. You may wish to review the alpha channel information regarding controls that set frame and field options (Interpret Footage), ratio settings, and audio information.

Alpha Output

There are two ways to output alpha channel information in After Effects. The first way is to render the alpha embedded within the file (RGB + Alpha, RGB+, or Millions+). The second is to render a separate pass of just the alpha information (Alpha Only).

You could benefit from creating a separate file of the alpha to allow you to apply the rendered file as another element or as a track matte (see Chapter 11), or for use in other applications capable of interpreting an alpha. This is useful when you need to use the alpha information in future compositions, and it gives you tremendous flexibility integrating parts of movies into your projects.

In broadcast production studios, many devices carry what is referred to as a Downstream Key, a normal video signal (the fill) that is complemented by a signal that carries transparency video (the matte). In video editors and switchers, this extra signal is used to superimpose an area within a shot over another. This is how editors or switchers composite video.

Outputting an alpha channel that is embedded in your movie gives you capabilities similar to those of professional switchers and on-line editors, but it's more advantageous because your downstream key isn't downstream—it's right there for you to use. With an alpha channel included in the movie, you can easily composite your movies with other movies and still images without having to worry about another signal that you're using for the alpha information.

You may output an alpha channel with every movie you render, but if your scene carries no transparency, your rendering time would be spent creating an empty alpha channel that would only take up unnecessary hard drive space.

As you build your composition, be aware of any transparency that it may contain. If you can see the background color through the open areas of your composition, you should consider rendering an alpha to accompany your RGB layers, particularly if you intend to bring the finished movie back into After Effects or if you want to composite it later.

 Studio Time: Rendering an Alpha with Your Output

1. Open any previously-created project and select Render from the Composition menu (Mac: Cmd-M, Windows: Ctrl-M). Open the Output Module by clicking the current module name.

2. Select Channels, then choose RGB+A or Alpha to output your movie with an alpha as shown in Figure 18-1.

3. The color depth should be at Millions+

4. Assign Color to Straight (unmatted).

Remember that compressed formats like Cinepak do not contain an alpha channel. Lossy or compressed formats are meant to be used real-time or near-real-time. Lossless or uncompressed formats are used for production work that must continue downstream. (Try not to save a file in a compressed format until you are sure that you no longer wish to edit it.) Video Compressors that do support an alpha channel are Animation, Planar RGB, and None, as

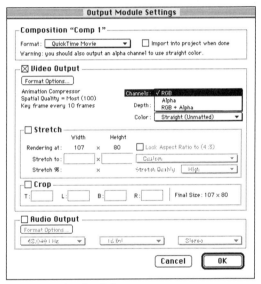

Figure 18-1: Render dialog.

well as some proprietary formats supported by third-party vendors for their own video boards.

For the purposes of this chapter, remember that compression should be reserved for the finished piece, and you should try not to compress a file that will need further visual processing.

Frame Rate

To create moving pictures, any animation program has to display the frames in succession. The sequenced pictures create a "Persistence of Vision" and simulate motion. The frame rate is the number of frames per second that are viewed to achieve the simulation of motion. Typically, the higher the frame rate, the smoother the motion.

Video, film, and multimedia do not share the same frame rate. Even video comes in different frame rates, depending on the standard chosen in a particular locality or country.

In the United States, Canada, and Japan, NTSC is the standard and specifies a rate of 29.97 frames per second. (See the section below for more details on NTSC, and charts of other rates.) This rate is referred to as "30 frames per second" in conversation, so don't be fooled into thinking there are two different rates. Video is always played at 29.97 fps (frames per second) or it is not to NTSC spec and cannot be broadcast in the USA, Canada, etc. In Europe, PAL is the standard, and operates at 25 fps. If you are producing for this format, create and output your compositions at the PAL standard rate.

If you are working to NTSC standard, you can produce at 30 fps and leave the final conversion step to your hardware. These are Interpret Footage issues. Just as you must properly interpret an alpha coming into and going out of After Effects, so you must properly interpret any footage coming in and going out.

Studio Time: Avoiding Stutter and Drift from Differences in Frame Rate

1. Create a new project (Mac: Cmd-Opt-N, Windows: Alt-Ctrl-N).

2. Import your footage items (File → Import File).

3. With a specific footage item highlighted in the Project window, select File → Interpret Footage. Set the frame rate in the Interpret Footage dialog to 29.97 (see Figure 18-2). This will avoid the frame rate mixing that causes the stutter and drift. You are interpreting the project to match the footage shot at 29.97, not adding or subtracting frames. This step makes After Effects see each frame in the source as having a duration of 1/(your project frame rate) of a second. So if your project is set to 30 frames a second, the interpretation sees each frame in the video footage as having a frame rate of 1/30 of a second.

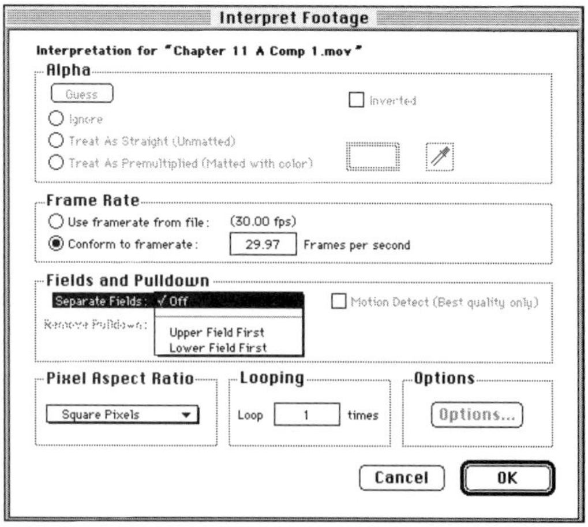

Figure 18-2: Conforming video input.

One caution: If your digitization and output hardware conform your incoming and outgoing footage for you, these After Effects settings will be unnecessary and might introduce a glitch. Check your hardware specifications.

After Effects also gives you the ability to change the output of a composition that has been constructed with a frame rate different than your chosen video and project format. To change the output, follow these steps from the Render Dialog.

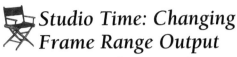

Studio Time: Changing Frame Range Output

1. Open a Project from any previous Studio Times.

2. Open a Comp within that project.

3. Select Composition → Make Movie.

4. Click on the Render Settings file. Set the desired frame rate in the box on the lower right as shown in Figure 18-3.

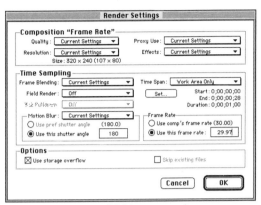

Figure 18-3: Frame and field output settings.

3:2 Pulldown, the Telecine Process, and Working with Film on Video

Matching the frame rate with film is more difficult. The frame rate for film is typically 24 frames per second, although film can be shot at rates that better match video rates (e.g., 25, 30, or 60 fps).

Transferring film footage to video usually involves the 3:2 pulldown process. Without going into the mechanics of the process, the 3:2 pulldown fits 24 frames of film information into 60 fields of video. This process involves interpolation and can give you a stuttering look every several frames. This technique is useful when transferring film that has an associated audio track that needs to remain in sync, or footage that has specific timing that can't be changed.

Footage without sync is sometimes transferred at 30fps, and if needed, time-remapped digitally to fit the motion into the original duration. Elements for compositing are good candidates for this method.

Scanning footage with a film scanner gives a very high resolution digital image and is used to maintain fidelity of a filmed image. This method works best when manipulating and compositing footage for output back to film resolution. After Effects will allow you to work at extremely high resolutions, but you will take a performance hit when doing so.

Using film is easy, especially if your output destination is also 24fps film. If you are working at 24fps and your film footage elements were transferred at 24fps, then no changes are needed in the Interpret Footage dialog. (Be sure to consider your resolution, however. You will still have to output the correct frame size, as is detailed below.) On the other hand, if the destination for your film-original is video, you will get the best result if you work at video frame rates.

Removing 3:2 pulldown isn't difficult. When you interpret the footage, you will confirm the transfer method and frame rate with the digitizer. You will also need to know the phase. Phase is based on the sequence of whole frames and split-field frames in the footage. During the application of 3:2 pulldown, 24 fps are distributed across 30 fps video, and non-interlaced film is converted to interlaced video, where it is divided into fields representing the even or odd lines in the image. (See the interlacing section later in this chapter.)

The conversion creates a repeating pattern of five video frames. Three are called whole frames, and two are called half frames. The whole (video) frames contain the two fields of a film frame and can re-create that one film frame. The half frames have a split field with two fields that come from different film frames, though they are always adjacent. Thus, the process is called 3:2 pulldown, and is the standard Telecine process used whenever film is shot for video or a feature is converted to videotape.

It is important that you know the history of any footage you may use. Footage that appears to be shot on video may actually have been filmed originally, then had a 3:2 pulldown applied. Knowing the history of the footage can prevent jitter and frame rate mismatches. If you are uncertain about the cause of jittery footage, try removing the 3:2 pulldown.

 Studio Time: Interpreting 3:2 Pulldown

1. Highlight the desired file in the Project window. Select File → Interpret Footage. In the Fields and Pulldown section of the dialog, click the Guess 3:2 pulldown as shown in Figure 18-4. Check to see if the jitter is gone. If so, your footage is actually from film and the problem is solved. If not, go to Step 2.

2. If you know who digitized the footage, contact them to determine how it was prepared. If this is not an option, proceed to Step 3.

3. From the same dialog, specify which field is first. Field order is explained in the NTSC section of this chapter.

4. For each of the two options (upper or lower field first) there are five possible 3:2 occurrences. You may have to try all ten combinations before you get the right answer. If you refer to Figure 18-4, you can see that uncertainty about the source of the file affects other factors. Clearly,

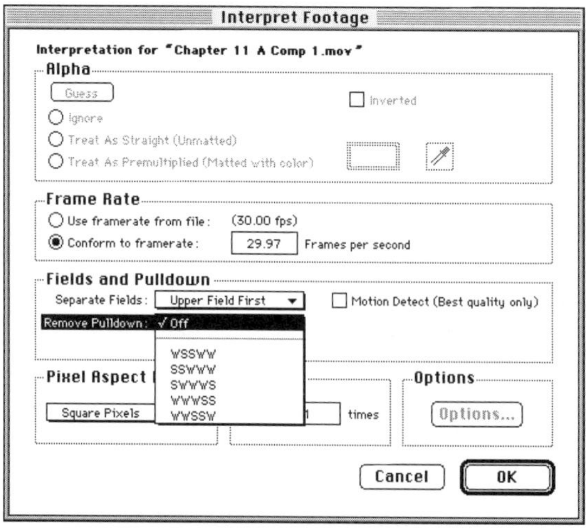

Figure 18-4: Interpreting 3-2 Pulldown.

the source frame rate is 30 fps, but if it were truly video footage, it would show a 29.97 rate. In this example, the animation file is interpreted as though it were at video's 29.97 rate.

5. Check the frame rate in the Fields and Pulldown section. In this example, it shows a frame rate of 23.96 which is not usable. Therefore, the source footage is not from film.

Note that your footage may or may not conform, depending on how your video hardware handles these things. If your hardware writes compressed movie formats, then it is pre-interpreted for you.

Multimedia output can have any frame rate. The rate you select depends on many factors, such as image size, platform for playback, and other issues related to the target medium. For example, if you are producing at 30 frames per second but want to output a smaller 15 fps file for preview or CD-ROM, you can set the new frame rate in the Render Settings dialog. In this case, After Effects drops every other frame, and doubles the duration of each remaining frame. Nonetheless most multimedia productions are output at 12 or 15 frames per second and are rarely larger than 320 x 240.

When you time-stretch or time re-map footage to a frame rate lower or slower than the original, the new layer does not have the same number of frames as the Composition, and any movement may stutter. After Effects has to fill the missing or discarded frames to keep the timing consistent. This is accomplished by omitting or duplicating frames. For Time Stretched or Slow Motion footage, you can smooth stuttering motion by using the Frame Blending Switch in the Render Settings dialog. This will interpolate new frames based on the originals to create a smoother transition.

Frame blending is not as effective if you are reducing the number of frames or if you are rendering a still or non-moving object. If images are being discarded, motion blurring would be a more effective method of smoothing any stutter.

Typically, new frame rates that are either half or double the original rate will not stutter. Therefore, a motion blur would be beneficial when going from 30fps to 12fps, but it would not help when going from 12 to 24fps. Remember that both frame blending and motion blur cost rendering time. You may want to consider disabling the process in the Time Layout window, then enabling it in the Render Settings dialog before your final render.

Images saved in the Gif89a format for Web distribution are generally said to be interlaced, but it's a different kind of interlacing than video. Gif interlacing is generally used in video format for Web animations.

Video Safe Areas

Video is the world of the television screen. Unlike a computer monitor where you see the entire image in a black border, video monitors and television sets do not allow you to see the entire image. This cropping is referred to as *overscanning*. Since television is an imperfect analog medium, broadcasters cannot guarantee that their images are centered and scaled correctly. Also, in the early days of TV, the edges of the image tended to be blurry. Therefore, television systems have always been designed to hide these imperfections to keep you from being offended by the black rough edges.

This is an important consideration because you must design your presentation with the understanding that overscanning prevents the viewer from seeing the entire image area. After Effects can show you where your design will be seen. In the Composition window, you can overlay an outline depicting the Title and Action Safe areas of a standard NTSC frame-sized composition. (See Figure 18-5.)

The Action Safe areas are the part of the screen that will always be seen. Do not set important motion events outside this border. The Title Safe area is within the Action Safe area. Text or still objects in this area are not subject to the distortion common along the edges. (To display the safe area overlay, click the grid icon in the bottom left corner of the Composition window.)

You may also want to tightly crop digitized footage placed within your Composition to eliminate the effects of over-scanning, particularly if you are going to reduce the footage within a new Composition.

Sometimes video carries image informa-tion from a previous production that is of no use to a subsequent production. Be sure to eliminate the edge effects and unwanted lines when you reuse video footage. If you are using

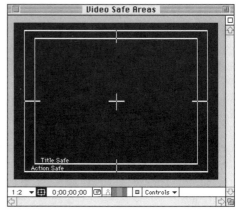

Figure 18-5: Video Safe areas.

video footage as a full screen element, these areas should appear outside the safe areas and need no adjustment. But if you are working on a multimedia project and your elements have artifacts or noise on the borders, make sure to scale your footage until the edges are beyond the border of your comp. Make sure to scale proportionately as it's easy to accidentally distort your original image.

Aspect Ratios

An aspect ratio is the horizontal size divided by the vertical size. It is expressed as the least common ratio of measure to both sides. Television is 1.33:1, but is generally referred to as 4:3. This also happens to be the aspect ratio of most computer monitors. This same aspect ratio works down the size scale into the typical multimedia sizes of 320 x 240, 240 x 180, and 160 x 120. They are all multiples of one another; these all share the aspect ratio of 4:3.

This seems to make everything quite simple, but be careful. Although the 4:3 frame aspect ratio is shared between NTSC and a 640 x 480 Macintosh monitor, specifications for the two use a different pixel aspect ratio. NTSC uses rectangular pixels at

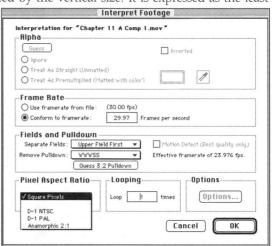

Figure 18-6: Setting D1 pixel aspect ratio.

a resolution of 720 x 486 which ends up as the same physical real estate as a Macintosh at 640 x 480. Some video capture and output hardware takes this into account and saves you the trouble of conversion.

When producing D-1 video, be aware that NTSC pixels are different. If you interpret or output the footage incorrectly, you may not get a 4:3 image. The pixels may be stretched, and your image may be distorted. Remember to use the Pixel Aspect Ratio pop-up in the Interpret Footage dialog when working with D-1 video. (See Figure 18-6.)

Motion pictures use a 16:9 ratio–much wider than both NTSC and the average computer monitor. Some video uses this ratio to playback on "widescreen" video monitors. Be aware that video and film at this ratio are different. There are almost four times as many pixels in the same area in film as there are in widescreen video.

Interlacing

As mentioned briefly before, interlacing is a method for producing an image in NTSC Video standard format. It is achieved by dividing each frame into fields representing the even or odd rows of pixels in the image.

We can contrast this with a computer monitor where a Progressive Scan method is employed. Pixels are drawn horizontally from edge to edge and from top to bottom. When the computer is done with all of the scan lines, it returns to the top and begins again.

Video, in its traditional NTSC form (broadcast, tapes, and cable television), draws every other horizontal line on its way down, and draws the remaining lines on a second pass. It then begins anew with its next even and odd set of lines.

Each odd or even pass is called a field. Two fields comprise a video frame. The fields are drawn at a rate of 59.94 per second, the frames at 29.97 per second. This number should look familiar: it is the NTSC standard output. This method of creating an image is called interlacing, or interlaced video.

The result is important to understand: with interlaced video, every frame has pixels from two different fields. If you display the fields in the wrong order, your picture will look as though you are viewing it through very fine horizontal lines that are in fact, displaying 2 incoherent images. This Field Ordering is critical to making a video image watchable. Different hardware sometimes use different methods for determining which field is drawn first. The methods are referred to as Upper Field First or Lower Field First . (Sometimes "dominant" is substituted for "First," or "Field 1, Field 2," or other names are used—and when you guess wrong, some of the names that you will want to use can be quite creative!)

The effect of seeing the fields is most pronounced whenever the frame contains motion, small detail, or fine edges in elements on screen. After Effects knows how to either throw away one field or split a field into a full frame to correct errors in the field order.

You should note that because of interlacing, any point or horizontal line in your Composition that is only a pixel wide will only be seen in every other field when it gets to video. Sometimes a single pixel line that has been anti-aliased to cover three lines will only resolve every other field, since the anti-aliased edge would only be sent to the television viewer every other field. To solve this, most applications require that the pixel width, including anti-alias drop-off, covers at least five pixels total. Any detail you plan that is smaller than this will shimmer when output to a destination in the television and videotape world.

However, remember that you can sometimes get away with great looking video without following strict rules. The best way to find out if your idea is going to flicker when output to an NTSC or PAL monitor is to test it. In fact, you should never assume that even if you do follow the rules that you will achieve perfection every time. The only way to really tell is to see it in its final form.

Interpreting Separate Fields

The Separate Fields option in the Interpret Footage dialog is necessary when working with interlaced footage. It marries the two fields in a frame. It prevents you from interlacing already interlaced video and possibly introducing a jitter that can't be removed. When you do import and remove the interlacing, your rendered output will take a small hit in quality. If you keep repeating the process with the same footage, you will be able to see the degraded quality.

If you don't know which field is dominant from the footage you're working with, render a test to check. It will save time fixing mistakes when you're closer to your deadline.

If you are fortunate enough to work with a disk recorder, be aware that some models work in both fields and frames. If you are outputting stills for use downstream, then use frames, otherwise interlacing makes moving elements easier to watch and gives it a cleaner look. Even if you are not doing the transfer yourself, your client may expect files that have been "readied" for such a transfer. The Render Settings window allows you to prepare a queued composition. You simply choose between Off, Upper, and Lower

Using the Reduce Interlace Flicker filter

Occasionally you may receive footage that flickers and continues to do so even after interpreting the footage to either upper or lower field interlaced video. You can try either the Reduce Interlace Flicker filter effect, or blurring the image.

To use the filter, select Effect → Video → Reduce Interlace Flicker. Adjust the softness until the interlace looks flicker-free. It is motion that makes flicker visible, so you might have to do a few test renders to get it right.

Other Transfer Options

Videotape is not your only output option, of course. Some of the other choices might make sense depending upon the application. There are many different types of devices that use video. This section will provide some introductory information.

Real Time

QuickTime or equivalent video capture hardware for personal computers are inexpensive alternatives to costly broadcast gear. Although some have reached high quality, the networks still have stringent broadcast standards. This "desktop" technology follows the more expensive gear at post production houses and broadcast stations, but its acceptance by consumers helps broaden the base of talent in video.

There are solutions for video effects and editing at many price levels. The price usually has something to do with the quality and ease of use. When looking for a solution for yourself, look for hardware capable of capturing and saving 30 frames, 60 field per second video.

Most real-time capture cards come with standard composite video connections like the ones found on a VCR or television. Others are equipped with S-Video connectors which provide a higher quality signal from camcorders and high-quality tape decks. If you have a choice, input and output with the S-Video connections to achieve better quality. Some video capture cards even offer 2 or 4 tracks of 16-bit, 44.1 kHz stereo sound. High-end products (professional) offer output to component video.

For professional work, make sure the capture and output hardware offers some form of 16-bit audio "capable of Genlocking" to video (genlocking makes sure that video signal between the computer and whatever device you're capturing from is in sync).

Video is compressed when it comes through the card, but not without losing some of the frames as it goes through the computer to a regular hard drive. It is 99% necessary to add a SCSI accelerator card and disk array to keep up with the flood of information coming into the computer through the card. We say 99% because some of the newer computers and some of the newer hard drives are good enough to get the information without any special formatting or other hardware. Follow the recommendations of the manufacturer of the capture hardware.

When you provide graphics and footage for an Avid editing session, you might output a QuickTime movie using the Avid codec. These can be imported by the Avid system seamlessly. If you are compositing something within the Avid, you need to render a separate matte movie because the Avid codec (as of this writing) does not support alpha channels. If you are finishing your project in the Avid, then you're done. However, if you need to finish in an uncompressed format, then you will need to output a PICT sequence or uncompressed QuickTime movie—depending on how you are finishing. If you finish on an online system that cannot read digital files, you need to output your project to a timecoded (frame accurate) tape.

SMPTE is a standard for videotape timecode. It specifies how video, film, and audio can be timed and offset in time. The format operates with the Hours, Minutes, Seconds, and frames standardized by 29.97 fps video. SMPTE timecode provides a standard format to coordinate all external elements.

There is a way to display timecode in After Effects. It appears as a series of numbers separated by colons or semicolons. You will generally need to know the frame rate used by your composition to display the timecode to match it. This is set with the Time preferences under the Edit menu.

Although the one percent speed difference between 29.97 and 30 fps is not much, the difference becomes substantial (as much as a minute and a half) over 24 hours. A counter that accommodates this difference provides a more seamless creative environment to time events and keyframes. It operates by dropping two numbers (not frames) every minute. The time display for timecode can now match that of a 30 fps comp.

Frame by Frame

Frame by frame services are available from most post-production facilities, and this kind of equipment is a purchase option for extremely serious users. You do not need the usual video card or hard drive array with this method, but you will still need a lot of storage space. This method lets you use uncompressed data, but you have to expect your footage to consume roughly one megabyte per frame. Frame by frame format can be transferred to tape or to D1 format in a disk recorder. This would require 1.1MB of disk space for each frame of 720 x 486 video.

You should provide numbered, uncompressed files with no more than 900 items, or 30 seconds worth of video in any folder. These services are usually billed by the hour and not by frame count. Remember to check with the post house to determine their submission requirements.

Additional digital disk recorder information and output options

A user who is preparing material for industrial or broadcast usage may be required to provide extremely high quality output. Diaquest makes excellent software that can control either a disk recorder or some professional video decks. You can use serial, network, or SCSI (the fastest) connections to move the video to a disk recorder, but you can use only a serial connection to move video to a video deck. The After Effects Production Bundle includes drivers for some popular DDRs. The primary advantage is the ability to output directly to a post-production standard.

An attractive alternative to a DDR is Exabyte. Exabyte is an 8mm DAT format that is common at many post houses and service bureaus. Abekas makes a DDR that accepts Exabyte tape. The tape also makes a handy backup device.

With an Exabyte tape, you can lay off uncompressed animation to any analog or digital tape format, including BetaSP, Digital Betacam, D1, and D2. Some facilities will even transfer your data to the tape from your hard disk or supply original footage in the DDR or Exabyte format. The quality surpasses most other transfer methods since the data is being converted directly into the target format.

You do need software to read these formats, and of course, you need the tape drive. For software, look for Knoll Software's Missing Link. For the tape drive, any model later than an Exabyte 8200 or 8500 should work well.

Other Considerations

Always use the highest video quality the project can support. Controlling the hardware choices and knowing the setups involved is the best way to achieve this, but understanding some specifics may also help.

Your finished footage must be in composite format before it can be broadcast, which is to say that the color signal must be combined with the luminance and sync pulses standard to composite video. It is at this point that you will get the greatest reduction in video quality.

Y/c, commonly referred to as S-Video and S-VHS, is available in the form of Hi-8 and S-VHS decks. This provides better quality than the composite signal, but it is still not a broadcast standard and serves best as a middle-ground between consumer and professional level video.

Component Video is the highest quality signal. It is not used for broadcast, but it is the superior format for routing video throughout most post facilities. It creates a high quality picture with color and luminance accuracy that is reproducible.

Film — The Final Option

As shown in Chapter 17, large frame sizes require more RAM and hard drive space. You must assess these resources carefully if you plan to work with and output film resolutions. Everyone involved in the project will understand and support concern for film process color accuracy.

There are two forms of scanned footage. Full aperture is 2048 x 1536, and consumes 9MB per 35 mm film frame. The Academy aperture is 1828 x 1332 and consumes 7MB. This size is nearly the 4:3 aspect ratio of TV and computers.

When a second of footage consumes 240+MB of drive space and the necessary RAM, larger systems equipped with equally fast networks and backups become essential. Consequently, film output (or creation) is not practical for most small operations without a significant increase in hardware speed and size.

Film producers select either film (full aperture, 35MM) or video (Academy aperture) according to their destination format. Generally, the service provider handling scanning and output prefers that color correction be avoided to keep the color and image quality in line.

When working with these large files, it is necessary to make motion proofs. These are done by rendering at half resolution, and stretching the output to a screen size of 640 pixels wide.

 **Rewind**

Here is a list of the standard video and film frame sizes that have been discussed in this chapter.

Standard	Frame Size	Used for
13 & 14" PC	640 x 480	Capture and output cards
NTSC:	640 x 480	Capture and output cards
NTSC:	648 x 486	US, Canada, Mexico, and Japan Broadcast
D1 NTSC	720 x 486	US, Canada, Mexico, and Japan Broadcast
D1 NTSC	720 x 540	Square Pixel, 4:3, 540 line
D1 PAL	720 x 576	European Broadcast
D1 PAL	768 x 576	Square Pixel, 4:3, 576 line
HDTV	1280 x 720	Proposed High Definition Television Standard
HDTV	1920 x 1035	Proposed High Definition Television Standard
Film	2048 x 1536	A standard resolution for Digital Film

Although our list of frame sizes would tend to indicate that almost any format conversion is possible, there are some general considerations that you should be aware of in planning and setup for After Effects.

You need not be an engineer to work with film, but some of their issues may provide a catalyzing component that will give you a final, cohesive picture of how to proceed. When confronted with the task of converting your creation into something that is allowed on the air, the engineers most often complain that:

- Computers use square pixels and television does not. To go between the two requires image conversion or processing.

- After Effects operates in RGB colorspace. NTSC comes in both RGB and composite and relies heavily on a luminance/chrominance model for advanced analog and digital systems. This bears little resemblance to computers.

- Computers tend to scale luminance from a 0 level for black to a 255 level for white. Once again, this is not according to broadcast practice where a 7.5% luminance is required to produce NTSC. Black and white is produced with a 225 to 235 value of grey.

▇ And finally, engineers complain that computers operate at an 8-bit resolution while digital video systems are standardizing on 10-bit systems. This requires sophisticated numerical rounding techniques to avoid the contouring effects (banding) and other artifacts of re-sampling and format conversion.

The answer is to provide video quality that is commensurate with the budget and client. With the new skills learned here, you should now be familiar with NTSC compliance, and understand about rendering for film. You can now set a frame rate, establish video safety areas, manage aspect ratios, set interlace, and deal with video transfer issues, making your work as high quality as possible.

Coming Attractions

In the final chapter, we will profile some of the users who keep After Effects on their toes. These folks regularly get more out of their tools than the manufacturer put into them. You will learn about their backgrounds and how they became involved with digital video. They will also share their views of the industry with you and offer advice for those of you who are just beginning to work with digital video and After Effects.

After Effects Experts

 ## Preview

This chapter allows you to meet four expert animators and graphic artists who use After Effects in their day-to-day work. They share the experiences that have led them to become animation artists, and their opinions on After Effects. Their work can be seen in the Color Gallery section of this book.

 ## Feature Presentation

The four artists that you will meet are, in alphabetical order, David Acosta, Richard Lainhart, Josh Laurence, and Dave Teich.

David Acosta

David Acosta is an unorthodox mix of skills and technical ability. He has always wanted to be the person behind the scenes who could help others put it all together.

Background

David has been interested in media and technology since the age of seven, when his father took him into a Sony store. Since that day, he has never stopped wanting to learn everything about how to make things work. If it has a button, knob, or dial, and can be connected to something mechanical that makes sound or shows pictures, David either knows about it now or will soon find out!

David left school early, before graduation, and joined the armed forces, where he became a satellite communications expert. He learned about large mainframe computer systems, and was trained to install a complete communications network within five minutes of arrival at a new site. Talk about working under time pressure!

After leaving the army, he moved to Oregon, where he produced a hit record that made the Billboard charts for two weeks. In search of more music, he went to try his fortune in the Big Apple. However, the music business is rough, and in 1985 and 1986, the music skill most needed in New York City seemed to be teaching musicians and their studios how to use the new MIDI technology. David helped to wire half of New York's music studios and to get them set up for MIDI.

David taught musicians how to use the equipment. He developed new techniques and taught musicians, producers, and technicians to use them. He became an expert of "dropping into" a project in the middle of the creative process and helping to fix the technical problems encountered. His understanding of both the technical and the creative side of the process helped him to be a sympathetic and non-interfering audience for the groups with whom he worked.

By the time QuickTime appeared in 1990, David was already pushing the envelope. One of his first projects was the creation of a digital business card, a very impressive use of the then-brand-new technology.

He also worked with Art Machines (NYC's first value-added video reseller), which was the first company to provide digital video solutions to the graphic arts and video community. He helped to install TARGA and other high-end (at the time) cards and trained people to use them. When the demand for Art Machines services became so overwhelming that the company could no longer cope, David restarted Silence, Inc., his business name from previous years.

Miles Tanaka, the art director for VH1, convinced MTV to create their own research labs, and they signed a five-year $4.2 million engineering agreement with Silence. David brought in SGI, Mac, and IBM equipment and built the lab to help MTV try new and experimental things. David trained the MTV folks to use and service the equipment so that he would no longer be needed. MTV is now part of Viacom, which still maintains the lab.

During the past year, David has converted Silence into a production company. He has built Web sites, helped people move into Web design, and created music animation. His ambition is to be the premiere music animation company (an occupation that he has created).

What is this career of music animation? David sees it encompassing all of the traditional elements that come into play, even when it concerns music videos or performing live concerts. He wants to design a graphic element for each sound—and incorporate that into the music video. He wants to finish an animation for broadcast, and then modify it for concert use (touring, supporting, etc.). A musician or group could hire his company to make the entire campaign for an album—the print graphics as well as the sound and video. He has the background, skills, and equipment to make this happen.

After Effects in the Field

When After Effects was still produced by its creators, CoSA, David met one of the founders of the company. He become interested in this fledgling product and implemented copies at MTV (along with copies of Premiere). He discovered that After Effects made the prettiest pictures.

David explained how various companies are using After Effects. MTV uses After Effects mostly to create *bumpers*—the 5, 10, or 15 second heads or tails to a TV program. ShowWorks has used After Effects to help create high definition images and animations for at least the last six Sony International dealers and distributors conventions. In the past year or so, they have also started using it to position and animate Photoshop and Illustrator elements, for special effects, and for titling and logo treatments. They do not edit video with it nor do they use any sound. VH-1 has a new look that is coming directly from their use of After Effects, ElectricImage, and Infini-D.

Most of his David's clients use the program for logo animations, creating backgrounds, making animated textures that offset and turn into sliding backgrounds, and for titling. It is typically *not* being used to create elements. Instead, After Effects is most often selected to modify existing elements, and to animate and manipulate them. In the print world, it is being used by artists to create a single frame to which a special effect has been applied.

Learning After Effects

David's first comment about learning After Effects is that it requires the same understanding (or lack of understanding) as Photoshop. In order to utilize either program effectively, you must comprehend what an alpha channel is and how it can be used. This is a tricky subject in Photoshop and if not mastered there, it is one that returns to plague you in After Effects. It is a critical skill, though, and you need to spend whatever time is needed until you feel comfortable with the topic.

If you are just starting out, David advises you to avoid taking courses in the software until you have a real goal. He says: "Until you know what you need to learn and why, you will only learn about things that you are not yet ready to learn. You will get much more out of going to every available trade show and mingling with the pros who attend them. Go to MacWorld, Siggraph, and any other trade or industry shows in your area. If you have no connection to the industry at all, you will only be able to obtain a job at an entry-level position. The idea is to create a niche for yourself where no one thought one existed and where you can differentiate yourself from all of the others who are also competing for the same jobs."

In order to do "wicked and good" work, he says you need to immerse yourself in the software and learn in the fire. "The best way, of course, is to learn-as-you-earn. There's nothing quite like the incentive of meeting production deadlines to teach you how to get work done."

"A musician—or a new artist—has to be nurtured. He or she does best when the music or art is allowed to be totally original, but when the newcomer has a group of trusting friends to critique it in a non-threatening manner. Too much critique can be taken too seriously. "The danger,"David says, "is that if you take too much criticism too seriously, your originality/music/vision dies unborn."

"You need to be able to see possibilities, and you need to learn where to apply your skills. Don't wait. Don't build and infrastructure. Just do it."

"If you aren't playing with After Effects on non-deadline projects, than you are not learning the product as you should be. Master the keyboard keystrokes and shortcuts; you will become much more productive. Fiddle with all of the dials, knobs, and controls in the program and see what happens."

"Watch television—the commercials, not the programs! After Effects is being used on many of the commercials aired today. You need to be able to recognize what effects were used in each commercial. If you have no clue how the 'magic' occurred, you need to go back and learn a lot more about After Effects."

"Don't try to make After Effects your only application. It is good for many tasks—but not *every* task. Think of it as the PageMaker of animation—the place where all the elements come together."

"Finally, reuse your old equipment." David's current music system is a Mac SE running System 6.0.7. It is an out-of-date machine running old software, but it still performs useful work. The pieces that you already have can often by recycled into doing another part of the job.

Future Visions

David is looking for a day when After Effects will work in real time, with no need to wait for rendering. There are $150,000 systems that will do this today, but it will someday be possible to do this on a desktop machine that is affordable. When that happens, After Effects will move into the Quantel class. Ultimately, there should be no need for post-processing because, in the real world, where time does indeed equal money, no one has the time to wait, he notes.

Richard Lainhart

Richard Lainhart started out as a professional musician and has become a computer animation specialist.

Background

Richard was always interested in animation, but he never had the skills or time to animate using traditional methods. He was trained as a jazz musician. In the mid-1980s, he acquired a deep understanding of digital media from working with Mac, Atari, and Amiga music software. When animation software began to appear—particularly QuickTime and Macromedia Director—Richard became much more interested in the topic since he could approach it from the computer side.

Richard began preparing animations by making sequential Photoshop files and modifying photographs. The first breakthrough came with the advent of Premiere and After Effects. His first chance to do digital video came with the use of the SuperMac digital film card.

He moved to New York City and began work for NovaWorks, providing tech support and training. He started out by providing support for DTP, ad agencies, and graphic designers. Then, some cable and post-production clients wanted to produce more active content (read "multimedia"). He then began to support more high-end systems and learned about them through the training and support he gave to these clients.

Richard is now most interested in 3D animation and in combining this with 2D animations (both video and desktop) using StrataVision and ElectricImage. His client list includes Showtime, HBO, and a number of other broadcast and desktop video users, and Richard has become an expert at production, animation, broadcast video, and CD-ROM and music production—all Mac-based and with recourse to very few traditional tools.

After Effects in the Field

Richard sees After Effects as an aide to 3D production. It is used to composite 3D elements in a less time-intensive environment. It is rare to render a 3D production in one pass. There is usually a need to assemble different elements into one piece—to composite them onto a background or onto moving video. Rendering 3D is a very lengthy process. Using After Effects, however, one can often simulate 3D animation with 2D tools—thereby saving a huge amount of rendering time.

Richard also sees After Effects as a tool for titling, text animation, and composition, for assembling, and as a way to create special effects for 3D animations. This is how Richard uses After Effects in his own work as a music and animation producer.

Learning After Effects

"When you start to use After Effects, the first thing that you really need to know is that it does not stand on its own. In order to have a complete studio, you must add additional pieces of software—at a minimum, you need to add Photoshop and Illustrator. These programs are the most common method of producing source material."

"You should have a good set of skills to bring to your After Effects work. You should know 3D animation—especially the concepts such as keyframe, layers, and lighting effects.

Knowing 3D can help you learn After Effects, and knowing After Effects can help you better learn 3D."

"One of the major problems today is being able to do professional work for real video and get it output. There seem to be two common approaches: you can work at low res and output in high res at a Service Bureau, or you can get a desktop system like Media 100 or TARGA 2000 to output directly to video. However, it is good to be able look at real NTSC video on the desktop—it can be very frustrating if you're not able to see your animations on a TV screen until you have them output by a Service Bureau. So, you really do need an output system of some type. Even a low-res system shows what your animation looks like on video; during the development process it is critical for you to know how your designs will look on NTSC video."

"You should also learn as much about digital media and traditional video world as you can. You will need to interface with traditional video people who are somewhat suspicious of the digital realm and who speak a different set of jargon. You must be able to understand the lingo and to explain to them in plain English what you are doing. Many desktop artists cannot explain about video production to traditional 'video guys' and this is not at all helpful on a project."

"If you are going to try to make a living from After Effects, you need to determine what kind of work are you going to do. If you are going to work for yourself, it is important that you master the commercial skills needed in a production environment—managing a business, bidding, competing with other independent producers. You need to develop the skills needed to accurately estimate a job, deliver it on time, and make a profit (usually trial and error teaches you that one!)."

"Also, be aware of what is going around you. Be alert to trends and watch the TV commercials. Of the current crop of commercials, Micotin and Martini and Rossi are both showing commercials made using After Effects. Big Pink (a New York agency) has a car commercial done with it, and A&E and Lifetime manipulate a lot of different layers and control them using After Effects for their network promos. One of the current trends is the moving of text that blurs slowly."

"While there is a difference between *good* and *fashionable,* you need to develop your own style but also be able to emulate other styles and reproduce them. Remain aware of the commercial environment around you."

"If you're not concerned with making a living from After Effects, but only to enjoy the tool and push at the envelope, then develop your own style. It only needs to be satisfying to you, even if it is not commercial."

Future Visions

One of the most intriguing things about After Effects is it ability to allow you to combine special effects in layers so that they interact in ways that are very interesting and not at all predictable. However, a current very weak part of After Effects is its text handling. Richard would like to see the ability to reshape letterforms, manipulate type outlines, and animate kerning. The other weak link in the program, according to Richard, is its audio, but he feels that this is not as important since you can "fix" the audio using other programs and bring the final tracks into After Effects. An alternate approach, which Richard uses fairly often, is to do the final compositing of audio with video in the Media 100 or Premiere environments.

Another major problem with After Effects is that you cannot see the results of your actions in real-time, and the more effects that you add, the slower the program previews.

After Effects should evolve as computers get faster, and it should eventually be able to work in real-time on the desktop. This would be a major breakthrough—real-time feedback is enormously significant and would allow you to experiment freely. It would produce a wonderful environment for creativity and allow you to invent never-seen-before effects. With the advent of new operating systems and faster processors, it should be possible.

Richard currently prefers a Mac-based system. He feels that, right now, it is more viable for broadcast work and that third party support is better, however, this may well change in the future (and in the near future). He also feels that After Effects, while slower than a high-end dedicated system, is much more flexible. While After Effects doesn't give you the production edge, you can do most of what a high end system does. In the future, Richard sees the end of closed, dedicated systems. With a super-powerful desktop system, you will no longer need them.

Josh Laurence

Josh Laurence is a computer animator who has worked for more than six years in the film industry doing technology and computer consulting. He was hired by Apple Computer and the BBDO advertising agency to produce the graphics seen on the Apple monitors in their print and on-air commercials. This task required him to know what was currently the "cool" thing to do on the Mac, so that he could show this on the monitor screens.

Background

Josh didn't start out as a digital guru—in fact, he started out as a drama major at Vassar. After graduation, he went to Hollywood to break into films. He did—but certainly not as he had originally envisioned. He helped to keep track of script pages, changes, and schedules with a computer, and worked with some of the early software aimed at the film industry. He learned about the backstage workings of the film industry and the production issues that were involved.

He then moved to New York City to consult for BBDO/NY using interactive TV, prime-time TV, and print graphics. He has since done animation for Gillette, Doritos, Apple Computer, Federal Express, and America Online. He is currently working on projects for Texaco and Sony.

Josh first started working with After Effects in 1994. He needed training and worked with Craig Talmy and David Miller in Los Angeles to get that initial training. He got better, he says, as he went along.

After Effects in the Field

Josh uses After Effects primarily for logo treatments and text animation (including character animation). He feels that it is a better design tool than it is a post-production tool. The Mac cannot compete in speed with Quantel and the other high-end production systems on the market. However, the Mac is a very diverse computer, and for some things, After Effects can do a better job than the dedicated systems.

Josh uses After Effects on a machine equipped with a DDR (Digital Disk Recorder), which stores from 30 seconds to 5-10 minutes of uncompressed video. This is a 132-Gigabyte SCSI device that is similar in concept to a video deck, but it is a hard disk. It can go directly to broadcast and is a very high quality. It is also very expensive—from $4000 to over $100,000 for one of these units (for corporate folks only—starving freelancers can only dream!). The nice thing about this unit is that you can render specific video elements to it as a "holding" device, and you can then merge them in with other footage.

Josh feels that After Effects' text handling provides a wonderful way to help convey a verbal and visual impression from a word: the meaning and shape of the letters in the word work together. After Effects provides the easiest and cheapest method for working with text.

Josh has also animated a number of logos rendered with ElectricImage and composited in After Effects. After Effects gives you a lot of control over the use of the 3D element. You can render a fog layer and add effects in After Effects for blurring, depth of field, and wide focus. It has a good feeling for lighting. He feels that you can also do excellent 2D character animation in After Effects.

Josh is impressed with the entire Adobe lineup of products. He feels that Adobe has little real competition in any of the niches that they have occupied. The only possible competition for After Effects is in the new Illuminaire Paint.

Learning After Effects

Josh feels that it is good idea to take a class to determine if you want to do anything with a particular piece of software. You need to realize that After Effects needs companion programs. Photoshop and Illustrator are indispensable. The combination of the three programs allows you to create the basic animations to get you started. Additional fonts are good to have for After Effects. Plug-ins are nice, but they are not necessary to do useful work. You just need to be sure that you have a 24-bit color card and enough RAM (if there ever is such a thing as enough RAM!).

If you are a more experienced After Effects user, Josh says "you should continue to play with the software. The current 'look' is for floating, blurry text, but you should try to advance your skills beyond that."

"In After Effects, the motion math attached to the Production bundle is probably the hardest thing to master—and most users won't bother. However, it is a wonderful tool for repeating commands. Don't start experimenting with it, however, until you have explored the other areas of the program and feel comfortable with them."

"Take time to learn the keyboard commands. They are a real speed-up and will save you a lot of time."

"For optimal results in After Effects, keep your system lean and mean. Pare down your system a lot and make sure that QuickTime is always there. Don't use any extensions that effect screen redraw (such as a screen saver). That takes too much processing power."

"Be organized! Make sure all your files are easy to find. Don't move files around after you have created your projects. Decide on naming conventions before you start a project and stick to them. Take time to type in name of movie. Don't just name it 'Comp 1 movie'—you will make yourself crazy with folders full of Comp 1 movies."

"Don't procrastinate by being over-organized though. Make sure that you get work done."

"If you work with Illustrator files, create outlines from the text so you can move from system to system and the font does not need to travel along. Use Illustrator files for text so that you can scale the text without worry."

"Don't be afraid of the computer. You can't break it. Back up—early and often! Think of the computer and the programs as tools—they are not a way of life; they are a way to express life. You need to have a life in order to do anything meaningful. Look at life. Watch how things move. Keep a sketch pad with you at all times and take the time to sketch things out."

Dave Teich

Dave Teich is the owner of the Mind of the Machine, a 3D illustration studio.

Background

Dave started out as a traditional illustrator and type designer. He started to illustrate electronically and became attracted to 3D. From 3D, it was a short step into animation. He was working with animation in 1991 when QuickTime was released, and he began to work with the beta version of Adobe Premiere.

After Effects in the Field

Dave has used After Effects since version 2. He uses After Effects for compositing and as a special effects tool. He uses ElectricImage first, to make 3D objects. He also uses Photoshop to create still images. Dave rarely uses moving video in his own work, however he does use a fair amount of stock footage of pyrotechnics, and sky and textural footage. Dave also uses After Effects for title treatments and logos.

Learning After Effects

Dave feels that you can improve your After Effects skills with good training. He sees books—like this one—as an excellent way to get that training. In addition, he likes the Total AE tape series created by Brian Moffat that offers advanced After Effects training (http://www.totalae.com).

If you are just getting started in digital video, try to get a job in the industry to learn in a production environment. This will give you a head start.

For hardware, begin with a fast Mac. (Dave does recommend a Mac over a PC right now, but may soon change his mind.) He feels that the best video tools, video cards such as the Media 100, filters, and add-ons are still Mac-only, however, with the introduction of After Effects for Windows and NT, this is likely to rapidly change. The other major piece of hardware that you need is a large, fast hard drive.

Future Visions

Dave feels that After Effects is currently the best tool for video compositing and special effects. It has the best interface of any animation program on any platform—an interface that should be the standard for all animation programs. In the future, the program can only get better and become more powerful.

Dave Teich can be reached at his website at: http://bird.taponline.com/mindma-chine/mom.html.

 **Rewind**

In this chapter, you met four talented artists who are using After Effects as part of their daily work. Their backgrounds are different—only Dave Teich comes from a "traditional" art background—but they have all been drawn into this exciting and promising new field. All four men emphasize the need to integrate After Effects with other graphics applications, and to keep playing with the program in order to refine your skills and to improve your creativity.

 Coming Attractions

And this, folks, is the end of the line. You should be much better at After Effects now than you were when you first picked up this book. If you have worked your way through all of the exercises, you have also seen the creativity of the featured artists in action: Josh in the Animation chapter (Chapter 10), and David Acosta and Richard Lainhart in Chapters 7 and 8 (Audio and 3D).

The next Coming Attraction should be your animation, coming soon to a client near you! Good-bye and good luck.

INDEX

A

B

C